THE UNKNOWN STALIN

THE UNKNOWN
STALIN

Zhores A. Medvedev and Roy A. Medvedev

Translated by Ellen Dahrendorf

I.B. TAURIS
LONDON · NEW YORK

Published in 2003 by I.B.Tauris & Co. Ltd
6 Salem Road, London W2 4BU
175 Fifth Avenue, New York, NY 10010
www.ibtauris.com

ISBN: 1-86064-768-5

A full CIP record for this book is available from the British Library
A full CIP record for this book is available from the Library of Congress

Library of Congress catalog card: available

Typeset in Carmine by A. & D. Worthington, Newmarket, Suffolk
Printed and bound in Great Britain by MPG Books Ltd, Bodmin

Contents

Glossary

Agitprop	Department of Agitation and Propaganda of the Central Committee.
apparat, apparatus	The machine or organization of offices and office-holders (for example, the Party *apparat*, the state *apparat*, etc.).
APRF	Presidential archive.
Central Committee	The chief policy-making body of the Communist Party during periods between congresses.
Central Executive Committee	The chief policy-making body of the Soviet government from 1917–36, when it was replaced by the Presidium of the Supreme Soviet.
Cheka	The first political police (1917–22) established by the new Soviet government to combat counter-revolution and sabotage. This Soviet acronym was taken from the initials of the organization – Extraordinary Commission.
Chekist	A member of Soviet security police. Although originally it meant 'agent of the Cheka', the term continued to be used for any operative of the security police agencies that succeeded the Cheka.
Council of People's Commissars (Sovnarkom)	The highest government body in USSR, equivalent to a cabinet in Western governmental structure. In 1946 the term 'people's commissar' was dropped in favour of the more traditional term, 'minister', and this body became the Council of Ministers. The chairman of the Council had a position roughly equivalent to that of prime minister in Western countries.
CPSU	Communist Party of the Soviet Union. In this book, 'the Party' refers to the CPSU.
dacha	Holiday house, usually in the country or at a resort. For officials it usually meant a special state-owned villa, given either for a certain period or indefinitely as the property of a family.
Dalstroi	Main Directorate for Construction in the Far East.
DVF	Far Eastern Front.
DVO	Far Eastern Military District.
FIAN	Physics Institute of the Academy of Sciences.
fond	A collection of documents. Each fond is divided into collections, collections into files, and files into numbered sheets. A reference to archive materials is therefore of the form: Fond No. 8, Collection No. 130, File 18, Sheet 21.
GKO	State Defence Committee.
Glavlit	The censorship organization.
Glavpromstroi	Main Directorate for Industrial Construction Camps of the MVD.
gorkom	The Party committee of a city or town (*gorod*).
Gosbank	The State Bank.

Gosplan	The State Planning Committee.
GPU	*see* State Security Agencies. The initials stand for State Political Administration.
gulag	The prison and labour camp network in the Soviet Union.
Izvestiya	Central government newspaper, second in importance to *Pravda*.
KGB	The Committee of State Security.
kolkhoz	Collective farm. An agrarian producers' cooperative which was obliged to make deliveries to the state at prices fixed by the state. Members also had small private plots around their family homes.
Komsomol	The Soviet Communist youth organization for ages 14 to 28, to which the majority of young people belonged.
krai	Sometimes translated as 'territory'; a large administrative unit, usually in an outlying part of the USSR near a past or present border, in which non-Russian ethnic minorities lived in autonomous regions.
kraikom	The Party committee of a *krai*.
MGB	Ministry of State Security; *see* State Security Agencies.
MVD	Ministry of Internal Affairs; *see* State Security Agencies.
narkom	People's Commissar.
NEP	New Economic Policy. Introduced by Lenin in 1921 in order to revive the economy after the Civil War and the system of War Communism (a policy followed by the Soviet government during the Civil War, 1918–21, involving notably a ban on private trade, forcible requisitioning of grain and centralization of economic institutions and activities). It permitted private enterprise and was expected to last many years. It was terminated by Stalin at the end of the 1920s and replaced by collectivization and the Five Year Plans.
okrug	Usually occurring with the adjective *voenny* and translated as 'military district'. Not the same as *raion*, which is also translated as 'district'.
PGU	First Main Directorate of the Sovnarkom to oversee the atomic project.
Politburo	Political Bureau of the Central Committee of the CPSU. The top decision-making body in the Soviet political system. It was called the Presidium between 1952 and 1966. It consisted of full members with voting rights and candidate members who attended meetings but could not vote.
Presidium of the Central Committee	The name of the Politburo from 1952 to 1966.
raikom	The Party committee of a *raion*.
raion	Usually translated as 'district', it is a smaller unit, a

	number of which make up an *oblast*; a city may also have several *raiony*.
RSDRP	Russian Social–Democratic Workers' Party.
RSFSR	Russian Soviet Federated Socialist Republic, the official name of Soviet Russia from 1917 to 1922, when the USSR was formed.
RTsKhIDNI	The Russian Centre for the Preservation and Study of Documents of Most Recent History.
SNK or Sovnarkom	*see* Council of People's Commissars.
soviet	The Russian word for 'council', the basic governmental unit of the Soviet system.
sovkhoz	A state farm.
State Security Agencies	The Cheka, 1917–22, was succeeded by the GPU (also called OGPU), which in turn was reorganized in 1934 as the NKVD (People's Commissariat of Internal Affairs). In 1941 a separate NKGB (People's Commissariat of State Security) was established, while police duties not directly involving 'state security' were left to the NKVD. In 1946 the NKVD was changed to the MVD (Ministry of Internal Affairs) and the NKGB to the MGB (Ministry of State Security). In 1954, after Stalin's death, the MGB was reorganized as the KGB (Committee of State Security) under the Council of Ministers; that is, it was reduced in status from a ministry to a 'committee' while still remaining very powerful.
Stavka	General headquarters of the Soviet high command.
Supreme Soviet	The Soviet parliament, consisting of elected deputies in two chambers, one based on nationalities, the other on demographic electoral constituencies. Only one candidate, usually proposed by the local Party organization, stood for each seat.
troika	A general term in Russian, meaning 'threesome'; in the Stalin era, a three-member board with special powers to sentence people without following normal legal procedures.
TsIK	Central Executive Committee.
VASKhNIL	Lenin Academy of Agricultural Sciences.
Vlasovites	Russian soldiers commanded by General Vlasov who served in the German army during the war. Vlasov recruited his men from Soviet prisoners of war and from Russian and Ukrainian exiles. After the German defeat the Vlasovites were tried as traitors and sent to the labour camps.
VTsIK	All-Union Central Executive Committee (replaced TsIK after the creation of the USSR in 1923).

Introduction

More than a hundred biographies of Stalin have been written in the USSR, in the new Russia and in other countries in the decades following his death in 1953. When Communist Party and state archives began to open after the collapse of the Soviet Union in 1991, yet more books and articles appeared, some examining specific aspects of the Stalin era: industrialization, collectivization, policies during the war, the terror, etc. Some authors have attempted to rehabilitate Stalin and justify his policies. Several pseudo-biographies have also been published, largely based on fictional 'information'. There have been books about Stalin's family, about his daughter Svetlana and his sons, Yakov and Vasily, as well as other relatives. Richard Harris's novel *Archangel* was a British bestseller in 1999. Stalin is the central figure in a number of memoirs, often published posthumously, by his close and not so close colleagues, ministers, generals, intelligence officers, interpreters and even his personal servants and bodyguards.

In view of this flow of literature about Stalin, the title we have chosen for the present volume, *The Unknown Stalin*, may seem rather surprising. However, after studying much of what has been written about Stalin since the opening of formerly top-secret archives, we remain convinced that so far only a surface layer of the new materials has been explored; a truly informed understanding of Stalin's era and his role in history is just beginning.

Lenin was the protagonist in a revolutionary process that led to the creation of an innovative social and political structure in a new type of state, the Soviet Union. The development of this state into a highly centralized, totalitarian, industrially developed military power was accomplished by Stalin. It was also Stalin who after 1945 established an external empire that extended from Berlin to Beijing. There is a certain irony in the fact that it was the disappearance of this empire and the disintegration of the Soviet Union itself that made it possible for scholars to analyse the role of the USSR in history more objectively and to arrive at a more accurate assessment of the historical significance of its founders. Until recently, the study of history in the USSR was less an academic discipline than a tool of state and Party ideology. Therefore the restoration of a more authentic picture of our history in the twentieth century coincides with the restoration of history itself as a proper academic subject. And this is of significance beyond the borders of the new Russia.

Among the new nation-states that have appeared on the ruins of Stalin's empire, there are some countries that have truly liberated themselves from communist oppression, but there are others that have not been able to develop their own statehood and whose people have experienced political and social degradation. Here it is hardly surprising to find nostalgia for the USSR, although not necessarily for its socialist system, which has given rise to public sentiment in favour of re-integration with the Russian Federation.

After Stalin, increasingly incompetent figures came to power in the Soviet Union, sometimes entirely by chance. Although the economic and military strength of the USSR continued to grow, it was largely inertia that preserved political unity, based on the strength of the early foundations. Not a single ruler of the USSR after Stalin's death contributed anything of substance to these foundations.

Stalin was a ruler, a dictator and a tyrant. But under the mantle of the despot's 'cult of personality' there was also a real person. He certainly was cruel and vindictive but he had other qualities as well: Stalin was a thinking, calculating, hard-working man possessed of an iron will and a considerable intellect; undoubtedly he was a patriot, concerned to uphold historic Russian statehood. This is the 'unknown Stalin' who is the subject of our book. He can only be understood in the context of uncharted aspects of his life and activity. The events analysed in this book have not been examined in detail in any existing biographies. The availability of new material (and no doubt there is more to come in the future) gives us the opportunity to revise certain stereotypes and extend our understanding of disputed episodes of the recent past.

Translator's note

I would like to thank Ralf, who helped to decipher the obscurities of Bukharin's Hegelian terminology. Professor Norman Cohn kindly read the entire text and suggested various stylistic improvements, for which I am extremely grateful. Zhores Medvedev provided crucial assistance with the scientific terminology and, along with Rita Medvedeva, much appreciated moral support.

PART I. AFTERWARDS

CHAPTER 1

Riddles Surrounding Stalin's Death

Zhores Medvedev

Illness or plot?

Was there a plot to murder Stalin? It has often been suggested that he died prematurely as a result of some slow-acting poison. A. Avtorkhanov developed a detailed theory to this effect in a book first published in 1976, naming Beria as the culprit.[1] Many versions of this story have continued to appear, most recently in the biography of Stalin by Edvard Radzinsky, who had entrée to previously inaccessible archive documents.[2] Nevertheless there is still no concrete evidence to substantiate the claim that Stalin's death was anything other than the result of illness.

His death was not unexpected. Although his health had noticeably been deteriorating in the course of 1951–52, he refused to take any medication or submit to medical examinations. His chronic afflictions – high blood pressure, arteriosclerosis and rheumatic pain in his joints and muscles – were all progressive. Towards the end of 1952, after an unidentified lung problem, Stalin suddenly gave up smoking. All these factors pointed to the approaching end. However, the fact that this was obvious to everyone, including Stalin himself, made him increasingly dangerous to all those in his immediate entourage as well as for the country as a whole.

It was in the period February–March 1953 that Stalin accelerated the preparations for trials and sentences relating to two of the most bizarre (even by Soviet standards) repressive campaigns that had ever taken place in the Soviet Union. Hundreds of people were arrested. In the past, Stalinist terror had been fundamentally political. Although there had been brutal operations against specific national groups, they were carried out in secret without the usual accompanying public hysteria, the manner in which the Muslim peoples were expelled from the Northern Caucasus and the Crimea being a perfect example. In 1952, however, the two ethnically based repressive campaigns were given full publicity. An anti-Semitic crusade pro-

1

claimed the existence of a 'Zionist–American conspiracy', linked to the 'Doctors' Plot', while repression in Georgia followed the 'exposure' of a secret Georgian or Georgian–Mingrelian conspiracy to withdraw from the Soviet Union. Even at the time it was quite clear that these campaigns were intimately bound up with Stalin's intention to make changes in the leadership of the country.

By the end of 1952 Molotov, Mikoyan and Voroshilov had lost their political influence and were no longer part of Stalin's immediate circle. The next group of comrades who were under the greatest threat were Malenkov, Beria and Kaganovich. Their fate would have been decided within the next few weeks, and for all of these men Stalin's illness and death did come as a salvation. Given this situation, speculation about a murderous plot by Stalin's closest collaborators is understandable, a Soviet version of a 'palace coup'. The fact that the official report falsified the time and place of Stalin's final stroke has also been used as circumstantial evidence to support the conspiracy theory – he died in his dacha at Kuntsevo and not in his Kremlin apartment as the public was told. And then there was the long, unexplained delay before any doctors were summoned – this too has been used to support the idea of a plot.

Although it is extremely probable that plotting went on at the time of his death, it was not a long-drawn-out conspiracy against Stalin himself but rather a spontaneous response to circumstances at the time of his fatal illness. Once he lost consciousness, paralysed by a massive stroke, Stalin lost power and was no longer part of the 'game'. This was the moment when his closest comrades-in-arms joined forces in order to regain the power they had lost at the Nineteenth Party Congress, convened in the autumn of 1952. This Congress ratified the decision to abolish the Politburo and approved the creation of an expanded Presidium of the Party's Central Committee. During the short interval between Stalin's stroke on 1 March and the summoning of doctors on the morning of 2 March, a redistribution of power was negotiated between two competing alliances, with Malenkov and Beria on one side and Khrushchev and Bulganin on the other. The rivalry between them prevented the emergence of a new supreme leader and laid the basis for the complex inner-Party struggle that went on from 1953 to 1957. It was during this period of instability that a series of crises took place within the CPSU: the arrest of Beria and his allies, Khrushchev's speech on the 'cult of personality' and finally the expulsion of the 'anti-Party group' (Molotov, Malenkov, Voroshilov, Kaganovich, Bulganin, and later the removal of Marshal Zhukov). Ultimately these events, taken together, undermined the authority of the Party and were the starting point for its ultimate demise.

Stalin's health, 1923–40

In the spring of 1923 the young Anastas Mikoyan, already the Secretary of the North Caucasus Party Committee at the age of 27, visited Stalin in his Kremlin apartment during a trip to Moscow. In his memoirs, Mikoyan wrote that Stalin's hand was bandaged. 'My hand gets painful,' Stalin explained, 'especially in spring. It must be rheumatism. After a while it goes away.' When asked why he did not get medical help, Stalin replied, 'And what can the doctors do?'[3] Mikoyan tried to persuade Stalin to go to Sochi for treatment, where the hot sulphur baths had long been thought to have a healing effect, particularly on painful joints, and in the autumn of that year Stalin followed Mikoyan's advice. Stalin did suffer recurring muscular pain in his hands and feet and assumed it was rheumatism brought on by his four-year exile in eastern Siberia, which probably was the case. The treatment did alleviate the pain, but it only provided temporary relief. Even today there is no radical cure for rheumatic or arthritic complaints. Stalin started going to the Matsesta resort near Sochi every year, at first staying in a house found for him by Mikoyan. By 1926 a place was arranged for Stalin on an annual basis in one of the local sanatoria where the head doctor was Ivan Valedinsky. Brief notes by Valedinsky about his meetings with Stalin were published recently, providing a clear picture of Stalin's physical state up until 1940.[4]

Stalin was examined by three doctors who did not discover any abnormal condition. Nevertheless he pursued the full course of mineral water treatments, and it helped. In 1927 Stalin returned with the same problems and remained for almost the whole of December. Before starting the mineral bath treatment, he was again given a thorough physical check-up including blood pressure, lung examination and a cardiogram. All the results were normal. At the time Stalin was 48, and the hot springs soothed his symptoms. In 1928 he spent the whole year in Moscow without a break and did not go south again for a vacation until the beginning of August 1929, first to Nalchik and then to Sochi. He was feeling unwell and only on 29 August was he able to write to Molotov, 'I'm beginning to recuperate.' A month later he informed Moscow, 'I think I'll stay in Sochi another week.' In 1930 and 1931 Stalin again extended his vacation in the south to two months, leaving Moscow at the beginning of August and returning only at the beginning of October. Several friends came to the sanatorium for lengthy visits, notably Voroshilov, Kirov and Gorky, while Molotov presided over meetings of the Politburo in Moscow. Stalin frequently sent him messages by courier, containing instructions on a whole range of questions. A note of 13 August 1930 concluded with the postscript, 'P.S. I'm getting better bit by bit.' A month later, on 13 September, Stalin informed Molotov,

'I'm now <u>completely</u> recovered.' In 1931 he also visited Tskhaltubo and from there wrote to Molotov on 21 August, 'The waters here are truly remarkable. Terrific. I'll tell you in detail when we meet.'[5]

Around this time Stalin appointed Valedinsky as his personal physician, not just in the south but also in Moscow, where on Stalin's orders Valedinsky was given a five-room apartment. He was additionally put in charge of the medical side of developing the Tskhaltubo area as a health resort. The whole Black Sea coast of the Caucasus was intensively developed as a result of Stalin's partiality for the region. Scores of new mineral springs were discovered and many sanatoria and rest houses were built. New factories produced bottled mineral water that was sold throughout the country.

In December 1936 Valedinsky was summoned to the dacha at Kuntsevo where Stalin lay ill with tonsillitis and a high temperature. The patient was also examined by Professor Vladimir Vinogradov, a cardiologist, and by Professor Boris Preobrazhensky, a specialist in throat infections. Stalin greeted Valedinsky as an old friend and asked him about the work of the recently established All-Union Institute of Experimental Medicine. In Stalin's view, the scientists of the Institute 'spend a lot of time on theory but come up with very little in practice and are not working on the problem of life-extension'.[6] Soon after this remark, which of course was relayed to those in charge of the Institute, life-extension became a central subject of Soviet medical research. In 1937 Professor Aleksandr Bogomolets, Director of the Institute of Physiology in Kiev, set up a permanent research unit attached to the Ukrainian Academy of Science to study the phenomenon of longevity in Abkhazia and Georgia. Stalin believed the legends about the inhabitants of the Caucasus, that they lived longer lives as a result of the mountain climate and water from melted glaciers but especially because their diet was rich in meat, dairy products, vegetables and fruit but contained a minimum of grain products. Water from glacial streams, known as the 'water of life', was regularly brought to Stalin in Moscow. He also thought that air quality was improved by wood vapours, which is why all the rooms in which Stalin lived and worked, whether in the Kremlin or at his dachas, had walls of unpainted wood. At the Kuntsevo dacha near Moscow, as well as at his other dachas, Stalin had his own Russian *banya* with steam and a Russian stove. Although there was central heating, in the winter he often liked to have open fires as well. At any sign of pain in his joints or muscles, Stalin turned to heat as a form of self-medication, climbing up to lie on the Russian stove. He continued this practice until the end of his life.

Valedinsky examined Stalin for the last time on 13 February 1940, again because of a throat infection. Stalin had a temperature but continued to work. Bitter battles were being fought on the Soviet–Finnish front, and a map of Finland was spread out on Stalin's desk. He explained the military operation to his doctor and then, tapping the table with his pencil, said, 'Any day now Vyborg will be taken.' (Vyborg was in fact 'taken', but not until a month later.)

In 1944 Professor Valedinsky moved to a government sanatorium near Moscow where he became head doctor, and Stalin chose the cardio-vascular specialist, Professor Vinogradov, to be his personal physician. This choice was determined by new problems with his health: the appearance of symptoms of high blood pressure and arteriosclerosis.

Stalin's work routine

It is well known that Stalin tended to work evenings in the Kremlin, often until late at night. When he arrived at his office, he first looked through and signed papers and then had various meetings. Every day anything from five to six up to 20 to 22 people visited Stalin's office. It was normally long after midnight, sometimes after watching a film, that Stalin drove to the Kuntsevo dacha where after a hearty supper, which was his main meal, he went to bed at three or four in the morning. Before sleep, he would read from books in his own library. He rose between ten and eleven in the morning, ate a light breakfast, worked on papers, dealt with various issues over the telephone and spent time with people who came to the dacha. This whole routine evolved gradually. When Stalin lived in the Kremlin in the 1920s, his office was right next door and he was usually there in the morning. At that time he only went to the dacha in the summer with his family. Like all southerners, Stalin liked to have a nap after his midday meal, and he then continued seeing people in his Kremlin office, finishing work at seven or eight in the evening.

During this period he had a conventional family – a wife, two sons and a daughter – and on the whole this meant a normal lifestyle. But things changed dramatically after the suicide of his wife in 1932, and he could no longer bear living in the Kremlin apartment or at his old dacha at Zubalovo. A new dacha was built for him in 1934 in the middle of a forest tract in the Kuntsevo district near Moscow, only a 15-minute drive from his office. From then on Stalin began to come to the Kremlin only once a day, usually between five and six in the afternoon and then worked until ten or eleven at night and sometimes later. He always slept at Kuntsevo and often invited friends and Party colleagues to late suppers there, which he called 'dinner'. Important government questions were often decided at these gatherings. Great quantities of alcohol were consumed, although according to many witnesses Stalin only drank Georgian wine, his own special remedy for the insomnia that tormented him. Some doctors do in fact recommend alcohol as a sedative.

This same routine continued during the 1941–45 war years, although with much less sleep. Crucial decisions had to be made instantly at any time of the day or night, and it was impossible to take time off or have a vacation. Stalin worked 14–15 hours a day in the Kremlin or at the dacha, which became a branch of military headquarters, with officials from the General Staff coming to report on the situation at the front. A large underground bunker equipped with offices had been swiftly constructed in the grounds of the dacha and anti-aircraft guns were positioned along the external perimeter of the property. During German air raids on Moscow, the guns were blasting away the entire night. Anti-aircraft machine gun installations were set up in the immediate vicinity of the dacha in case of a German attempt at an airborne landing. For three to four months at the end of 1941 and the beginning of 1942, Stalin's main office in Moscow was transferred to an underground location that was part of the Kirov metro station, not far from the Kremlin.

The beginning of serious illness

Stalin suffered his first minor stroke on 9 October 1945. However, no medical details about the exact nature of his illness have been preserved. Possibly it was not a stroke at all but an attack of high blood pressure, i.e. a sharp rise in blood pressure which can be accompanied by spasms in the brain vessels, a temporary loss of consciousness and partial, temporary paralysis.

The Kremlin Hospital kept a file labelled 'J.V. Stalin: Medical History' containing a record of Stalin's health problems over the years. It was normal medical practice for every hospital to keep a dossier on all its regular patients. But after the arrest of Stalin's personal physician, Professor Vinogradov, in 1952, Stalin ordered all his medical records to be destroyed, evidently determined to make sure that no one had access to objective data about his physical condition. In her memoirs, Stalin's daughter Svetlana wrote that in the autumn of 1945, 'father fell ill and was quite unwell for months. The tension and fatigue of the war years and of his age were beginning to tell. He was sixty-six by this time.'[7] However, Svetlana really knew nothing about what had happened to her father, since she was not allowed to visit him or even speak to him on the telephone. For more than a month it was impossible to ring him, which gave rise to rumours that he had temporarily lost his power of speech. On 10 October Moscow papers published a short TASS statement that 'Comrade J.V. Stalin has gone away on holiday.' The announcement appeared in order to allay the spread of rumours after the cancellation of several important meetings with foreign diplomats to discuss the future of Japan. Nevertheless, the foreign press began to speculate about Stalin's health and the question of succession.

In cases of a minor stroke, the patient usually recovers but with a diminished capacity for work. Although the symptoms may disappear, the underlying cause is still there, and the patient is normally advised to change his or her habits and to work fewer hours. In 1945 reliable methods to stabilize or lower blood pressure had not yet been discovered, and doctors usually recommended rest along with sleeping tablets for insomnia. Stalin refused to take sleeping tablets, but he did reduce his workload. From 1946 he began to appear in the Kremlin less frequently and seldom remained for long. Visitors were invited to come at 8, 9 or sometimes 10 pm, and meetings never went on for more than two or three hours. Sometimes current issues were dealt with at the dacha during the day or at dinners in the evening. The number of papers requiring Stalin's official stamp or signature was reduced. According to Svetlana, after his illness in 1945 Stalin spent a large part of his time walking in the woods and parkland that surrounded the Kuntsevo dacha. Several pavilions with little tables were built for him in the park.

> My father spent hours roaming the garden as if he were seeking a quiet, comfortable spot and not finding it. In summer he spent days at a time wandering out of doors and had his official papers, newspapers and tea brought to him in the park. This was luxury as he wanted and understood it. It showed his healthy appetite for life, his enduring love of nature and the soil. It showed his common sense, too, for in later years he was determined to remain in good health and live longer.[8]

In the autumn of 1946 Stalin travelled to the south to have a vacation for the first time since 1937. The holiday began in the Crimea and was extended to three months. A large sanatorium complex was specially built for him in 1949 on the shore of the beautiful mountain lake Ritsa in Abkhazia, making it possible for him to spend several months a year in the mountains, 1,000 metres above sea level.

Svetlana visited her father for the last time at the Kuntsevo dacha on 21 December 1952, the day of his official birthday. He was 73:

> He did not look well that day. Apparently he was feeling the signs of illness, perhaps high blood pressure, because he had suddenly stopped smoking and was very proud of it – he had certainly been smoking for not less than 50 years.[9]

Svetlana noticed that her father's complexion had changed colour. Normally he was pale but on that day his face had a ruddy look. She correctly suspected that it was a sign of severe high blood pressure.

But by then his personal physician was in prison, and there were no regular medical check-ups.

Stalin had stopped smoking when he had pain in his lungs and found himself gasping for breath – these were signs of the beginning of emphysema or chronic bronchitis. But when people addicted to nicotine suddenly stop smoking, it leads to a process of physiological and psychological change that continues over several months, including changes of metabolism that lead to the deposit of fat. Irritability increases along with a loss of concentration. Stalin had always been slim, and he did put on weight at the beginning of 1953, which in turn led to a rise in blood pressure. The destructive process suffered by the body could have been slowed down by a sanatorium regime of total rest. But for the first time in the post-war period, Stalin refused to take a break in the autumn or winter of 1952 despite the enormous amount of time and effort he spent on organizing the Nineteenth Party Congress in October. Immediately after the Congress, with a new Party structure in place, Stalin turned his attention to pursuing two wide-ranging repressive campaigns, later known as the 'Doctors' Plot' and the 'Mingrelian conspiracy', which ultimately were intended to bring about major changes in the highest leadership of Party and state. In November and December 1952 the most frequent visitors to Stalin's Kremlin office were the Minister of State Security, Semyon Ignatiev, and his deputies Goglidze, Ryasnoi and Ogoltsov.

In the first half of February 1953 Stalin had meetings with several members of the state security apparatus to discuss the reorganization of the foreign intelligence service. Among those he sent for was General Pavel Sudoplatov, at that time deputy head of the First Directorate (intelligence) of the MGB. In recently published memoirs, Sudoplatov wrote:

> I entered Stalin's study feeling agitated until I looked at him. I was startled to see a tired old man. Stalin had changed greatly. His hair was thinner, and although he had always spoken calmly and slowly, now he talked with difficulty and his pauses between sentences were longer.[10]

1–2 March 1953: eyewitness accounts

Visitors were admitted to the Kremlin office for the last time on the evening of 17 February 1953. From 8 to 8:30 pm Stalin received a delegation from India led by the Indian ambassador, Krishna Menon. At 10:15 Bulganin, Beria and Malenkov arrived, but they only stayed for a short time, approximately 15 minutes. On 27 February, Stalin attended a performance of *Swan Lake* at the Bolshoi. On the 28th, a Saturday, he went to the Kremlin in the evening to watch a film with his four most frequent companions, Khrushchev, Bulganin, Malenkov and Beria. Afterwards he invited them to a late supper at Kuntsevo. The meal began around midnight and ended towards four in the morning of Sunday 1 March. According to Khrushchev, Stalin was in high spirits and seemed in good health.

On the next day, Sunday 1 March, Khrushchev was expecting another invitation. It had become a tradition, particularly on Sundays when things were quieter, since Stalin hated being on his own. 'As soon as he woke up, he would ring us – the four of us – and either invite us to see a film or start some long conversation about a question that could have been resolved in two minutes.' Khrushchev waited at home, reluctant to begin his lunch. 'I didn't eat for the whole day, thinking, perhaps will he ring? Finally I gave up and had a meal. The call never came.'[11]

Khrushchev's son Sergei, who at that time was a student living with his parents, confirmed this account in his own memoir of his father:

> My father knew very well that Stalin could not bear to be on his own on an empty day, that he would summon them to come. He did not sit down to eat with us and went for a stroll, telling us to get him immediately if a phone call came from there. ... It began to get dark. He had a bite to eat and started looking at his papers. It was well into the evening when Malenkov rang, saying that something had happened to Stalin. Father left in a hurry.[12]

At the end of February it began to get dark in Moscow at around 5:30 pm. It was approximately 11 pm when Malenkov telephoned Khrushchev.

On Sunday 1 March several members of staff were on duty from 10 am in the service quarters of the dacha, adjacent to Stalin's rooms: MGB Lieutenant-Colonel Mikhail Starostin, who was a senior member of Stalin's bodyguard, Pyotr Lozgachev, assistant to the commandant of the dacha, and Matryona Butusova who served as a waitress and looked after the linen, described by Khrushchev as 'Stalin's devoted servant who worked at the dacha for many years'. There were also other employees present in the house: the cook, gardener and librarian, all those who might be called upon to satisfy any of Stalin's personal needs. The actual physical protection of the dacha was the responsibility of a special unit of the MGB that kept the whole area under surveillance and guarded all approaches and entrances to the dacha. Two high, thick wooden fences surrounded the entire periphery of the property, and the space between them was patrolled by guards with dogs. The duty officer who stood at the entrance gate was always a senior member of the guard. All visitors underwent an extremely thorough examination. The turning into Stalin's dacha was off the Mozhaisky highway with a barrier across the road which the guards only raised for government cars. A second check took place at the gate and a third at the entrance to the dacha, where the officer on guard was a state security colonel in military uniform. A two-storey building adjoining the grounds of the dacha provided housing or barracks for ordinary members of the guard numbering around 100 soldiers and officers.

All the rooms of the dacha and its service quarters were linked by an internal telephone system, including, of course, all of Stalin's rooms, even the bathroom and toilet. Stalin used this line to order food or tea or to ask for newspapers or the post to be brought. Additionally, almost every room that Stalin might conceivably use contained special government and Kremlin telephones as well as an instrument linked to the ordinary Moscow network. Top Party and government officials were connected to each other by two or three special 'Kremlin' telephone lines, and in any urgent situation they could ring Stalin direct. These included members of the Politburo, the most important members of the government, ministers in charge of the MGB and the MVD, the Minister of Defence, the head of the General Staff, the heads of principal departments of the Central Committee, the first secretaries of regional Party committees and Party leaders in the republics, commandants of border military districts, secretaries of the Central Committee and certain others.

Certainly no one ever contacted Stalin unless it was absolutely necessary, and according to Starostin and Lozgachev, who were on duty at the dacha, Stalin received no telephone calls on Sunday 1 March. Edvard Radzinsky has recorded Lozgachev's account of the sequence of events on that day. At around 10 am the guards and service staff gathered in the kitchen, waiting for Stalin to ring. He usually gave his first orders between 10 and 11 in the morning. Butusova would bring him breakfast in what was called the small dining room. But on 1 March there was only silence. According to Lozgachev: 'At 10:00 a.m. there was "no movement" in his rooms. ... 11:00 a.m. came, 12:00 and still no movement. It began to seem strange.'[13]

The expression 'there was no movement' referred to the fact that in addition to the internal telephone, a special signalling system had been installed in all Stalin's rooms so that the guards could be sure of his exact whereabouts at any time; this included sensors fitted into the soft furnishings and on the doors between rooms. (After Stalin's death, when discussing the possibility of turning the dacha into a Stalin museum, a group of officials from the Marx–Engels–Lenin–Stalin Institute visited the dacha. Yevgeniya Zolotukhina, a member of the group, later recalled: 'Springs were sticking out of all the soft furnishings, the remnants of the special sensors which had signalled Stalin's location to the guards.'[14])

To continue Lozgachev's story:

> 1:00 p.m. came – and there was still no movement. We began to be
> alarmed. 3:00 p.m., 4:00 p.m. – no movement. ... I was sitting there
> with Starostin and he said: 'There's something wrong, what shall we
> do?' We wondered whether to go in there ... 8:00 p.m., still nothing.
> We didn't know what to do. 9:00 p.m., no movement. 10:00 p.m. still
> nothing.

Lozgachev's account has been corroborated by the testimony of
Starostin, recorded in 1977 by Stalin's former bodyguard A.T. Rybin,
who had become head of the guards at the Bolshoi Theatre (also a
special 'object' for MGB protection) and was no longer working at
the dacha in 1953. On his own initiative after retirement, he began to
collect witness accounts relating to various incidents of Stalin's life
and also the circumstances at the time of his death. Rybin published
several booklets in 1995, including one devoted to the events of
March 1953. He quotes Starostin as follows:

> At 10:00 p.m. I tried to send Lozgachev to Stalin because by this time
> Stalin's behaviour seemed very strange indeed. But Lozgachev urged
> me to go instead, insisting, 'You're the more senior, you should be the
> first one to go.' We argued back and forth and time passed.[15]

Lozgachev, quoted by Radzinsky whose book was written much
later, confirms this picture:

> I said to Starostin: 'You go, you're in charge of the guard, you ought
> to be getting worried.' And he said, 'I'm afraid.' I said, 'You're afraid –
> what do you think I am, a hero?' About then they brought the mail –
> a packet from the Central Committee. It was usually our job to take
> the mail straight to him. Or rather my job, the mail was my responsi-
> bility. 'Oh well,' I said, 'I'll go.'[16]

The scene described above, which is meant to be a genuine description of what actually took place, certainly sounds very peculiar
and is also extremely improbable. Men, who at the slightest indication of any cause for alarm were required to alert their immediate
superior and take whatever measures were necessary, waited for
hours doing nothing while knowing something had happened? They
were afraid to open Stalin's door as if in danger of an armed am-
bush? The argument between Starostin and Lozgachev was supposed
to have taken place in the special service building connected to the
dacha by a long corridor of about 25 metres. The doors leading to the
living quarters of the dacha were never locked, and Stalin enjoyed
easy and informal relations with the servants and others on duty at
the dacha. As evening approached on 1 March all members of staff,
including the guards, were quite naturally increasingly concerned,
and it would not have been normal for the staff to be afraid of entering Stalin's room or even to ring him on the house line. Dmitry

Volkogonov attempted to explain the source of this fear in his short biography of Stalin, published in 1996: 'after mid-day, the servants became extremely alarmed. However, no one dared to go to the Boss without being summoned; this was because of Beria's orders.'[17] But it was virtually impossible for the guards to have been given such an order by Beria. He had not been in charge of the MGB or the guards service since 1946 and, in accordance with government and Politburo lines of authority, only the MVD was under his control.

Lozgachev stated that he finally entered Stalin's quarters with the packet from the Central Committee at about 10:30 pm. What he found in the small dining room has been described many times, often in slightly different versions, as Lozgachev had a tendency to modify his story. The basic picture, however, remains the same – Stalin lay on the floor next to the table in an undershirt and pyjama bottoms, wet from reflex urine. It was clear that he had been lying there for some hours and that he was extremely cold. There was a glass and a bottle of mineral water on the table. Apparently Stalin had got out of bed and went to the table for a glass of water, but at that moment he had had a stroke. It was clear from the scene that all this had taken place in the morning, in any case before 11 am. Lozgachev called for help on the internal phone. Starostin, Tukov and Butusova came running. The four of them carried Stalin to the other room, the big dining room as it was called, where they laid him on the sofa and covered him with a rug. He was paralysed and did not respond to questions although his eyes were open.

What happened next has been described both by Starostin (as told to Rybin in 1977) and Lozgachev (recorded by Radzinsky in 1995), and on the whole their accounts corroborate each other. MGB Lieutenant-Colonel Starostin was the senior officer of the guards and it was his responsibility to summon assistance. According to Svetlana Alliluyeva, who during the next days talked to other members of the staff working at the dacha, 'All the servants were extremely upset and urged them to call a doctor. ... But the senior officers of the guard decided to inform their own superiors first and ask for instructions.'[18]

According to Starostin:

> The first thing I did was ring the Chairman of the MGB, Semyon Ignatiev, to report Stalin's condition. Ignatiev told me to contact Beria. I kept ringing Beria but got no answer. I rang Malenkov and told him what happened. Malenkov murmured something into the receiver and hung up. About 30 minutes later Malenkov rang back and said, 'Try and find Beria yourself, I can't get hold of him.' Soon after that Beria rang to say 'Don't tell anyone about Comrade Stalin's illness,' and he put the phone down.[19]

Why would Ignatiev have told him to contact Beria? Ignatiev was afraid of Beria and they were enemies. Could it be that this whole story was invented to make Beria seem responsible? We have no way of knowing. Lozgachev recalls these conversations to have taken place between 10 and 11 at night:

> I sat beside Stalin, counting the minutes, assuming that Beria and Malenkov would have called the doctors and that they would soon arrive, but no one came. The clock struck 11:00 but other than that, there was dead silence. I kept looking at the clock – the hands showed that it was 1:00, then 2:00 ... finally at 3:00 in the morning I heard the sound of a car pulling up to the dacha. I was heartened by the thought that soon I would be able to hand Stalin over to the care of the doctors but was cruelly mistaken. Stalin's comrades, Beria and Malenkov appeared. ... Beria, his pince-nez gleaming, came up to me and said, 'Lozgachev, why are you in such a panic? Can't you see, Comrade Stalin is sleeping soundly. Don't disturb him and stop alarming us.' They stood there for a while and then turned and left.[20]

Neither Starostin nor Lozgachev mention the arrival of Khrushchev and Bulganin. This can be explained by the fact that although they had come to the dacha a little earlier, they had restricted themselves to a conversation with the guards on duty at the gate and never entered Stalin's quarters. After their chat with the Chekists (as the guards were called), they left without giving any instructions. In his memoirs, Khrushchev wrote that he had been informed about Stalin's condition by Malenkov at about midnight after he had already gone to bed:

> I immediately sent for my car and quickly got dressed. I got there within about 15 minutes. We agreed that we would first talk to the guards before going to Stalin.

The guards gave Khrushchev and Bulganin a general picture of the events of the day and described Stalin's condition. Khrushchev continued:

> When they told us what had happened, we decided that it wouldn't be suitable for us make our presence known while Stalin was in such an unpresentable state. We separated and went home.[21]

When Khrushchev wrote, 'We agreed that we would talk first to the guards', it seems that he was referring to an understanding with Malenkov and not with Bulganin, who accompanied him to the dacha. Malenkov and Beria, having delayed their arrival for some reason, wanted to be the first to inspect the scene and then decide what had to be done. But in the end they did nothing, at least not as far as Stalin was concerned.

Resuming Lozgachev's story:

Once again I was left on my own beside Stalin. The clock on the wall continued to chime – 4 o'clock, 5:00, 6:00, 7:00, 8:00 – and nothing happened. It was the worst night of my life. ... At 8:30 Khrushchev arrived and said: 'The doctors will be here right away.' They finally came at around 9:00 in the morning, among them Dr. Lukomsky, and they started to examine the patient.[22]

In the end, the doctors had come as a result of Starostin's repeated phone calls to Malenkov and Beria at about 7 am. The bodyguards had not been contacted during the night nor did they receive any inquiries about Stalin's condition. But they knew that if Stalin were to die, they would be the ones who would be held responsible and blamed for delaying the arrival of medical help. For some time all the employees at the dacha had been demanding that the doctors be called immediately, and the main building of the Kremlin Hospital was quite nearby. According to Svetlana Alliluyeva, 'the servants and the guards were extremely upset, insisting that the doctors should be summoned at once. When they heard that Beria had been there and said, "Nothing's happened, he's sleeping soundly," they all became quite furious.'[23]

Khrushchev wrote in his own memoirs that he went to the dacha for the first time at around midnight. This is corroborated by his son Sergei, who went on to say:

I was rather surprised by my father's speedy return, he had been away only for one and a half or two hours. However, no one asked him any questions and without a word he returned to his bedroom and again busied himself with his papers. ... I never heard him go out again, I must have been asleep. This time my father was gone for a long time and did not return until morning.[24]

Khrushchev's movements during this second absence are far from clear, and according to his own version, he only left home again when it was already morning, in response to a new phone call from Malenkov. What is certain is that neither Khrushchev nor any of the other members of the 'quartet' ever went to bed that night.

1–2 March 1953: additional details

From the account they received from the guards at the gate soon after midnight, it was absolutely clear to Khrushchev and Bulganin that Stalin had suffered a stroke, or a 'blow' as it was called at that time. It was also obvious to Malenkov and Beria after Starostin's phone call. The fact that for many hours Stalin had lain on the floor, undressed, paralysed and unable to speak, provided more than enough evidence for them to come to that conclusion. Therefore Khrushchev's and Bulganin's unwillingness to go to Stalin or talk to Lozgachev and Starostin, Beria's 'he's only sleeping soundly' as well as Beria's earlier order that no one be informed of Stalin's illness – none of these reactions could have had any justification if there was an intention to help the victim. Clearly Stalin was in a critical condition, and there were other reasons for the delay in summoning medical assistance. The problem was that once the doctors were called, news of Stalin's illness inevitably would spread beyond the inner circle, but for the Party leaders it was crucial to have some time to come to an agreement about the governance of the country and the future distribution of power. They also may well have been hoping that the undoubtedly serious stroke would lead to Stalin's death sooner rather than later. His sudden death would certainly be preferable to the prolonged uncertainty that followed Lenin's paralysis in 1922. An extended illness would stop them from going ahead with a reorganization of the leadership.

Neither Khrushchev nor, needless to say, Malenkov, had any idea which doctors should be contacted. Therefore they called the Minister of Health, A.F. Tretyakov at about 7 am on 2 March, and he selected a group of *Russian* doctors (it was specified that they must be Russian) for the first consultation. On the morning of 2 March Voroshilov and Kaganovich were informed of Stalin's illness, and a little later, Stalin's daughter Svetlana and his son Vasily.

As has been mentioned previously, during this period the guards at the dacha as well as in the Kremlin were under the command of the Minister of the MGB, Semyon Ignatiev, and *not* Beria, as many have mistakenly written. Ignatiev, in turn, reported personally to Stalin – after the death of Dzerzhinsky at the end of the 1920s, Stalin maintained direct personal control over all the security organizations. Furthermore the proposition that Starostin and Lozgachev stood at the door of Stalin's quarters from 10:30 in the morning until 10:30 at night, in a state of distress and taking no action, simply does not make sense. Khrushchev, as we have seen from his own memoirs and also those of his son, was quite disturbed by the absence of the expected phone call from the dacha. Undoubtedly his other comrades were also waiting for Stalin's call, particularly Beria, Malenkov and Bulganin. Stalin's personal office in the Kremlin continued to function, even on Sundays. Since Khrushchev and Beria were both known to be extremely impatient men, it is difficult to imagine that neither of them phoned Stalin's dacha to find out what was going on. But the fact that neither Starostin nor Lozgachev recollected any such phone calls does not mean that they never occurred. As well as the direct Kremlin telephone line between most senior Party officials, Party leaders would also have been able to contact the senior guards on duty at the dacha as well as the personal bodyguards. They could ring Stalin on his direct line, the

Kremlin *vertushka*, and only Stalin would have lifted the receiver. But of course Stalin was not answering any phone calls that day.

If any unusual situation were to arise, Stalin's bodyguards were required to report to Semyon Ignatiev, the Minister of State Security, and carry out his instructions. Ignatiev had been put in charge of the MGB's guard service in May 1952 after the removal of General Nikolai Vlasik, who for many years had been the head of Stalin's personal bodyguard. Several of Stalin's biographers have attributed the removal of Vlasik to a conspiracy by Beria. Vlasik was transferred to work as a deputy to the commandant of one of the labour camps in the Sverdlovsk region where he was subsequently arrested. Radzinsky has suggested that Stalin could have been poisoned on the night of 1 March by one of the dacha guards, Ivan Khrustalev, on Beria's orders. He bases his theory precisely on the fact of Vlasik's convenient absence: 'After Vlasik's arrest, Beria of course had recruited support for himself among Stalin's guard, which was no longer under proper supervision. ... Beria had seized his last chance of survival.'[25] This is a rather whimsical suggestion, however. There were many reasons for Vlasik's dismissal, and he would not have been arrested without Stalin's personal approval. The order for arrest could only have come from Ignatiev and not from Beria. It is highly unlikely, and almost impossible in fact, that Stalin could have been poisoned by Khrustalev, whom he treated in a particularly friendly manner.

Stalin knew Vlasik from the days of the Civil War and trusted him completely. In 1934 Vlasik became the head of Stalin's personal bodyguard and from 1946 was in charge of the entire guards unit of the MGB, which turned the bodyguards of other members of the Politburo and the government into subordinates. This enabled Vlasik to serve also as Stalin's private 'informer', but he played the role with a growing lack of conscientiousness; his own moral and material corruption made him vulnerable and a likely subject for blackmail. Stalin undoubtedly lost confidence in Vlasik, and his arrest was not entirely arbitrary. He was not released after Stalin's death or Beria's arrest in June, and eventually was put on trial in 1955. When Vlasik was dismissed in 1952 and Poskrebyshev removed as head of Stalin's personal office, it actually became *more* difficult for Beria to have access to information about what Stalin was planning with the MGB, and he was unable to follow the progress of the investigation of the 'Doctors' Plot' or the 'Mingrelian conspiracy'. From the middle of 1952 Stalin was relying on Ignatiev to implement these wide-ranging repressive campaigns. He was made a member of the Presidium of the Central Committee after the Nineteenth Party Congress, but apart from all his senior positions it was definitely Ignatiev who was head of the Guards Directorate at the beginning of 1953 and in charge of Stalin's personal bodyguard, and he was certainly the first person whom Starostin would have rung. But Ignatiev would also have been receiving reports from the senior officers in the special subdivision of the MGB Guards Directorate at the dacha.

When Stalin's dacha was built in 1934 in a dense, mixed forest not far from Volynskoe, this village was well beyond the limits of the city. But by 1953 Moscow had expanded and Volynskoe was already on the outskirts of the city – hence the need for the very tight security structures described previously. Stalin led a rather physically active life at the dacha. Dressed in a warm sheepskin coat and felt boots, he was able to go out for winter walks. Sometimes he went for rides on a horse-drawn sled along the 'ring' passage between the two fences surrounding the property. He could order the heat to be turned on in the Russian bath-house and he also liked to spend time in the dacha's greenhouse-conservatory. The plan for the day, including meals and the names of guests to be invited, would be arranged in the morning or on the previous evening. But he could also suddenly decide to go to the theatre or see a film in the Kremlin. Each of these options required distinct security operations, particularly as Stalin did not like his bodyguards to be too close. Obviously the Kuntsevo dacha was a priority 'object' for the MGB protection service, and therefore Ignatiev received regular reports about Stalin's plans from the dacha so that he could ensure that all necessary arrangements were made. Sunday 1 March would have been no exception. Ignatiev certainly would have been rung from the dacha and informed that the daily routine had changed, since Stalin did not get up in the morning as usual and had not given any instructions for the day. This phone call evidently was made by the senior duty officer. Ignatiev surely would have telephoned later in order to check the situation.

It is very likely that Ignatiev, via his own channels of communication with the dacha, would have known much earlier than the others that Stalin did not rise as usual on that Sunday and was not answering any of the special government telephone lines. The situation must have been fairly clear to Ignatiev, but to raise the alarm and call the doctors, which he certainly could have done without any instructions from Beria, would have had complicated ramifications. Above all he had to think about how to save his own skin.

In November 1952 the Bureau of the Presidium of the Central Committee resolved that if Stalin were absent (at the time this referred to absences on holiday), chairmanship of the government would be taken in turns. Stalin was exercising power largely through the government structure during this period, and the post of General Secretary no longer existed. If Stalin was away, government meetings would be chaired in turn by Beria, Pervukhin and Saburov. Beria would come first, and in that case Ignatiev unquestionably would be his very first victim. Malenkov headed the list of alternate chairmen of the Bureau of the Central Committee Presidium and of the Secretariat; therefore the Beria–Malenkov 'duo' would be in charge if Stalin's phones suddenly went silent, at least until the Presidium of the Central Committee was summoned. For this reason it was definitely in Ignatiev's interest to delay the news of Stalin's illness or possible death – it would be helpful for his potential allies while putting Beria and Malenkov at a certain disadvantage.

After Stalin's death, although Ignatiev lost his position as Minister for State Security as a result of Beria's temporary rise, he nevertheless was promoted to the post of Secretary of the Central Committee in charge of supervising the organs of state security and internal affairs. Beria made several unsuccessful attempts to have Ignatiev expelled from the Party and put on trial for his criminal role in the 'Doctors' Plot' operation. But this whole affair had not been resolved by Beria; it was probably Ignatiev himself who closed the case on 1 March, just around the time that Starostin and Lozgachev were in a such a state of distress because of the absence of movement in Stalin's quarters.

1–2 March 1953: the sudden end of the 'Doctors' Plot'

The investigations into the 'Doctors' Plot' and the 'Georgian–Mingrelian Conspiracy' were approaching completion towards the end of February. Although more people had been arrested in connection with the Mingrelian case, it was considered to be largely of local significance, and the trial was scheduled to take place in Tbilisi. Beria was a Mingrelian, the majority of those arrested were his protégés and some were good friends; therefore no one could have any doubts that the conclusion of the case would signal the end of his career. The 'Doctors' Plot' had much broader implications because of its anti-Semitic overtones and its relevance to national relations within the USSR. The sentencing and execution of prominent physicians inevitably would lead to an unprecedented anti-Semitic campaign and an international outcry; there were widespread rumours of the possibility of mass deportations of Jews from Moscow to remote regions of the country. Several historians have suggested a link between the 'Doctors' Plot' and Stalin's alleged intention to provoke a new world war. However, there is no evidence to support this theory.

It is generally assumed that the initial stimulus for the case against the doctors was provided by a letter from Dr Lydia Timashuk, the cardiologist at the Kremlin Hospital, who had claimed that the treatment being given to Politburo member Andrei Zhdanov was unsuitable. But the story is rather more complicated. In his 'secret speech' to the Twentieth Congress in February 1956, Khrushchev crudely and deliberately distorted the facts:

> Let us also recall the case of the doctor-saboteurs (a buzz of excitement in the hall). ... Actually there was no 'case' whatsoever outside of the statement by the woman doctor Timashuk, who was probably influenced or ordered by someone (she was, after all, an unofficial collaborator of the organs of state security) to write a letter to Stalin claiming that doctors were applying improper methods of medical treatment. For Stalin such a letter was sufficient for him to come to the immediate conclusion that there were doctor-saboteurs in the Soviet Union. He gave orders for the arrest of a group of eminent Soviet medical specialists.[26]

The true circumstances were quite different. Timashuk's letter, which had not been addressed to Stalin but to the head of the Guards Directorate of the MGB, Vlasik, was written on 29 August 1948. It concerned the diagnosis of Zhdanov's illness and was not inappropriate in view of the fact that Zhdanov was still alive at the time. It was a handwritten letter, hurriedly prepared on the advice of Zhdanov's own personal bodyguard, Major Belov. On 28 August 1948 Zhdanov had suffered a heart attack while on vacation at a Central Committee sanatorium in the Valdai hills, north-west of Moscow. He had already suffered a coronary thrombosis at the end of 1941, so the heart problem was nothing new. Timashuk was summoned urgently from Moscow to take a cardiogram and make a diagnosis. The preliminary report by other doctors had found only a 'heart inadequacy', while the electrocardiogram done by Timashuk showed a massive heart attack and determined its exact location. This diagnosis indicated a strict bed-rest regime. However, the principal doctors involved – the head of the Medical-Sanatorium Department of the Kremlin, Pyotr Yegorov, the senior cardiologist, Vladimir Vinogradov, Professor V. Kh. Vasilenko, and the doctor in charge of treatment, G.I. Mayorov – refused to accept Timashuk's diagnosis or modify the patient's previous regime, allowing him to go for walks and to the cinema, etc. In her letter Timashuk defended her own diagnosis, attached a copy of the electrocardiogram for a second opinion and warned that without constant bed rest, 'there could be a tragic outcome.'[27] Timashuk's diagnosis was not recorded in the case notes. Two days later on 31 August, getting out of bed to go to the toilet, Zhdanov died. The results of the post-mortem examination confirmed Timashuk's original diagnosis, but this was not made public in the official communiqué announcing the illness and death of Zhdanov. Timashuk was certainly the one who got it right in this medical dispute and the diagnosis of the other doctors was erroneous. But there was no question of Stalin coming to any 'immediate conclusion', and it is not even known whether or not he was aware of Timashuk's letter in 1948. In several studies of the 'Doctors' Plot' it is alleged that Vlasik was removed in 1952 precisely because he concealed Timashuk's letter. But all the doctors that she mentioned were in fact Russian, and a 'Zionist conspiracy' could hardly have been conjured up on the basis of her letter.

The whole notion of a 'Zionist conspiracy' against the Party leadership had been invented by Stalin at the end of 1948 as a continuation of the campaign against 'cosmopolitans' begun in 1946. Scores of people were arrested in 1949 as part of this anti-Semitic campaign along with almost all the members of the Jewish Anti-Fascist Committee, including Molotov's wife, Polina. The celebrated Jewish theatre director, Solomon Mikhoels, was killed during a visit to Minsk in January 1948, according to a special scenario devised by Stalin. The murder was disguised as an automobile accident and personally organized by the Deputy Minister of State Security, Sergei Ogoltsov, and the Belorussian MGB chief, Lavrenty Tsanava. The anti-Semitic campaign continued throughout the whole period 1948–52, with the 'discovery' of a mounting number of plots. When the investigation of the Georgian–Mingrelian case began sometime later, several of the accused were compelled to testify that Beria was concealing his Jewish origins. Stalin initiated the 'Doctors' Plot' episode in October 1952, ordering the arrest of Dr Yegorov, the director of the Kremlin Hospital, followed by the arrest of his personal physician, Professor Vinogradov, and another doctor, Professor Vasilenko. Only then was Timashuk's letter retrieved from the archives. It was also Stalin who invented the Zionist aspect of the 'Doctors' Plot'. Viktor Abakumov, who had been appointed in 1946, was still the Minister when the MGB embarked on the fabrication of a huge American-Zionist conspiracy. Although officially Abakumov reported directly to Stalin, since Abakumov was a professional Chekist, Stalin feared that he might have secret links with Beria. In July 1951 Abakumov was arrested and accused of allowing too many Jews to occupy leading positions in the central apparatus of the MGB. The new Minister for State Security, Ignatiev, was a professional Party worker who had been head of the Cadres Department of the Central Committee. With the appointment of Ignatiev, Stalin removed the MGB from Beria's influence, although Ignatiev made only a few personnel changes and most of the professional staff members were retained.

The case of the 'Doctors' Plot' was in the process of taking shape with a new Zionist slant added on. More doctors from the Kremlin Hospital were arrested, one of whom, Miron Vovsi, was a brother of Solomon Mikhoels. The whole case was an extremely crude concoction, based on the 'testimony' of Yakov Etinger, a doctor who died under torture and was therefore unable to confirm his evidence in court.

On 13 January *Pravda* reported that the security organs had uncovered a 'group of terrorist doctors who aimed to cut short the lives of active public figures in the Soviet Union by means of sabotaged medical treatment', and from then on earlier anti-Semitic cases were simply lumped together with the 'Doctors' Plot'. The story named the Jewish doctors who had allegedly been recruited by the international Jewish bourgeois-nationalist organization 'Joint'. Among the arrested doctors were some who were actually Russian and also rather prominent, and they were linked to other organizations. Stalin's former personal physician, Professor Vinogradov, and the head of the Kremlin medical service, Dr Yegorov, were said to be long-term agents of British Intelligence.

These entirely absurd accusations provided the basis for an unrestrained and increasingly hysterical crusade in the press, particularly in *Pravda*. Every day the major papers published some item or other exposing subversive activity in the USSR by American, British, Israeli and various other secret services. The evident signs of an incipient pogrom aroused anxiety throughout the world. Sunday 1 March, however, turned out to be the last day of this anti-Semitic, anti-Western onslaught. On that day one could still read about the 'dispatch of spies, saboteurs, wreckers and murderers to the USSR' or that 'Zionist organizations are used for espionage activities' or how the Jewish organization 'Joint' engaged in espionage-sabotage activity. But on Monday 2 March neither *Pravda* nor any other central paper contained a single anti-Semitic remark or any trace of anti-Zionist material. Nor did anything of that kind appear in the days that followed. The anti-Semitic campaign was over.

In the Soviet Union, national newspapers were typeset on the evening before the day of publication. The editor signed the dummy after the whole text had been examined by the censor, and during the night the typeset was dispatched by air on special planes to the capitals of the other republics and to large cities, where papers such as *Pravda* and *Izvestia* appeared on the street or reached their subscribers only several hours later than in Moscow. The Moscow edition was ready at 6 am and was delivered to subscribers with the morning post. This means that the instruction to stop the anti-Semitic, anti-American campaign linked to the forthcoming trial had to have been received by newspaper editors and the censorship organ, Glavlit, by the early afternoon of 1 March at the latest. Analogous directives would have had to be sent to state television and radio. In fact the necessary instructions would have had to reach not only the editors of *Pravda* and *Izvestia* but also all editors in all vehicles of mass communication as well as the instructors and propagandists at every level of the Party. There was only one service that would have been capable of so abruptly putting an end to such a massive propaganda campaign that had already gained considerable momentum. It could only have been the Agitprop Department of the Central Committee, the same body that had directed and co-ordinated the whole campaign in the first place.

One of the first authors to suggest that Stalin had been murdered by Beria, Abdurakhman Avtorkhanov, placed special emphasis on the sudden absence of anti-Semitic material in the press on 2 March. This provided the main circumstantial evidence for his theory that Stalin was murdered during the night of 1 March, with all members of the 'quartet' at the 'last supper' taking part in the conspiracy. He wrote:

> By March 1st, power was already to all intents and purposes in the hands of the 'quartet'. ... The objective proof of this lies in the sudden end of the campaign against 'enemies of the people' in *Pravda* on March 1–2.[28]

Avtorkhanov is of course right to claim that a change in Party and state policy took place on 1 March and was reflected in the press on 2 March. However, neither Beria nor Khrushchev had a direct channel to the entire mass communications network. Only one person, the Central Committee Secretary for Ideology, Mikhail Suslov, could have organized a general directive from Agitprop, while an instruction to Glavlit could only have come from Ignatiev, the Minister for State Security. The censorship organization of the USSR, acting as a system to prevent the publication of state secrets, received constantly updated lists of forbidden topics and subject matter compiled by the state security organs in collaboration with the Agitprop Department. There would have been no way of issuing a general directive to the press and censorship without the involvement of Suslov and Ignatiev. In November 1952 Dmitri Shepilov, who had once been close to Zhdanov, was appointed to be editor-in-chief of *Pravda*. On Malenkov's orders, Shepilov had been removed from all his posts at the time of the 'Leningrad affair' in 1950 and he spent several months without work, expecting to be arrested. It was Stalin who brought him back to the Central Committee apparatus as part of his preparations for a reorganization of the entire ideological system. Stalin was intent on promoting educated Marxists to the Party leadership which would mean putting the manager-administrators, including all members of his closest circle, in a subordinate role. (Malenkov, when he became aware of this general plan, immediately ordered new bookshelves to be built in his main office in the Central Committee Building and had them filled with over 700 volumes on philosophy, political economy and history.)

We still have no way of knowing exactly how the anti-Semitic campaign was stopped on 1 March or who was ultimately responsible. In posthumously published memoirs Shepilov totally evaded the question, although any relevant directive must have come to him as the editor of *Pravda*. It is clear, however, that the end of the propaganda campaign was associated with a decision to abandon preparations for the trial of the doctors. The actual order could only have come from Ignatiev. It is also conceivable, however, that Stalin had given the instruction himself on 27 or 28 February. An indication that Stalin might have been considering this option is provided by the fact that a special letter to *Pravda* was being prepared in February at his behest, signed by a number of prominent Soviet Jews.

Semyon Ignatiev: the organizer of terror saves his own life

During November and December 1952 Stalin had summoned Ignatiev to the Kremlin several times. Possibly he was also invited to the dacha where more confidential conversations could take place without witnesses. On 3 November 1952 Stalin had a meeting with Ignatiev and his two first deputies, Sergei Goglidze and Vasily Ryasnoi, along with Mikhail Ryumin, the head of the MGB Investigation Department. They talked for almost two hours. According to Sudoplatov, who at that time headed one of the departments of the MGB, Stalin was extremely critical of the 'Doctors' Plot' case as prepared by Ryumin, regarding it as primitive and unconvincing. Ryumin was removed on Stalin's orders and transferred to reserve duty on 14 November. Stalin then decided to reconstruct the 'script' himself. All the Jewish Chekists working in the central apparatus of the MGB, about 30 people, were arrested. It was in this wave of arrests that Andrei Sverdlov, an MGB colonel and son of Yakov Sverdlov (the first Soviet head of state), wound up in the Lubyanka. In its second stage, the 'plot' organized by the Jewish doctors would be expanded into a general 'Zionist conspiracy'. Ignatiev and his deputy Goglidze were put in charge of orchestrating what was intended to be a pogrom on a massive scale.

On 5 March 1953 the MGB and MVD were combined into one ministry, to be headed by Beria. The first person to be released from prison was Molotov's wife, Polina; it was the day of Stalin's funeral and also Molotov's 63rd birthday. The arrested doctors were released and rehabilitated shortly afterwards, and others soon followed, while the organizers of the whole trumped-up campaign were arrested, including Ryumin and Ogoltsov. From recently published documents relating to the activities of Beria, it can be seen that each of these arrests was sanctioned by the Presidium of the Central Committee.[30] In a note on the 'Doctors' Plot', written for the Presidium, Beria demanded that Ignatiev and Ryasnoi also be brought to justice for the violation of legal norms and the fabrication of false accusations. However, the Presidium, for reasons that have never been disclosed, did not approve the arrest of Ignatiev and Ryasnoi. Ignatiev was, however, relieved of his post as a Secretary of the Central Committee. He was ordered to 'present explanations to the Presidium of the Central Committee concerning the falsification of evidence and the most crude perversion of Soviet Law by the MGB', but the content of these 'explanations' has not been disclosed. In any case Ignatiev continued to be a member of the Central Committee and only received a Party reprimand for 'lack of vigilance'. He was then given the post of First Secretary of the Bashkir Regional Party Committee (*obkom*) and subsequently moved to the same position in the Tartar obkom two years later. Selected to be a delegate to the Twentieth Party Congress, Ignatiev helped Khrushchev to prepare his speech on the 'cult of personality', in which he was presented as one of Stalin's victims rather than as an executor of Stalin's policies. Ignatiev died at the age of 79, having received the usual decorations on his 70th birthday in 1974. The fact that Ignatiev was treated in this way and managed to survive all Party purges unscathed suggests that he enjoyed the protection not only of Khrushchev but also of Suslov as well.

Ryasnoi, Ignatiev's First Deputy, had worked with Khrushchev in the Ukraine in 1943–46. He had been Commissar of the Ukrainian MVD. In 1954 he was given the post of head of the MVD Directorate for the Moscow region and from 1956 was put in charge of various major construction projects. Most puzzling of all was the fate of Ogoltsov. He was arrested after Beria's report to the Presidium of the Central Committee in April 1953 in connection with the circumstances around the murder of Mikhoels in 1948; Ogoltsov had been in charge of the MGB special operations detachment that had carried out the mission in accordance with Stalin's instructions. But he was released in August 1953, together with others who had participated in this 'liquidation' and was retired on a pension. Khrushchev's attachment to the principles of 'socialist legality' proved to be highly selective.

The unusual consideration shown by Khrushchev and other members of the new Party leadership towards several of the organizers of the last brutal and highly dangerous wave of Stalinist terror can hardly be explained away on humanitarian grounds. It is more plausible to suggest that on that critical day, 1 March 1953, it was they who were the first correctly to assess the reasons for Stalin's 'telephone silence' and the 'absence of movement' in his quarters, and they took the decision to inform Khrushchev and Bulganin, giving them a head start in the resolution of power questions. Next they contacted Suslov for instructions on the anti-Semitic propaganda campaign. On this day, during those crucial hours, an enormous amount of power to influence future events was concentrated in the hands of Ignatiev and the MGB system. Their behaviour ultimately helped Khrushchev (aided by the strength of Bulganin, the head of the military) to become Party leader when the time came for the final distribution of posts in the new regime. Within Stalin's entourage, it was Malenkov and Beria who had been most involved in devising the reorganization of Party bodies; according to a document issued by the Bureau of the Presidium in November 1952, if Stalin was absent for any reason, Malenkov would take charge of the Party *apparat* while Beria would become Chairman of the Council of Ministers. The third most influential person in the leadership, in accordance with the wishes of Malenkov and Beria, would be Molotov. (Molotov was important as the only member of the leadership, aside from Stalin, who was genuinely popular in the Party and in the country at large.) Khrushchev was never regarded as a potential successor to Stalin during this period, neither within the Party nor among the general public. On the whole Bulganin was a rather unpopular figure, particularly within the military. But as it turned out, these were the two men who were in the strongest position to influence the first decisions, thanks to the support of the MGB and the army.

2 March 1953: two plots

Khrushchev and Bulganin, arriving at Stalin's dacha at around midnight on 1 March, stayed only for about an hour and a half, basically limiting themselves to a conversation with the head of the guards in the commandant's office near the massive gates. Although the dacha was not very far away, it could not be seen from that vantage point. The asphalt road leading to the dacha passed through a thick forest tract, with a sharp bend in the final approach to the main entrance. The tyres of any vehicle making this turn could be heard by the household staff as well as the guards on duty. All the windows of the dacha had thick blinds, which meant that light in the rooms was not externally visible. These security precautions had been introduced by Stalin himself. After 60–90 minutes in the MGB duty room, Khrushchev and Bulganin, as described previously, decided against taking a look at Stalin at the dacha. They had been told that he was paralysed and not responding to questions, but for some reason they were reluctant to verify this for themselves. Khrushchev's explanation, that he did not want to 'embarrass' Stalin, can hardly be taken seriously. We can only speculate. It could be that they went to the MGB duty room at Kuntsevo simply in order to use the secure telephones of the emergency government line as well as to have a safe place to discuss and agree their next moves. From there they could also speak to Ignatiev, undisturbed. When Khrushchev recalls that 'we agreed that we would not go to Stalin but to the guardhouse', this could have been referring to an understanding with Ignatiev. On 2 March Bulganin secretly ordered several elite units of the Moscow garrison to come to the city 'to preserve order'. The Ministry of Defence and the General Staff also had to be given instructions in view of the incapacity of the Commander-in-Chief and Chairman of the Council of Ministers.

During the last years of Stalin's rule, even Politburo members were sure that their home telephones and apartments were bugged by the security services. Therefore they tried to avoid any confidential conversations within their own walls. Also we cannot exclude the possibility that Ignatiev was with Khrushchev and Bulganin at Kuntsevo. It would have been obvious for him to arrive as soon as Starostin reported Stalin's illness. What is clear is that between midnight and 2 am, under the protection of the guards, Khrushchev and Bulganin (and possibly Ignatiev as well) took some important decisions which to this day remain obscure. Beria finally became aware of it, but only much later. This explains the punitive measures taken against the dacha guards after 5 March, which many people found puzzling and unexpected. According to Svetlana Alliluyeva, the entire staff of the dacha was dismissed several days after Stalin's death, on Beria's orders:

> Servants who had worked for my father devotedly for ten or fifteen years were simply thrown out. Every one of them was sent away. A good many officers of the bodyguard were transferred to other cities. Two of them shot themselves. No one knew what was going on or what they were guilty of or why they were being picked on.[32]

Malenkov and Beria also received a report about Stalin's illness from the dacha at about 11 pm on 1 March. But it may be that Beria was the last to get the news – sometime around midnight. As has already been described Starostin tried to ring Beria after talking to Ignatiev but was unable to contact him either at home or through the government telephone network, and Malenkov had experienced the same problem. After 30 minutes (!) he rang Starostin back and said, 'You find Beria yourself, I haven't been able to reach him.' But 'soon' Beria somehow turned up and rang Starostin himself. Possibly it was already after midnight. It took Malenkov and Beria three more hours before they arrived at the dacha, and they were both obviously in a state of uncertainty and indecision. According to Lozgachev, 'Beria brazenly went through to the room where Stalin lay; Malenkov's new boots were squeaking, so he took them off and carried them under his arm. He approached Stalin in his socks.'[33] This account does not rule out the possibility that Malenkov genuinely thought Stalin was asleep and was concerned not to disturb him. It was just at that point that Beria told Lozgachev, 'Stalin is sleeping soundly.' A third bodyguard, Vasily Tukov, has added some additional details to the story:

> Beria left the room and started swearing at Starostin. He was no longer speaking, he was shouting. 'I'll deal with you personally. Who assigned you to Comrade Stalin? You're a bloody idiot.' He left the dacha in a rage. The Second Secretary of the Central Committee, Malenkov, padded after Beria, and their car took off.[34]

Everyone commented on Beria's agitation and capricious behaviour – the doctors, Svetlana, and the bodyguards. Clearly in an over-excited state, he was in turn elated, triumphant, fearful and at all times impatient. He threatened almost everyone and behaved as if he were in charge.

Khrushchev left home for a second time in the early hours of 2 March, while his family slept. Evidently he went to meet Malenkov and Beria in the Kremlin after they had been to the dacha. Issues to do with power had to be discussed as well as the question of calling the doctors. There had already been a serious delay. Although Stalin's bodyguards were undoubtedly to blame and Ignatiev even more so, Beria has come to be thought of as the sole culprit. All the biographies of Stalin written in the last 25 years quote his assertion that the dying Stalin was merely sleeping soundly.

It would seem that the first decisions about the division of power were taken by Khrushchev and Bulganin with the participation of Ignatiev during the night of 1 March at Stalin's dacha. Ignatiev was guaranteed a new post in the Central Committee Secretariat. None of them could aspire to what was considered to be the top job, Chairman of the Council of Ministers, i.e. head of the government. Although Malenkov had been ranked 'second' in the leadership, his actual base was in the Party hierarchy. The two First Deputies of the Chairman of the Council of Ministers were Bulganin and Beria, the person who would have aroused the most anxiety among his colleagues. His undoubted organizational skills combined with ruthlessness and an unlimited capacity for work created the danger of a new dictatorship. If Beria were to succeed to the leadership post, Ignatiev and Suslov would have reason to fear for their lives. The decision to make Malenkov the Chairman of the Council of Ministers was evidently an unavoidable compromise. Beria could consent to this arrangement since Malenkov was pretty much under his control and could be 'managed'. The decision to abolish the new Presidium of the Central Committee, created by Stalin in October, must have been taken collectively by the members of the old Politburo. It was not a step that could have been taken on the initiative of Khrushchev and Bulganin alone. A formal meeting of the former Politburo took place at the Kremlin at 10:40 am on 2 March.

In October 1952 the Nineteenth Party Congress had adopted Stalin's proposals for an alternative Party leadership structure. The Politburo was replaced by an enlarged Presidium of the Central Committee with 25 members (selected by Stalin) and 11 candidate members. But in order to ensure the 'efficient leadership' of the country, Stalin unexpectedly called for the creation of a compact, nine-member Bureau of the Presidium, which did not include Molotov or Mikoyan. The Bureau actually met only twice after the Congress, on 31 October and 22 November, in Stalin's office without the participation of Voroshilov, although he was a member. However, the Bureau was not really a 'legitimate' body, in the sense that the revised Party Rules made no mention of a Bureau of the Presidium. The published account of decisions taken at the 16 October Central Committee plenum reported the establishment of the new Presidium and listed its members but did not mention a Bureau. There were never any public announcements of decisions taken by the Bureau nor were any Bureau pronouncements ever circulated within the Party network. Thus it remained unclear whether or not this smaller, 'efficient leadership' body actually existed or what the functional responsibilities of its members might have been.

The problem for Malenkov and Beria was that a government reorganization would not be regarded as legitimate unless it was approved by a plenum of the Central Committee. Officially any proposal for such a reorganization would have had to come from its Presidium. However, this body had not yet met in formal session, and since they intended to abolish it they were reluctant to give it proper status by calling a meeting.

Towards the morning of 2 March a new ruling organ of the Party leadership had come into being, and its members later met in Stalin's Kremlin office. Stalin's junior secretaries were at their desks and as usual continued to record the names of all visitors. The first to arrive was Beria at 10:40. They all took their places along the table in the usual way, with Stalin's chair left empty. There was no official chairman. The participants included all members of the Bureau of the Presidium as well as Molotov, Mikoyan and Shvernik from the former Politburo whom Stalin had excluded from the inner leadership. M.F. Shkiryatov, the Chairman of the Party Control Commission, was also present. The meeting was over in 20 minutes and its agenda is not known. Presumably there was only one issue to be decided – that of their own self-empowerment. The new body met again in the evening of the same day. This time the session went on for exactly an hour, from 20:25 to 21:25. Evidently several questions were settled: the abolition of the enlarged Presidium, the reorganization of the government, and the date (5 March) for a plenum of the Central Committee.

A full plenum of the Central Committee and the Central Control Commission involved approximately 300 people – it would have been impossible to convene a group of this size within one or two days. 5 March was probably chosen as the first realistic date for getting everyone to Moscow and was unrelated to the progress of Stalin's illness.

Beria chaired the second gathering of the new leadership on the evening of 2 March, and again he was the first to enter Stalin's office, but evidently a specific distribution of 'portfolios' still did not occur. The doctors had only just begun to treat Stalin, and there could only be the most tentative, preliminary discussion of the question of succession. The Minister of Health, Tretyakov, was asked to report on Stalin's condition and would certainly have given them an extremely pessimistic prognosis, but he would have been unable to predict how much time was left before the end.

2–5 March 1953: politics, doctors and Stalin's death

The Minister of Health led the first group of physicians who came to examine Stalin on 2 March. The party included Professor P.Ye Lukomsky, the chief doctor of the Ministry of Health, professors of neuropathology, P.A. Tkachev and I.N. Filimonov, and another doctor, V.I. Ivanov-Neznamov. Immediately and unanimously they diagnosed a massive cerebral haemorrhage in the left side of the brain caused by high blood pressure and arteriosclerosis. As he lay prostrate on the sofa, Stalin's blood pressure was 220/110, a dangerous level even for a much younger man. The doctors were told that Stalin had been stricken in the early hours of 2 March, and that during the evening of 1 March he was, as usual, at work in his study. The following story was invented in the expectation that it would subsequently be passed on to the press:

> The officer on duty, looking through a keyhole, saw Stalin still at his desk at three in the morning of March 2nd. The light was on the whole night, but that was not unusual. Stalin usually slept in the next room but also often rested on the sofa in his study. At seven in the morning the guard again looked through the keyhole and saw Stalin lying on the floor between the table and the sofa. He had lost consciousness. They carried him to the sofa where he was now lying.[35]

The doctors requested that Stalin's medical records be brought straightaway from the Kremlin Hospital, quite naturally assuming that such records must exist. But no trace could be found of any documents relating to Stalin's previous illnesses. Nor could they find even the most basic medication anywhere in the dacha. The large household staff did not include even a single nurse. 'They could have hired a nurse posing as one of the maids or a doctor pretending to be one of the officers,' exclaimed one of the astonished specialists during the consultation, 'after all, he was 73 years old!' No one seemed to know exactly when Stalin had began to suffer from high blood pressure.

In the course of 2 March a stream of luminaries from the Academy of Medical Sciences arrived at the dacha including, towards evening, a group of experts with life-support systems. But the possibilities for treating someone in Stalin's condition were extremely limited. An attempt was made to lower the blood pressure and stimulate the activity of the heart. Beria and Malenkov set up absurd working conditions for the doctors: before any medical procedure was carried out, it had to be approved by those Party leaders who were present at the time. On the morning of 3 March a larger group of consultants was appointed and ordered by Malenkov to make an official prognosis. Malenkov was evidently rushing ahead with the Party reorganization, and although so far no one had objected, a formal prognosis would provide legitimacy for urgent action. The conclusion of the consultants was unanimous: death was inevitable, and it was a question of days rather than weeks. This provided sufficient justification for sending an urgent summons to all members of the Central Committee in order to discuss essential measures that were necessary in view of the impending death of the head of state.

It was clear, however, that a realignment of political power had already taken place; only members of the pre-Nineteenth Party Congress Politburo were allowed at the bedside of the dying Stalin, while none of the new members of the expanded Presidium were summoned to the dacha. According to Professor Myasnikov, one of the consultants called on the evening of 2 March who remained at the dacha until the end, one could observe a hierarchy among the visitors to the bedside. Malenkov and Beria arrived most frequently, always together, and next came Voroshilov and Kaganovich. A third pair, Bulganin and Khrushchev, were followed by Mikoyan and Molotov, although Molotov came only rarely as he himself was unwell with a post-flu lung inflammation.

Could Stalin have been saved if doctors had been summoned on 1 March immediately after the stroke occurred? Biographies of Stalin have often included speculation along these lines, echoing views expressed by members of his family, but it is extremely unlikely that anything could have been done. It was a very severe cerebral haemorrhage, and even today a stroke of this kind is nearly always fatal or is at the very least seriously debilitating. Earlier medical attention or attempts at life-support, then only in an experimental stage, could have prolonged the agony but would not have saved the patient.

Risky surgical intervention to remove a blood clot from the brain is only appropriate for relatively young people.

The meeting of the CPSU plenum was scheduled for 8 pm on 5 March; the timing was unrelated to Stalin's immediate physical condition, which was poor and deteriorating, but he was still alive at 8 pm. In addition to members of the Central Committee (who might well ask questions about the abolition of the enlarged Presidium created by Stalin at the Nineteenth Party Congress), the gathering included members of the Council of Ministers and the Presidium of the Supreme Soviet. It took place in the Sverdlov Hall of the Kremlin with approximately 300 Party and state officials present. Almost everyone who participated in this historic occasion arrived 30–40 minutes early. No conversation took place in the hall; uninformed about the specific agenda, they all sat waiting in silence. Few of those present were aware that Stalin was dying at the Kuntsevo dacha, that he was not right there in his Kremlin apartment as had been announced in the first reports of his illness on the morning of 4 March. At exactly 8 pm the stage door opened and the members of the Bureau, with the addition of Molotov and Mikoyan, walked on to the platform and sat down at the table (i.e. not the 25 people chosen by Stalin to be members of the new Presidium). One of the most recent commentators on this event, the historian N. Barsukov, was in 1989 the first person to gain access to the secret archive holding the protocol of the meeting. He wrote:

> Stalin may have been envisaging collective leadership as an alternative to his own absolute power, while simultaneously trying to forestall a possible usurper among his associates. Hence, his new Presidium with 36 members and candidates that included only a minority of the 'old guard', not more than a third.

> However, there was too little time between the Nineteenth Party Congress and Stalin's death for the members of the new Party leadership structure to bond and become firmly established. This is why it was possible for Stalin's closest subordinates so quickly and easily to restore their supremacy in the Party and government on the day of his death. This indicates a considerable degree of careful preparation. To expel 22 people from the Presidium in the course of an hour would hardly have been possible without a pre-arranged deal. It was crucial to take swift action while they still could take advantage of the shock effect of Stalin's departure from the scene. As justification, they could point to the exceptional situation, which required maximum efficiency and the strengthening of authority. Their calculation proved to be correct. Certainly no member of what had been intended to be the new Party leadership was prepared to engage in a struggle for power at the graveside of the 'great leader'; there had been no opportunity for them to exchange views. And so the 'operation' was executed without any complications.[36]

The meeting lasted only 40 minutes, but the decisions taken were regarded as final at all levels of both Party and state institutions. It was Khrushchev who presided over the meeting, just as it was he who had initiated the basic political changes on that memorable day, 1 March. First the assembled delegates heard a brief report from the Minister of Health, Tretyakov, so that there could be no doubt about the inevitable outcome of Stalin's illness. Next came a short speech by Malenkov, who reminded those present about the need for 'firm leadership' and unity. At this point Khrushchev called upon Comrade Beria to talk about the candidate for Chairman of the Council of Ministers. In the name of the Bureau of the Presidium, Beria proposed Georgy Malenkov for this post. There was no vote – the nomination was approved by acclamation. Malenkov then proposed a sweeping programme of reorganization consisting of 17 points, the main one being the reduction of the Presidium of the Central Committee to 11 members for the sake of greater efficiency. Stalin was included, since he was still among the living. Beria, Molotov, Bulganin and Kaganovich were named as First Deputy Chairmen of the Council of Ministers. Voroshilov replaced Shvernik as Chairman of the Presidium of the Supreme Soviet. The MGB and the MVD were amalgamated into one ministry to be headed by Beria.

Khrushchev's new position was not considered to be a clear promotion. He remained a Secretary of the Central Committee but left his post as First Secretary of the Moscow Party Committee. When the list of members of the new Presidium of the Central Committee appeared, drawn up according to rank as was customary at the time, rather than in alphabetical order, Khrushchev came sixth, after Stalin, Malenkov, Beria, Molotov and Voroshilov. Bulganin was moved down to seventh place. All members of the new Presidium of the Central Committee, except Khrushchev, also sat in the Presidium of the Council of Ministers.

The nature of the reorganization clearly suggested that the apex of power in the country had shifted again from the Central Committee of the Party to the Council of Ministers. Until the end of 1953 Malenkov also chaired meetings of the Presidium of the Central Committee, having kept his post as a Central Committee Secretary. These arrangements were understood to mean that Malenkov had become the new leader of the country and Stalin's heir. The restoration of Beria as the head of state security in control of the entire military and semi-military MVD system was a defeat for Khrushchev and Bulganin, but they were unable to prevent it from happening. But as compensation, the Ministry of Defence was strengthened. Point seven of the reorganization plan confirmed the appointment of Marshal of the Soviet Union, Comrade N.A. Bulganin as the Minister

of Defence with Marshals Vasilevsky and Zhukov as his First Deputies.[37]

All the nominations were approved without debate or discussion.
According to Simonov, there was no sign of sorrow or 'mourning'
among the members of the Presidium on the platform, only relief.
'One sensed that right there, within the Presidium, they had all been
liberated from an oppressive force, and it was a feeling that united
them.'[38]

At 8:40 pm Khrushchev declared the meeting over. The members
of the Presidium rushed off to the dacha and got there just in time.
Approximately half an hour after their arrival, at 9:50 pm, the
doctors announced that Stalin had died. Only then did they enter the
room where he lay and stand in silence for about 20 minutes beside
the body of their late leader. Afterwards they all went to the Kremlin,
again to Stalin's office, where the members of the Party and state
leadership had urgent questions to discuss. A new historical epoch
had begun. The former members of Stalin's Politburo came to his
office for the last time during the night of 9–10 March after the
funeral. The first to enter the office was Malenkov followed by Beria.
Khrushchev was the last.

CHAPTER 2

Stalin's Secret Heir

Zhores Medvedev

Stalin's testament

Over the years Stalin annihilated various members of his immediate entourage whom he considered to be unsuitable as potential successors. Historians are familiar with their names. However, Stalin undoubtedly was relying on certain Party and state leaders to maintain the Stalin cult and preserve his creation, the Soviet empire, although we cannot be certain of their identity.

Lenin evaluated the political and personal qualities of his closest disciples and colleagues in a document composed during his last illness that has come to be called his 'political testament', but he found himself unable to recommend one person out of the group to be the new leader of the Party. Lenin's 'testament' was intended for a future Party Congress rather than the restricted audience of a Central Committee meeting. Evidently he had no sense of urgency about nominating a successor, since during the whole of 1923 he was no longer running Party or state institutions, which is why it seemed there would be no immediate need for reorganization after his death. In the event, the Party elite moved a new leader forward gradually on the basis of his political programme; policies were seen to be more important than any considerations of service to the Revolution, closeness to Lenin or special personal abilities. If the Party chieftains had been intent on the international expansion of the Revolution or the triumph of Marxism in large parts of Europe and Asia rather than in Russia alone, then Trotsky most certainly would have become the leader. But the members of the Party elite wanted stability and were above all concerned with building socialism in the one country where they actually held power.

Since Stalin was the man who personified this policy to a maximum degree, it is deceptive to brand him as a usurper. It took several years for him to ascend to the role of dictator, from 1923 to the end of 1929. He was able to extend his power as part of a process of acquiring personal authority and creating a 'cult of personality'. Lenin had been a leader rather than a dictator, a leader whose power rested on that luminous quality which is the mark of 'political genius', authority. His greatness 'incorporated' the genius of Marx, and his achievement was not merely the seizure of power in Russia; it was also a turning point in human history, the beginning of a new historical era as foreseen in the teachings of Marx. The source of Lenin's power came from the leading role he played in the October Revolution, from his crucial contribution to its strategy and organization.

After Lenin's death, Stalin may have become the 'first among equals' but he was by no means already in charge, largely because he still had no claim to any major 'historic' achievements. The New Economic Policy (NEP) of the 1920s was popular and very successful. But improved living standards and economic development took place spontaneously, in the context of a capitalist market and the law of supply and demand, rather than as a result of a planned economy based on socialist principles. Stalin became the real 'boss' of the country only after he inaugurated the new 'revolution from above' – the collectivization of agriculture (1929–31), the dissolution of NEP and the introduction of the first Five Year Plan for socialist industrialization. After the victory over Germany in 1945, the leader of the Soviet Union also became the head of an unprecedented Soviet empire, a vast bloc of socialist countries stretching from Berlin to Hanoi. But by this time there was not even one truly impressive, talented or well-educated person among the 'faithful comrades' within Stalin's immediate entourage. Ageing and undoubtedly sensing the approaching end – he spoke about it more and more often – Stalin was unable to follow Lenin's example and prepare a detailed assessment of the positive and negative qualities of his closest subordinates to be read out at a posthumous Party Congress. None of the four Party leaders closest to Stalin in 1952, Malenkov, Beria, Khrushchev and Bulganin, were in any way outstanding. Their authority rested on their proximity to Stalin rather than any personal capabilities. Therefore if Stalin were to think about leaving a political testament, he would have been unable to name the most erudite Marxist-Leninist in the Politburo, since there was no one in this elite body answering to that description. Among the Party rank and file as well as within broad sections of the population, Molotov was still thought to be Stalin's most likely successor. But few were aware of the fact that Molotov had lost his former influence, that he no longer played an important role in the Party or had any significant function in the government apparatus. Nor was it generally known that Molotov's wife, Polina Zhemchuzhina, had been arrested at the beginning of 1949, accused of 'links with Zionism' and 'betrayal of the Motherland'. Molotov's dismissal as Minister of Foreign Affairs in 1949 marked the beginning of his 'disgrace'.

Without an obvious successor Stalin certainly understood that unlike the situation at the time of Lenin's death, his departure would leave the country in the hands of a considerably less stable 'collective leadership'. In 1924 conflicts between the closest colleagues of the deceased leader were largely based on genuine political disagreement. Within Stalin's inner circle, however, there were no political differences; all that mattered was the pursuit of power and influence in a context of personal rivalry that Stalin himself had always encouraged.

Yet the problem of succession was acquiring an ever pressing urgency. Only six formal meetings of the Politburo took place in 1950, five in 1951 and just four in 1952. Stalin was spending an increasing amount of time in the south to rest and have treatment. In 1949 he was in the south for three months, living in different dachas; in 1950, five months went by, from the beginning of August until the end of December, without an appearance in his Kremlin office. In 1951 his leave, which began on 9 August, was extended to a total of six months and only came to an end on 12 February 1952.[1]

In June 1952 Stalin suddenly informed his colleagues of his decision to convene the Nineteenth Party Congress in the autumn. According to Party rules, Congresses were meant to take place every three years, but even though there had been no such gathering since 1939, Stalin's announcement took the other Party leaders by surprise. The Congress was scheduled for October. According to Khrushchev's memoirs, after revealing his decision to hold the Congress, for some time Stalin said nothing about its agenda or whether he intended to present the General Report.[2] It was obvious that it would be too difficult for him to speak for several hours, but it was rather crucial for the others to know exactly to whom this role was to be given. There was of course the possibility that Stalin would draft the Report and have it printed and distributed among the delegates, but in the end he chose to arrange things differently. Malenkov was told to prepare the General Report, while Khrushchev would speak on changes in the Party rules; Kaganovich was given the task of outlining the Politburo's proposals for a revision of the Party programme; Mikhail Saburov, the Chairman of Gosplan and final speaker, was to give an account of the new Five Year Plan.

Shortly before the opening of the Congress, *Pravda* published several articles by Stalin under the general title 'Economic Problems of Socialism'. These articles were intended to be the basis for a new textbook on the political economy of socialism. In view of Stalin's inability to deliver the keynote address, perceptive observers considered this Congress to be a symbolic occasion, in a sense his final legacy. The articles on the economy of socialism were declared to be programmatic blueprints for the building of communism. It was reasonably assumed that the choice of the main speakers would reflect the roles they would be playing in the leadership in the immediate future. The overall leadership of the Party would be entrusted to Malenkov. Khrushchev would supervise the organizational work of the Party *apparat.* Kaganovich, the old revolutionary who had been at Lenin's side, symbolized the continuity of the central goals of the Party. Although Saburov was not yet a member of the Central Committee in 1952, he was the representative of the new technocrats in the government.

Everyone certainly understood that Stalin was behind each of the four reports at the Congress. The texts had been prepared by special commissions and were then checked and edited largely by Stalin, while the speakers themselves made a much smaller contribution. As at all previous Congresses, the selection of members of the Central Committee was of key importance. The number of Party members in the USSR had doubled since the Eighteenth Party Congress in 1939 and had now reached a figure of almost seven million. Correspondingly the size of the Central Committee was enlarged to 125 members and 111 candidates. In accordance with Stalin's proposal, the actual name of the Party was changed from the 'Party of Bolsheviks' to the 'Communist Party of the Soviet Union'. The new Party rules altered the structure of the Party organs, with a Presidium of the Central Committee replacing the traditional Politburo. Neither its size nor its composition had been discussed in advance before the meeting of the Congress, and no one imagined that these changes, seemingly just a matter of protocol, concealed Stalin's secret plans for a radical reshaping of the leadership. Evidently Stalin had decided to implement his political testament personally. It was his intention to promote new people to the national and international stage, above all people who would preserve and promote the Stalin cult in the same way that he himself had nourished the cult of Lenin. Although his designs were still disguised, he was determined to ensure that 'the great epoch of Stalin' retained its place in history.

The first steps

The Nineteenth Party Congress was opened by Molotov on 5 October 1952. The general public would have had no idea of the real distribution of power within the highest leadership. Voroshilov brought the Congress to a close. These were the two members of the Politburo who had served the Party longer than all others except Stalin, which was the reason for their formal roles in the proceedings. Where sessions of the Congress were open to guests and to the press, it was crucial to maintain an image of total unity. On the first evening all members of the Politburo were there on the platform, even Kosygin, although for some time there had been no public mention of his name. In the accounts of the first day published the next morning, it was reported that 'when Comrade Stalin and his loyal comrades-in-arms, Comrades Molotov, Malenkov, Voroshilov, Bulganin, Beria, Kaganovich, Khrushchev, Mikoyan and Kosygin appeared on the podium, the delegates greeted them with prolonged applause', with the order of names indicating the relative position of each member of the Politburo. Western analysts knew this to be the case, and so, of course, did delegates to the Congress. Therefore many of them could not help but focus on the surprising demotion of Beria from his usual third place to fifth position. Previously he had always come after Malenkov, but he was now superseded by both Voroshilov and Bulganin.

An even more telling sign of the attitude towards Beria was the fact that certain of his close collaborators, such as Vsevolod Merkulov and Vladimir Dekanozov, were excluded from the new, substantially expanded Central Committee, although they previously had been members. Merkulov and Dekanozov were Beria's friends since their student days at the Baku Polytechnic in 1915–16 and they stuck close to him for the next 35 years, usually working as his first deputies. In 1940–41 Dekanozov was the Soviet ambassador to Germany while Merkulov was First Deputy Commissar of the NKVD. But by 1952 Merkulov had become USSR Minister of State Control and Dekanozov headed the MVD in Georgia. These changes were an indication of the fact that Beria's power was on the wane. Although he was allowed to make a speech at the Congress, his position certainly was affected by the investigation into the 'Georgian affair', just then drawing to a close. A number of Georgian state and Party officials had been arrested in 1951, including a large contingent of Mingrelians, many them protégés of Beria. They were accused of separatist tendencies, i.e. of seeking the withdrawal of Georgia from the USSR.

The new Central Committee of the CPSU met for the first time on 16 October in order to choose the members of its executive bodies. The posts to be filled included the Secretaries of the Central Committee and the Chairmen of both the Party Control Commission and the Presidium of the Central Committee (which replaced the Politburo and the Orgburo). Malenkov presided and called on Stalin to speak. To the amazement of all those present, Stalin's speech went on for almost one and a half hours. He spoke clearly, passionately and without notes, and obviously the speech had been well prepared. Either no minutes were taken at this meeting or, if they were, they were subsequently destroyed. Therefore what we know of the contents of Stalin's speech comes from the recollections of those who were present. Khrushchev has written about it in detail as has Dmitri

Shepilov. The writer Konstantin Simonov, who was selected at the plenum to be a candidate member of the Central Committee, used his professional skills to provide the most vivid, authentic account of the speech, and he was in no doubt that it had the quality of a testament:

> His main theme (if not verbatim, then his train of thought) was that he was old, that the time was approaching when it would be up to others to continue his work, that the state of the world was complex and a bitter struggle with the capitalist camp lay ahead. The greatest danger in this struggle would be to waver, to take fright, to retreat, to capitulate. This was the central message that he wanted not merely to convey but to imprint on the minds of those present. ...

> The odd thing about Stalin's speech was that when he mentioned courage or fear, resolution or capitulation, his remarks were not general but were directed concretely towards two members of the Politburo who were sitting there behind him only two metres away, men about whom I certainly would have least expected to hear what Stalin said.

> First he came down on Molotov with accusations of irresolution and unreliability, cowardice and defeatism. It was so astonishing that at first I hardly believed my own ears and thought I must have misheard or misunderstood. It turned out that this was not the case. ...

> With all Stalin's anger, his words at times seemingly out of control, there was nevertheless a characteristically solid quality in the construction of the speech. The next part dealing with Mikoyan was similar; it was shorter but perhaps subtly expressed an even greater degree of malice and contempt.

> I have no idea why Stalin chose to single out Molotov and Mikoyan as his main objects of attack in his last speech at a Central Committee plenum. Clearly there can be no question that he intended to compromise them both, to humiliate them and to depose one of the Party's last remaining great historic figures from his pedestal. ...

> If and when something happened to him, for some reason Stalin did not want Molotov to remain as the most important Party-state figure. His speech put an end to that possibility once and for all.[3]

According to Shepilov:

> With a scornful expression on his face, Stalin recalled how Molotov had been intimidated by American imperialism, how on a trip to the United States he had sent panicky telegrams to Moscow. Such a leader was not worthy of respect and there was no place for him in the leading body of the Party. ... Political distrust of Mikoyan and Voroshilov was expressed in a similar tone.[4]

L.N. Yefremov, a member of the Central Committee who also left an account of the speech, wrote that one of Stalin's accusations against

Molotov was that he, as Minister of Foreign Affairs, had given permission for several British newspapers and magazines to be published in Russian in the USSR.

Stalin also attacked Molotov for disclosing information to his wife, including details of secret Politburo meetings. 'It has turned out that there has been some kind of invisible thread linking the Politburo to Molotov's wife, Polina Zhemchuzhina, and her friends. And she is surrounded by friends who are totally untrustworthy. Clearly such behaviour by a member of the Politburo is impermissible.'[5] By this time Zhemchuzhina was already in custody, convicted in the case of the Jewish Anti-Fascist Committee, which was thought to be working for Israel.

No other members of the Politburo were subjected to criticism or evaluated in any way. None of them except Malenkov were regarded as possible successors. In view of the rapidly expanding anti-Semitic campaign, Kaganovich could have no pretensions to the highest office, and neither Stalin nor the members of the Central Committee ever regarded Khrushchev as a serious contender for power.

However, in order to test the intentions and ambitions of Malenkov, Stalin came up with a singular, rather intricate manoeuvre. By 1951–52, Stalin was no longer supervising the work of the Central Committee Secretariat. This job was being done by Malenkov, while Stalin remained a Secretary of the Central Committee along with others. Although there never had been any official decision, in effect the position of General Secretary had been abolished. Stalin exercised power largely as Chairman of the Council of Ministers and Chairman of the Politburo, and Malenkov presided over meetings of the Secretariat, thus coming second in the Party hierarchy. However, Stalin was aware of Malenkov's limitations. According to Khrushchev, Stalin often said that Malenkov was a man who had to be led. 'He's a clerk. He can produce resolutions quickly enough and if he doesn't always do this by himself, he's very good at organizing others, but he's not capable of any kind of independent thought or initiative.'[6]

In the course of his speech Stalin referred to his age and said that it had become difficult for him to combine the posts of Chairman of the Council of Ministers and Secretary of the Central Committee. He was prepared to remain in the government and on the Presidium of the Central Committee, but he asked for permission to relinquish his post of General Secretary. Malenkov, chairing the plenum, was obliged to present Stalin's request for discussion. For Simonov, a newcomer to the Central Committee, Stalin's suggestion seemed logical, but later, in his memoirs, he described the effect produced by Stalin's statement, particularly on Malenkov:

> I caught sight of a terrible expression on Malenkov's face – not fear exactly, no, not fear – but an expression which a man might have

when it was clearer to him than to others, or in any case, to many others, that mortal danger was hanging over everyone in the room although the others had not yet understood this. It was impossible to approve Comrade Stalin's request, impossible to let him relinquish what was his definitive position of power, impossible. On Malenkov's face, in his gestures and the way he raised his hands, there was a direct appeal to everyone present that they immediately and absolutely reject Stalin's request. And then, drowning out the chorus that had already begun on the podium behind Stalin's back, came shouts of 'No, you must stay!' (or something like that). Throughout the hall their were cries of 'No!', 'Impossible!', 'You must stay!', 'You must withdraw your request!'

The spontaneous, agitated reaction in the hall apparently did save Malenkov. Simonov wrote:

I can so clearly remember Malenkov's face when the shouting began in the hall. It was the face of a man who had just managed to evade an immediate and tangible threat to his life ... if Stalin had been given the feeling that either in the rear, behind his back, or in the audience before him there were any prepared to agree to his request, the first who would have answered with his head would have been Malenkov.[7]

It was only after the plenum in a united outburst had rejected his request to relinquish the post of General Secretary, that Stalin took a sheet of paper out of his pocket and read out a previously prepared list of the 25 members and 11 candidate members of the new Presidium of the Central Committee. The names were approved without discussion, and although a sense of relief could be felt in the hall, a degree of confusion was apparent on the podium. The list had been drawn up in alphabetical order rather than according to rank. Only nine members of the existing Politburo were included in the new Presidium. A.A. Andreyev was excluded without any explanation. Kosygin was demoted to the level of candidate member, although to everyone's gratification, Molotov and Mikoyan were on the list. But with such a large number of new members in the highest leadership body of the Party, removals of the old guard could take place at any time and were likely to happen in the near future. The Secretariat of the Central Committee was also doubled in size.

In his memoirs Khrushchev describes his colleagues' reaction to these changes:

When the Plenum session was over, we all exchanged glances. What had happened? Who had put this list together? Stalin himself couldn't possibly have known most of the people he had just appointed. He couldn't have put the list together himself. I confess that at first I thought Malenkov was behind the new Presidium and wasn't telling the rest of us. Later I quizzed him about it in a friendly way. ... Malenkov answered, 'I swear, I had absolutely nothing to do with the list. Stalin didn't even ask for my help, nor did I make any sugges-

tions at all about the composition of the Presidium.' Malenkov's de-
nial made it even more mysterious. I couldn't imagine that Beria was
involved, since there were people on the list whom Beria never would
have recommended to Stalin. ... Molotov and Kosygin were out of the
question. Bulganin did not know anything about it either. ... So we
were stumped. ... Some of the names were hardly known in the Party,
and Stalin certainly had no idea who they were.[8]

Stalin established one more body at the plenum in addition to the
enlarged Presidium, a small Bureau of the Presidium for which there
had been no provision in the revised Party rules. Its members would
include some of his closest colleagues, but unlike the Politburo, there
was no division of responsibilities. Strangely, accounts of the plenum
meeting made no mention of this Bureau nor was there any reference
to its existence in the press. The Bureau is not known to have ever
taken any formal decisions. Once the plenum was over, only four of
the Party leaders – Malenkov, Beria, Khrushchev and Bulganin – were
regularly invited to the Kuntsevo dacha for the traditional late-night
meals. Evidently Stalin wanted to keep these four under constant
observation. On 20 October he received the ten new Central Committee secretaries in his Kremlin office, among them the young
Leonid Brezhnev who had been made a candidate member of the
Presidium. Stalin got to know Brezhnev for the first time during this
meeting and liked him.

Having dealt with the Party Congress and the reorganization of
the leading Party organs, Stalin did not go to Abkhazia for his usual
autumn–winter break as had been expected. This seemed to indicate
still more changes to come. In November 1952 Stalin was particularly interested in speeding up the investigation of the 'Doctors' Plot'
and the 'Mingrelian Conspiracy'. He got to know the new members
of the Presidium and convened two meetings of its Bureau.

For the first time since 1945 Stalin attended the 6 November
ceremonial meeting at the Kremlin to commemorate the October
Revolution – it was the 35th anniversary. In 1952 Pervukhin had
delivered the main speech and, according to custom, almost all the
elected members of the Presidium of the Central Committee took
their places on the podium. However, at that time it had not yet
become the norm to sit in sequence according to rank. On 7 November 1952 Stalin reviewed the traditional parade of the Moscow
garrison in Red Square from the stand on top of Lenin's mausoleum,
wearing his Generalissimo's winter uniform. On his right and left
stood Marshals Bulganin and Timoshenko, but by then other members of the leadership were placed according to rank: Malenkov,
Beria, Khrushchev, Kaganovich, Molotov, Shvernik, Pervukhin,
Saburov, Mikoyan, Ponomarenko, Suslov, Shkiryatov, Aristov, Pegov

and Brezhnev. It was customary for Voroshilov to stand alongside Budenny in the group of marshals to the right of Bulganin.

According to General Sudoplatov, there was a large turnover of cadres in the MVD and MGB in December–January 1952–53. The two Ministers, Kruglov (MVD) and Ignatiev (MGB) had become members of the Central Committee, and their deputies Serov and Masslennikov (MVD) and Goglidze and Ryasnoi (MGB) were made candidate members. Simultaneously all Jews were removed from the leadership of the security services, even those in very senior positions. In February the anti-Jewish expulsions were extended to regional branches of the MGB. A secret directive was distributed to all regional directorates of the MGB on 22 February, ordering that all Jewish employees of the MGB be dismissed immediately, regardless of rank, age or service record. Certainly the purge of MGB Jewish employees, carried out with such urgency, suggested that something serious was about to happen. As a rule all of Stalin's previous repressive campaigns started out with arrests and liquidations within the central organs of power and only afterwards were followed by waves of arrests and deportations in the various republics and regions. Any campaign devised by Stalin always began in Moscow.

There can be no doubt that Stalin intended to rely on certain new members of the Central Committee Presidium once he swept away some of his old comrades, particularly Beria and Malenkov. The following members of the former Politburo were included in the new Presidium: Beria, Bulganin, Kaganovich, Khrushchev Malenkov, Mikoyan, Molotov, Shvernik, Stalin and Voroshilov. The new additions were: Andrianov, Aristov, Chesnokov, Ignatiev, Korotchenko, Kuznetsov, Kuusinen, Malyshev, Melnikov, Mikhailov, Pervukhin, Ponomarenko, Saburov, Shkiryatov and Suslov – 15 people in all. Undoubtedly Stalin regarded one of these men as his most reliable potential successor, and this person would have been the one who helped him put together the list that so astonished Khrushchev and Malenkov. In 1952 there was no one in Stalin's closest circle who was not bewildered by his choice of people nor could they single out any individual who would have been capable of consigning them, the 'Stalinist old guard', to retirement, without hesitation or regret (which, incidentally, would have been the most optimistic scenario).

Today, because of what we know with hindsight, it is rather less difficult to determine the name of the person whom Stalin had decided to trust. He was a convinced Stalinist and leading conservative, who for 30 years after Stalin's death continued to be the chief ideologist of the CPSU; as chief censor he was powerful enough to curb the flow of revelations about the 'cult of personality', and ultimately, although only over time, he was able to oversee the removal of the entire old guard, including Khrushchev himself. Stalin was not mistaken in his choice. He picked a reliable, ruthless, clever, well-educated Marxist as his ally, a fanatical believer in the communist ideal. Stalin's only error was an overestimation of the state of his own health and the amount of time he had left. He was counting on years or perhaps it was months, but it had become a question of weeks or days. The fact that neither Malenkov nor the more intelligent Beria were able to work out Stalin's hidden agenda saved the life of his secret ally. Subsequently this chosen heir was able to rise to the summit of power without any patronage from above, thanks to his own abilities. He never became the boss of the Party but found it gratifying enough to be its first cardinal.

Problems of succession

The question came up every time Stalin went on leave during the 1930s – who would take his place as the leader of the country? It can be seen from Stalin's letters to Molotov, Ordzhonikidze, Kirov and other colleagues, sent from various health resorts, that at the time they all regarded the highest post in the country to be Chairman of the Politburo rather than General Secretary of the Party. All major decisions were taken collectively at Politburo meetings. It was hardly democracy, but there was some kind of mutual guarantee. The Secretariat and Orgburo of the Central Committee were executive bodies, while the Council of People's Commissars also had executive functions and was the organizational link between Party and state in the governance of the country. The Politburo and the Central Committee were the policy-making organs, although the plenum of the Central Committee was never convened in Stalin's absence. It was Molotov who chaired meetings of the Politburo when Stalin was away. If he was unable to carry out this function for reasons of illness or travels of his own, the chair was taken by Kaganovich or Kuibyshev. Kirov also enjoyed Stalin's full confidence.

The institutional power hierarchy just described changed significantly in May 1941 when Stalin assumed the post of Chairman of the Council of People's Commissars, with Molotov, the former head of government, as his Deputy. It was quite apparent by then that war with Germany was inevitable. A large contingent of the German army was concentrated along the western borders of the USSR. Intelligence reports left no doubt that Hitler was planning to attack, although there were differences of opinion about timing. In these circumstances it was no longer expedient to have a structure of governing where policy-making and executive functions were split, since all major decisions would require immediate action. Once Stalin became Chairman of the Sovnarkom, this automatically became the most powerful post in the country. New arrangements now had to be made for the periods of his inevitable absences from Moscow (e.g. the Teheran Conference in November 1943 or Yalta in February 1945). Stalin no longer left one person in charge to fulfil all his functions and responsibilities. His First Deputy was put in charge of the State Defence Committee (GKO) and the General Headquarters of the Soviet High Command (Stavka); Party affairs were left in the hands of Andrei Zhdanov, who had taken on the functions of Second Secretary after the Eighteenth Party Congress. During this period, the role of the nine-member Politburo became less important, and there were almost no formal sessions. Many issues were settled on the telephone or via military communication links.

The question of an actual successor to Stalin initially came up in the autumn of 1945 when after all the stress of the war years, Stalin fell seriously ill for the first time. His daughter Svetlana wrote that her last meeting with her father in 1945 took place in August. 'It was some time before we saw each other after that.' Her father was ill 'for months'.[9] The visitors' book from Stalin's office, published in *Istorichesky archiv* (Historical Archive) in 1994–97, shows that Stalin was in the Kremlin on 8 October but after that was absent until 17 December. It has recently become known that Stalin was taken to Sochi for treatment. Later, in 1949, when Svetlana married Yuri Zhdanov, he told her that there had been days when Stalin's condition was so critical that his father, Politburo member Andrei Zhdanov, spent all his time in the Kremlin, expecting that the Party-state leadership would temporarily be his. At that time Zhdanov had actually been chosen by Stalin to be number two in the Party. Andrei Zhdanov was then 49 years old, and he and Stalin were good friends. He was in charge of the Ideological Department of the Central Committee but was also carrying out a number of other Party and state functions. Within the government, Stalin's successor unquestionably was Molotov. Before the war Molotov had been Chairman of the Sovnarkom for ten years, and in 1945 he was the First Deputy Chairman of the Sovnarkom and also the Commissar of Foreign Affairs. Zhdanov was an absolutely convinced Stalinist, a conservative who advocated almost total cultural isolation from the capitalist world. Both Molotov and Zhdanov had been active participants in the Stalin terror of the 1930s (events in Leningrad after the murder of Kirov have sometimes been known as the 'Zhdanov terror'); therefore any rehabilitation of victims would not have been in their interest. Zhdanov died on 31 August 1948 in circumstances that remain somewhat opaque to this day, and his departure from the scene shifted the balance of power in Party and state. At the end of 1948 Molotov's wife, who occupied important positions in the Ministry of Light Industry as well as in other public organizations, was accused of having Zionist links and was expelled from the Party at a

Politburo meeting following a report by Beria. Polina Zhemchuzhina was arrested at the beginning of 1949, but the Party membership at large knew nothing about it, and Molotov continued to be regarded as the man in second place after Stalin, although this was no longer the case.

Malenkov started to occupy the key position in the Party apparatus after Zhdanov went to a sanatorium for medical treatment in July 1948. His overall power was less than that of Zhdanov, who in addition to his ideological role had been head of the International Department of the Central Committee. Questions of foreign policy were now handed over to Suslov, a Secretary of the Central Committee who also took charge of ideological issues. Suslov immediately was made the head of two departments when he entered the apparatus of the Central Committee: Agitation and Propaganda (Agitprop) and International Relations. In addition to controlling travel abroad by Soviet citizens, the Department of International Relations carried out various secret operations supporting communist parties in other countries and had close links with the MGB. There was also a close relationship between the MGB and Agitprop, since the Central Committee and the MGB jointly controlled the enormous all-embracing censorship structure (dealing with the press, radio, television, international correspondence, films, theatre, etc).

Thus towards the end of 1948 changes had taken place in the pyramid of power. Stalin remained at the summit as before. Malenkov had become his potential successor in the Party apparatus, but he was largely a technocrat without any ideological expertise (Malenkov had a technical higher education). Within the government structure, Stalin promoted Nikolai Voznesensky to second place. He was the Chairman of Gosplan and had been a member of the Politburo since 1947. Voznesensky had proved to be brilliant at organizing industry during the war and had become Stalin's deputy in the GKO. He was an educated economist and at 44 the youngest member of the Politburo. On several occasions Stalin emphatically and openly remarked that he considered Voznesensky to be his most appropriate successor as head of the government. Most historians believe that it was this that made Voznesensky the target of a conspiracy organized by Malenkov and Beria. At the time of Voznesensky's 'disgrace', the accusations against him were so blatantly phoney that even in those days they could not appear in the press, and very few people were aware of what had happened. In March 1949 Voznesensky was removed from his posts and expelled from the Politburo; he was arrested in October and shot at the end of 1950. The liquidation of Voznesensky was not part of the 1950 'Leningrad affair', in the course of which many prominent Party officials also were put to death. The MGB put together a special

'Gosplan case' for Voznesensky, accusing him of losing certain secret government documents and deliberately downgrading the industrial output plans for several branches of heavy industry. However, it would be naïve to think that the murder of Voznesensky could have been solely the result of a plot organized by Beria and Malenkov. In situations where such a prominent person was involved, only Stalin himself could have taken the initiative using Beria and Malenkov to carry out the operation, although in this particular case they were also interested parties.

My personal interpretation is as follows: once Stalin came to realize that Voznesensky was a popular figure, someone whose talent and capabilities gave him a real chance of becoming leader of the country, he could think of no way of blocking that possibility other than liquidation. It was clear to Stalin that Voznesensky would never be the one to preserve the Stalin cult. An independent person of outstanding quality, Voznesensky was not an ideological fanatic, and undoubtedly he would have aimed for reform. That he had never been associated with the political repressions of the 1930s, the fact that his hands were not stained with the blood of the terror, was a crucial consideration. Voznesensky would be quite capable of having unorthodox views about the arrests and executions that took place in the pre-war period, and Stalin could hardly allow himself to be succeeded by a man who might be inclined to favour a reassessment of Soviet history. During Politburo sessions the only two members who ever allowed themselves to disagree with Stalin, in a very cautious way, were Molotov and Voznesensky. Since Voznesensky had risen to the top during the war on the basis of his own professional competence rather than through patronage, perhaps he was too independent. In any case, he certainly could not be considered to be a diehard Stalinist.

In the recently published stenographic record of the June 1957 plenum of the Central Committee, at which Khrushchev condemned the activity of the 'anti-Party group' (Molotov, Malenkov, Kaganovich and others), a typical exchange took place between Khrushchev and Malenkov, in this instance concerning Voznesensky.

> Khrushchev: I'll tell you about it. Malenkov, a Secretary of Central Committee of the Party, was one of the people Stalin trusted most, and he systematically provided misinformation on a number of issues. When Stalin suggested to promote Voznesensky up to the post of Chairman of the Council of Ministers, Malenkov together with Beria did everything possible to destroy him. I want to ask Comrades Malenkov, Kaganovich, and Bulganin – how many times did Stalin raise the question in our presence – maybe we should put Voznesensky in charge of Gosbank [the State Bank]? And this was already after Beria and Malenkov had cooked up the case against him.

Bulganin: It's true.

Khrushchev: But all the same, Voznesensky was never sent to Gosbank, stuff kept swirling round and round against him and led to his arrest and then finally to his destruction.

Malenkov: It would have been enough for Stalin to say so and he would have been appointed. Who would have made a sound?

Khrushchev: That's not what Malenkov told Stalin.

Malenkov: And I'm telling you, if Stalin had said – why not appoint Voznesensky? he would have been appointed the next day.

Khrushchev: You kept whispering to Stalin, in his last years he was a sick man.

Malenkov: What, that I was managing Stalin? You must be joking.[10]

There are details that are difficult to explain in the whole story. Removed from all his posts and expelled from the Party, Voznesensky spent more than seven months waiting to be arrested. This was extremely unusual. Stalin apparently was hesitating. Having lost Zhdanov and moved Molotov aside, Stalin was patently unhappy about the prospect of leaving the country in the hands of Beria and Malenkov. It was just at this time, in December 1949, that he summoned Khrushchev from Kiev in order to counteract the power of Malenkov. Stalin also spared Aleksei Kosygin, who had been one of the accused in the 'Leningrad affair'. Without any political ambition, Kosygin was an outstanding organizer who would be useful to the country. He could become the new Voznesensky while having no pretensions to being a Marxist theorist, and in this case Stalin certainly was not mistaken.

However, in 1950–52 Stalin's clear favourite in the government was Vyacheslav Malyshev, the Deputy Chairman of the Council of Ministers. In 1939 Stalin personally had promoted the young Malyshev, at the time only the manager of a metallurgical factory, to the post of Commissar of Heavy Machine Construction. During the war years Malyshev was Commissar for Tank Construction and he was able to provide the Red Army with a supply of tanks that were considered to be the best in the world. By the beginning of 1943 a larger number of tanks were being produced in the Soviet Union than in Germany, and after the war production levels were higher than in the whole of western Europe. Malyshev was summoned to Stalin at the Kremlin more than a hundred times, much more frequently than any other Narkom or minister. He was a brilliant organizer, particularly when it came to heavy industry or machine construction, although, unlike Kosygin, he was less effective when it came to light industry. However, since his talents were practical rather than theoretical, Malyshev clearly was not the appropriate person to lead the

Party. Nevertheless he was brought on to the Presidium of the Central Committee in 1952. (Malyshev became responsible for the Soviet missile, rocket and atomic weapons programmes in 1953. As a result of his own carelessness, he was exposed to radiation during the H-bomb test in 1953 and died of radiation sickness in 1957 when he was 55. He decided to inspect the epicentre of the H-bomb blast too soon after the test. His absurd trip to the bomb site is described in Andrei Sakharov's memoirs.)

Within the Soviet elite, it was generally accepted that the centre of power had shifted from the Party to the government, since Stalin governed the country as Chairman of Council of Ministers and in this role also headed the 'socialist commonwealth'. No Party congresses were held in the immediate post-war years, and plenums of the Central Committee took place only rarely. All routine business was mainly dealt with by the government. Therefore it was the prospective head of government rather than Party leader who was regarded to be the potential successor. There were virtually no appropriate candidates for the Party leadership. This position demanded a person who was educated, well versed in Marxism and ideologically adept – it could not be someone who was merely an experienced apparatchik, and there was no such person to be found among Stalin's Politburo colleagues. When he decided to convene the Nineteenth Party Congress, Stalin was concerned once again to enhance the role of ideology within the Party and throughout the country; he believed this to be crucial in view of the fact that during the post-war years political confrontation with the capitalist world, and above all with the United States, had intensified.

After the execution of Voznesensky, there were only two men in the Politburo whose base primarily was in the Party rather than the government   Malenkov and Khrushchev. But the semi-literate Khrushchev had not even had a primary school education, while Malenkov was by training an engineer. When Shepilov visited Malenkov's office in the Central Committee Building towards the end of 1950, he observed that something strange was happening:

> I found work going on in his huge office that seemed most unusual. High bookcases with glass doors had appeared, and Malenkov's assistant, N. Sukhanov, was filling them with books. On the floor, already arranged in rows, there must have been several hundred volumes. I saw the familiar spines of works by Adam Smith, Ricardo, Saint-Simon, etc. ... Coming up to me near the shelf where I was standing, Malenkov, looking rather embarrassed, said: 'Well, Comrade Stalin requires me to study political economy. What do you think? How long will it take me to master it?'[11]

Stalin was already over 70 at the time, and he could hardly postpone all his plans until Malenkov managed to read even a small part of this library, supplied by bibliographers from the Higher Party School and the Academy of Social Sciences. Stalin was not about to wait. As he embarked on the reorganization of the Party *apparat*, he had already singled someone out within his own, absolutely dedicated team; these were people who owed their ascent to him alone and were prepared to put all their skills at his disposal, whatever he asked of them.

The keeper of the cult

The cult of a leader can never be based exclusively on terror and the falsification of history, although Khrushchev tried to claim this to have been the case in his 'secret speech' of 1956. Other elements must be present as well, above all, actual achievement on a historic scale. There is usually also that rather rare quality of psychology and personality that has come to be called 'charisma'. Max Weber brought this term into circulation towards the end of the nineteenth century, arguing that there was a fundamental difference between authority derived from law and tradition and authority generated by a charismatic personality. Today the term 'charismatic leader' is firmly established in the political lexicon although it is often inappropriately applied to ordinary popular politicians. But originally the quality of charisma was attributed only to individuals capable of attracting mass adulation and engendering new values. Familiar examples include Alexander the Great, Jesus, Mohammed, Napoleon, Lenin, and no doubt Trotsky and Mao as well. But there is also a different phenomenon, 'pseudo-charisma', which is largely the product of effective propaganda or 'mega-propaganda' rather than a sign of extraordinary intellect or unique prophetic gifts. 'Mega-propaganda' helped to create a charismatic aura around Hitler, and this was also true of Stalin. In both cases propaganda persuaded the masses of their brilliance, of their prophetic vision, although in reality these qualities were minimal or nonexistent. Unlimited power may have been grounded in fear and supported by an apparatus of terror, but it was enhanced by the existence of genuine mass devotion, encouraged and nourished by an all-embracing and extremely effective network of propaganda and censorship, capable of stifling any criticism. For pseudo-charismatic leaders, it is vital to be able to rely on people of absolute loyalty, and this is particularly true for subordinates in charge of the propaganda system or the punitive organs. The latter needs to be someone who is brutal, amoral and totally without principles while at the same time possessing considerable organizational skills. Different qualities are required of the head of the propaganda machine: here there has to be a genuine fanatic, totally and unselfishly devoted to the leader and dedicated to

the propagation of his 'teaching'. Himmler and Goebbels served as
the two pillars of Hitler's regime, while for Stalin from the end of the
1930s it was Beria and Zhdanov.

Andrei Zhdanov, the First Secretary of the Leningrad obkom and
gorkom (city Party committee), was political commissar in Leningrad
from the beginning of the war until the termination of the blockade
in 1944. Ideological work in the country as a whole during the war
years was led by Aleksandr Shcherbakov, a candidate member of the
Politburo and a Secretary of the Central Committee. He was simultaneously the First Secretary of the Moscow regional and city Party
committees. The person in charge of the Agitation and Propaganda
Directorate of the Central Committee at that time was G.F. Aleksandrov, a professor who later became an Academician. Shcherbakov
additionally was given the rank of general and put in charge of the
political administration of the Soviet army, which meant that the
entire military counter-propaganda effort was in his hands. He
turned out to be so effective in his job that in Germany they started
to call him 'the Russian Goebbels'. As the youngest Party leader in
Stalin's inner circle (he was born in 1901), Shcherbakov was considered to have a very promising future, but in May 1945 he died of a
sudden heart attack. (His premature death was later ascribed to
improper medical treatment and was used as part of the indictment
in the 'Doctors' Plot'.)

It was the death of Shcherbakov that led Stalin to bring Zhdanov
to Moscow where he was put in control of all ideological questions.
Shortly after his arrival it became necessary to dismiss Aleksandrov
from his post as head of the Department of Agitation and Propaganda (the 'Directorate' had been renamed 'Department' by Stalin).
As was explained in a confidential Central Committee letter circulated
to Party organizations, it was a question of moral rather than political misdemeanours (too many young ladies). It was on Stalin's
personal recommendation that Suslov was brought in as his successor. After Zhdanov's death, Suslov became Central Committee
Secretary in charge of ideology and took over all ideological work
throughout the country. In the course of 1949–52 Suslov considerably extended the ideological empire bequeathed to him by
Shcherbakov, Aleksandrov and Zhdanov. He began to exert a greater
influence on Soviet life than any other member of the Politburo with
the exception of Stalin, although he preferred to remain in the shad-
ows. Within the Politburo itself, Stalin of course was still the
'ideologist-in-chief', but in practice all ideological decisions taken by
the Politburo could only be implemented through Suslov. As long as
he remained outside the Politburo, Suslov was able to feel extremely
secure, but if he joined the Politburo with the same functions and
responsibilities that previously had belonged to Shcherbakov and

Zhdanov, he would have found himself thrust into the middle of the intense, if veiled, power struggle going on between two major factions – Malenkov and Beria versus Khrushchev and Bulganin. Stalin was well aware of the situation and apparently was holding Suslov in 'strategic reserve'.

Suslov was only 46 years old in 1948. He had joined the Party in 1921 after two years working in a district Komsomol organization near Saratov. He went to Moscow to study in 1922, at that point having had only a primary school education. He enrolled at a workers' faculty (*rabfak*) and after completing the course entered the Plekhanov Economics Institute. Here too he was successful and then went on to gain higher qualifications at the Economics Institute of Red Professors. At that time he had no intention of working in the Party *apparat*, and he became a professor of political economy at Moscow University, also teaching at the Industrial Academy. In 1931 the Central Committee appointed Suslov to be an inspector in the Party Central Control Commission and in this position he was involved in various regional Party purges. He was sent to the Rostov obkom in 1937 and became one of the Secretaries of the obkom a year later. In 1939 he was sent to work in Stavropol as First Secretary of the *kraikom* (territorial committee). At that time the city was called Voroshilov, and the territory Ordzhonikidze. (These strange names continued to be used until the end of the war.) The job of First Secretary of a kraikom guaranteed a place for Suslov on the Party Central Committee. During the war he was a member of the War Council of the Northern Caucasian front and as Secretary of the kraikom took part in the deportation of the Muslim Karachai people from Stavropol.

The expulsion of the Karachai from Stavropol to 'special settlements' in Central Asia, which began on 2 November 1943, was the first incident in the evacuation of the entire Muslim population from the North Caucasus. A secret decree by the Presidium of the Supreme Soviet on 12 October 1943 ordered the liquidation of the Karachai-Circassian Autonomous Oblast (region). Although the initiative for these deportations must have come from Stalin and their technical execution carried out by NKVD military units, the whole operation was organized in collaboration with the local authorities. This is obvious, if only from the fact that as the deportations were going on, local villages and districts were immediately renamed. There were also territorial changes. The northern part of the Karachai Autonomous Oblast remained in the Stavropol krai, while the southern part was included within the territory of Georgia. A total of 14,774 families were deported – 68,938 people in all.[12]

During the war and especially from 1943, Stalin actively began to pursue a policy of Russian nationalism, and he could fully rely on

Suslov's support. Neither Old Bolsheviks nor non-Russian members of the Party leadership could have approved this rather acute shift in Stalin's attitude towards Russian nationalism. In 1944 the Politburo appointed Suslov to head a special bureau of the Central Committee for Lithuanian affairs. The task of this bureau was to ensure the 'sovietization' of Lithuania and the elimination of Lithuanian nationalists. After the liberation of the Baltic republics from German occupation in 1944, a civil war raged throughout the region with partisan units fighting the Soviet army. In this period Suslov was regarded as Stalin's chief emissary not only in Lithuania but in the neighbouring Baltic republics as well. He established Soviet power in the region by means of massive repressions that affected all strata of society and it was in this period that Stalin got to know Suslov well and was able to evaluate his ability and also his loyalty. Suslov continued to work in Lithuania until the end of February 1946 and spent the next two years carrying out secret missions for Stalin, about which very little is known. In the first two-volume, and later three-volume collection of speeches, reports and articles by Suslov that were published in the 1970s and at the beginning of the 1980s, we see that after a speech in Vilnius on 1 February 1946, he made no further public appearances until 21 January 1948 when he was unexpectedly given the special honour of delivering the main address at the remembrance ceremony on the 24th anniversary of Lenin's death. In the two most detailed biographies of Suslov, one published in Russia and the other in the West, there is virtually no information about the nature of his activity during the period 1946–48.[13,14] Yet Suslov was summoned to see Stalin in the Kremlin six times in 1947 and 20 times in 1948.

It was around this time that Suslov began to attract the attention of Sovietologists and Western intelligence agencies. The research department of the CIA and its branch at Radio Liberty in Munich started to analyse the context of each mention of Suslov's name in the Soviet press as well as his position vis à vis other leaders in photographs of various ceremonial occasions. This technique for evaluating the status of Soviet leaders had existed for some time, but it was first applied to Suslov in 1946. His rank was then thought to be 18th in the hierarchy. In 1947, on the basis of an analysis of a photograph of Soviet leaders at a session of the RSFSR Supreme Soviet and published on 21 June, Suslov was promoted to 12th place, the first person after the 11 members of the Politburo. It was known that Suslov had been appointed to the Orgburo of the Central Committee in March 1946, then consisting of 15 members. In this period Suslov was officially attached to the staff of the General Department of the Central Committee, rather than the Ideological Department. Essentially, this was all that the Western intelligence services managed to find out. Their great interest in Suslov was motivated by the fact that on the basis of circumstantial evidence they came to the conclusion that after Lithuania Suslov had become Stalin's secret emissary and was engaged in overseeing the process of sovietization in one of the major eastern European countries, possibly Hungary or East Germany or both. As these were the years in which the countries of eastern Europe were forced to introduce one-party systems on the Soviet model, Suslov's experience in the Baltic states was extremely useful. Because the job had to be done in conditions of secrecy, it would have been impossible to use one of the better-known members of the Politburo. Suslov was also involved in the creation of the Cominform in 1947. Again on the basis of circumstantial evidence, it was thought that Suslov attempted to settle the emerging conflict with Yugoslavia.

It was only after the death of Stalin that Suslov devoted his attention entirely to ideological work. But as the only Secretary of the Central Committee dealing with ideology, he was able to extend his sphere of influence considerably. Even the Political Administration of the Soviet army, headed by Shcherbakov during the war, now came under the control of his department. He supervised Soviet relations with other countries in the socialist bloc as well as all questions to do with censorship. Educational and cultural institutions, the press and publishing organizations, radio and television, and even the writing of history itself came under his authority, and the list could be extended. Suslov undoubtedly was the conductor-in-chief of the Cold War.

However, despite the fact that he had an enormous influence on the life of the entire country, to some extent greater than certain Politburo members such as Andreyev, Voroshilov or Kaganovich, Suslov did not even become a candidate member. Apparently he preferred genuine power to public prominence. As the struggle for power continued, his position had greater stability as long as he remained outside the Politburo, particularly in view of his special ally inside it, namely Stalin himself. In any case, it would have been rather awkward to have two ideologists sitting at the table during Politburo meetings. However, when he understood that his own time was drawing to an end, the elder of the two was prepared to give way to his younger lieutenant.

After Stalin's death Suslov remained at his main posts in the apparatus of the Central Committee. In 1956 it was he who was sent by the Central Committee to Hungary as political 'commissar' when it was decided to back up military intervention with the installation of a new political leadership and the restoration of the Hungarian Communist Party. Suslov supported Khrushchev in his conflict with Malenkov because he considered Malenkov to be dangerous to the future of the country. In the end, however, Suslov did begin to engage in cautious preparations for Khrushchev's removal. Khrushchev could only have delivered his well-known speech on the 'cult of personality' at the Twentieth Congress after the death of Stalin. But it was in Khrushchev's presence that Suslov presented the report on Khrushchev's 'cult of personality' in October 1964 at an enlarged meeting of the Presidium of the Central Committee. After Khrushchev was forced to retire, criticism of Stalin virtually came to an end. The Soviet empire again began to expand, primarily at the expense of countries in Asia, Africa and South America.

When Khrushchev was removed in 1964, the choice of Brezhnev to replace him as leader was not regarded as final. Brezhnev was not a large-scale political figure, and his organizational skills were limited. But he was neither a power-hungry nor an ambitious man, and his behaviour towards his colleagues was amiable and predictable. He disliked conflict. When Aleksei Kosygin became Chairman of the Council of Ministers, Brezhnev almost never interfered with his work. He had little understanding of ideological problems and was a person who was on the whole incapable of sustained activity or systematic work. Although Brezhnev was not slow in reviving the former designation of the key political body, the Politburo, and restoring for himself the post of General Secretary, the normal work of the Central Committee apparatus was directed by Suslov. At the time of the 90th anniversary of Stalin's birth in 1969, Suslov initiated a series of measures that amounted to a partial rehabilitation.

During the entire subsequent period until his death at the beginning of 1982, Suslov came second in the Party hierarchy and was given the unofficial title of 'chief ideologist of the Communist Party'. In so far as the Soviet Union was an ideological state, the ideological leader of the USSR during the whole post-Khrushchev period was in fact Suslov. It was the ascetic and inconspicuous Suslov rather than the more flamboyant Brezhnev or the pragmatic Kosygin who determined the extremely conservative political course of the USSR from the end of the 1960s to the beginning of the 1980s. The term 'period of stagnation' is associated largely with the cultural-ideological life of the country rather than with the economic sphere. The standard of living of the population rose considerably in the 1970s as a result of the moderately reformist policies pursued by the very competent Prime Minister, Aleksei Kosygin. Yet a sense of degradation pervaded the moral life of the country, the political persecution of 'dissidents' was resumed, and in the international arena the aggressive tendencies of communism were on the rise. Stronger control was established over the countries of the Warsaw Pact, in particular Poland, with a special 'Suslov Commission' set up to enforce it. This whole range of ideologically conservative policies was Suslov's 'contribution' to Soviet history. After Stalin's death, he was able to give Stalinism approximately 20 additional years of active life.

Suslov died on 25 January 1982. He was given burial honours of a kind that had not been accorded to any other leader since the funeral of Stalin. Brezhnev did not attempt to hide his tears. He knew who had been the secret General Secretary of the CPSU after the death of Stalin. Fortunately Suslov left no heir, secret or otherwise.

CHAPTER 3

Stalin's Personal Archive: Hidden or Destroyed? Facts and Theories

Zhores and Roy Medvedev

Lenin, Stalin and the archives

Lenin's archive is housed in thousands of special document cases containing the manuscripts of handwritten resolutions, notes, letters and articles as well as a huge collection of documents that he signed, including various orders, instructions, drafts and decrees. All originals are protected from the effects of light and humidity. A large part of this meticulously preserved treasure has been published in the *Collected Works of Lenin* and in various editions of *Collected Lenin*; documents are also available on microfilm. But there were also a variety of Lenin's unpublished papers that for one reason or another were placed in secret archives. After the process of opening these archives began in 1991, the author of a new biography was able to have a look at them.[1] Two monographs were published, analysing the new materials,[2,3] and scores of articles and studies appeared, devoted to various episodes of the October Revolution, the Civil War, NEP and the last year of Lenin's life. Access to the entire archive enabled historians to have a better or different understanding of the past.

Lenin's life and activity can be studied comprehensively, but in the case of Stalin the situation is unfortunately quite different. No comparable archive exists, nor will it ever be possible to recreate one in the future, since a significant portion of Stalin's papers were deliberately destroyed by his political heirs, including a large number of documents and a considerable part of his personal archive.

Stalin's claim to political legitimacy was based on continuity with Leninism and the traditions of the Revolution. Throughout his life he continued to lean on the authority of Lenin. All documents with any connection to Lenin were painstakingly collected and safeguarded with what virtually amounted to religious zeal. The Stalin epoch in the USSR encompassed a complex interweaving of contradictory phenomena: major socio-economic and political achievements took place against the background of a relentless power struggle and mass terror; there were military defeats but even more dramatic military victories. Stalin's crimes, about which many volumes have been written, were also the crimes of the entire Stalinist regime. They were perpetrated collectively. Stalin's comrades within the Politburo, the Orgburo, the Secretariat and, most crucially, in the state security organs were also his accomplices in the execution of all his repressive campaigns.

After Stalin's death, the members of his immediate circle derived their legitimacy in the public consciousness from the fact that they had been his intimates. However, although his heirs were eager to share the credit for all the achievements of the Stalinist period, they were anxious to disassociate themselves from its crimes. No evidence was required to demonstrate Stalin's involvement in the mass repressions; his role and guilt were obvious. But the exalted leader and dictator, no longer among the living, could only await the verdict of history. When it came to his closest comrades, however, their participation in the crimes of Stalinism was less overt, with the exception of Beria; on the whole, incriminating evidence could be found only in secret archives, largely Party archives but also in Stalin's personal files, since he had always made sure that there were documents recording collective responsibility. In the political situation following Stalin's death and the struggle for power among his successors, it was in no one's interest for the contents of Stalin's personal archive to become an object of 'religious' veneration. It would have been extremely inconvenient to repeat the Lenin experience. After Stalin's archive had been destroyed, most of Beria's archive received the same treatment, along with Beria himself. The new leaders of the Soviet Union were intent on acquiring an historical alibi.

The destruction of Stalin's personal archive: circumstantial evidence

When previously secret Party and state archives began to be accessible in 1989 (the process rapidly accelerated after the break-up of Soviet Union), Russian and foreign historians were immediately attracted by the chance to examine them and begin a process of systematic organization. The extraordinary international interest excited by these archives was not simply a question of something once forbidden now being permitted. It was seen as an opportunity to shed light on questions of current political relevance, but perhaps even more importantly, scholars were hoping to find explanations for events that were still part of living memory. Several British and American universities and libraries actively participated in the process of sorting out and systematizing the archives, putting them on microfilm and creating catalogues. During the first years of this work, which certainly will continue for many years to come, separate fonds (collections of documents) were created to house material relating to the most important aspects of Soviet history, and the protocols of all sessions of the Politburo from 1919 to 1940 were made available to scholars. Archives of the NKVD-MVD, along with several other People's Commissariats and Ministries, were declassified and put in order. Separate archive fonds were allocated to various key figures of the past, including Trotsky, Ordzhonikidze, Kalinin, Kirov, Zhdanov and many others. Microfilm versions of the archives of prominent non-Bolsheviks were made available for purchase by libraries or individual scholars: Martov, Akselrod, Zasulich, Plekhanov, etc. Archive fonds also were established for victims of the Stalinist terror, including figures from the arts, science and literature as well as political figures and military personnel. A large part of these archive collections was assembled by dedicated researchers and biographers and was not simply the work of archive employees dismantling secret dossiers. In some cases small library-museums were set up to house the new archive fonds of prominent individuals (e.g. Kapitsa, Sakharov, Bulgakov, Vavilov, etc). Essentially, a reassessment of our national history had begun, a history which in the past had not merely been distorted but often entirely falsified. This whole process was promoted by the elimination of censorship.

Unfortunately the restoration of our history could only be a partial exercise for the simple reason that crucial parts of the archives had disappeared, including documents relating to many eminent individuals, above all people who had suffered repression. Whenever a political figure, writer or scholar was arrested, all personal papers were routinely confiscated. After the investigation was over, documents that turned out to be irrelevant to the case were never returned to relatives; instead they were destroyed, usually burned, in accordance with authorized rules of procedure. Novels, manuscripts, diaries, photograph albums, marginal notes, letters – they all vanished. In the case of Academician Nikolai Vavilov, NKVD Lieutenant A. Koshelev and his boss Senior Lieutenant A. Khvat burned 90 notebooks in which Vavilov had recorded in detail the results of his botanical-geographical expeditions to collect samples of cultured plants throughout the world; there were maps of plant distribution and also several manuscripts of unfinished books. Whatever materials the NKVD investigators considered to be 'of no value' (i.e. unrelated to the accusation) were consigned to the flames.[4] There is a certain irony in the fact that Stalin himself turned out to be a victim of this practice.

From 1934 to 1953 Stalin lived and worked in his country residence at Kuntsevo for a large part of the time. It was not far from Moscow and was usually called the *blizhnaya* (nearby) *dacha*. Specially designed for Stalin, the dacha had about 20 rooms, a greenhouse and a solarium, as well as substantial auxiliary accommodation for guards and domestic staff. Stalin also transferred a large part of his library there. He only came to work in his Kremlin office in the evening; after looking through official papers, he spent the next several hours seeing the people he had summoned, holding meetings, and discussing various questions with members of the Politburo. More confidential conversations took place at the dacha, where Stalin also read his most important post and wrote letters, articles and speeches. As an insomniac, Stalin would keep several books on his night table which he would read or glance through until the early hours of the morning, always making copious notes in the margins.

He had an office at the dacha, but he also worked in other rooms, even the dining room, and used them for longer meetings. In 1952 Stalin received Dmitri Shepilov, at that time the editor of *Pravda,* in a room that was sometimes called the 'small library' to discuss the production of a textbook on the economics of socialism. Stalin was writing a great deal on this theme at the time, largely critical notes, reviews and articles. Since it was clear to him that he could not write a textbook himself, he decided to entrust this task to a group of writers personally selected by him, including Shepilov. Their conversation went on for about three hours. In his memoirs Shepilov wrote that while they were talking,

> Stalin suddenly asked me: 'When you're writing your articles or scholarly works, do you use a stenographer?' I replied in the negative. 'But why not?' he asked. I explained that I often had to make corrections in the text as I was working. Stalin then said: 'I never use a stenographer either. I can't work when someone is hanging around.'[5]

And that really was the case. He wrote grammatically correct texts in a clear, legible hand, always when on his own. To this day, however, nothing is known about the fate of the manuscripts and notes that must have been left behind at the Kuntsevo dacha. In her memoirs written in 1963, *Twenty Letters to a Friend,* Stalin's daughter describes the following incident, but at the time even she could not properly assess its meaning:

> Strange things happened at Kuntsevo after my father died. The very next day – it was well before the funeral – Beria had the whole household, servants and bodyguards, called together and told them that my father's belongings were to be removed right away – no one had any idea where – and that they were all to quit the premises.

> No one argued with Beria. Men and women who didn't have the slightest idea what was happening and who were practically in a state of shock packed up my father's possessions, his books and furniture and china, and tearfully loaded them on trucks. They were all carted

off somewhere to the sort of warehouse the secret police had plenty of. ...

Later, in 1955, when Beria himself had 'fallen', they started restoring the dacha. My father's things were brought back. The former servants and commandants were invited back and helped put everything where it belonged and make the house look as it had before. They were preparing to open a museum, like the one in Lenin's house at Leninskiye Gorki. But then came the Twentieth Party Congress. After that, of course, any thought of a museum was dropped.[6]

Svetlana, of course, was unaware that the writing tables, various secretaires, cupboards and other pieces of furniture had been returned with all papers removed. Although a part of Stalin's library was preserved, all manuscripts, letters and other documents had simply vanished. A special commission was set up at the Marx–Engels–Lenin–Stalin Institute in October 1953 (Stalin's name was added on immediately after his funeral on 9 March) to make arrangements for a Stalin museum at the restored Kuntsevo dacha. They first had to undertake a fact-finding mission, since all the furniture had not yet been returned to the appropriate rooms. Some of it was still in packing cases, while carpets were rolled up and kept in the kitchen. For various reason the final decision to establish a museum at the dacha was continually postponed. There are several possible explanations for this, but it is likely that the main obstacle turned out to be the impossibility of recreating the authentic 'working' atmosphere of the dacha. Stalin's felt boots could be placed by the door, but there could hardly be an exhibition without any manuscripts or papers.

In 1955, having buried the idea of a Stalin museum, Khrushchev decided that the dacha would be transferred to the Central Committee to serve as an isolated location where groups of Central Committee employees could get together to prepare various reports and analyses for the Politburo. They then began to refurnish the building for this purpose. Much of Stalin's furniture was removed and taken to the vast underground chambers that had been built before and during the war as air raid shelters. Aleksei Snegov, an acquaintance of ours who had been an aide to Khrushchev, told us that when Stalin's desk was being moved from his former study, they accidentally came across five letters addressed to him that he had hidden under a layer of newspapers in one of the drawers. Snegov could only recall three of them. One had been dictated by Lenin on 5 March 1923. He demanded that Stalin apologize for his abusive manner towards Krupskaya. Not long after it was found, Khrushchev read out this letter to the delegates at the Twentieth Party Congress during his secret speech on 'the cult of personality'. The second letter was from Bukharin, awaiting death, written shortly before he was shot. He finished with the words: 'Koba, why do you need my death?' The third came from Marshall Tito in 1950. The text was brief: 'Stalin. Stop sending assassins to murder me. We have already caught five, one with a bomb, another with a rifle. ... If this doesn't stop, I will send one man to Moscow and there will be no need to send another.'

Dmitry Volkogonov, working in the Central Committee archives, was the first professional historian to report the disappearance of Stalin's personal Kremlin archive. And even he only made this discovery in 1988 when he was writing the first detailed biography of Stalin to be published in the USSR under the auspices of the Propaganda Department of the Central Committee. After Stalin's death, a special 'commission on the Stalin heritage' was set up to examine his personal papers; it included senior staff from the Marx–Engels–Lenin–Stalin Institute along with employees of the Ideology Department of the Central Committee. This commission was meant to take charge of all Stalin's papers, including the contents of his Kremlin office and apartment as well as whatever was found in his dachas outside Moscow or in the south where he had been spending considerable amounts of time between 1948 and 1951. It was thought that Stalin kept his most important documents in his Kremlin office, locked up in a large safe to which no one else had a key, not even the long-serving Poskrebyshev.

The Central Committee commission began its work approximately two weeks after the funeral. Its first obvious task was to examine Stalin's office and official residence in the Kremlin. However, someone had apparently been there before them. According to the recollections of many who had visited these rooms in the past, they were always overflowing with piles of paper; clearly a large number of documents had been taken away. 'Stalin's safe was empty, aside from his Party card and a small packet of unimportant papers,' wrote Volkogonov, 'and despite many attempts, I was never able to discover what it had contained or what had happened to his personal papers.'[7] Volkogonov made the point again in a later study of Stalin, published in 1996: 'After his death, Stalin's personal archive was combed out repeatedly.'[8] During the seven years between the first and second versions of his Stalin biography, Volkogonov, who was a key figure on the commission established by the President to declassify Party archives, says that he was only able to find a few 'insignificant' Stalin papers. There were several notebooks containing preparatory thoughts 'for buro meetings', consisting of rough drafts of questions he intended to raise at regular sessions of the Politburo or at some other meeting. It was clear from the contents that these notebooks were from 1932–34: there were references to the OGPU, Gorky was still alive, and they were discussing the introduction of an internal passport system. At present this small collection of notebooks is still kept in a classified Stalin fond in the Presidential Archive (APRF). But if Stalin prepared for every meeting of the Politburo in this way, and there can be little doubt that he did, then his personal archive must have contained several hundred notebooks of this kind. In the course of the 1930s alone, there were approximately 500 sessions of the Politburo at which tens of thousands of issues were decided.

Remaining archive materials

The Stalin fonds available to historians largely contain papers that were once deposited in various secret archives during Stalin's life-time, including originals of reports and drafts that were sent to him for a decision or signature or possibly just for information. During the years 1944–53 the secretariat of the NKVD–MGB kept copies of all reports sent to Stalin in its 'Special Stalin File'. As part of a Rus-sian-American project, the Russian Federation State Archive and the University of Pittsburgh jointly published a catalogue of these docu-ments in 1994.[10] We can see from this catalogue that within ten years Stalin received almost 3,000 items from the NKVD–MVD. Some were purely informative, for example accounts of earthquakes in different regions of the USSR; others evidently required Stalin's approval and return to the security organs (e.g. the numerous post-investigation sentences imposed by 'special boards' of the NKVD or MVD on large groups of people who had been arrested in territories of the USSR liberated from the Germans); a third category included draft resolutions sent for signature (e.g. a GKO resolution to release 708,000 foreigners from NKVD camps, sent to Stalin on 10 August 1945). Stalin may well have stored some of these documents in his own archive. He did so with a report dated 28 May 1949 informing him that the NKVD–MVD had discovered proof in the State Archive of the October Revolution 'that N.A. Govorov and L.A. Govorov had served in Kolchak's army'. L.A. Govorov was a Marshal of the USSR who had been in charge of the Leningrad front at the end of the war and was one of Stalin's favourites. However, Stalin collected secret dossiers on all his marshals, including Zhukov, and the new infor-mation about Govorov's past would have been stored in Stalin's 'marshal collection'.

A large number of reports and draft resolutions also arrived from other commissariats and ministries. According to various witnesses, Stalin read or looked through anywhere from one to 200 documents every day. But towards the end of his life, when his capacity for work had diminished, complete sets of unexamined papers and even packets with their seals intact began to pile up in the Kremlin and at the dacha. In due course the flow of papers was reduced. Ministries were sent a directive telling them to limit the number of questions requiring Stalin's personal intervention.

Stalin took an enormous interest in how his own activities were portrayed in books dealing with Soviet history, the Second World War and the history of the Party. He allowed historians to use archive material, although of course only with special permission. In order to assist them in their work, he sent a large number of the various documents passing through his hands to Party and military archives. Particularly sensitive material was sent to the Politburo archive or to the 'Special Files', a top-secret archive where papers were kept in sealed packets and could only be examined with the permission of the General Secretary. After Stalin's death, during all the years from Khrushchev to Gorbachev, only the leaders of the CPSU had access to the 'Special Files'. Even in the 1980s the documents in this archive were considered to be so 'hot' for the Party that declassification only took place when the Communist Party itself was proscribed after the break-up of the USSR. The 'Special Files' contained the originals of documents the very existence of which had been denied for decades: the secret protocols attached to the Molotov–Ribbentrop Pact of 1939 confirming the division of Poland and outlining future 'spheres of influence'; materials on the liquidation of Polish prisoners, including army officers, police, priests and government officials, carried out by the NKVD in the autumn of 1940; the decision by the GKO to exile the Muslim peoples of the North Caucasus and the Crimea in 1943–44; plus a variety of original documents signed by Stalin, Beria, Molotov, Voroshilov and other leading figures. Whenever he dispatched papers to the 'Special Files' Stalin could be certain that absolutely no one, not even members of the Politburo or the Central Committee, could have access to a sealed packet without his personal authorization. In 1990 the document collection of the 'Special Files' was transferred from the Central Committee building to the Kremlin, where it was housed in Stalin's former apartment. Later, after the attempted coup by conservatives in the Party, army and KGB, Gorbachev moved the 'Special Files' to the secret archive of the General Staff. Following Gorbachev's resignation, all these documents exposing the whole secret history of the CPSU as well as hidden aspects of the Stalin era were returned to the Kremlin and became part of the newly created Archive of the President of the Russian Federation (APRF), known as the Presidential Archive.

Working on his first biography of Stalin, *Triumph and Tragedy*, published in 1989, Dmitry Volkogonov largely used the Central Party Archive, which by then had been amalgamated with several other archives including the archive of the Marx-Lenin Institute (TsPAIML), the Central Archive of the Ministry of Defence (TsAMO) and the Central State Archive of the Soviet Army (TsGASA). By the time Volkogonov was preparing his later book on Stalin, published in 1996, all the archives had been reorganized. His main archival source was now the Russian Centre for the Preservation and Study of Documents of Most Recent History (RTsKhIDNI), which combined the Marx-Lenin Institute archive with various other Party archives. Judging by Volkogonov's book, there turned out to be two fonds (17 and 558) in this archive containing documents that included Stalin's instructions or bore his signature; however, these were the same papers that Volkogonov had studied earlier. All the new materials found by Volkogonov for the 1996 volume are now kept in the Presidential Archive, where access is only possible by permission of the President's head of administration. We tried several times to obtain this permission from Sergei Filatov in 1994 and 1995, but were always refused.

The Presidential Archive contains secret documents from the Politburo and the 'Special Files' as well as part of the archive of the former KGB. There are also some of Stalin's personal papers, such as the notebooks from 1932–34, referred to previously. A special Stalin fond was created in this archive as well, which in 1994 included more than 1,700 files. However, most of these papers are of little significance and have a certain value only because of some direct link with Stalin. They include participants' credentials issued to Stalin for conferences or congresses, congratulations received on various personal or official anniversary celebrations, and books sent to Stalin with dedications from their authors. Complete sets of war-time front-line maps, annotated by Stalin, were sent to the archive of the General Staff, while the RTsKhIDNI was given several film scenarios containing Stalin's marginal notes. All together 1,445 items have been removed from the Presidential Archive and deposited elsewhere.[11] Approximately 300 restricted files remain in the Stalin fond. Because no list has ever been compiled, it is impossible to determine their content. This has led several historians to assume that there are crucially important documents hidden away in this fond. However, we think this unlikely and are inclined to believe that there is nothing of much importance in this last collection of Stalin documents closed to most historians. (After all, neither Radzinsky nor Volkogonov, who did have access, found anything of major interest.) But the fond could contain manuscripts, notes or letters that somehow escaped the general onslaught in Stalin's offices, apartment and dachas.

Although Volkogonov did not discover anything of significance for his new biography of Stalin, it should be said that he was under time pressure. His second 'short' biography of Stalin is only a superficial supplement to his earlier, vast, four-volume work, *Triumph and Tragedy*. As can be seen from the very title of the book, written in collaboration with the staff of the Institute of Military History where Volkogonov was director in the 1980s, the author was striving to maintain a balanced approach in what ultimately amounted to a positive assessment. Colonel-General Volkogonov was the product of a military-political education and in the 1970s had been head of the Main Political Administration of the Soviet army. At that time he was to some extent a Stalinist and was the author of many books reflecting the official view of Stalin's place in Soviet history. Towards the end of his life, seriously ill but possessing full access to the archives, Volkogonov was hastening to complete biographies of all seven Soviet leaders from Lenin to Gorbachev. However, his outlook had shifted considerably, and he was now mainly concentrating on the exposure of negative material, without aspiring to objectivity or analysis.

A more detailed, although one-sided, negative biography of Stalin has been attempted by the well-known Soviet playwright Edvard Radzinsky. This book, with the straightforward title *Stalin*, was published in 1997, but as the author explains in the introduction, he first began writing it in 1969.[12] Like Volkogonov, Radzinsky was given access to all the archives, including the APRF. In a bibliographical note, he lists the archive documents he examined. Radzinsky looked at 25 files in the Stalin fond of the Presidential Archive; 20 are related to Stalin's family problems (correspondence with his mother, letters from his wife, Nadezhda Alliluyeva, news about his son, Yakov Dzhugashvili, information about the death of Alliluyeva, etc) and had already appeared in a monograph published by the archivists. The contents of the other five files are also in the public domain and were published before the appearance of Radzinsky's book (Stalin's visitors' book, his letters to Molotov, Bukharin's letter to Stalin, and Marshall Tukhachevsky's letter to Stalin concerning the reconstruction of the Red Army). In short, the book does not contain any fundamentally new material.

The best new biography of recent years is that by Yevgeny Gromov, *Stalin. Power and Art*, published in 1998.[13] Its approach is original and it is a truly serious work, interesting and objective and based on a comprehensive use of both archival and previously published materials. The book covers the entire course of Stalin's working life but deals with only one aspect of his activity: his role in the formation of Soviet culture as a distinct phenomenon, different in form and content from what was then called Western or 'bourgeois' culture. We are given a comprehensive picture of Stalin as a young poet, as an author and editor, and as a harsh censor and critic of plays and films, music and literature. The book virtually ignores the major events of Soviet history – the Party battles of the 1920s, collectivization, industrialization, terror, the war – where Stalin played a rather more direct and decisive role than in music or ballet. The author set himself a quite different task and has succeeded admirably in accomplishing it. Approximately 1,000 sources are cited in the book, almost half of them from the archives. However, practically all the cited archival documents are from various fonds of the RTsKhIDNI without a single reference to any file in the APRF. This suggests that the author either could not gain access to the still restricted Presidential Archive or that he found nothing in it relevant to his theme.

In 1994 the *Bulletin of the Presidential Archive* was established as a new journal, by order of the President. The aim was to publish annotated material from the APRF, which was then going through a process of gradual declassification. This *Bulletin of the APRF* came out as a supplement to another new journal, *Istochnik* (Source), which published material from other archives, including the RTsKhIDNI, GARF (the State Archive of the Russian Federation, formerly the Central Archive of the October Revolution), the archives of the MVD and the KGB, etc. All of these archives contained Stalin fonds that had been established during his lifetime. The Director of the APRF, A.V. Korotkov, became chief editor of its *Bulletin*. In the course of five years the two archival journals published a great deal of fascinating material on Russian and Soviet history and also several interesting documents concerning Stalin.

But however valuable these documents may be for any biographer of Stalin, they did not emerge from Stalin's personal archive. Among them, perhaps the most important text is the memoir-diary of Vyacheslav Malyshev, appointed Commissar for Heavy Machinery in 1939 and from 1941 the commissar in charge of tank production. Because Stalin was determined to achieve tank superiority over the Germans as rapidly as possible, qualitatively and quantitatively, Malyshev was summoned by Stalin to the Kremlin or the dacha more frequently than any other commissar. Tanks played a major role in the German blitzkrieg strategy. In the period 1939–50, Malyshev talked to Stalin around 100 times, with a large part of their meetings taking place during the war. After each encounter or telephone conversation, Malyshev made notes in his diary. The diary provides a sense of Stalin's leadership style and gives a good idea of the kind of effort it took to supply the Red Army with new tanks by the end of 1942, tanks that prevailed over the German tank armada and secured victory for the Russians in the battles of Stalingrad and Kursk. The tank combat at Kursk in July 1943 took place on a scale that was without precedent; approximately 4,000 Red Army tanks withstood 3,000 German ones. The fighting went on for more than a week and when it was over, the battlefield was littered with damaged or burned-out tanks (2,900 German and 1,700 Soviet).[15] Among the documents about Stalin published in the journal *Istochnik,* perhaps the most interesting are the memoirs of Ivan Valedinsky, who was Stalin's personal physician during the years 1926–44.[16]

From the middle of 1999, however, the *Bulletin of the Presidential Archive* ceased publication. Undoubtedly the fund of materials in the APRF had been exhausted. Anything that remained could appear in other journals such as *Voprosy istorii* (Questions of History) or *Istoricheski Arkhiv* (Historical Archive). From the end of 1994 to the beginning of 1997, it was the latter journal that published the lists of visitors to Stalin's Kremlin office between 1924 and 1953, of such crucial interest to historians and based on records held in the Presidential Archive.

Taking an overview of the Stalin fonds in various archives, we can be almost certain that Stalin's correspondence with his mother was kept either in the Kremlin apartment or at the dacha until 1953. These were extremely short letters, sometimes containing only one or two sentences and written in Georgian. After the death of Yekaterina Dzhugashvili in Tbilisi in 1937, the letters undoubtedly would have been sent to Moscow by the Georgian authorities. There could have been no question of exhibiting them in the existing Stalin museum at Gori without Stalin's permission. Stalin's correspondence with his wife, Nadezhda Alliluyeva, also ended up in the APRF and must have come from the apartment; the letters were written during Stalin's trips to the south for mineral water therapy. He frequently took breaks alone, leaving his wife and children in the dacha or at the Kremlin. Similarly, the APRF holds documents relating to the capture and imprisonment of Stalin's son Yakov by the Germans, prepared specially by the NKVD in a single version with no copies. There are letters to Stalin from Bukharin, written in 1937 shortly before his arrest, which had been kept in the Kremlin office. The visitors' book from Stalin's Kremlin office, which also wound up in the APRF, must have come from there as well because there is no other place where it could have been found.

A large part of the Stalin fond in the RTsKhIDNI consists of documents that apparently were sent to the Central Party Archive (TsPA) during Stalin's lifetime. After his death, most of his books were moved to this archive. (In March 1999 yet another reorganization of the archives was carried out. The RTsKHIDNI was combined with the archive of the youth organizations and is now called the Russian State Archive of Social-Political History (RGASPI).)

The missing fonds

The well-known Soviet poet-satirist Demyan Bedny was for many years a favourite of Stalin and was called the 'poet of the Party'. But suddenly in August 1938 this 'proletarian' poet was expelled from the Party and even from the Soviet Writers' Union. This was done on Stalin's orders, but neither Bedny nor his friends had any idea why he had fallen into disfavour. One of the poet's friends, Ivan Gronsky, who in the 1930s was first the editor of the *Bulletin of the VTsIK* (All-Russian Central Executive Committee) and subsequently the editor of *Novy Mir*, shed light on the story in his memoirs, *Out of the Past*. He wrote that during a meeting with Stalin, they had

> a confidential conversation in which he explained what it was all about. He took an exercise book out of his safe. Written in it were some rather unflattering remarks about inhabitants of the Kremlin. I said that the handwriting was not Demyan's. Stalin replied that these were the sentiments of the slightly-tight poet, taken down by a certain journalist.[17]

This episode once again confirms the widespread view among Stalin specialists that he had his own network of secret informers, independent of the NKVD. An extremely suspicious man who mistrusted virtually everyone, Stalin liked to have the maximum amount of information, often of a personal nature, about people with whom he associated or had to meet. When a person was suggested for some important post, Stalin would always send for the NKVD dossier on the candidate. Any objective assessment of Stalin's lieutenants makes it clear that what he valued above all in his subordinates was their personal loyalty; this was certainly far more important than any individual's 'moral qualities'. Once he was informed about the moral shortcomings of a Party or state official, Stalin found it rather easy to manipulate that person, to bend him to his will. This explains how the Politburo largely came to be Stalin's obedient agent by the beginning of the 1930s, although its members were not devoid of intellect or organizational abilities. During the 1930s and up to his death in 1935, Valerian Kuibyshev, a member of the Politburo and Chairman of Gosplan, was one of those who were most devoted to Stalin. However, shortly before his departure from Moscow in September 1933, Stalin learned that Molotov, whom he usually left in charge, also intended to go on leave at the same time. He immediately sent Molotov an urgent letter: 'Is it so hard to understand that you simply can't leave the Politburo and the Council of Commissars to Kuibyshev (he may start drinking) or to Kaganovich for long?'[18] After Kuibyshev died in 1935 from delirium tremens during a drinking bout, it was later said that he had been poisoned by his enemies, since the medical report on the cause of death had been falsified.

In an article entitled 'Behind the Walls of the Kremlin' published in 1938 in the émigré journal *Bulletin of the Opposition*, Trotsky claimed that Stalin possessed a considerable amount of compromising material on Kalinin and Voroshilov and was therefore able to blackmail them into full submission. Kalinin, who became Chairman of the TsIK (Central Executive Committee) after Sverdlov's death in 1919, was in formal terms the head of state; within the Politburo he was meant to represent the interests of the peasantry. According to Trotsky, during the first years of his chairmanship Kalinin behaved well and was extremely modest.

> However, with time and under the influence of the formal attributes of power, he assumed the role of a statesman and no longer was timid in front of professors, actors or especially actresses. Hardly acquainted with life in the Kremlin behind the scene, I found out about Kalinin's new way of life belatedly and from a totally unexpected source. I think it was probably in 1925 that a Soviet satirical magazine published a cartoon depicting the head of state in a very intimate situation. The resemblance left no room for doubt. In addition, in an extremely licentious text, the initials M.I. were used to identify the Kalinin figure. I could hardly believe my eyes. 'What's this about?' I asked several close acquaintances, including Serebryakov. 'It's Stalin giving a last warning to Kalinin', he replied. 'But why?' 'Of course it's not about safeguarding his morals. Kalinin must have been obstinate about something.'[19]

According to Trotsky, as a result of this 'warning', Kalinin stopped being difficult and gradually became completely submissive, approving all of Stalin's schemes and signing any decree put before him. Decrees of the Central Executive Committee, signed by the Chairman and the Secretary, had the force of law. For many years the Secretary of the TsIK was Stalin's friend, Avel Yenukidze, who was also completely under his control. Only these two signatures were necessary in order for a decree to come into effect. Formally it was considered that the new statute had been approved by all members of the Presidium of the TsIK, although in practice majority consent was sought by telephone. Decrees of the Presidium of the Supreme Soviet were usually approved in the same way, and it was Kalinin who guaranteed this rapid method of transforming Stalin's orders into legislative acts.

Trotsky also claimed that around 1928 he found out that 'Stalin had a special archive containing documents, bits of evidence, and discreditable rumours about all prominent Soviet figures, without exception. In 1929 at the time of the open break with the members of the 'right' in the Politburo – Bukharin, Rykov, and Tomsky – Stalin kept Kalinin and Voroshilov on his side only by threatening to expose their depravity.

This method of ensuring the total subservience of subordinates is rather widespread as a power technique. Stalin may have had only a small group of secret informants, but crucially these people had access to any archive (including that of the GPU) and could use bribery or threats in order to collect information from the servants and bodyguards of the Kremlin elite. According to the memoirs of Stalin's former personal secretary, Boris Bazhanov, who fled abroad through Turkistan and Persia in 1928, the chief organizers of this network of informers in the 1920s were two of Stalin's personal aides, Grigory Kanner and Lev Mekhlis.[21] Kanner was shot in 1937. Apparently he knew too much, although Mekhlis continued to enjoy Stalin's trust. From 1930 to 1937 Mekhlis was the editor of *Pravda,* a post considered by Stalin to be of crucial importance. Subsequently, Stalin's informer network operated through what was called the Secret Department of the Central Committee, later (as of 1934) known as the 'Special Section'. From 1930 until 1952, the permanent head of this department was Aleksandr Poskrebyshev, one of Stalin's most loyal subordinates. However, his political vulnerability served to cement this loyalty. Poskrebyshev's wife had been arrested and later shot because she was the sister of Trotsky's daughter-in-law. Poskrebyshev himself was 'provided' with a new wife via NKVD channels. Stalin's chief of personal security, General Nikolai Vlasik, was also used as a private source of information from the NKVD. Since Vlasik was simultaneously in charge of the entire NKVD body-guard service, ordinary guards and drivers who served other members of the Politburo were his subordinates. He had been Stalin's bodyguard since the days of the Civil War. Vlasik had problems with both women and money, but up until 1952 Stalin forgave him everything.

The key figures of Stalin's apparatus of repression, Yagoda, Yezhov and Beria, all had some dark shadow in their pasts (i.e. the years before 1920) as well as certain 'moral' weaknesses, which as we now know in the cases of Yezhov and Beria amounted to sexual pathology. Stalin did not promote these people to the highest position in the NKVD out of ignorance but because he understood that their vulnerability would make them willing executors of any criminal enterprise. In comparison with the official crimes carried out in the course of their work, their sexual offences could only amount to a minor footnote in the judgement of history. People could hardly be chosen to participate in the organization of mass terror on the basis of moral criteria. Historians of Stalinist repression have suggested that similar factors explain the total subservience of the USSR Procurator General, Andrei Vyshinsky, during the terror. Until 1921 Vyshinsky had been a Menshevik. His professional career as a lawyer began in 1913 and he was working as procurator at the time of Kerensky's provisional government. It was known that in the summer of 1917 he had issued an order in Moscow for the arrest of Bolsheviks.[22] After the Bolshevik victory in October 1917 there were sufficient grounds to accuse him of counter-revolutionary activity. However, having known Vyshinsky since they were imprisoned together in Baku in 1908,[23] Stalin always protected him and insisted that the accusations were false. He did the same for Beria with regard to his role in counter-intelligence between 1918 and 1920 in independent Azerbaijan. Stalin helped to create the myth that when in Baku, Beria had in fact been acting as a secret agent on behalf of the Bolshevik organization.

In his 1976 book, *The Technology of Power*, A. Avtorkhanov writes of other similar cases, based on rumours as well as 'unidentified sources', where moral blackmail ensured the devotion of several highly placed Party and state officials. One example was Andrei Andreyev, a loyal Stalinist member of the Politburo from 1926 to 1952 (candidate member in 1926–32). But before 1917 he had been a Menshevik and a 'Defencist' (i.e. he supported Russia's continued participation in the war) and after the Revolution had been convicted of embezzling money from one of the trade unions.

The members of the Politburo who were closest to Stalin in 1952 – Malenkov, Beria and Khrushchev – certainly were aware of the methods he used to secure total loyalty. Although they were firmly bound to him by the mafia principle of mutual guarantee, they were also certain that Stalin possessed secret dossiers on them as well. Beria himself was involved in supplying Stalin with this kind of information when he was working in the Georgian NKVD and also later in Moscow. When Malenkov was in charge of the Central Committee department dealing with senior Party personnel (1934–39), it was his job not only to assemble personal dossiers but also to make active use of them when deciding the fate of senior functionaries. At this time Malenkov was neither a member nor even a candidate member of the Central Committee, but he played a key role in the repressions of the 1930s. Stalin endowed Malenkov with extraordinary powers, and often together with Yezhov he was responsible for planning repressive campaigns in various republics and regions of the country. Malenkov was in effect the representative of the Party *apparat* in the NKVD. After the war it was Malenkov and Beria who organized the 1949–50 repressive campaigns in Leningrad and Moscow, culminating in the physical liquidation of Nikolai Voznesensky, a Politburo member, and Aleksei Kuznetsov, a Secretary of the Central Committee, along with a large number of senior Leningrad Party officials. Khrushchev also actively participated in the repressive campaigns of the 1930s and 1940s – he certainly was not a passive spectator. In 1935–38 he directed the repressions in Moscow where, as First Secretary of the Moscow city and regional Party committees, he was a member of the Moscow troika that confirmed the death sentences imposed by the NKVD. After he became First Secretary of the Ukrainian Central Committee in 1938, Khrushchev took charge of the repressive campaigns in that republic as well and also supervised deportations from the western provinces of the Ukraine that had been annexed by the Soviet Union in 1939. He organized a particularly ruthless battle against Ukrainian nationalism during the years 1944–49.

There was certainly ample evidence in the archives of the NKVD–MGB, the Politburo, the Ukrainian Politburo, and in many secret regional archives to prove that Malenkov, Beria and Khrushchev had been overt participants in the terror, frequently acting on their own initiative and often motivated by a desire to enhance their own power. However, Stalin's lieutenants were unconcerned about the existence of these archives, since it would have been inconceivable for anyone to even think of declassifying them. When Stalin died, there was no particularly urgent need to be concerned about their existence. There was only one vital question at the beginning of March 1953: what should be done with Stalin's personal archive? All of it, or perhaps just a part, could be destroyed with impunity, since at that point none of the branches of power – and certainly not the Procuracy, MGB, MVD or the Ministry of Defence – had an interest in making the documents subject to general scrutiny. Only among the broad masses of the population, hypnotized by the 'cult of personality', was there a widespread conviction that Stalin must have left some kind of instructions, a 'political testament' that would map out the future according to his own plan. The decision to add a Stalin section to the Marx–Engels–Lenin Institute was taken in order to placate this public mood.

There was a growing hostility between Stalin and his senior generals after the end of the war and particularly in 1946–47, which was not widely known about at the time and usually is ascribed to Stalin's 'jealousy', his desire to appropriate all the laurels of military victory and be recognized as the greatest war leader of all time. This is thought to explain why Marshal Zhukov, having been appointed commander-in-chief of the Soviet land forces after his return from Germany in April 1946, was a year later relegated to the command of the Odessa military district. The marshals and generals were extremely displeased by the appointment of Bulganin as the military minister, a man without military credentials whose former positions had largely been within Party and state structures. In the pre-war period (1938–40) he was chairman of the board of Gosbank. He could never have commanded the respect of the military.

This interpretation of Stalin's conflict with Zhukov as well as with other senior officers is, however, mistaken. Several illustrious marshals and generals suffered considerably greater penalties than Zhukov. The air force chief marshal A.E. Golovanov, who had been a favourite of Stalin, was discharged from the military in 1947 and given an insignificant job at the Vnukovo airport. The commander of the cavalry-tank corps, Lieutenant General Vladimir Kryukov, after distinguishing himself in the final phase of the war during the offensives in Poland and Germany, was arrested in 1946 and sentenced to 25 years' imprisonment together with his wife, Lyudmila Ruslanova, a celebrated singer and 'people's artist' well known throughout the country. At the time no one had any idea why a famous singer wound up in the gulag. There were also other marshals and generals who were demoted and sent to various provincial military districts.

But this whole episode had less to do with rivalry for military prestige or acclaim than with the enthusiasm exhibited by the generals for appropriating rather extravagant 'trophies' in Germany and exporting them as personal property, including old-master paintings and other valuables that should have been handed over to the state depository (Gokhran). Marshal Golovanov transported Goebbels' entire country villa, in parts, with the assistance of long-range aircraft under his command. General Kryukov and his wife Ruslanova took 132 original canvases from Germany along with a huge collection of other valuables.[25] Apparently even Marshal Zhukov, who commanded the Soviet occupation troops in 1945–46, could not resist the general passion for removing and appropriating German trophies. On Stalin's personal orders, agents of the MGB carried out a secret search of Zhukov's apartment and dacha and discovered not only a considerable number of souvenirs (carpets, furs, gold watches and other 'trifles') but also '55 valuable classical paintings in handsome frames'; some of which, it turned out, 'had been taken from Potsdam and other palaces and houses in Germany'. Stalin was informed about the results of the search in January 1948 by the Minister of the MGB, Viktor Abakumov; a copy of the report was discovered in the KGB archives by the historian Pavel Knishevsky who was doing research on the question of German reparations and confiscated trophies.[26] There continued to be finds of this kind for many years after Stalin's death. In 1945 General Ivan Serov was the deputy of the supreme commander of the occupation forces in Germany and was also in charge of NKVD units there; he was responsible for the disposition of trophy property. Serov was a Khrushchev man rather than a Beria loyalist. From 1938 until the beginning of the war he had been in charge of the NKVD in the Ukraine. In 1954 Khrushchev appointed Serov to head the new KGB. But in 1958 it was discovered that Serov had stolen the crown of the King of the Belgians, which had disappeared from the collection of trophy property, along with many other valuables. The Procurator General gave approval for a search of his apartment. Subsequently, Serov was removed as Chairman of the KGB but became the head of the Main Intelligence Directorate (GRU).

Certainly it was not only army generals who were carried away by the temptations of trophy export, free of charge. Generals of the NKVD and SMERSH also gave in to avarice. Ordinary soldiers and junior officers were not forbidden from taking souvenirs or sending parcels home from occupied Germany, and there were specific secret directives about this. But there were no special regulations for generals. Yet for Stalin, who decorated the walls of his rooms at the dacha with photographic reproductions cut out from *Ogonek*, the trophy plundering was disagreeable and even shocking. The phenomenon had also spread to the Party and state elite. A number of Party and state officials replaced the government-issue furniture in their apartments and dachas with luxurious German suites. Only the most extreme examples of this kind of theft were punished severely, while moderate indulgence was usually forgiven. Certainly it was obligatory to hand over works by famous painters, which were then stored in various secret gallery collections. On an even larger scale, German property was confiscated without any proper registration and used to augment government finances as well as to provide material support for industrial enterprises, universities and research institutes, clubs and sanatoria; even *kolkhozy* and *sovkhozy* benefited from the distribution of hundreds of thousands of German horses, cattle and pigs. All this was done with Stalin's knowledge and approval.

Stalin's personal archive also contained his correspondence with his closest comrades over many years. Both Lenin and Stalin tended to write a large number of letters and notes giving instructions – it was a leadership style that they shared. These notes were handwritten without a copy and delivered to the recipient by a special state courier or sometimes a pair of messengers in order to guarantee total security. This service was established early on by the Cheka and expanded by the GPU and the NKVD where a special courier department was established. Among all the publications of the last ten years relating to Stalin, the most valuable for any biographer surely must be *Stalin's Letters to Molotov*, which appeared in 1995.[27] It is an annotated collection of letters written between 1925 and 1936 during the autumn months when Stalin travelled to the south to rest and take the waters, leaving Molotov in Moscow in charge of the Politburo. Molotov kept these letters at home in a safe. In December 1969 at the age of 79, he gave the originals to the Central Party Archive. That year marked the 90th anniversary of Stalin's birth, and Suslov was preparing to use the occasion as a pretext for a partial rehabilitation, in conjunction with a series of articles in the press. Molotov thought that several excerpts from the letters could be published. However, the major rehabilitation never materialized and, unknown to historians, Stalin's letters to Molotov remained in the secret archives for another 25 years. They were deposited in the

'Special Files' until 1992 when they were transferred to the RTsKhDNI. The editors of the collection suggest that Molotov may have only given the Party archive letters up to 1936 because he had destroyed any letters of 1937, 1938 or later years that would have referred to events of the terror; their theory, however, is ill founded. From the beginning of 1937 until the autumn of 1946 Stalin worked continuously without a break, which meant that there was no need to communicate with Molotov by post. The content of the letters shows that many of them were replies to information that had come from Molotov about Party or state affairs or events in Moscow that had not appeared in the press. Several of the letters were written when Molotov was on holiday while Stalin remained in Moscow. In one letter Stalin even joked:

> Hello Molotshtein,
> Why the devil have you burrowed into your lair, like a bear, and why are you not talking? How are things there good or bad? Write something.[28]

In the introduction, the editors wrote:

> This collection of letters from Stalin to Molotov is uniquely valuable. ... The letters contain unparalleled information, and they enable us substantially to broaden and refine our understanding of the nature and mechanism of the Soviet Union's Party-state leadership in the 1920s and1930s. They also offer an invaluable source for studying Stalin as an individual.[29]

Undoubtedly the letters would have been even more valuable if we had both sides of the correspondence. Perhaps the letters from Molotov were kept in Stalin's personal archive, but no one has ever been able to find them. They must have been destroyed, and it is hardly likely that Stalin himself would have destroyed letters from a colleague, received by special courier.

Letters from Stalin have also recently been found in the archives of other Party leaders – Kalinin, Ordzhonikidze, Kirov, Mikoyan, Kuibyshev, Kaganovich, Voroshilov – as well as letters written by members of the Politburo to each other. Three letters from Ordzhonikidze to Stalin in 1930 and 1931 were found in the Ordzhonikidze archive, but these were more in the nature of reports. Two of them were addressed both to Stalin in Moscow and Stanislav Kosior in Kharkov, while only one was handwritten and sent personally to Stalin.[30] It can be found in the Ordzhonikidze fond of the RTsKhIDNI.

The special courier service was only used for absolutely confidential correspondence; in the course of 30 years, millions of letters relating to Stalin's regular Party and state activities were sent in his name either by normal post or via the dispatch office of the Central

Committee. The Central Committee had a special correspondence section where quite a few Party officials, called Instructors, did a preliminary sorting and analysis of letters and decided what needed to be done. Some letters could be given a conventional reply; others would be forwarded to various departments, to local organs, etc. There was an enormous flow of letters to Stalin from relatives of people who had been arrested as well as from prisoners themselves with complaints about groundless accusations and requests for their cases to be re-examined. Obviously letters of this kind never actually reached Stalin and on the whole remained unanswered. However, functional letters with serious suggestions or letters from well-known members of the Soviet intelligentsia frequently did arrive on Stalin's desk. From time to time he answered them, and his reply might appear in the press. More often he responded by telephone. Sometimes the writer was invited to the Kremlin or the dacha for a chat. It is known that Stalin read letters from Gorky, Sholokhov, Fedin, Ehrenburg and Fadeyev as well as several other leading Soviet writers. On several occasions Mikhail Bulgakov wrote protest letters to Stalin, which must have reached him, judging by the results, including a phone call to the writer.

Stalin received and read letters from prominent film directors, particularly as he followed their work with considerable interest. Yevgeny Gromov, in his study of Stalin's relationships with writers and artists, wrote that in the 1930s, 'letters from figures in the world of art and culture, even from those who were less well known, were put on Stalin's desk without delay. The situation was different during the war and the post-war years; Stalin was much less interested in such letters, and they tended to accumulate within the apparat.'[31]

In 1945–51, years when science was playing an increasingly important role in the development of new branches of military technology, Stalin read letters from scientists more frequently than he had done in the past. Academician Pyotr Kapitsa wrote to him regularly. Between 1937 and 1950 Kapitsa sent Stalin 42 detailed letters, some of which were published in 1989 in a volume entitled *Letters about Science*. However, all the published letters were reproduced from copies that had been kept in Kapitsa's personal archive. Not a single original was found in any of the archives, although it is known that Stalin received and read them. This was confirmed by Malenkov in a telephone conversation with Kapitsa in 1949. On one occasion Stalin did reply to Kapitsa and acknowledged his previous letters. Only one original letter from Kapitsa to Stalin has been discovered; it was dated 28 April 1938 and was found in the NKVD archives rather than in one of the Stalin fonds. Kapitsa's letter began with the words: 'This morning a member of the Institute, L.D. Landau, has been arrested. Despite the fact that he is only 29, he and Vladimir Fock are the greatest theoretical physicists we have.'[32] Stalin sent the letter on to the NKVD without any written orders but apparently there was an oral instruction to 'sort this out properly'. In the end Landau was released 'into the custody' of Professor Kapitsa, i.e. without rehabilitation. By this time Landau had already confessed to non-existent 'crimes', and the NKVD was concerned with saving face.

The majority of the letters written to Stalin by figures in the arts and sciences, letters which he actually received and read, have been preserved and occasionally reproduced from copies kept by their authors. Some have been found in the archive of the Politburo with Stalin's instructions: 'Show members of the PB'. This was for Poskrebyshev, who prepared the agenda for Politburo meetings. After a letter was discussed at a Politburo meeting, it would be deposited in the Politburo archive. In the 1930s Stalin read a great number of denunciation letters, made notes on them and instructed that the Politburo be informed. Several denunciations of Academician Nikolai Vavilov were found in the Politburo archive and subsequently transferred to the APRF. No decision was taken to arrest him at that time. Denunciations of Vavilov were also sent to the NKVD, to Yezhov and later to Beria.

It is extremely unlikely that Stalin would have destroyed some of the letters that he received through his private office but not others. The head of the Party and state could hardly deal with the flow of incoming and outgoing papers in a spontaneous manner, without a system. His secretariat kept a record of all letters and documents that reached his desk. If papers were sent on to a department with his instructions or retained for discussion in the Politburo or Central Committee Secretariat, this too, inevitably would be recorded. In cases where Stalin had no further need of the materials in question, he would himself instruct Poskrebyshev to deposit them in the relevant archive – it could be the archive of the Ministry of Defence, the Party, the Politburo or the 'Special Files'. Possibly a few documents were destroyed, but this could only have happened where 'special actions' were concerned, such as the plans to assassinate Trotsky. Letters like those from Academician Kapitsa, in view of their very nature, would not have been sent to some other archive, and there was certainly no reason to destroy them. Along with letters from Gorky, Sholokhov, Romm, Fadeyev and other leading members of the intelligentsia that were kept in Stalin's personal archive, Kapitsa's letters could only have a positive influence on the judgement of future historians. Stalin was always concerned about how he would be remembered by future generations. He thought he deserved to be placed alongside Marx, Engels and Lenin.

Stalin had a certain amount of creative talent, in the sense that he wrote all his own articles and speeches himself, by hand. He worked at a fairly slow pace, often making changes to what he had written. His manuscripts would almost certainly have been kept in his safe or in his desk. But few of these manuscripts can be found today in any archive. Somehow they have simply disappeared.

As mentioned previously, the visitors' books from Stalin's Kremlin office have survived. The lists of visitors were recorded by junior secretaries sitting in the reception room outside the office. There was no fixed style. Frequently entries were made in school exercise books in different coloured inks and handwriting, and sometimes 'Com' (for 'Comrade') was written before a name, or just 'C'. There were spelling mistakes in the surnames and never any initials. All this suggests that the visitors' book was seen as a formality and not taken very seriously. The registration of documents reaching Stalin's desk, however, was regarded as a much more important task and was performed by the 'special section' headed by Poskrebyshev. There was an endless stream of papers flowing towards Stalin's office, and certainly only the most important documents merited his personal attention. Papers leaving the office containing Stalin's instructions were treated with equal care. There was a considerably larger volume of paper going in and out of the office every day than visitors. But despite the fact that every document passing through Stalin's hands was meticulously noted down, these records are nowhere to be found. The published lists of documents received by, or rather sent to Stalin from the NKVD-MVD from 1944 to 1953 were compiled from copies of records kept in the *apparat* of the security services. There is no way of knowing which of these papers actually reached Stalin's desk.

Stalin was scrupulous about preparing himself for various meetings – not only for the Politburo but also the Orgburo, and for meetings of different commissions and committees (for example, the committee dealing with the Stalin Prize). Notes like the ones found in the Presidential Archive (APRF) – 'for meetings of the Buro' (1932– 34) – must have been made for many other meetings as well. As a rule, there were no shorthand records or minutes of such meetings; only final decisions were recorded. Talks with foreign officials or conversations with certain foreign writers were treated differently. Here more formality was observed and a stenographic record would be produced in two languages, but Stalin would not have kept it in his own archive. Stenographic records of this kind were deposited in the archives of various institutions such as the MID, the Sovnarkom, the Central Committee, the Ministry of Defence, etc. Therefore they have survived and can be studied by historians, and this also applies to Stalin's diplomatic correspondence.

Stalin took particularly long breaks in the years 1947–51. In the autumn of 1951 he left Moscow for the new dacha complex on Lake Ritsa and spent six months there until the beginning of 1952. Following his usual practice of sending letters and notes to his Politburo colleagues, Stalin undoubtedly would have written to Malenkov, Beria, Khrushchev, Bulganin, Kaganovich, Voroshilov, Shvernik, and possibly to Suslov who headed the Ideological Department of the Central Committee, the MGB Minister S.D. Ignatiev, and others. Obviously all these lieutenants could hardly have left Stalin's letters unanswered. A few letters have survived from Stalin's correspondence with his colleagues in the 1930s when his vacations were much shorter. However, virtually nothing remains from his last years, during which he spent almost 15 months in the south.

The destruction of Stalin's personal archive: a hypothetical reconstruction

The removal of all furniture from the dacha at Kuntsevo on 7 March 1953, as described by Svetlana Alliluyeva, obviously included all the desks, cupboards, secretaires and safes; the whole operation could well have been carried out on the orders of Beria, who was then Minister of the MVD (which had been combined with the MGB on 5 March). As the entire staff as well as the guards were employed by the MVD, they had all become subordinate to Beria. It would have been extremely awkward to carry out a thorough search of the dacha, removing only papers and documents, as this would have revealed the central purpose of those behind the exercise. It was less obvious simply to remove the furniture, and even Svetlana failed to understand that Beria had no interest in desks but was only concerned about what papers they might contain. However, it was virtually impossible to remove all the furniture and the large safe from Stalin's Kremlin office in a similar, clandestine manner. Unlike the dacha, the Kremlin office and apartment were neither isolated nor under the control of the MVD. Many other government organizations were part of the Kremlin structure, and there was a double security system in place. Some of the Kremlin guards were part of an army unit rather than the state security services. In the army it was regarded as the highest honour to serve as a guard at the Lenin Mausoleum. Therefore it remains a riddle to this day: how was it possible to clean out all the papers from the Kremlin office and apartment?

In his 1989 Stalin biography, Dmitry Volkogonov was the first to suggest that it was Beria who destroyed the papers in Stalin's Kremlin safe on 2 or 3 March while Stalin was still alive but clearly beyond any hope of recovery in view of the doctors' report. According to Volkogonov:

> Beria made a dash for the Kremlin, leaving the other leaders at the deathbed for several hours. ... It is reasonable to assume that he was desperate to clean out the boss's safe which he feared might contain instructions regarding his own future. ... Stalin might well have left some kind of testament, and given his unlimited authority at that time, no one would have questioned the last will of the dead leader.[33]

Working on his shorter biography several years later when he had access to new material in the Presidential Archive, Volkogonov slightly modified his account of what might have happened. When the Bureau of the Central Committee Presidium was preparing for the Central Committee meeting set for the evening of 5 March, it was proposed that Malenkov, Beria and Khrushchev be charged with putting Stalin's papers 'in proper order' (which in fact meant official Party permission to examine Stalin's personal archive). Beria decided to get there first. On his own, without Malenkov or Khrushchev, he went to Stalin's office sometime during the day on 5 March.

> Beria left for the Kremlin once again. He would now have the chance to go through Stalin's private safe, undisturbed. He could 'put Stalin's papers in proper order' without Khrushchev and Molotov. This state butcher could well have suspected the existence of some kind of Stalin testament; Stalin had at one time hinted that it was necessary 'to write something for the future'. And since the 'old man's' attitude towards him had recently cooled, he could expect nothing good in any testament. ... And furthermore, Stalin had an old, thick notebook with a black cover in which he jotted things down from time to time. ... Could there be something in it about him? As I wrote in my first book about Stalin, the dictator apparently was thinking about leaving a testament for his comrades.[34]

By the time Volkogonov produced this version, he presented it as a factual account rather than as a theory of what might have happened. However, it would seem that the story is an invention. Beria may well have visited the Kremlin, but we have no way of knowing whether he went to the Kremlin or not or what he might have done there. In 1945 Beria's own office had been moved to the Kremlin from the NKVD building on Dzerzhinsky Square when he became First Deputy of Chairman of the Council of Ministers. During Stalin's illness, there was a round-the-clock roster of secretaries on duty in his office. How could Beria have got the key to Stalin's safe? There were two meetings of Stalin's comrades in his office on 2 March. The names of all visitors to the office continued to be recorded in the usual manner. Within an hour of Stalin's death, there was a large meeting to organize the funeral with 23 people taking part. This meeting went on until 4 o'clock in the morning of 6 March. During the evenings of 6 and 7 March and the night of 9 March after the funeral, members of the new Central Committee Presidium along with several other senior officials met to discuss various immediate issues.[35] Stalin's office in the Kremlin continued to function in the normal way until after the funeral on 9 March and it was only then that the registration of visitors was discontinued. This suggests that Stalin's papers could only have been taken from the Kremlin after the sarcophagus containing his embalmed body had been installed in what now became known as the Mausoleum of Lenin and Stalin.

As a rather experienced political operator, Beria certainly understood that the 'succession to the throne' would not be determined by the contents of Stalin's black notebook. On 4 March the Bureau of the Central Committee Presidium had put together detailed proposals to be submitted to a joint meeting of the Central Committee, the Council of Ministers and the Presidium of the Supreme Soviet, set to take place in the evening of 5 March. Once Stalin's doctors had declared him to be incapacitated, there were sufficient grounds for calling the meeting in order to take urgent measures to ensure continuity of leadership.

The meeting began at 8 pm on 5 March. Stalin was still alive, but the Minister of Health, Tretyakov, who was the first to speak, reported that his condition was hopeless. Khrushchev was in the chair. He did not intend to allow any kind of discussion; the assembly had been convened only in order to give formal approval to the proposals of the Bureau of the Presidium. Power was to be concentrated in the hands of Malenkov (as head of the government), Beria (in charge of the MVD and MGB) and Khrushchev (as head of the Party Secretariat). Voroshilov would become Chairman of the Presidium of the Supreme Soviet. Stalin's other old comrades, Molotov, Kaganovich and Bulganin, would become First Deputies of the Chairman of the Council of Ministers. The proceedings were over after 40 minutes, with 17 important questions resolved during that time. At the very end of the meeting Malenkov reported that 'the Bureau of the Central Committee Presidium had entrusted comrades Malenkov, Beria and Khrushchev with the task of putting the documents and papers of Comrade Stalin, his archive as well as all current materials, in proper order.'[36]

The recommendation concerning Stalin's papers was the final proposal, and it was not included among the others, which were numbered. All the proposals were voted on simultaneously, and the result was unanimous. However, when the record of this meeting appeared in the central press on 7 March, it was published with certain abridgements. There was no mention of the date of the meeting, Stalin's name was excluded from the list of new members of the Presidium, and the paragraph about putting Stalin's papers 'in proper order' was missing, as it was considered to be confidential. The original text was marked 'top secret' and was deposited in the Politburo archive.

Malenkov, Beria and Khrushchev had now been legitimately authorized to look through all Stalin's papers and documents including his private archive. They could open his safes (it is not known how many there were in the various dachas) and do whatever they liked with what they found. Undoubtedly the expression 'put in proper order' was intentionally imprecise in order to allow the Party leaders quietly to destroy any papers containing information that they believed to be dispensable, information that posterity could well do without.

On 7 March some unknown 'special group' from the MVD removed all the furniture from the Kuntsevo dacha. However, in addition to documents and papers, Stalin always had cash, piled up in packets in his desk drawers and cupboards. He never had any need for cash nor did he think it necessary to put it in a safe. Stalin received a salary for each of his ten official positions (Chairman of the Council of Ministers, Secretary of the Central Committee, member of the Politburo, deputy of the Supreme Soviet of the USSR and of the Russian Republic, deputy of the Moscow Soviet, member of the Presidium of the USSR Supreme Soviet, Supreme Commander-in-Chief, member of the Central Committee, and, until 1947, Minister of Defence). In the Soviet Union at that time, it was normal practice for salaries to be paid in cash twice a month. As the envelopes with banknotes regularly arrived, he would put them away in his desk or cupboard without even bothering to open them. Occasionally he gave large sums to his daughter Svetlana or to other relatives who sometimes visited the dacha, and he also sent money to the widow of his eldest son Yakov, who had died as a prisoner of war; she lived with her daughter, Stalin's first grandchild, who had been born in 1938. There were also stories of gifts being sent to childhood friends in Georgia. All these packets of cash, which even according to Soviet law at that time rightfully belonged to Stalin's heirs, disappeared along with the papers. But there is only circumstantial evidence to suggest what might have happened to the papers in Stalin's safes.

Two people we knew in the 1960s, Aleksei Snegov and Olga Shatunovskaya, have provided the most plausible account of how a large part of Stalin's personal archive was destroyed. Snegov was a longstanding friend of Khrushchev from the days when they worked together in the Ukraine in the 1920s. Shatunovskaya was a colleague and friend of Mikoyan since the time of the Baku commune in 1918. Snegov also knew Beria – they both worked in the Transcaucasian kraikom in 1930–31. Snegov was arrested in 1937 but managed to survive. On the initiative of Khrushchev and Mikoyan, he was released in the summer of 1953, and he appeared as a witness in the investigation of the 'Beria case'. In 1954 Khrushchev appointed Snegov to be deputy head of the political administration of the gulag and later enlisted his aid when preparing the secret speech on the 'cult of personality' for the Twentieth Congress. By the 1960s Snegov was a pensioner and happy to share his reminiscences with people he trusted. After a heart attack in 1967 he asked Roy Medvedev to come to see him with a tape recorder. They spent three days together, and he gave permission for the contents of their conversations to be made public after his death.

Shatunovskaya also spent almost 15 years in the camps. After full rehabilitation in 1955 she became a senior official in the Party Control Commission and afterwards a member. This led to her being appointed to head several special commissions including the investigations into the murder of Kirov, the death of Ordzhonikidze, the murder of Khandzhian (the Party leader of Armenia who died in prison in 1938) and others who suffered a similar fate. In the 1960s, after the removal of Khrushchev, Shatunovskaya, like Snegov, was a pensioner, but she continued to visit the family of Mikoyan.

When Snegov and Shatunovskaya talked to us at the end of the 1960s, they alluded to stories, told to them in confidence by Khrushchev and Mikoyan, which made it clear that Stalin's personal archive had been deliberately destroyed. Rumours to this effect were circulating among historians by the end of March 1953, but without any details or reference to possible motives. There is no way of being absolutely sure about the precise timing of the process. Certainly the designated trio would not have been inclined to delay. Malenkov, Beria and Khrushchev went to the Kremlin office shortly after the funeral, i.e. on 10 or 11 March. According to Snegov and Shatunovskaya, without even looking through the papers in Stalin's safe, they proceeded to burn them en masse. The three comrades evidently had no desire to study the contents of the boss's safe, particularly in the presence of each other. Their own confidential letters to Stalin might have been among the papers, as well as dossiers on each one of them, compiled over the years by Stalin's 'Special Section'. Others close to Stalin who were not part of the triumvirate were also anxious for their own dossiers to be destroyed. Neither Molotov, Mikoyan nor Kaganovich had any illusions about the nature of the archive in Stalin's safe. Their own private letters must have been there as well, letters they would hardly be inclined to leave behind for the benefit of future historians. The papers may have been burned in the beautiful old-fashioned tiled stoves which attracted the attention of visitors. For Stalin, fireplaces and stoves were not simply a matter of decoration. He loved to sit in front of a real fire and particularly liked to warm his legs. It was a pleasure he learned to enjoy during the years of Siberian exile. It was because of his aching joints that he preferred to walk around during meetings rather than sit.

Stalin was a well-organized person; therefore it is likely that his papers would have been kept in a certain order. Notebooks and exercise books from the end of the 1920s and the beginning of the 1930s were no longer of any interest to anyone, which is why they survived. The rest of the papers, and in particular the correspondence and sealed packets, were earmarked for liquidation. No one was inclined to open them or sort them out – a job that in any case would have taken many days or weeks to complete. If the three leaders had needed help from trusted bodyguards or drivers in the process of 'ordering' Stalin's archive, there was enough cash in the desks to buy their absolute silence. Among the 'current materials' referred to in the Central Committee resolution, documents relating to the 'case of the Zionist doctors' certainly were priority objects for destruction; Stalin had personally been supervising the investigation, which was approaching an end just before his fatal stroke.

Several days later perhaps, Malenkov, Beria and Khrushchev paid a similar visit to Stalin's apartment in the Kremlin. Stalin never slept there during the last years of his life, but old family letters were kept in the apartment along with other family relics. Part of Stalin's personal library remained there as well. There were also school reports and other documents relating to Stalin's children, Svetlana, Vasily and Yakov. These were sent to a secret archive rather than to the children themselves or their relatives. At the beginning of the 1990s some of these family papers were collected by staff of the APRF and published in a volume entitled *Stalin in the Embrace of his Family*.[37]

Even after the dachas were cleared out, searches continued and more papers were destroyed. Over the next years, as Stalin's comrades died, their archives were also seized and partially destroyed. The first in line was to be Beria.

The destruction of the archive continues

Malenkov, the new Chairman of the Council of Ministers, wasted little time before demanding to see the MVD files on the 'Leningrad affair' (1949–50) in which he, together with Beria, had played a major, very active role. Beria certainly did not hand over everything; in order to make sure that particular materials would never be made public, he destroyed them himself. When Malenkov was excluded from the Presidium of the Central Committee several years later in July 1957, it emerged that a number of documents relating to the 'Leningrad affair' had disappeared.[38] An even more radical purge of Beria's private archive took place after his arrest in June 1953. According to Dmitry Volkogonov, who interviewed former heads of the KGB as part of his research:

> When Beria was arrested, Khrushchev ordered his personal archive to be confiscated, including a large number of documents sent by Stalin to the NKVD. Without much deliberation, the commission established to deal with this affair considered it a 'blessing' when 11 sacks of what must have been unique documents (!) were consigned to the flames, unread ... the members of this senior Party group felt personally threatened by the compromising revelations which the papers were likely to contain. Many of Stalin's orders and instructions, addressed to Beria, also disappeared in the bonfire and will thus remain forever hidden from history. In April 1988, talking to Aleksandr Shelepin, a former head of the KGB, I learned that MVD general Ivan Serov had taken charge of a huge clean-out of Stalin's archive on Khrushchev's orders.[39]

Khrushchev appointed General Serov to be the Chairman of the recently created KGB in 1954. They had worked together over a number of years, and Serov enjoyed Khrushchev's total confidence. Serov was instructed to destroy any archive materials containing information about Khrushchev's role in the repressive campaigns of the past. Since Serov had been the main executor of these campaigns, in Moscow (1936–37) as well as in the Ukraine (1938–41), there can be no doubt that he did as thorough a job as possible. The destruction of compromising archives continued up until the Twentieth Party Congress.

After his removal from government and Party posts in October 1964, Khrushchev also handed over or possibly destroyed part of his own personal archive. When he had become a pensioner and decided to record his memoirs, he spoke into a tape recorder from memory without the use of documents. As the archives were declassified during the 1990s, there was no attempt to create a Khrushchev fond containing his personal papers. However, in this case it was not a question of yet another special bonfire; it merely confirmed something that was well known in Party circles – that Khrushchev himself hardly ever wrote letters, articles or reports. After he dictated a draft to a stenographer, numerous aides would then edit the text. Khrushchev's Russian was that of an uneducated man. He came from a poor peasant family and only went to a village school for about two years. Although he could read, he was unable to write grammatically, which explains why no handwritten documents were found after his death in 1971.

The next of Stalin's closest comrades to die was Anastas Mikoyan on 21 October 1978. On his 70th birthday in 1965 Mikoyan voluntarily retired from the post of Chairman of the Presidium of the Supreme Soviet. But he continued to be a Deputy of the Supreme

Soviet and a member of the Central Committee for another ten years. In his free time he began to write his memoirs. The first two volumes, *The Path of Struggle* and *At the Beginning of the 20s*, published in 1971 and 1975, made it clear that the author had a large quantity of documents at his disposal. At the time of his death, the third volume had been completed, but he had not yet made arrangements for publication. Several incidents that took place at the time of Mikoyan's death are described in the memoirs of Viktor Pribytkov, a former aide of Konstantin Chernenko, who was at the time head of the General Department of the Central Committee. Chernenko summoned Pribytkov on 22 October 1978 and gave him a rather unusual task:

> 'This is what you have to do, Viktor ...,' he said thoughtfully. 'Mikoyan's dead ... take some boys from the *apparat* who can hold their tongues and ... you'll be told the locations ... go today and start picking up the archives. Sort it all out and make a list. The list will go to the very top, together with whatever documents you find. There could be anything. He was stowing things away even before the revolution. Do you understand the responsibility?' ... We collected documents from various spots – the dacha, apartment and some other places. It was an immense quantity of paper, not less than three huge truckloads.[40]

According to members of Mikoyan's family, the gathering up of this respected pensioner's papers amounted to compulsory confiscation. When even professionals from the KGB were unable to open the ancient safe, it was finally cut apart with the help of a blow-torch. Only a small part of Mikoyan's documents reached 'the very top'. Chernenko made sure that any particularly interesting papers, especially originals relating to Lenin and Stalin, were put aside for his own use. How much of Mikoyan's legacy has survived? What proportion of his papers were destroyed, returned to the family or finally transferred to the Party archive? It will never be possible to answer these questions precisely.

According to Viktor Pribytkov, arrangements were made to remove personal papers after the deaths of all the Old Bolsheviks who had worked with Stalin. Archives were simply confiscated by compulsory order, analysed, sorted and then deposited in the top-secret archive fonds of the Central Committee, with only two exceptions: Stalin's former secretary, Poskrebyshev, who died in 1965, and Central Committee Secretary Suslov, who died at the beginning of 1982. No personal archives were ever discovered after their deaths. Neither Poskrebyshev nor Suslov ever attempted to write memoirs, and possibly neither man kept a diary. It is most unlikely that anything was intentionally hidden away for the sake of future historians. These two men were known to have phenomenal memories, which largely explains why it was unnecessary for them to write anything down. Perhaps this also partly explains why they enjoyed Stalin's special trust over such a long period of time.

The fate of Stalin's private library

Writers and scholars very much rely on their own collections of books and papers, and this is also true of politicians who write their own speeches and articles. The private library of a person in power serves as an additional special source of authority and information. Stalin was always a great reader, particularly during his exile. Although he may have owned quite a few books at that time, there was nowhere to keep them and he hardly could have accumulated a 'library'. In 1918 Stalin and his family were given their first apartment, located in the Kremlin. Only then could he begin to amass his own collection of books which numbered some 20,000 volumes at the end of his life. When he moved to the dacha specially built for him outside Moscow in 1934, two years after the death of his wife, a major part of his Kremlin library was transported there as well. A small building was constructed to house the books with ordinary open shelves. The staff of the dacha would include a new category of employee – a librarian.

All Bolshevik leaders of the older generation gradually acquired considerable libraries, including Trotsky, Bukharin, Zinoviev, Kamenev, Molotov, Kirov, Zhdanov and others. Needless to say, they were not in the habit of going to Moscow bookshops to buy whatever they needed. In the early period of the Soviet state, many public libraries – central, regional and local – were established and supplied with books from the collections of former middle class and aristocratic owners whose libraries had been confiscated along with their houses. Tens of thousands of well-off inhabitants of Moscow and Petrograd either emigrated or were killed or exiled. Their books were stored in special depositories where librarians from various new Soviet institutions could select the volumes they needed. As the censorship regime intensified during the 1920s, a new practice was introduced, known as 'the delivery' (*raznoska*), which required advance copies of all books to be distributed to top Party and state officials. Every publisher had a list of officials to whom he was obliged to send advance copies before any book could be put on sale to the public. It was a special additional form of censorship. All members of the Central Committee were also sent advance copies of any book published in Moscow or Leningrad. The recipient could return his copy to the publisher with notes or critical comments or keep it. In the latter case, the publisher could assume that the rulers of the country had no objection to the appearance of the book in question. Naturally Stalin also received advance copies from most publishing houses, particularly books dealing with politics, economics, history or the arts. He also received a large number of books from the authors themselves with personal inscriptions. Visitors to Stalin's apartment in the Kremlin were always struck by the extensive range of his library.

When preparations were under way to establish a Stalin museum at the Kuntsevo dacha in 1955, staff of the Stalin section of the Marx–Engels–Lenin–Stalin Institute had the opportunity to have a look at his collection. The commission in charge of the whole enterprise included Yevgeniya Zolotukhina, a bibliographer employed in the inquiry section of the institute's library. In her recently recorded recollections, she stated:

> The atmosphere at the dacha was stiff and formal, the only agreeable room was the library, which had a cosy feel. ... The books were housed in a neighbouring building ... and brought to Stalin according to his requirements.

After the war Stalin spent very little time in the Kremlin apartment, but he had accumulated a large number of books there as well. From 1918 it was his third apartment and rather spacious, unlike the first which had been extremely modest. Zolotukhina describes the Kremlin apartment as

> a suite of vaulted rooms, with a spiral staircase leading to Stalin's study. Three rooms had belonged to Svetlana, her dolls were still there as well as a diploma in her married name of Zhdanova, and family photos. There was a large old trunk filled with the belongings of Stalin's wife. Neither this nor the photographs were given to the children. The library was furnished with a large number of old-fashioned bookcases that were filled with books on a great variety of subjects. All writers made a point of sending their books to Stalin, often with a personal inscription. Clearly Stalin was an educated person. He got extremely irritated whenever he came across grammar or spelling mistakes, which he would carefully correct with a red pencil. These books, therefore, all the ones he marked, were transferred to the Central Party Archive.

After studying the collections of both libraries, in the Kremlin and at the dacha, Zolotukhina was above all struck by Stalin's interest in Pushkin, apparent

> from the large assortment of books about Pushkin, all published during the Soviet period, as well as individual old editions – a number of books had slips from second-hand bookshops. He was also interested in books about Peter the Great and Ivan the Terrible. There were also a few books in German ... (Stalin did study German when he was young, but never became proficient in the language). ... He read all the émigré literature that appeared in Russian ... including the celebrated biographies by Roman Gul of Voroshilov and others. In the

post-war years he became interested in books and magazines about architecture, which must have been related to the construction of tall buildings in Moscow. These books could be found on his bedside table.[41]

Stalin owned all the editions of Marx, Engels and Lenin that were published during the 1920s through to the 1940s. It is clear from his assiduous notes that he read Lenin with dedication. He had an almost complete collection of the works of Karl Kautsky and Rosa Luxemburg as well as other German socialist writers. His library also contained the books of his most serious political opponents: Trotsky, Bukharin, Kamenev, etc. Stalin possessed that rare gift known as speed-reading as well as an excellent memory. During the 1920s he sent for approximately 500 books a year from the Kremlin library service, which he read or glanced at; in the 1930s his rate declined somewhat, but even during the war he continued to read a great deal, largely books dealing with military questions. Even in 1940 Stalin managed to read the first volume of the Russian edition of the collected works of Bismarck, making a number of corrections and comments in the margins of the introductory article. Publication had to be delayed so that the introduction and notes could be rewritten, incorporating Stalin's revisions. Several of Stalin's biographers, and in particular Dmitry Volkogonov, Robert Tucker and Yevgeny Gromov, have written about his library and commented on his habit of making notes while he read. If it were possible to undertake a serious analysis of Stalin's library, examining the kind of books he collected, his marginal notes and even the paragraphs he underlined, it would certainly contribute to our understanding of his personality. However, in the present context we are only concerned with the ultimate fate of his books. Officially the entire collection was transferred to the Marx–Engels–Lenin–Stalin Institute. However, when the Stalin section of the institute was closed after the Twentieth Congress, the library was transferred to the Central Party Archive where it was kept in a restricted fond. Dmitry Volkogonov, working on his 1988 biography, was the first prominent historian to have access to this fond, and in 1989 the American biographer Robert Tucker also had the opportunity to inspect Stalin's books. He was then working on the second volume of what to this day remains the best and most comprehensive account of the life of the Soviet leader.[42] When the Party archive was reorganized in 1992 Stalin's library was moved to a fond in the RTsKhIDNI and thus became more accessible. It turned out, however, that by this time many books were already missing. Yevgeny Gromov, who examined Stalin's library when he was working on his book about Stalin's relationships with people in the arts, tells us that during Khrushchev's time, at the height of the struggle against the cult of personality, the bulk of Stalin's library amounting to thousands and thousands of books was destroyed. Happily some enthusiasts at the Central Party Archive were able to save hundreds of books and articles that had been annotated by their owner.[43]

According to Gromov, the story of Stalin's record collection, which also contained brief handwritten assessments on album covers, is even more unfortunate. To this day it has never been found. The records were removed from the dacha in March 1953 along with the furniture and seem to have utimately disappeared without trace, although, as we shall see, there were some sightings of them along the way.

Judging from the above account, once it was finally decided not to establish a Stalin museum, the Central Party Archive continued to keep only those books that had been annotated. According to L. Spirin, who did a special study of the fate of Stalin's library, the majority of books acquired in the 1920s and 1930s bore the stamp: 'Library of Stalin'. Approximately 5,500 volumes were marked in this way. But many editions of Russian and foreign classics as well as art books or books dealing with science were never stamped and usually had no marginal notes; all of these books, approximately 11,000 volumes, were sent to the Lenin Library and dispersed throughout its various collections. Around 500 books were given to the nearest school and also to a local Party Agitprop centre. School textbooks and other books that had belonged to Stalin's children, approximately 400 volumes, were pulped, and several books that had come from other libraries were returned. In the collection now held by the RTsKhIDNI, there are exactly 391 books containing Stalin's marginal jottings and underlinings. Spirin is convinced that many more volumes of this kind once did exist and then subsequently 'disappeared', but there is no way of knowing how many there might have been.[44] In view of the fact that Stalin always read with a pencil in his hand, never simply for pleasure or relaxation, there should be thousands of books containing his notes and comments, but, unfortunately for historians, it seems that most of this private library has simply vanished forever.

Certain other personal effects

In addition to his own papers and personal possessions, Stalin's apartment and dachas also contained objects that had belonged to his wife, Nadezhda, and his children, Yakov, Svetlana and Vasily, particularly from the period when the children were still living with their father. There was also a large collection of family photographs. After Stalin's death, his children Svetlana and Vasily became the rightful owners of all these things. However, only a few days after the death of her father, Svetlana's Kremlin pass was withdrawn, which meant that she was deprived of access to many of her own belongings still in the Kremlin apartment. During the years before her escape from the Soviet Union in 1967, she was never allowed to visit this apartment again. Towards the end of the 1950s and during the 1960s, pictures from the Stalin family album surfaced abroad. Some were photos of Stalin and his family that had been kept in the private archive of General Vlasik, who for 30 years often played the role of Stalin's 'house photographer'. Almost all these photographs somehow or other made their way to private collections, mainly in the West. During the last ten years a number of the most interesting pictures have appeared in various books including photographic narratives of Stalin's life and the history of his family.[46-49]

The gramophone record collection, which Gromov described as lost, was in fact returned to the dacha in 1955 in the course of the arrangements to turn the dacha into a Stalin museum. But when the plan for a museum was discarded after the Twentieth Party Congress, the records, together with other possessions, were moved to the underground bunker. At that time all of Stalin's possessions were still classified as 'museum pieces'.

In the course of 1956 and 1957 there was a considerable toning down of the exposure of the 'cult of personality', largely because of pressure from the Chinese Communist Party and from Mao Zedong personally. It was not until the Twenty-Second Party Congress in 1961 that they decided to remove Stalin's embalmed body from the Lenin–Stalin Mausoleum and re-bury him outside the Kremlin wall. Only then did Stalin's personal effects lose their 'museum' status. A special commission was created within the Administrative Department of the Central Committee – the names of its members are not known – to dispose of all objects that were thought to have been Stalin's personal property. Portraits, pictures and prints from the walls of the apartment and dachas were sent to different archives. The gramophone records were given to the Household Section of the Central Committee in 1961, but by then, apparently, only a small part of the original collection remained. Stalin had been sent a copy of virtually every record produced in the USSR. After listening to a record on his own gramophone, he would write one of the following on the album cover: 'good', 'so-so', 'bad' or 'rubbish'. Records judged to be 'rubbish' were quickly taken away, and it may well have been the case that their distribution was stopped throughout the country. According to an official document, 93 recordings of opera, eight of ballet music and 57 of Russian and Ukrainian songs were transferred to the Household Section of the Central Committee in 1961.[50] However, their subsequent fate is unknown: the Central Committee

Building was comprehensively looted in August 1991 after the coup, and Yevgeny Gromov, who was collecting material for his book between 1993 and 1997, was unable to find anything.

Although Stalin owned nothing made of gold, he possessed many silver objects, including busts presented to him to mark various special anniversaries, cigarette cases and also plates to be given as gifts. All this silver was sent to the Goznak factory to be melted down. Most of Stalin's other possessions (furniture, crockery, carpets etc.) were 'listed', but their fate remains unknown. It was decided that the Household Section would keep only his marshal's uniform and some of the more interesting examples of 'gifts from the workers'. Much of his clothing was described as 'worn out and worthless', while items still in a relatively good state (trousers, scarves, jackets and boots) were donated to homes for the disabled.

Stalin's archive and the 'cult of personality'

The new leaders of the country certainly were alarmed by the thought that various inconvenient documents might turn up in Stalin's personal archive, but this was not their only motive for destroying his papers. When they decided to get rid of current materials as well as archive documents, what they in fact were doing was posthumously dismissing Stalin from the leadership of the country.

Given the intensity of the Stalin cult in the USSR, his power over people's thoughts and behaviour could easily have continued long after his own death, particularly if his papers had included some kind of explicit instructions; many were convinced that at the very least there must have been some directives or guidelines for the future development of socialism. People were mindful of the process that took place after the death of Lenin in January 1924. Stalin had been able effectively to exploit archive material, including Lenin's correspondence with various contemporaries, in his struggle with the Left and Right Oppositions and particularly with Trotsky during the second half of the 1920s; references to Lenin's thoughts and ideas were cleverly used to authenticate his own political positions.

Stalin died just as a new wave of terror was spreading across the country, this time against 'Zionists'; the campaign had begun with the 'Doctor's Plot' and had aroused widespread anti-Semitism, signalling an ominous turning away from socialist and internationalist principles. It clearly was Stalin and not one of his subordinates who was the active instigator of this campaign, and no one favoured its continuation. Overt anti-Semitism would severely compromise the entire ethos of the CPSU. The destruction of Stalin's private papers proved to be the first step in the process of liquidating the Stalin cult. The new approach led to a number of unanticipated developments –

very soon those who invented it were themselves swept from the
political arena, starting with Beria, followed by Malenkov, Molotov,
Kaganovich, Voroshilov and Bulganin. Ultimately their fate was
shared by Khrushchev as well. If Stalin's personal archive had not
been destroyed, selected items certainly would have surfaced and
been used to support the moves to rehabilitate Stalin in 1965. Of
course historians continue to lament the loss of documents that
might have increased our understanding of the Stalin era. However,
for the Soviet Union and its people, the disappearance of Stalin's
papers was no great loss. Indeed, it can be argued that the absence of
a vast collection of unpublished documents was in fact beneficial for
the country, since ultimately it contributed to the whole process of
overcoming Stalinism.

CHAPTER 4

The Twentieth Party Congress:
Before and After

Roy Medvedev

The secret speech

The Twentieth Party Congress of February 1956 had already formally come to an end when delegates were told to return to the Great
Hall of the Kremlin for an additional 'closed' session, with special
passes distributed to those eligible to participate. Journalists and
guests from fraternal communist parties were excluded. Khrushchev
personally approved the list of approximately 100 former Party
activists, recently rehabilitated and released, who were invited to
attend. The Chairman of the Council of Ministers, Bulganin, opened
the session and then immediately gave the floor to Khrushchev. For
almost all the delegates in the room, even the title of Khrushchev's
report seemed extraordinary and was entirely unexpected: 'On the
Cult of Personality and its Consequences'. The astonished delegates
and specially invited Party veterans listened to Khrushchev in
stunned silence, only occasionally interrupting the speaker with
exclamations of amazement or indignation. Several people became
unwell and had to be carried or escorted out of the hall.

Khrushchev immediately declared that he did not intend to discuss
Stalin's merits or achievements, about which so much already had
been written. He would be concentrating on phenomena only recently discovered by the Presidium and hitherto unknown to the
Party. He began with an account of the conflict between Lenin and
Stalin during the last months of Lenin's life, which had led to Lenin's
proposal that Stalin, whom he accused of being too rude, capricious
and disloyal, be removed from the post of General Secretary. Khrushchev spoke of the dubious circumstances surrounding the murder of
Kirov and produced evidence that unambiguously hinted at the
possible involvement of Stalin. The speech went on to describe the
illegal mass repressions, sanctioned by Stalin, the cruel tortures
experienced by prisoners, including men who shortly before had been
members of the Politburo; as they were about to die, they wrote to
Stalin, who read their letters but ignored their entreaties. Amid
resounding shouts of indignation, Khrushchev reported that Stalin

had annihilated more than half of the delegates to the Seventeenth
Party Congress, ironically known as 'the Congress of Victors'; more
than two-thirds of the members of the Central Committee, chosen by
the Congress, were also eliminated. Khrushchev accused Stalin of
flagrant errors in the pre-war years and attacked him for destroying
the best commanders in the army and navy. Stalin was responsible
for the defeats of the Red Army in 1941–42 that resulted in the
occupation of large parts of Soviet territory. During the war years it
was Stalin who ordered Kalmyks, Karachai, Chechens, Ingush and
other peoples to be exiled from their lands. After the war, Party
activists in Leningrad became victims of illegal repression and several
members of the Central Committee were shot. At the beginning of
the 1950s Stalin was preparing new repressive measures while figures such as Molotov Mikoyan, Kaganovich and Voroshilov were
effectively pushed aside and prevented from participation in the
leadership. Khrushchev declared Stalin to be largely responsible for
the critical state of Soviet agriculture and for serious mistakes in the
direction of foreign policy. He had encouraged the development of the
cult of his own personality, falsified the history of the Party and
personally inserted whole pages of extravagant praise into his own
biography.

There was no stenographic record of this closed session of the
Congress, nor was any debate allowed after Khrushchev's report.
Delegates left the hall in a state of confusion. The final resolution of
the Twentieth Party Congress, ratified unanimously but published
only several months later, stated that the Congress had approved
Khrushchev's report and authorized the Central Committee 'reso-
lutely to carry out measures to ensure the total removal of the cult
of the individual, alien to Marxism-Leninism, and the liquidation of
its consequences in every aspect of Party, Government, and ideological activity.' On the evening of 25 February 1956 the delegates from
foreign communist parties were finally invited to the Kremlin and
given the opportunity to look through Khrushchev's report, having
been warned in advance that the document was top secret.

Khrushchev's speech, however, did not remain secret for very
long, and in fact he made no great effort to prevent the disclosure of
its contents. On 1 March the text of the speech, with a few minor
editorial corrections, was distributed to senior functionaries of the
Central Committee, and on 5 March, the 'top secret' stamp on the
front page was replaced by the milder 'not for publication'. The
Central Committee printing press immediately produced several
thousand copies of the report in the form of a pamphlet with a red
jacket, which was then distributed to all regional, city and district
Party committees throughout the Soviet Union. In accordance with
the recommendation of the Central Committee, Khrushchev's report

was read out at thousands of meetings held all over the country by Party and Komsomol organizations that included non-Party activists as well as their members.

How well I remember those days! At the time I was the principal of a small rural school near Leningrad, and a sudden instruction arrived: I was told to assemble all the teachers at 4 pm in the club of the nearby brickworks on the following day. Many of the factory's workers as well as managers from the local kolkhoz and sovkhoz came as well. Only a minority of those present were Party members. A member of the raikom opened the meeting. He told us that he would read out the full text of a secret report made by N.S. Khrushchev at the Twentieth Party Congress, but that afterwards there would be no questions or debate. We were not allowed to take notes. He then began to read from a small pamphlet – it took several hours. We paid close attention and listened in silence, almost in horror. He finished the last sentence, and for several moments there was not a sound in the room. And then we all silently left.

There were places where the reaction to the speech was not quite so calm. At a number of gatherings there were demands for a discussion. In different parts of the country, people returned to their homes and committed suicide. The Party organizer of *Kommunist*, Yevgeny Frolov, a man whose history was complex and inconsistent, read out the text at a Party meeting and then locked himself in his office and by morning had typed two copies of the entire report. He had decided to write a book about Stalin that would be based on Khrushchev's revelations. In Georgia, Khrushchev's report was read out on 6 March to a select group of the Party and state leadership. However, rumours about it had already been circulating widely, particularly among young people, and some sections of Georgian society were upset and indignant. On 5 March a demonstration took place at the Stalin monument on the bank of the Kura River in the centre of Tbilisi to commemorate the third anniversary of Stalin's death. The demonstration continued through 6 and 7 March, and as the general tension grew, absurd rumours were spreading around the city and the number of demonstrators swelled to 70,000. On 8 March many enterprises and institutions were no longer functioning, and by the 9th the city appeared to be out of control. Open appeals to Georgian nationalism could be heard among the traditional slogans paying homage to Lenin and Stalin. On the night of 10 March, during an attempt to seize the Central Post Office, shots rang out for the first time. Barricades appeared in the centre of the city and there were clashes with soldiers and the police in front of Government House on Lenin Square as well as in other parts of the city. The army, police and KGB soon regained full control, although there were still sporadic attempts to hold demonstrations. Even according to the official figures of the Georgian MVD, 15 people were killed and 54 were wounded on the night of 10 March in Tbilisi.[1] Unofficially, however, it is believed that the number of dead reached between 250 and 300, while not fewer than 1,000 people were wounded. Several hundred participants in the demonstrations were arrested. It is virtually impossible to check the figures, since many of the wounded and possibly even the dead were taken away by their families and then treated or buried in secrecy.

There was absolutely no mention of the events in Georgia in the Soviet press, nor was the Stalin question discussed anywhere in print. Although the Twentieth Party Congress had no effect on the external rituals of the state, the Party or any other public bodies, this might create a misleading impression. Since the foundations of our state were based on ideology rather than on national or historical tradition, the strength of the state was closely bound up with the potency of ideology; the whole edifice was never preserved by repressive methods alone. But the Twentieth Congress delivered a major blow to the dogmas of Marxism-Leninism. Several large chunks of this ideology fell by the wayside, the foundations of the building were weakened and it slowly began to tilt like the Tower of Pisa. The Twentieth Congress was like the explosion of a neutron bomb – it affected people while leaving structures apparently intact. An enormous change took place in the country, but above all it was in the hearts and minds and consciousness of individuals that this change was felt. Some rejoiced at finding out the truth; it gave them hope that life would improve, that their friends and relatives who had suffered would return and that those who died would at least be rehabilitated. Others were very troubled. Prisoners were overjoyed at the thought of imminent release, but there were many people who were uneasy and afraid of what might come next.

Before the congress

The Twentieth Congress came as an enormous shock to the delegates, to all members of the CPSU and to all citizens of the country who by the end of February or March had heard the speech. Astonished foreign observers, specialists and politicians were able to see the text of the 'secret speech', which soon reached the West via various channels. According to several accounts, it was Khrushchev alone who was responsible for the speech, which was thought to be part of the power struggle going on within the Presidium. Certainly for Soviet citizens the Twentieth Congress is firmly linked with the name of Khrushchev, but in fact his speech was not a surprise personal initiative or improvisation. Before the Twentieth Congress was convened, various meetings, discussions and arguments took place behind the scenes involving tough political battles. I can only deal with a few of the relevant incidents here.

From a medical point of view, Stalin's death on 5 March 1953 was hardly unexpected: alarming symptoms of the deterioration of his health existed from the end of the 1940s, but Stalin almost never had appropriate medical tests and rarely sought help from doctors. Yet no political preparations had been made and there had been no discussion about contingency arrangements; there was no mechanism to deal with the situation and no designated heir apparent. Stalin used to change his favourites, and circumstantial evidence suggests that in the autumn of 1952 he had begun to think of Suslov as his possible successor, which certainly would not have suited the old members of the Politburo. While Stalin was alive, there were no opportunities to discuss the question since members of the Presidium almost never met except at Stalin's dinners and suppers, after which they left for their own departments or for home. They were finally able to talk to each other in private once Stalin had disappeared from the scene, and the first triumvirate came into being, as described previously.

The totalitarian system evolved gradually, reaching its apogee after the war, and it was based on the total and absolute power of one man – Stalin. A huge number of questions relating to the army or military industry, the punitive organs or the gulag system were decided by Stalin alone with none of his colleagues allowed to interfere. Less obviously he also took unilateral decisions about certain of the gigantic enterprises built after the war as well as the entire system of manufacturing nuclear weapons. Many issues of foreign policy were dealt with personally by Stalin. He did consult the relevant ministers about foreign trade, state finances and foreign currency, but no member of the Politburo or Deputy Chairman of the Council of Ministers had the right to intrude on any area of the life of the country controlled by the boss himself. Therefore the three men who took charge of the country after Stalin's death were landed with problems and issues that came as a complete surprise to them. There had been no transparency in the system, even for its most senior players, and this was as much a source of Stalin's absolute power as the use of terror or the cult of personality.

Thus only Beria was familiar with the gulag system and knew something about the production of nuclear weapons. But even these systems were divided into a number of sectors, with those in charge reporting exclusively to Stalin. In 1945 the NKVD Commissariat, until then a single body, was divided in two – the NKVD and the NKGB – and as Deputy Chairman of the Sovnarkom, it was Beria's role to supervise both commissariats as well as several other related departments. However, several of the Commissars (they became

'Ministers' in 1946), as well as certain others in senior positions, had direct access to Stalin and took orders only from him. In 1948 Beria almost lost control of the state security organs of the country, and a number of repressive actions undertaken at that time by the MGB presented a substantial threat to him personally. Beria never had control over the army nor did he ever attempt to acquire it. Malenkov's knowledge of the system of government was even more limited. For a large part of his career he was concerned with organizational work within the Party apparatus and the ideological sector, although from time to time he was called upon to deal with difficulties occurring elsewhere, in the aviation industry, for example, or in agriculture. Among the Party leaders, Khrushchev was regarded as an expert on agriculture, but he also had the experience of being in charge of a large republic, the Ukraine. He had the best links with the army high command, and his close friend, Nikolai Bulganin, was the Minister of Defence. He was acquainted with nearly all the regional and republican leaders of the country, but knew almost nothing about the disposition or organization of military and nuclear plants in the eastern parts of the USSR or the gulag system. Nothing of that kind ever existed in the Ukraine.

The whole system of totalitarian dictatorship relied on a single leader who could have no deputy. This allowed Stalin to keep a firm hold on absolute power even from one of his southern residences near Sochi or in Abkhazia, where he spent so much time during the last period of his life. A struggle for power within the triumvirate was therefore inevitable and each member of the new leadership with their allies paid the greatest attention to every move or pronouncement by any one of the others. It is significant that not one of the trio raised the Stalin banner or vowed to continue his work and follow his policies. Within a narrow circle, Malenkov and Beria raised the question of the need to overcome the 'cult of personality'. There are new declassified documents that show that it was actually Beria who was the first to speak out against the Stalin cult more forcefully and consistently than either Malenkov or Khrushchev.

Cautious rehabilitations got under way immediately after Stalin's funeral, and probably the first person to be released was Molotov's wife, Polina Zhemchuzhina. Many members of the leadership had close relatives or friends who were prisoners, and Beria had no intention of continuing to keep these people in detention, nor would it have been possible. In any case, he was in a similar predicament with regard to quite a few of his own personal associates. Among those who were rehabilitated and released was Khrushchev's daughter-in-law, the widow of his eldest son, a pilot who had perished returning from a mission somewhere over occupied territory. Because his plane was never found, Leonid Khrushchev was listed as missing, which in those days was considered tantamount to treason, and the families of traitors were arrested and exiled to the east. Lazar Kaganovich began to press for the rehabilitation of his brother, Mikhail Kaganovich, the former Minister of the Aviation Industry who had been accused of wrecking and had committed suicide. Beria himself quickly put an end to the 'Mingrelian affair' in Georgia, where his supporters and henchmen in the Party and security organs had been arrested. It was also particularly urgent for him to stop the proceedings in the case of the 'Doctors' Plot'; a large contingent of MGB officers had been arrested along with the many doctors working in Kremlin medical institutions. Within a month of Stalin's death, all central newspapers published a short report that attracted widespread attention among astonished readers: it stated that the large group of leading doctors had been wrongly arrested, that the whole operation had been carried out illegally by the 'former MGB' and that in order to secure the 'necessary' confessions, the MGB had 'applied methods of investigation that are impermissible and strictly forbidden by Soviet law'. A leading article in *Pravda* announced the rehabilitation of the 'outstanding Soviet actor, Mikhoels' and referred to the attempts by 'provocateurs in the former MGB' to inflame national discord in the country.

By the end of April more than a thousand people had been released from imprisonment, almost all of whom had only recently occupied senior posts in the government or Party hierarchy. Among them was a large group of generals and admirals who had been arrested and convicted of various offences after the war and were now rehabilitated at the insistence of Marshal Zhukov. With Khrushchev's backing, he had recently become First Deputy Minister of Defence and in fact was in control of the Soviet armed forces. After Beria's arrest in the summer of 1953 and later his trial and execution together with his 'gang', the process of rehabilitation accelerated and was applied to many thousands of Party and state officials who had fallen victim to the post-war repressions. The first convictions to be repealed were those of the 'Leningrad affair': in 1949–50 thousands of Party and state officials were arrested in Leningrad and Moscow and accused of 'separatism' and 'nationalism', including Politburo member Nikolai Voznesensky and Secretary of the Central Committee Aleksei Kuznetsov; many of the accused had worked in Leningrad in the war years and distinguished themselves during the siege. The anti-Semitic campaign against 'rootless cosmopolitanism' was stopped, having claimed many victims, and other small-scale terror campaigns also came to an end. The authorities began to review cases and accusations from the pre-war period in response to individual private petitions. Survivors who had been sent to the camps in the 1930s began to appear in Moscow.

Almost no information about these rehabilitations or about people returning to their families appeared in the press. But those who were released described their experiences to friends and relatives. In the course of 1953–54 decisions on each case were made by various boards collectively after detailed consideration of the evidence. From March 1953 until the end of 1954 there were meetings in the Central Committee, in the Procuracy, in the Supreme Court and even at different levels of the state security organs to examine papers and also hear testimony by witnesses and prisoners demanding rehabilitation. Sometimes accusers were invited to the Procuracy to justify their original denunciations. The appeal cases proceeded slowly, but by the end of 1954 more than 10,000 recent prisoners, largely former senior officials, had been rehabilitated. There were also a large number of posthumous rehabilitations. Pressure was growing on the Party leadership to accelerate the process; at all levels of Party and state there were hundreds of thousands of applications for rehabilitation, and it was increasingly difficult to ignore this stream of documents. Almost every rehabilitation and in particular each case of a prisoner released from the camps had an affect on the prisoners who remained. Camp administrators who previously had unlimited power over their inmates were becoming extremely uneasy. There were still thousands of camps in the country, and Khrushchev and other members of the Party leadership had to come to some decision about the prisoners. It was dangerous to delay, as strikes and protests were rippling across the northern camps as early as 1954. In 1955 there were separate uprisings in several of the larger camps, including the most well-known major uprising at Kengir, described by Solzhenitsyn and savagely put down by tank units. However, by this time it was impossible to stop the spread of resentment among the prisoners and the growing tension within the camps. Nothing was known about these events either within the Soviet Union or abroad, but in the highest echelons of the Soviet leadership, they were well aware of the unstable situation and were becoming increasingly concerned.

In December 1954 a show trial was held in Leningrad, a city which had experienced particularly brutal repressions both before and after the war. The accused were the former Minister of State Security, Viktor Abakumov, and the head of the investigation section of the MGB, Major-General A.G. Leonov, along with a group of other MGB generals. The trial took place in the City Officers' Club and was attended in shifts by thousands of Party and Komsomol workers. Many relatives of those who perished in the 'Leningrad affair' as well as a number of prominent individuals were given passes to attend the court sessions. But the press published only a very brief account of the trial after the verdict was announced. The sentences were harsh –

the majority of the former MGB generals were shot. Similar trials took place in Baku and Tbilisi. Among the accused were not only MGB generals but the Party leader of Azerbaijan, Mir Bagirov, who had been a protégé and old friend of Stalin as well as of Beria. Although the case was widely talked about, there was nothing in the press and no public explanation of any kind.

Meanwhile the next (Twentieth) Party Congress was set to meet in February 1956. Clearly it would be difficult to hold the Congress without saying anything about the repressions of the 1930s, 1940s and 1950s. Towards the middle of 1955 a large number of Central Committee members were rehabilitated and also quite a few former commissars, generals and marshals. Scores of Civil War heroes and hundreds of prominent writers, artists and intellectuals were also rehabilitated. Was it possible simply to remain silent or speak of 'mistakes'? The Presidium decided to establish a special commission to study the mass repression of members and candidate members of the Central Committee elected at the Seventeenth Party Congress in 1934 as well as other Soviet citizens arrested between 1935 and 1940. The commission did its work rapidly, and by the beginning of 1956 its chairman, Central Committee Secretary Pyotr Pospelov, presented the Presidium with a report amounting to 70 typed pages. The report not only recognized the existence of illegal mass repressions but also pointed to the direct responsibility of Stalin. The members of the Presidium were particularly shocked to learn that more than two-thirds of the members of the Central Committee elected at the Seventeenth Party Congress were annihilated on Stalin's orders, as well as more than half the delegates to this 'Congress of Victors', among whom there were almost no former oppositionists or so-called 'Trotskyists' or 'Bukharinists'. It would hardly have been possible to ignore these figures; the discussion within the Presidium was now about what form the revelations should take and how best to present the information about illegal repressions.

In February 1956 this question was debated beyond the narrow confines of the Presidium within certain groups of the Central Committee and the Supreme Court. Various opinions were expressed. As might be expected, the most hesitant of the leadership were Molotov, Voroshilov and Kaganovich. For many years they had been deeply implicated in the repressions, and numerous documents contained their instructions for the accused to be shot. Khrushchev was more insistent, and he was supported by Mikoyan, Bulganin, Zhukov, Aristov, Saburov and Shepilov. The chairman of the KGB, Ivan Serov, also was on Khrushchev's side despite the fact that he had directly participated in many acts of repression. But he had worked with Khrushchev for a long time and was very much part of his team. As a military man he could also plead that he was merely following orders. In the end there was no major dispute about the report that had to be made.

Among the legends that have arisen around this whole episode is the claim that Khrushchev had prepared his report in absolute secrecy, without informing other members of the Presidium. In fact his speech was based on Pospelov's material, and then with the help of Dmitry Shepilov he considerably expanded the subject to include the war years and the post-war repressions. It was decided that his report would be read to a closed session of the Congress after elections had been held for the new Central Committee. All members of the Presidium and the Secretaries of the Central Committee received the text on the morning of 23 February, but only a few reacted in any way or suggested changes.[2] While ordinary delegates listened to Khrushchev on 25 February in a state of horror and alarm, or some with bewilderment and fear, the members of the Presidium who sat on the platform with blank expressions on their faces already knew exactly what the speech contained.

Afterwards

Khrushchev's speech had an enormous, in a sense contradictory effect on the international communist movement. Some communist parties welcomed the speech (e.g. in Italy), while others greeted it with barely concealed disapproval. The most displeased were the Chinese Party leaders. In the United States, France and several other countries where the materials of the Twentieth Congress were publicly discussed, a large number of ordinary members left the Communist Party. As we know, the Twentieth Congress served as an impetus for the disturbances in Poland in the autumn of 1956 and also the Hungarian uprising in Budapest in October–November of that year, although a number of other factors played a part as well.

Much has been written about the international consequences of the Twentieth Congress, and the first book dealing with the influence of the secret speech on the international communist movement appeared by 1958. However, few scholars have studied its effect on society in the Soviet Union and on the Soviet Communist Party and its ideology. It would seem that Khrushchev's speech affected the Soviet people least of all. But this impression, even if partly true, is rather misleading. A huge, truly profound transformation had begun, although its effect was felt only gradually. It was a process that unfolded over the next years, indeed over the next decades and came to be called 'the line of the Twentieth Congress'. Here I will discuss only a few episodes most closely related to the period of the Congress itself.

During the meetings of Party members and activists that took place in March, it was by no means always possible to avoid a discussion of Khrushchev's speech or attempts to expand criticism of the personality cult and crimes of the Stalin era. A special secret communication from the Central Committee to subordinate Party organizations gave an account of a two-day Party meeting at the laboratory of heat engineering of the Academy of Sciences on the 23 and 25 March, where several researchers spoke of the degeneration of the Party and the regime and criticized the dictatorship of a small group of leaders; others said that the Stalin personality cult had been replaced by a similar cult of Khrushchev, that the Soviet Union was moving towards fascism and that it was necessary to arm the people. The speakers were expelled from the Party and dismissed from their positions. Denunciations of similar outspoken remarks and conversations reached the Central Committee via the KGB from various cities, from Kiev, Chkalov (now Orenburg), South Sakhalinsk and other places. Within the Moscow intelligentsia, it was known that there had been speeches at the Party meeting of the Writers' Union that may have been less radical but were no less painful for the Central Committee. Many writers spoke of the difficult situation for literature during the years of the cult and alluded to the illegal repressions of writers including prominent figures of Russian and Soviet literature. The 70-year-old writer P.A. Blyakhin, a Party member since 1903, said at this meeting:

> Lenin's testament and principles have been trampled on and have still not been restored. The Stalin epoch delivered a blow to the brotherhood of peoples, to socialist legality. So far some seven to eight thousand people have been rehabilitated. What Khrushchev said about the number of prisoners left a painful impression. How many more innocent people are still languishing in prison? It is necessary to have a mass rehabilitation. The only guarantee against a repetition of what happened under Stalin – is a Leninist Party and Soviet democracy.[3]

Khrushchev himself spoke at many meetings of Party activists in Moscow and Leningrad. He seemed unashamed to admit that he had been aware of many of the improper proceedings that went on under Stalin but had been afraid to express any disagreement or protest. At one of these meetings someone in the hall sent Khrushchev the following note: 'How could you, a member of the Politburo, allow such terrible crimes to take place in our country?' Khrushchev read out the note in a loud voice and then said: 'This note is not signed. Whoever wrote it, stand up!' No one in the room got up. 'The person who wrote it,' said Khrushchev, 'is afraid. And that's just how it was for us with Stalin.' It was only a very partial answer, but nevertheless an honest one. Other members of the Presidium found it more difficult to deal with such questions, particularly those who had been part of Stalin's inner circle from the middle of the 1920s, well before Khrushchev. It was their support that allowed Stalin to amass his power. Thus, far from being able to claim that they had been only silent witnesses, they clearly were accomplices in the many crimes of the regime. Certainly Khrushchev had hardly been a silent witness in Moscow or the Ukraine. But now he was in power, in control of the Party and the security organs, and he hoped it would be possible to strengthen this power in the aftermath of the Twentieth Congress. This was not a hope that could be shared by Molotov, Voroshilov, Kaganovich or Malenkov.

Painful political and psychological difficulties were also experienced by people at the middle and lower levels of the Party in direct contact with ordinary Party members. Those who worked in the ideological apparatus of the Party or the Party press often had no idea what to do, what to say, how to explain the events of the past. Party activists as well as many ordinary Party members found themselves unable to adjust to the new ideological platform or to accept the 'line of the Twentieth Congress'. It would be necessary to promote new people and replace a large part of the Party cadres. This kind of renewal did take place here and there, but it was the exception rather than the rule. The higher echelons of the military leadership were also extremely resentful; the Stalin cult was particularly strong among the generals and marshals who had been promoted during the war. Khrushchev found himself under growing pressure and he was not always able to contain it.

By April and May 1956 many attempts to extend the examination of the Stalin cult were cut short. One of the Old Bolsheviks who sharply condemned Stalin's crimes at a Party conference was expelled from the Party several days later. When a teacher of Marxism-Leninism in one of the technical institutes attempted to touch on some of the causes that gave rise to the personality cult, he was summoned to the Moscow city Party committee and was severely reprimanded. News of this incident quickly reached all district Party committees. *Pravda* reprinted without commentary an article from the main Chinese paper, the *People's Daily*, which maintained that Stalin's achievements were much greater than his mistakes and that even many of his mistakes were useful because they enriched the 'historical experience of the dictatorship of the proletariat'. It was said in Party circles that the author of this article was Mao Zedong himself. On 30 June 1956 the Central Committee adopted a resolution 'On overcoming the cult of personality and its consequences', which was published in all newspapers. This resolution both in form and content was a retreat from Khrushchev's speech at the Congress. On the other hand it represented progress since it was actually published and thus became a document that was binding on the Party.

Khrushchev's report was never circulated in printed form; at all Party meetings the text was withdrawn as soon as it had been read aloud, and even Party activists unable to be present had no way of gaining access to the little booklet in its red paper jacket. Moreover during the summer of 1956 even Khrushchev himself referred to Stalin in a number of public speeches as that 'great revolutionary' and 'great Marxist-Leninist'; the Party, he said, 'would not allow the name of Stalin to be given up to the enemies of communism'.

From the summer of 1956 it seemed as if the life of the country was divided into two very different streams, one of which was reflected in the press, while the other, often of even greater significance, was ignored by all the organs of mass communication. The extraordinarily important socio-political process that began in the second half of 1956 – the release of almost all political prisoners from the camps and places of exile – was never publicly mentioned. Simultaneously a large-scale and rapid review of cases was under way, followed by the posthumous rehabilitation of the majority of prisoners who died between 1935 and 1955. The walls of the gulag came tumbling down in Kolyma, Vorkyta, Karelia, Siberia, Kazakhstan, Mordovia, the Urals and Primorie. A new system of rehabilitation was instituted. As proposed by Khrushchev, more than 90 special commissions were set up and sent to the camps or places of 'settlement for life' to examine the cases of all prisoners. Each commission included one member of staff from the Procuracy, one representative from the Central Committee apparatus and one newly rehabilitated member of the Party. These 'troikas' were temporarily endowed with the powers of the Presidium of the Supreme Soviet and could grant rehabilitations, pardons or a reduction of sentences. Their decisions did not have to be approved by higher authorities and came into force immediately. Even before these commissions got to work, people who had been imprisoned for critical remarks about Stalin, for telling anecdotes about him or similar petty offences, were rehabilitated and released according to instructions sent by telegraph from Moscow.

The special commissions worked for several months. Cases were dealt with rapidly – it was usually enough for the members of the commission to have a chat with the prisoner and a brief look at the file. The case notes, which had been kept in a special section of the camp, were destroyed. Thus the files that bore the infamous instruction 'to be preserved permanently' were emptied of all content except for the original sentence by a court or Stalinist 'troika' and the new certificate of rehabilitation. I have only seen the materials of one of these commissions, copied and brought to Moscow by Lev Portnov, an Old Bolshevik who took part in the October Revolution in Petrograd. To this day the records of the commissions have not been made public nor has there been any final assessment of their work, at least not for publication. It is not known how many people were released and rehabilitated. According to some witnesses, the commissions dealt with something like 500,000 cases; others put the figure at 1.5–2 million. The first to be freed were former members of the Party and also family members of communists who had perished. Also rapidly released were prisoners who had served their sentences but continued to be held in custody. In more complicated cases, people were released but without rehabilitation, which would be granted later on an individual basis. The commissions next began to free non-Party victims falsely accused of anti-Soviet activity. The few surviving Mensheviks, anarchists and socialist-revolutionaries who had been arrested at the end of the 1920s or the beginning of the 1930s were also released, having spent 25–30 years in prisons, camps and exile. I met some of these people seven or eight years later in order to record their testimonies.

After the Twentieth Congress, in addition to political prisoners, many former prisoners of war and 'displaced persons' (i.e. Soviet citizens who had been taken to work in Germany and arrested after repatriation in 1945–46) who were 'not compromised by active collaboration with the enemy' were also rehabilitated. The fate of people in this category was not dealt with by the special commissions of the Central Committee but by other bodies. But the labour camp system of the Ministry of Medium Machinery (the ministry in charge of the military-nuclear industry and the uranium mines) continued to exist after the Twentieth Congress, and the archives of the 'special administration' in charge of these camps have not been opened to this day.

The return of hundreds of thousands of gulag prisoners to their families and homes, the rehabilitation of millions who perished – all this affected the internal life of the USSR no less than the Twentieth Congress. Anna Akhmatova expressed apprehension at the time, attempting to imagine how the two Russias would meet, how they would look one another in the eye: the imprisoners and the imprisoned. Khrushchev obliged all government organs to pay maximum attention to those who had been rehabilitated. In the first instance it was necessary to provide accommodation, work and pension entitlements. I know of a case of three women who were not related but spent 17 years together in one camp where they slept on the same plank bed and worked side by side. They wanted an apartment in Moscow with three separate rooms so that they could remain together after rehabilitation. But only one of the women, Maria Solntseva, had been arrested in Moscow, which meant that only she had the right to live there. The women appealed to Khrushchev, who personally arranged for their request to be granted. Matilda Fishman, a well-known Party activist in the Crimea, had been part of a partisan detachment of German settlers set up by her father during the Civil War, but she was arrested in 1941 as 'a person of German nationality'. Her release from the camps came earlier than that of the majority of Russian Germans who had been deported to special settlements in 1941. When they refused to offer Fishman a place to live in Moscow, she spent seven months in the city's German cemetery. No one wanted to help her, and only the intervention of Ivan Papanin, the famous polar explorer who had known Matilda years before in Crimean revolutionary circles, allowed her to return to normal life. There were many similar 'collisions' in those days of the two Russias.

For a number of reasons the rehabilitation process was not only marred by bureaucratic failings but also by fundamental injustice. Prisoners who had been shot or who died in the camps were rehabilitated only if there was an application by relatives or friends. Otherwise cases were not examined. When people were rehabilitated as part of a group, no attempt was made to inform relatives or children of the deceased who would have been entitled to receive a small compensation. No formal rehabilitation was available for oppositionists of the 1920s, although any survivors were released. Neither was there any review of the open show trials of the 1930s. After the Twentieth Congress it took the widow of Nikolai Krestinsky seven years to secure the rehabilitation of her husband who had been tried as a member of the 'right-Trotskyist-bloc' together with Bukharin. When she finally was informed that her husband had been rehabilitated and restored to the ranks of the Party, she died of a heart attack, falling to the floor with the telephone in her hand. For 25 years Bukharin's widow could not gain rehabilitation for her husband. Although he ceased to be officially branded as an 'enemy of the people', he remained on the list of anti-Party figures that included Tomsky, Rykov, Kamenev, Pyatakov, Shlyapnikov, Ryazanov and many others who had once played a major role in the Party and state.

No one was brought to justice – neither the NKVD investigators who used torture on their victims nor the heads or warders of camps and prisons. The names of those who made blatantly false denunciations were never revealed. Nevertheless, as soon as former prisoners began to return home, many of the informers and investigators were seized by panic. There were instances of such people going mad or even committing suicide. The prominent Komsomol activist, Olga Mishakova, whose false denunciations led to the arrest of many leading Komsomol figures in 1937–38, wound up in a psychiatric hospital. After the posthumous rehabilitation of her victims, Mishakova was removed from her positions and expelled from the central *apparat* of the Komsomol. However, by that time she was no longer capable of understanding what had happened, and she continued to arrive at her office every morning as usual. When her entry pass to the building was taken away, she became violent and had to be hospitalized. A former investigator who became a colonel in the troops of the MVD, after recognizing one of his victims on the street, fell to his knees and begged forgiveness. Another former investigator, finding himself in the same hospital ward as a prisoner whom he had interrogated, had a heart attack and died. There were many other similar situations. When the director of a school in Northern Ossetia, after many years of imprisonment and rehabilitation, visited his Ministry and recognized the Ossetian Minister of Education as the man who had been his interrogator, it was he who had the heart attack and not the Minister. In Kiev a rehabilitated officer who returned to the army encountered his torturer and shot him on the spot. But this kind of incident was rare, and NKVD officers who had taken part in the repressions as well other active participants in the lawlessness of the Stalinist times soon calmed down and stopped worrying. Society woke up very slowly from its totalitarian torpor. And by that time the majority of the prisoners of Stalin's camps had for many years already been lying in common graves.

At first most of those who returned from the camps experienced fears of new repressions and re-arrest, rather than anger or a thirst for revenge. The attitude of many of the authorities they encountered, as well as the content of the official press, only served to re-enforce this fear. Returnees were often afraid to tell their friends and relatives about what they had suffered. Many felt that they were being watched, that their telephones were being tapped, that they were surrounded by informers. People arrested for the first time after the war, who spent only five to eight years in the camps, found it easier to escape this kind of persecution mania. They were more rapidly reinstated in their former professional occupations. But the majority of those who spent 17 or 20 years in inhuman conditions were psychologically broken and suffered serious health problems. They were hardly in a state to become politically active. The former First Secretary of one of the obkoms in Kazakhstan, N. Kuznetsov, went to work as an ordinary forester. He simply wanted to avoid other people. Just to walk freely in the streets of one's town, to eat one's fill, including meat, fruit, sweets, ice cream, to take a bath, to go to the cinema and theatre, to have a vacation in the south – all this meant enormous happiness for the majority of recent prisoners. It was also true that the authorities were less than enthusiastic about re-employing former prisoners. Only a negligible number of camp inmates returned to work in the Party or state *apparat.*

But some former prisoners began to write memoirs or works of fiction about the camps and the repressions. The first were Solzhenitsyn in Ryazan, Shalamov in Moscow and Yevgeniya Ginsburg in Lvov. Keeping it secret even from his own family, the former Chekist from Tbilisi, Suren Gazaryan, started to write his memoirs. The former philosopher and Party worker P.I. Shabalkin began to analyse the Stalinist repressions in his diary. Aleksandr Todorsky, the only survivor among the generals who were sent to the camps at the beginning of the 1930s, embarked on the task of restoring the good names of many military commanders who had not yet been rehabilitated. These efforts, however, came up against powerful opposition within the Party and the ideological *apparat*. They would refer to a remark, attributed to Khrushchev, that the Party could not and never would prepare a 'Bartholomew's Night'. An anonymous poet wrote the following lines in 1957 or 1958:

With no mourning flags on the towers of state
Or funeral candles or speeches
Russia forgave her innocent victims
And also forgave their executioners

At the end of the 1950s Khrushchev publicly declared on several occasions that the Soviet people and Party would remember Stalin and do him justice and that the term 'Stalinism' had been invented by the enemies of socialism. Stalin's body continued to lie in the mausoleum next to Lenin. At the Twenty-First Party Congress in 1959 there was no mention of Stalin's crimes. Everything rapidly and unexpectedly changed at the Twenty-Second Party Congress at the end of 1961. However, that is the beginning of another story.

PART II. STALIN AND NUCLEAR WEAPONS

CHAPTER 5

Stalin and the Atomic Bomb

Zhores Medvedev

The uranium problem

In September 1942 Stalin chose the codename *Uran* for the counter-offensive operation at Stalingrad. Physicists have tended to assume that he was thinking of the explosive force of a nuclear bomb, since he had recently approved the resumption of research on uranium. Various accounts of the history of atomic energy in the USSR also mention the Stalingrad connection. What Stalin had in mind, however, was Uranus, the seventh planet of the solar system. In Russian *uran* can mean either uranium or the planet Uranus. The strategic battle that followed *Uranus*, the encirclement and rout of the German armies at Rostov-on-Don, was given the codename *Saturn*.

The extraordinary potential of an atomic weapon was mentioned in the Soviet press for the first time on 13 October 1941. *Pravda* published an account of an anti-fascist meeting that had taken place in Moscow the previous day, attended by scientists, and reproduced a statement by Academician Pyotr Kapitsa which astonished its readers:

> Explosive materials are one of the basic weapons of war. ... But in recent years, new possibilities have opened up – the use of atomic energy. Theoretical calculations show that if a powerful contemporary bomb can destroy an entire neighbourhood, then an atomic bomb, even a fairly small one, would be able to destroy a large capital city of several million people.[1]

By the beginning of 1939, after the publication of experimental results obtained by Otto Hahn and Fritz Strassmann in Germany showing that the nuclei of uranium-235 disintegrates when bombarded by neutrons, physicists considered the construction of a nuclear bomb to be feasible. Subsequent experiments carried out in various countries showed that when the nucleus of uranium-235 is struck by a single neutron, it becomes unstable and fragments, a process that was termed 'fission'. The fission of one uranium-235 nucleus not only produces several isotopes of lighter elements, some of them radioactive, but also releases three or four new neutrons. If these new, secondary neutrons hit other nuclei of uranium-235, the fission is repeated. Where there is only a small quantity of uranium-235, a large proportion of the new neutrons miss their targets, but it was calculated that if the mass of neutron-irradiated uranium-235 is larger or if the fission neutrons are slowed down by first hitting some small and stable nuclei, the splitting of one nucleus of uranium-235 could initiate the splitting of more than one additional nucleus of uranium-235, thus creating a self-sustaining chain reaction. This chain reaction, if produced by fast neutrons in a solid block of uranium-235, would result in an instant atomic explosion. The amount of uranium-235 large enough to sustain a chain reaction is known as the 'critical mass'. If uranium-235 is mixed with a substance that can slow the neutrons down (a 'moderator'), the fission chain reaction can also be slowed down and regulated. The best moderator for this process, which also releases huge amounts of energy, was thought to be heavy water (a composition of oxygen and deuterium). The crucial problem was to determine the size of the critical mass. Calculations, some of them carried out by the young Moscow physicists Yakov Zeldovich and Yuli Khariton, showed that critical mass could be reached with 10–40 kilograms of uranium-235. There was great excitement around this discovery, which pointed to the potential use of nuclear energy for practical purposes as well as the possibility of creating a powerful atomic explosion.

Natural uranium is a mixture of isotopes – uranium-238 and uranium-235 – in which the fissionable uranium-235 constitutes only 0.72 per cent of the whole. The main part of the uranium in uranium ore is the heavy isotope, uranium-238. Both isotopes are radioactive and disintegrate slowly. Georgy Flerov and Konstantin Petrzhak, Soviet physicists working in Professor Igor Kurchatov's laboratory in Leningrad, measured the radioactivity of uranium isotopes in 1939–40. It was found that the 'half-life', the time it took for half the nuclei to disintegrate, is several billion years for uranium-238 but only seven hundred million years for uranium-235. This meant that the proportion of uranium-235 had been much higher when the earth was born several billion years ago.

The physicists were convinced that it would be possible to construct an atomic bomb on the basis of uranium-235, but the project would need large amounts of natural uranium and the invention of a process to separate uranium-235 from uranium-238. This would involve highly complex technological operations but was technically feasible. By April 1939 German scientists were telling their government that an atomic bomb could be constructed. In the United States, at the urgent request of his fellow physicists, Albert Einstein sent a letter to President Roosevelt on 2 August 1939 informing him about the potential of a nuclear 'super-bomb' and warning him that Germany might have already embarked on practical work in this direction. In France it was not until March 1940, after war had already broken out in Europe, that Frédéric Joliot-Curie informed his government that there was a realistic possibility of constructing an atomic weapon. In the course of 1940 even newspapers in the United States began to refer to the atom bomb and the likelihood that this new weapon would determine the final outcome of the war.[2] From the middle of 1940, however, all developments in the work on uranium became classified information.

Nuclear physics was a priority area of research in the USSR. There were institutes in Moscow, Leningrad and Kharkov specializing in the study of the nucleus of the atom. However, it was only after the beginning of the war that the Soviet government received the first reports on the possibility of constructing an atomic bomb, reports that came from the intelligence service rather than from its own scientists.

Recently published declassified documents reveal that an agent of the Soviet secret service in London sent a coded message by radio at the end of September 1941 informing Moscow that Britain had established a special 'Uranium Committee' to develop an atomic bomb. It was thought that such a bomb might be ready in two years. A second communication from this agent, received in Moscow at the beginning of October, contained technical details of the project to build a plant for the separation of uranium isotopes along with calculations relating to the critical mass of uranium-235, the 'stuffing' of the bomb. A whole dossier on this question, which had been prepared for the British War Cabinet, was soon received in Moscow.[3]

The first Soviet physicist to write several letters directly to Stalin about the possibility of creating an atomic bomb was Georgy Flerov at the beginning of 1942. He also expressed certainty that the project was under way in Germany, the United States and Great Britain. Flerov had been called up for military service at the beginning of the war, and in the autumn of 1941 was a lieutenant in the Air Force Engineers at a military airfield near Voronezh. He did not fail to notice the publication of Kapitsa's remarks in *Pravda*. Flerov immediately began to write to his former colleagues, including Kurchatov, pointing out the need to resume the research on uranium that had been interrupted by the start of the war. When he visited a university library and discovered that scientific journals had stopped publishing anything about nuclear physics, he realized that this whole area of research had become secret. Receiving no clear response from his colleagues who had been evacuated to Kazan, he started to write to the State Defence Committee and also to Stalin.

Science and the intelligence service

According to the procedures of the Soviet secret service, information received from agents could only be acted upon after it had been evaluated by Stalin personally. This is another example of the fact that all important decisions were under his absolute control, and this was the effective source of his unlimited power. On the eve of the war with Germany, it was Stalin alone who possessed the full range of facts necessary to determine what needed to be done. Communications from the intelligence directorates of the Red Army and the NKVD were sent first to him and then to the General Staff. According to Marshal Zhukov, who was head of the General Staff at the beginning of the war, the officer in charge of the General Staff Intelligence Service, General Filipp Golikov, often reported to Stalin personally, bypassing Zhukov and the Commissariat of Defence. 'It is possible to say,' wrote Zhukov, 'that J.V. Stalin knew significantly more [about the situation on the western border] than the military leadership.'[4] Stalin would certainly have been the first to assess intelligence reports about the atomic bomb. It was his monopoly on information rather than any special intellectual gifts that made Stalin so exceptionally knowledgeable about a wide variety of subjects; he seemed to possess a universal expertise that certainly impressed his subordinates and was an important source of the 'cult of personality'.

During 1942 the Soviet secret service received a large number of documents concerning uranium. In Britain the two most valuable informants were Klaus Fuchs, an atomic physicist who left Germany in 1933, and John Cairncross, the secretary of one of the ministers of the War Cabinet, Lord Hankey. At the same time information began to arrive from Bruno Pontecorvo in the United States, an Italian émigré and close collaborator of the eminent Enrico Fermi, who in 1942 was the first person ever to construct a nuclear reactor. Cairncross, Fuchs and Pontecorvo were all convinced communists who sent information to the Soviet Union voluntarily and on their own initiative. The role of Soviet secret agents was only one of transmission rather than the obtaining of information. The material arrived in the form of actual scientific data, complex mathematical calculations and copies of research reports that were distributed as special classified publications among participants actively engaged in the uranium project in the United States and Britain. Each new technological process or technical solution was patented, and copies of the patent documentation were passed to the Soviet Union. Only scientists with a knowledge of higher mathematics and theoretical physics could have understood these materials. Some of the data would have been comprehensible only to chemists or physicist–chemists. For more than a year all this information lay unread in the safes of the NKVD.

Almost nothing came from Germany. Various works on the history of Soviet atomic research mention the notebook of a major in the German engineer corps who was killed not far from Taganrog in February 1942. This notebook contained calculations and formulae that indicated an interest in the uranium bomb. It was sent from the front to Sergei Kaftanov, the Chairman of the Committee on Higher Education and scientific consultant of the State Defence Committee (GKO) but was never submitted to expert analysis.

Surviving documents and recollections of contemporaries suggest that Stalin received brief oral reports about the atomic bomb for the first time in May–June 1942, presented independently by Beria and Kaftanov. The official written report to Stalin from the NKVD, dated March 1942 and cited in a number of recent publications, was too complex and technical to be signed by Beria. In his oral account, Beria reported on the findings of the intelligence network. Kaftanov informed Stalin about the letter from Flerov which, unlike the NKVD report, explained the basic structure of the atomic bomb in clear language as well as the reasons why it was likely that Germany or the US would possess this weapon in the not too distant future. According to Kaftanov's memoirs, Stalin walked about in his office for a short time, thought about it and said, 'We need to get started as well.'[5]

The promotion of Kurchatov

Appointments to important state or Party positions were always determined by Stalin. Officially the decision may have been taken by the Politburo, the GKO or the Presidium of the Supreme Soviet, but this was just a formality. Someone had to be chosen to direct the atomic bomb project and Stalin understood that it would have to be a highly respected major scientist. On one occasion before the war, Stalin had met Academicians Vladimir Vernadsky and Abram Joffe; he had also corresponded with Academicians Nikolai Semyonov and Pyotr Kapitsa. Apparently this was the source of the story that Stalin summoned these four Academicians to his dacha at Kuntsevo in October 1942 for consultations on the question of the atomic bomb, but in fact no such meeting ever occurred. Consultations about a possible leader for the programme took place in the offices of both Kaftanov and Beria. The NKVD had an important role in this appointment, above all because the head of the project would have to have access to the large number of documents in its possession, many of which had remained incomprehensible even within that organization: formulae, diagrams, calculations and explanations in English. By this time the NKVD had accumulated approximately 2,000 pages of specialized scientific materials. The physicist entrusted with the leadership of the project would have to spend his first months working at the NKVD rather than in the laboratory. His most important first task would be to brief the intelligence service and compile a list of concrete questions for 'sources' in the United States and Britain. Only by specific questions from the USSR, linked to the documents that had already been received, would it be possible to show Fuchs, Pontecorvo and other scientists who had agreed to help the Soviet Union that specialists were actually working with the materials they had sent.

Several physicists were called for consultations in Moscow in the autumn of 1942. They were asked to note down their thoughts about what needed to be done in order to renew research into atomic physics as well as their ideas about the military applications of nuclear energy. Naturally checks were carried out on the 'reliability' of the physicists in question, particularly in view of the fact that almost none of them were Party members. Among the Academicians, the most suitable in terms of their prestige were Abram Joffe, Vitali Khlopin and Pyotr Kapitsa who, as directors of institutes, already had the experience of being in charge of large scientific organizations. However, these members of the Soviet Academy of Sciences were not particularly enthusiastic about the bomb and had little inclination for close co-operation with the NKVD. That autumn a number of younger atomic physicists were summoned to Moscow for separate consultations, including Georgy Flerov, Igor Kurchatov, Isaak Kikoin, Abram Alikhanov and Yuli Khariton.

It was during this period, on 28 September 1942, that Stalin, as Chairman of the GKO, signed the secret GKO Directive No. 2352, 'On the organization of work on uranium', which had been drafted by Molotov in consultation with Academicians Joffe and Kaftanov. Molotov was then entrusted with the general leadership of the 'uranium project' in his capacity as Deputy-Chairman of the GKO. The secret order provided for only relatively modest arrangements that mainly concerned the Academy of Sciences; inevitably attention was focused on events at the front as the war entered a critical phase with the German army continuing its attack in the south at the approaches to Stalingrad. The intention was to create a special centre within the Academy of Sciences to investigate the uranium problem, but the scientific director was still to be chosen.

In a note dated 9 July 1971 Molotov reminisced about his decision:

> We were engaged on this work from 1943, and it was my task to find the man who could make the atomic bomb become a reality. The chekists gave me a list of reliable physicists who could be depended on, and I made the choice. I summoned Kapitsa, the Academician. In his view we were not ready, the atomic bomb was not a weapon for this

war but something for the future. We asked Joffe, but his response
was also rather vague. In short, I was left with the youngest and least
known, Kurchatov. They didn't think he had a chance. I asked him to
come, we talked, and he made a favourable impression. But he said
that he was still very unclear about the project. I then decided to give
him the materials from our intelligence service – the secret agents had
done a very important job. For several days Kurchatov sat in my
room in the Kremlin, going through these materials.[6]

Molotov recalls presenting Kurchatov to Stalin; however, this
apparently refers to a written recommendation rather than a personal meeting. On 11 February 1943 the GKO formally approved the
appointment of Kurchatov as the scientific head of the uranium
project. His report on the secret service documents that he had studied in Molotov's Kremlin office was dated 7 March 1943. In his
detailed analysis he began by saying that the materials obtained by
the secret service 'have huge, incalculable significance for our state
and our science'. In conclusion he wrote that 'summing up, the
intelligence materials show that it may be technically possible to
solve the entire uranium question in significantly less time than
envisaged by our scientists, who are not familiar with the progress of
work taking place abroad.'[7]

Three days later, on 10 March 1943, an atomic energy institute
was established in the Academy of Sciences, which for reasons of
secrecy was given the codename 'Laboratory No. 2'. Kurchatov was
appointed 'chief' of the laboratory (not the 'director' or the 'supervi-
sor') in order to emphasize the special military objectives of this new
academic centre.

The atomic tsar

The GKO and Stalin provided Kurchatov with extraordinary powers
to mobilize whatever human and material resources were needed for
the project. During the whole of March 1943 Kurchatov studied
numerous intelligence documents at the NKVD. At the beginning of
March he had familiarized himself in detail with the materials received from Britain in Molotov's study. He was now given
documents from the United States containing huge amounts of data.
Kurchatov had to evaluate 237 scientific reports, largely concerned
with the construction of the uranium–graphite pile (as the reactor
was then called) and the possibility of constructing an atomic bomb
using plutonium as well as uranium. Kurchatov produced an expert
analysis of the material and also, as the head of the project, put
together a detailed list of questions to be sent abroad, requesting that
appropriate 'instructions be given to the intelligence services'.[8]

The documents that Kurchatov studied in the Kremlin and at the
NKVD did indeed contain a great deal of unexpected information.

Soviet atomic physicists were surprised to learn that it might be possible to construct a nuclear reactor with graphite as a moderator of fast neutrons. Until then physicists thought that only heavy water could be used. German physicists had tried to build a reactor using heavy water in 1942, but their work was held back because of a shortage of this material.

Kurchatov had also been unaware of the discovery of plutonium in the USA and the possibility of using this new element for the creation of an atomic bomb. Since the critical mass of plutonium was considerably lower than that of uranium-235, a smaller plutonium bomb could have greater explosive power. Research in the United States and Britain into the separation of natural uranium into isotopes 235 and 238 by gas diffusion was also very important. There were so many papers covering such a wide spectrum of data that even if Kurchatov had been a super-genius it would have been impossible to assess all the information or take the responsibility for translating it into action. Despite the opposition of Beria, who was reluctant to widen the circle of those 'initiated' into the secrets of the intelligence service, Kurchatov insisted on sharing the NKVD documents with the scientists who headed the various departments of Laboratory No. 2. From April 1943 Academicians Joffe, Alikhanov and Kikoin were given access to the materials, and subsequently Lev Artsimovich, Yuli Khariton and Kirill Shchelkin were added to this group of trustworthy physicists. Each of them was put in charge of a different scientific-technical question. Kurchatov concentrated on the building of a uranium-graphite reactor and the isolation of plutonium. Alikhanov led the work on the construction of a heavy-water reactor. The practical task of working out how to separate uranium isotopes by gas diffusion was entrusted to Kikoin, while Artsimovich tried to use electro-magnetic fields. Khariton and Shchelkin were given particularly important assignments to do with the actual construction of uranium and plutonium bombs.

Neither Kurchatov nor his colleagues who had been given access to the secrets of the intelligence service were allowed to reveal the source of their knowledge. The fact that any kind of concrete information was obtained in this way was regarded as top secret, since its revelation could lead to the exposure of the entire network of agents as well as the inevitable removal of the leadership of the NKVD. Therefore Kurchatov and his colleagues had to pretend that any data they received via the NKVD was in fact their own discovery or a result of their own insight. This provided them with the halo of genius, which on the whole was helpful to the task in hand. Kurchatov's subordinates were astounded by his apparent ability to solve complex problems of atomic physics at once, without calculations. The biographies of Kurchatov describe many incidents involving

instantaneous solutions of this kind. One day, for example, Kurchatov asked for data on the slowing down of neutrons in uranium-
graphite prisms. Yakov Zeldovich, an expert on this problem, made
the necessary calculations and presented Kurchatov with the results.
'Lost in thought, Kurchatov suddenly announced, to the astonish-
ment of those present: "It's clear, even without the calculations", and
he produced a solution without the aid of complex formulae.'[9]

German uranium trophies

Although the secret service continued to provide the physicists with
large amounts of information showing how close the United States
was to creating a real atomic bomb, there was only modest progress
in this direction in the Soviet Union. The reason was simple: the
country did not have supplies of uranium. Tens of tonnes of pure
uranium were necessary for even the smallest uranium reactor, but
Laboratory No. 2 had only a few kilograms at its disposal. Uranium
ore had not been found anywhere within the USSR, and although
geological exploration was already under way, quick results were
unlikely. It was known that uranium for the German project was
being mined in Bulgaria, Czechoslovakia and eastern Germany. The
Bulgarian mines were brought under Soviet control at the beginning
of 1945, almost immediately after the country was liberated. However, uranium ore in Bulgaria was of poor quality, and there were no
enrichment plants. The uranium mines in the western part of
Czechoslovakia and in Saxony were destroyed by American bombs
prior to the arrival of the Soviet army. After the Allied forces landed
in Europe, the Americans set up a special forces group called the
'Alsos Team' whose job was to seize any equipment on German
territory connected with the uranium project, along with German
stocks of uranium and heavy water. In the first months of 1945 two
as yet unfinished experimental heavy-water uranium reactors were
dismantled and sent to Britain. One of these had been located near
Leipzig in the future Soviet zone of occupation. The Alsos Team also
organized the arrest and deportation of German nuclear scientists to
Britain.

The NKVD and Laboratory No. 2 were rather slow in forming
their own team for the same purpose. A group of German-speaking
nuclear scientists, accompanied by NKVD officers headed by the
deputy chief of the NKVD, Avrami Zavenyagin, went to Berlin in the
middle of May 1945 after the capitulation of Germany. The group
included Flerov, Kikoin, Khariton and Artsimovich. They all wore the
uniform of colonels in the Soviet army. Professor Nikolaus Riehl, the
main German expert on the production of pure uranium, was in
Berlin at the time and voluntarily agreed to help his Soviet col-

leagues. Riehl had been born in St Petersburg in 1901 into the family of a German engineer working for Siemens. He lived in Russia until 1919 and spoke fluent Russian. He took the Soviet scientists to Oranienburg, a town north of Berlin and the site of the main factory in Germany producing pure uranium for reactors. It turned out, however, that the factory had been deliberately destroyed by American bombers only days before the end of the war. Nevertheless the damaged remains of the factory's equipment were dismantled and transported to the Soviet Union. As a result of their inquiries, Kikoin and Khariton did manage to find a store of uranium oxides in another town, almost 100 tonnes. A further 12 tonnes were found elsewhere. Nikolaus Riehl and his family, together with several engineers from the German uranium factory, followed the uranium to Moscow. They went of their own free will, since there was nothing for them to do in Germany, whereas the nuclear physicists who were found in the American–British zone were arrested and detained in Britain for more than a year without the right to correspond with family or friends. In July Nikolaus Riehl's German team began to convert the 'Elektrostal' factory in Noginsk, a town near Moscow, into a uranium plant. By the end of 1945 the transformation of oxides of uranium into pure uranium had begun. The first batches of uranium ingots began to reach the Kurchatov laboratory in January 1946, and the assembly of a uranium-graphite experimental reactor got under way.

The Elektrostal factory was immediately turned into a special 'zone' enclosed by two rows of barbed wire. In his memoirs published in Germany in 1988, Riehl explained why he had not been surprised by the barbed wire, which was necessary

> so that the construction workers engaged in the conversion of the factory could not wander off. ... On the whole the work was carried out by prisoners, largely Soviet soldiers who had been captured by the Germans. On their return, they were not received with flowers and dancing. ... Instead they were sentenced to several years' imprisonment, charged with being cowards in the face of the enemy.[10]

Elektrostal became one of the first 'islands' of the atomic gulag. Within the NKVD it was referred to by the codename 'Construction 713'. The number of prisoners in this camp grew in proportion to the growth of uranium production. By 1950, when the production of pure uranium reached one tonne a day, there were 10,000 prisoners working in the factory.[11] In order to speed up production, a ten-hour working day was established for prisoners and also for 'free workers'.

In addition to Nikolaus Riehl, Avrami Zavenyagin's team concluded contracts with two other groups of scientists in the Soviet zone of occupation in Germany. One of them was led by the eminent physicist Gustav Hertz, who had received the Nobel Prize in 1925. Manfred von Ardenne was in charge of the other. The composition of these groups included famous as well as unknown physicists and chemists. The main task for both teams was to work out various methods for separating the uranium isotopes 235 and 238. Institutes were established for them on the Black Sea near Sukhumi. Some time later another German institute was set up for radiochemical and radiobiological research. Between 1945 and 1955 some 300 German scientists and engineers were working on the uranium project in the Soviet Union.

Yuli Khariton, one of those who had located the German uranium stocks, subsequently recalled: 'I remember one day when we were going to the installation, Igor Kurchatov said to me that those hundred tonnes helped us speed up the time for launching the first industrial reactor by about a year.'[12]

Stalin after Hiroshima

The first American atomic bomb was tested successfully in the desert of New Mexico on 16 July 1945, which was also the opening day of the Potsdam Conference. Soviet Intelligence informed Stalin of this test on 20 or 21 July, some three days before President Truman told Stalin and Molotov that the United States possessed a new, mega-powerful weapon. Stalin, however, did not expect that the atomic bomb would be used so soon, only two weeks later. At the Yalta conference in February 1945, the United States and Britain had insisted that the Soviet Union join the war against Japan within three months after the capitulation of Germany and no later. A secret protocol attached to the Yalta agreements confirmed that the USSR would accede to this request; in return the Soviet Union would regain possession of the southern part of Sakhalin and the Kurile Islands and be granted the use of Port Arthur as well as the China–Eastern Railway which had belonged to Russia before 1904. By the beginning of August there was a build-up of 1.5 million Soviet soldiers on the Manchurian border, and Stalin informed his allies that the Soviet Union would enter the war with Japan within a few weeks. At the beginning of 1945 the United States sought Soviet help in bringing about a more rapid Japanese surrender, thus minimizing American casualties. But by summer the strategy had changed: Japan would be forced to capitulate with the help of the atomic bomb. This would guarantee the United States full sway throughout the Asiatic region.

From Stalin's point of view, entry into the war with Japan meant a great deal more than simply helping his allies. He had serious strategic designs in Asia, and the advance of the Soviet army into

Manchuria, which had been a colony of Japan since 1933, was only the beginning. News of the explosion of the atomic bomb over Hiroshima on 6 August reached Moscow on the morning of the 7th. That afternoon, at 2:30, Stalin and the Chief of the General Staff, Aleksei Antonov, signed an order for military action against Japan to commence on 9 August along the entire Manchurian border in the early hours of the morning, local time. On that same day, by order of President Truman, the American air force dropped a second atomic bomb, this one on Nagasaki. On 14 August the Emperor of Japan announced on the radio his country's surrender. By the time of the formal surrender on 2 September the Soviet army had occupied almost all of Manchuria and half of Korea, which had been a Japanese colony since 1905. The opportunity to influence the political future of the far-eastern region of Asia had now passed to the Soviet Union.

After Hiroshima and Nagasaki

The atomic projects of the USA and the USSR were initiated in response to the nuclear potential of Hitler's Germany. With the end of the European war in sight, scientists who had been working on the construction of the bomb assumed that it would never actually be used. Shortly before his death in April 1945 Roosevelt did consider the possibility of deploying a nuclear weapon against the Japanese fleet, but after uranium and plutonium atomic bombs were dropped on the civilian populations of the two cities, killing between 200,000 and 300,000 people, all perceptions changed; it became conceivable that this new weapon could be used in other places as well. According to information received from Fuchs and Pontecorvo, the United States was producing enough uranium-235 and plutonium to produce eight atomic bombs per month. Understandably the atomic project became Stalin's number one priority.

The first of a series of meetings with the main leaders of the uranium programme took place on 12 August at the Kuntsevo dacha. Stalin tended to have confidential meetings there, although occasionally he used a more distant dacha at Semenovskoye, about 110 kilometres from Moscow. His official residence in the Kremlin, with its complex system of admissions, guards and a large number of different services and officials, was hardly suitable for top-secret or intelligence discussions. From 12 to 16 August Stalin arrived at the Kremlin only towards midnight in order to receive visitors with urgent business, and he worked there until two or sometimes three in the morning. Chinese diplomats came to see him at the behest of Chiang Kai-shek, anxious to find out about Soviet intentions in Manchuria. They feared, and it soon became clear, not without reason, that the Chinese communists would be the first to enter the Soviet zone of occupation. During the day and evening Stalin met the leaders of the atomic project and the members of the State Defence Committee at the Kuntsevo dacha. Kurchatov did not participate, but various questions were discussed with him on the telephone. We have brief, largely oral recollections of these meetings from Boris Vannikov,[13] who at the time was Commissar in charge of ammunition supply. From 1943 he and Mikhail Pervukhin, Commissar of the Chemical Industry, had been Molotov's deputies on the GKO commission responsible for the atomic project. Beria was not then playing a major role, since at the end of 1943 the external security service had been transferred from the NKVD to a separate new People's Commissariat of State Security (NKGB), with Vsevolod Merkulov in charge. Beria had remained head of the NKVD, controlling the police and the gulags.

As a result of the meetings at Kuntsevo, Stalin signed State Defence Committee Resolution No. 9887 on 20 August 1945, creating a new structure to preside over the atomic project. The GKO established a 'Special Committee' with emergency powers to supervise all those working on the use of atomic energy, a kind of 'atomic Politburo', with Beria appointed as its chairman. The members of the Committee, chosen personally by Stalin, were Malenkov, Voznesensky, Vannikov, Zavenyagin, Kurchatov, Kapitsa, Vasily Makhnev and Pervukhin. Their role was to ensure 'the large-scale development of geological prospecting within the USSR in order to create a raw material base for the extraction of uranium ... and also the utilization of uranium deposits found outside the Soviet Union'. They were to guarantee 'the effective organization of the uranium industry, ... the construction of atomic energy plants ... and the production of the atomic bomb'. The Special Committee established an executive organ, the First Main Directorate (PGU) of the Sovnarkom, to be headed by Vannikov. A large number of enterprises and institutions (scientific, planning, building and construction) were transferred from other departments and put at the disposal of the PGU, including Kurchatov's centre which had been established within the Academy of Sciences. The scientific-technical department of the secret service was also put under the control of the Special Committee. Orders coming from the Special Committee or the PGU to other Commissariats requesting the manufacture of equipment, the delivery of construction materials or the provision of technical services had to be given first priority; payment came from an 'open account' in the State Bank, which meant unlimited financing. Construction projects approved by the Special Committee were paid for by the Bank in accordance with 'production expenditure', and all enterprises involved in the atomic project were exempt from the obligation to register their employees with the financial organs. The PGU had become a vast, secret super-commissariat.

The largest, highest-capacity construction organization transferred to the PGU was the NKVD's First Main Directorate industrial production labour camp system (GULPS). Towards the end of 1945 this industrial gulag consisted of 13 camps holding 103,000 prisoners. The Main Directorate of the mining-metallurgy camps (GULGMP) was also assigned to the PGU and amalgamated with the industrial camp network. At the beginning of 1946 it held 190,000 prisoners, a third of them designated as 'special contingent' (former prisoners of war, people who had been repatriated from Germany and others who had fallen into the gulag without court sentence). NKVD Directive No. 00932 declared this unified camp system, later known as *Glavpromstroi*, to be 'a special construction organization for the enterprises and institutions of the First Main Directorate'.[14] According to the classification code of NKVD directives at that time, two zeros before the number of a directive meant that it was issued on Stalin's personal instructions. This did not mean, literally, from his own lips, but rather a document that might have come from the State Defence Committee, the Sovnarkom or the Politburo, but which had been signed by Stalin. There would usually be a preamble to the directive referring to the body that had issued the instructions.

Approximately 125,000 people participated in the American atomic project. The figure for the Soviet Union towards the end of 1945 was twice that number. And by 1950 the number of people drawn into the PGU system had grown to over 700,000. More than half of them were prisoners, and about one-third were from the army construction battalions of the MVD. Only about 10 per cent were 'free workers', whose freedom of movement was in fact heavily restricted.

Towards the end of 1946 there already were 11 specially constructed nuclear installations. The prison camps serving these installations were removed from the authority of the NKVD and came under the control of the PGU. Certain allowances that sometimes were made within the NKVD system, such as the release of prisoners suffering from serious or chronic illnesses, pregnant women or the elderly who were unable to work, did not apply in the atomic gulag. Here prisoners were never allowed to leave, as they were the bearers of exceptionally important state secrets.

Stalin gave the PGU a deadline: the Soviet Union was to possess uranium and plutonium bombs by 1948.

Stalin and Kurchatov

It has been reported that there were frequent meetings between Stalin and Kurchatov, but this was not the case. Nor was there ever a demonstration model of the atomic bomb or of a plutonium 'bead' which Kurchatov and Khariton were said to have brought to the Kremlin shortly before the first test. Kurchatov was in fact invited to see Stalin only twice, on 25 January 1946 and 9 January 1947. At the first meeting, Stalin included Beria, Molotov, Voznesensky, Malenkov, Mikoyan and Zhdanov. S.F. Kaftanov and the President of the Academy of Sciences, Sergei Vavilov, came as well. Kurchatov entered Stalin's office along with the others at 8:15 pm and left 50 minutes later together with Vavilov. The other participants remained for another two hours.[15] Kurchatov wrote down his impressions as soon as he returned to the institute, and his notes, deposited in his safe, have only recently been published. Their contents make it apparent that it was the first time Kurchatov had ever been in Stalin's office. I reproduce an extract here, dated the day of the meeting:

> On the future development of the work, Comrade Stalin said that it was not worth paying attention to minor matters, that it was necessary to take a broad view in grand Russian style so that help from every corner would be brought to bear on the project. ...

> With regard to the scientists, Comrade Stalin was preoccupied with the thought of how to ease and improve their material living conditions. By awarding bonuses, for example, for achievement. He said that our scientists are very modest, that they sometimes don't even notice that they are living badly – it's already bad, that our state suffers so heavily, but it's always possible to ensure that (several thousand?) men live well, with dachas, so they can rest, that cars are available. ...

> We also have to use Germany in every possible way - there are people, equipment, experience, and factories. Comrade Stalin was interested in the work of German scientists, how useful they had been for us. ...

> (Then?) there were questions about Joffe, Alikhanov, Kapitsa, and Vavilov and about the expediency of Kapitsa's work.

> (Opinions?) were expressed about (those?) who were involved and whether their activity was directed towards the good of the Motherland or not.

> It was suggested that we make a note of whatever measures we thought would help speed up our work – everything that was necessary. And which new scientists should be recruited.

> The furnishings of the office show the (originality?) of its occupant: tiled stoves, a wonderful portrait of Ilyich, and portraits of Suvorov and Kutuzov.[16]

Kurchatov's second encounter with Stalin, on 9 January 1947, was at a meeting that in part discussed atomic questions and went on for almost three hours. Khariton, Kikoin and Artsimovich, the scientific heads of what had by now become atomic cities, were invited as well. Also present were Molotov, Beria, Malenkov, Voznesensky and Pervukhin, and also Vannikov, Zavenyagin and Makhnev as members of the Special Committee. NKVD Major-General Aleksandr Komarovsky, the head of *Glavpromstroi* – the atomic gulag – was also there.[17] No one at that meeting left any notes, and no record would have been kept for reasons of secrecy. Only many years later one of the participants, Mikhail Pervukhin, revealed that at this meeting, Kurchatov reported the successful launch of Europe's first experimental 'physical' reactor in December 1946 at Laboratory No. 2. 'Stalin eagerly questioned Kurchatov and the others about the significance of this event. When he became convinced of the reliability of our information and judgement, he ordered us to maintain the strictest secrecy.'[18]

Uranium and plutonium for the bomb

Detailed notes and sketches of the plutonium bomb dropped on Nagasaki had been received from Fuchs in 1945 and also from Pontecorvo, independently. But the production of plutonium had not yet begun in the Soviet Union. They could use uranium taken from Germany in the small experimental reactor built by Laboratory No. 2, but a large, industrial reactor would require 150 tonnes of uranium. At the end of 1945 work resumed at the uranium mines in Czechoslovakia and eastern Germany. A Soviet joint-stock company, Vismut, was created to operate the German mines in Saxony. Germans who had been interned in the Balkans along with German prisoners of war were brought to work in these mines.

In 1946 uranium deposits were found in various parts of the Soviet Union. Mining uranium is an extremely difficult job, particularly in remote places. The first domestically produced uranium only became available in 1947 from the Leninabad mining-chemical complex in Tadjikistan, which had been built in record time. Within the atomic gulag system this complex was known as 'Construction 665'. The location of all uranium production sites was kept secret until 1990, and even the miners were kept in ignorance of the nature of their work. Officially they were extracting a 'special ore', and the documents of the time always referred to 'lead' or 'product A-9' rather than to uranium. Although the deposits of uranium in Kolyma were of poor quality, a mining complex was set up nevertheless, including a labour camp known as Butugichag. Anatoly Zhigulin, who spent two years here as a prisoner, wrote about it in his novel *Black Stones*, but even he was unaware of the fact that uranium was being extracted. In 1946 uranium ore from Butugichag was taken to the 'mainland' by air, but this was an extremely expensive operation. A local enrichment processing plant was built in 1947.

In the Urals near Kyshtym, 100 kilometres north of Chelyabinsk, building began on the first industrial reactor and radiochemical plant, called 'Mayak' (Beacon). Nikolai Dollezhal, the director of the Institute of Chemical Machinery Construction, was put in charge of the engineering project for the reactor. Kurchatov personally directed the loading of uranium. The construction of the whole centre, later known as Chelyabinsk 40, was supervised by the head of the PGU, Vannikov. An enormous amount of building work was involved. More than 30,000 prisoners from various camps were set to work along with three regiments from the army construction battalions of the Ministry of Internal Affairs.

In 1947 a further three 'atomic cities' were built: two in the Sverdlovsk region, Sverdlovsk 44 and 45, for the industrial separation of uranium isotopes, and one near Gorky, Arzamas-16, to make plutonium and uranium bombs. Kikoin and Artsimovich were the scientific directors of the Sverdlovsk installations, while Khariton and Shchelkin were put in charge at Arzamas-16. All of these men, who later became eminent scientists, were virtually unknown at the end of the 1940s, and at the time their names were kept secret. The construction work progressed rapidly. There were never any complaints about a shortage of workers. But there was not enough uranium. Even at the beginning of 1948 the first industrial reactor could not be launched. Nor was there enough uranium for the Sverdlovsk installations. The deadline for the production of the first atomic bombs was slipping by.

When in December 1946 Laboratory No. 2 successfully started up an experimental reactor (F-1), it had been an extremely simplified version without a water cooling system. This allowed a very compact arrangement of the uranium blocks, with graphite used as a moderator of neutrons; 45 tonnes of uranium, largely brought from Germany, was enough for the beginning of a controlled chain reaction. It was expected that a certain amount of plutonium would be received so that its properties could be studied in this experimental reactor. But without a water cooling system, the experimental reactor rapidly overheated and therefore could only run for very short periods.

The industrial reactor designed for the Urals centre was a much more complex structure with a permanent cooling system. In order to start a regulated fission chain reaction, they needed 150 tonnes of uranium to be placed in special aluminium channels containing permanently circulating cooling water. The main fission product of this reactor would be uranium-235. However, neutrons produced during fission could also hit and merge with the uranium-238 nuclei, forming a new element with a mass of 239. This new element had been named plutonium. After its separation from spent nuclear fuel, it could be used for the construction of plutonium bombs. The advantage of plutonium was that its critical mass was about ten times less than that of uranium; therefore a smaller quantity of this element would be required to make a bomb.

Towards the beginning of 1948 they finally succeeded in accumulating the 150 tonnes of uranium needed to load the industrial reactor. However, around that time it was discovered that the system for unloading the reactor, until then checked from a stand on a single canal, was unsuitable for a reactor that had more than a thousand canals. It was urgently necessary to work out how to construct a new system for unloading the reactor. This held the start back by several months. Test starts of the reactor at low power finally began on 8 June 1948, almost a year later than the original plan. On 22 June the reactor was brought up to its designed capacity – 100,000 kilowatts. The reactor began to work around the clock, although there were interruptions when repairs were necessary as a result of rather frequent accidents. Some of the repair work, carried out in accordance with the orders of Kurchatov and Vannikov, 'led to the contamination of the premises and the irradiation of shifts of workers and repair personnel'.[19]

A particularly serious accident took place at the end of 1948, and in 1949 the reactor was stopped for major repairs for a period of almost two months. They had to produce replacements for all the canals, virtually dismantling and then reassembling the whole reactor. During this process several thousand people were exposed to radiation because of the need to 'enlist the entire male staff of the unit to carry out this "dirty work"'.[20]

During the whole of 1948 and almost half of 1949 Kurchatov, Vannikov and Zavenyagin were in the Urals taking decisions on the spot as problems arose. Beria, who had to keep explaining the reasons for the delays to Stalin, visited the site several times. 1948 was also a year of decisive battles in the Chinese Civil War, and in the summer Stalin began the blockade of West Berlin, provoking a very serious post-war crisis between the USSR and the West. The lack of a nuclear weapon prevented Stalin from conducting his foreign policy from a position of strength.

In May 1949 the radiochemical factory Mayak began separating plutonium from the reactor's spent uranium fuel blocks, but there was a failure to anticipate the full decomposition of the short-lived products resulting from the fission of uranium-235; the blocks usually needed to be submerged in water for at least three months. This exposed the radiochemists to dangerous levels of radiation. Professor Angelina Guskova was a young doctor working in the laboratory for isolating uranium at the Urals unit from 1947 to 1953. According to her recent testimony:

> Mainly young women worked there. This was the group at greatest risk, and 120 cases of radiation sickness were recorded among them – they called it 'plutonium pneumosclerosis'.[21]

Radioactive waste from the Mayak complex was discharged into the Techa, a small river flowing through the industrial zone. This led to the heavy pollution of the river for tens of kilometres downstream beyond the perimeter of the installation, causing a large number of cases of radioactive illnesses among the local peasant population.

By June 1949 they had ten kilograms of plutonium, the amount used in the American bomb over Nagasaki (a uranium bomb had been used at Hiroshima). According to the physicists' calculations, it would have been possible to create an explosion with half the amount of this precious metal. But Stalin had demanded that they make an exact duplicate, and no one wanted to take any chances.

Rewarding the victors

The successful explosion of the first Soviet atomic bomb took place at a specially built testing ground in the Semipalatinsk region of Kazakhstan on 29 August 1949. In engineering and scientific terms the plutonium bomb was a more complex achievement – the uranium bomb had a simpler design. By the middle of September, after examining the radioactive fallout from the explosion which spread into the upper levels of the atmosphere throughout the world, the Americans came to the conclusion that the Soviets had made a virtual copy of the bomb that had been dropped on Nagasaki. The Soviet Union had not given any advance warning of the test because Stalin feared that the United States might attempt a preventive strike against Soviet atomic facilities.

A secret unpublished decree of the Supreme Soviet awarded decorations to a large number of those who had participated in the creation of the atomic bomb. The scientists Kurchatov, Flerov, Khariton, Shchelkin, Zeldovich, Khlopin, Dollezhal and Academician Andrei Bochvar, the director of the radiochemical plant for the separation of plutonium, along with several others received the highest award – the title of Hero of Socialist Labour and the Gold Star medal. Nikolaus Riehl received the Gold Star and the title of Hero. They were all given dachas near Moscow and Pobeda cars (Kurchatov, exceptionally, was given the superior ZIS) and were awarded the Stalin Prize as well.

The head of the PGU, Vannikov, and his deputy, Pervukhin, also received the title of Hero of Socialist Labour, a gold medal and the Stalin Prize. Eight generals from the Ministry of Internal Affairs were given the title as well, along with the Gold Star medal. These included: Deputy Minister Zavenyagin; the head of Glavpromstroi, Aleksandr Komarovsky, and his deputy, Pyotr Georgievsky; the head of building No. 859 (the reactor), Mikhail Tsarevsky and his deputies, Vasily Saprykin and Semyon Aleksandrov. Also in this group of heroes from the MVD were the two heads of the uranium mining complex, Boris Chirkov (the Leninabad complex in Tadjikistan) and Mikhail Maltsev (the German *Vismut* project). They were decorated for 'exceptional achievements' and 'participation in the building of the atomic bomb'. Lavrenty Beria, the head of the Special Committee, received only the Order of Lenin. His name appeared in the second long list of those who 'took part' in the construction of the units of the atomic industry. Beria certainly regarded this as a slight and found it offensive, but Stalin apparently wanted to make it clear that it was he, himself, who had been responsible for organizing the work on problem Number One and that it was he who deserved the credit.

Epilogue

After initial surprise in the United States and Britain that the Soviet Union had been able to explode a complex plutonium bomb, American and British experts became convinced that basic information crucial to the construction of the bomb must have been obtained by espionage. It was clear from an analysis of the fallout and from the fission coefficient of the plutonium (the proportion of intact and split plutonium nuclei) that the Soviet bomb was an exact replica of the American version. An urgent investigation was begun in order to discover the source of the leak. With the help of new computers, the Americans were able to decipher several old Soviet radio codes that had been used seven or eight years before. Klaus Fuchs was arrested in Britain in January 1950. He admitted sending the Soviet Union information about the bomb but did not reveal his channels of communication with Soviet Intelligence. Fuchs was sentenced to 14 years in prison and was released in 1959 'for good behaviour'. He went to the GDR where he was put in charge of the Berlin Institute of Nuclear Physics. Bruno Pontecorvo, fearing arrest, fled with his family to the Soviet Union via Finland in 1950. In the USSR he 'assimilated', was given a laboratory at the Institute of Nuclear Physics at Dubna, and soon became a full member of the Soviet Academy of Sciences. The British agent of the Soviet secret service, Cairncross, who had been the first to inform Moscow about the uranium project in 1941, was not discovered until the mid-1980s. He was exposed by the KGB agent Oleg Gordievsky when he defected to the West. By this time Cairncross was a pensioner and living in France. He was not put on trial but lost his pension and was compelled to make a confession. Three other British agents who had been involved in the transmission of information to the Soviet Union were also able to avoid arrest by fleeing to the USSR via other countries. They lived in Moscow for the rest of their lives, were given the rank of colonel in the KGB and worked as consultants in the security service. The most important figure among this notorious 'Cambridge group' was Kim Philby, who until 1949 had been First Secretary at the British Embassy in Washington, serving as the link between the British and American secret services. His escape to the Soviet Union did not take place until 1963. A series of postage stamps was issued in 1990 honouring those who had been the most successful Soviet spies, and Kim Philby was among them. Philby became the personal adviser and friend of the Chairman of the KGB, Yuri Andropov. Nikolaus Riehl and other German scientists who worked on the Soviet atomic project were not allowed to return to East Germany until 1955. Within four weeks, together with his family, Riehl crossed into West Berlin and flew to Munich, where he lived and worked until the end of his life. He died in 1990.

It was not until 1951 that the Soviet Union was able to produce and test a uranium bomb. By this time it was an original Soviet model, more compact and sophisticated than the earlier American version. The Soviet Union's status as superpower was guaranteed by its possession of a nuclear arsenal.

CHAPTER 6

Stalin and the Hydrogen Bomb

Zhores Medvedev

The beginning of the project

The atomic bomb was a product of human ingenuity. Plutonium is not a natural substance nor does uranium-235 ever spontaneously accumulate in quantities that would allow the start of a fission chain reaction. The theory behind the hydrogen bomb, however, is based on the most widespread phenomenon in the universe – nuclear synthesis, a process in which the nuclei of comparatively light elements combine to form the nucleus of a heavier element. Almost all the elements of the earth's crust originally came into being in this way. Nuclear synthesis releases hundreds of thousands of times more energy than the fission of heavy atoms. Interest in the question of nuclear fusion arose in the 1930s, particularly after Hans Bethe, a German physicist who emigrated to the United States in 1934, developed his ideas about the origin of the energy of the stars, including the sun. According to his theory, which gained rather widespread support at the time, the energy output of the stars results from synthesis, an exothermic (i.e. at high temperatures, in the order of hundreds of millions of degrees) fusion reaction in which four nuclei of hydrogen unite to form one nucleus of helium. This synthesis takes place after several intervening stages. Hydrogen is the most abundant element in the universe, accounting for 75 per cent of the mass of all matter.

During the explosion of a uranium or plutonium bomb, it is thought that the temperature at the epicentre reaches some millions or tens of millions of degrees. Many physicists were aware of the possibility of using an atomic explosion to serve as a detonator for a much more complex nuclear fusion bomb. But it seemed inconceivable that there could ever be any use for such a bomb. If an atomic bomb with an explosive power of 15–20 kilotonnes of TNT could destroy a large city and kill hundreds of thousands of people, what need could there conceivably be for a bomb that was thousands of times more powerful, the equivalent of millions of tonnes of conventional explosives? What circumstances could ever justify the use of a bomb that would instantly kill not hundreds of thousands of people but many millions at one stroke?

Nevertheless among the American physicists working on the development of the atomic bomb (the Manhattan Project), one rather highly regarded figure decided to concentrate his efforts on building a hydrogen bomb and as early as 1942 began to make preliminary calculations to prove that it could be done. The physicist in question was Edward Teller. He was born in Budapest in 1908 but was educated in Germany and began his research in Munich. In 1935 he moved to the United States where he was invited to join the laboratory of Robert Oppenheimer at the University of California. Teller's first calculations showed that a temperature of some millions of degrees produced by a nuclear explosion would not be high enough to cause the nuclei of ordinary 'light' hydrogen to fuse. But this temperature would be sufficient to bring about a fusion of the nuclei of deuterium, the 'heavy' isotope of hydrogen, producing the 'light' isotope of helium. In this case a thermonuclear reaction would take place according to a very simple formula:

$$D + D = {}^3He + n + 3.27 \text{ Mega electron volts (MeV)}$$

Fusing the two nuclei of deuterium forms one nucleus of the light isotope of helium, releasing one neutron and a vast amount of energy in the process. Easier still would be the fusion of the deuterium nucleus with the nucleus of tritium – the heavier isotope of hydrogen. In this case the nucleus of 'heavy' helium (${}^4He$) is formed, releasing one neutron and five times more energy – 17.3 mega electron volts.

Despite its colossal power, the hydrogen bomb would not need to be any larger than an atomic weapon. Furthermore, fusion products, unlike those of fission, are not radioactive and would not contaminate the earth's atmosphere. At the same time, if measured in terms of equivalent kilotonnes of TNT, the explosive power of a potential hydrogen bomb (soon known among the physicists as the 'super-bomb') turned out to be much cheaper to produce. It would therefore cost less to destroy a large city with one hydrogen bomb than with several atomic bombs aimed at the same target.

In September 1945 most of the physicists who were working at Los Alamos and other American atomic military centres began to return to their former universities and laboratories, preferring to live a normal life with the chance to publish, travel and teach. Los Alamos was threatened with temporary closure. Obsessed with the notion of the hydrogen bomb, Teller decided to create new projects for the laboratory at Los Alamos and secure them with government grants. With this goal in mind he convened a secret seminar at Los Alamos in April 1946 to discuss the feasibility of constructing a hydrogen, or thermonuclear bomb. About 40 scientists took part in the seminar, including Klaus Fuchs, who after starting the work on the British atomic project in 1941 had moved to the United States in 1944 where he became part of Oppenheimer's group at Los Alamos. At about this time the United States and Britain decided to unite their efforts. Britain was more advanced in research on the uranium bomb, while the US was in front on plutonium. The British delegation returned home at the end of 1946, and Fuchs went back to his work at the British atomic centre at Harwell. He also resumed his former links with Soviet Intelligence. This meant that the Soviet government heard about the seminar on the hydrogen bomb that had taken place at Los Alamos.

We know very little about whether or not or to what extent American research on the hydrogen bomb reached the Soviet Union, since in contrast to the almost full publication of relevant data about the atomic bomb, a considerable amount of the information on the construction of the hydrogen bomb remains classified. In any case the actual successes of Soviet Intelligence were rather modest after 1945, when the American atomic programme was put under military control.

By the summer of 1946 Kurchatov and the other leading participants in the Soviet nuclear project were aware, in general terms, of the new direction of research at Los Alamos. The theoretical possibility of creating a thermonuclear weapon was of course obvious to Soviet physicists as well. However, before any practical work could begin, it was first necessary to construct an atomic bomb, and the Soviet Union was still totally without an adequate industrial base to support this effort. It was nevertheless clear that the production of a hydrogen bomb would require new factories and new materials, particularly in order to acquire significant quantities of deuterium.

It was impossible to create the conditions for a thermonuclear reaction experimentally since it takes place at astronomical temperatures; therefore all research demanded a colossal amount of calculation. It was decided to mobilize the theoretical resources of virtually all the mathematical institutes and departments of the Soviet Academy of Sciences. The co-ordination of this work was entrusted to a talented young physicist, Yakov Zeldovich, who headed the theoretical department of the Institute of Chemical Physics. Lev Landau, the head of the theoretical department of the Institute of Physical Problems, was enlisted as a member of the team. The director of this institute, Pyotr Kapitsa, had refused to continue working on the atomic bomb after a conflict with Beria towards the end of 1945 and afterwards openly explained his reasons in two detailed letters to Stalin. The fact that Kapitsa stepped aside from work on the atomic bomb did not lead to his immediate dismissal as director of the institute, which was not playing a key role in the atomic project. However, as preparatory steps got under way in 1946 towards building a hydrogen bomb, the scientific potential of Kapitsa's institute could not be ignored. It was always obvious that the construction of the bomb would require liquid or even solid deuterium. It was at the Institute of Physical Problems, using a unique apparatus invented by Kapitsa, that physicists had worked out technologies for obtaining large quantities of liquid gas, particularly oxygen and helium. Research into the physical properties of gases, condensed by cooling to temperatures close to absolute zero, brought Kapitsa worldwide acclaim. But it was decided to change the focus of the institute: it would now concentrate on the problems of separating hydrogen isotopes and isolating deuterium, storing it in its liquid form or in the form of heavy water. This made it inevitable that the director would have to be replaced.

Stalin, Beria and Kapitsa

Kapitsa had been recruited to work on the building of an atomic bomb shortly after the appointment of Igor Kurchatov as the overall head of the whole project in February 1943. It had been vital to mobilize the best scientists in the country; however, physicists with more experience, greater authority and a higher academic standing than the young, little-known Professor Kurchatov, might have been reluctant to work as his subordinates. Therefore instead of attempting to enlist their participation in the atomic project on the basis of his own authority, Kurchatov preferred to rely on resolutions from the Sovnarkom, signed by Stalin, for which he prepared the drafts.

Kurchatov's main advantage over his better-known colleagues was that he had been given the opportunity to analyse data collected by the intelligence service and was fully conversant with all the achievements of Britain and the United States. During this period Molotov and Pervukhin were in charge of the uranium project at the State Defence Committee. On 20 March Kurchatov sent Pervukhin a memorandum 'Concerning the necessity to enlist L.D. Landau and P.L. Kapitsa to join the work'. It was proposed that they become consultants to Kurchatov's laboratory – Kapitsa to work on the separation of isotopes and Landau on the development of the explosive process in the uranium bomb.[1]

On 20 August 1945, after the explosion of American atomic bombs over Hiroshima and Nagasaki, a resolution of the GKO, signed by Stalin, established a Special Committee on atomic energy in order to speed up the work in the Soviet Union. The Committee was given emergency powers and Beria was put in charge. Only two scientific representatives were included – Kapitsa and Kurchatov. The other members of the Committee represented the leadership of the country: the Politburo (Malenkov), the government (Voznesensky), the NKVD (Zavenyagin) and the two Commissariats which would be playing the main role in establishing the nuclear industry – Ammunition (Vannikov) and Chemical Industry (Pervukhin). Stalin knew Kapitsa best of all the Soviet Academicians. It was not that they were in the habit of meeting, but from the mid-1930s Kapitsa had been writing to him regularly on a whole range of questions. Kapitsa was the first Soviet scientist to be honoured with the title Hero of Socialist Labour on 30 April 1945.

During the first weeks of feverish activity, Kapitsa vigorously participated in all the discussions and decisions of the Special Committee and its Technical Council. But Stalin and Beria had decreed that the Soviet bomb was to be an exact replica of the American model, and unlike Kurchatov and his closest collaborators, Kapitsa was not allowed access to the vast quantity of NKVD intelligence materials. This led to an inevitable conflict between Kapitsa and Kurchatov and also with other members of the Special Committee. Kapitsa began on the assumption that it was necessary to solve certain scientific problems, such as the method of separating uranium isotopes, while Kurchatov, Beria and others knew that these problems had already been dealt with in the United States. It was now mainly a question of checking, clarifying and absorbing the American data.

On 3 October 1945 Kapitsa sent Stalin a letter through the secret dispatch office of the Kremlin, cautiously critical of Beria and requesting 'release from all appointments by the SNK, except my work in the Academy of Sciences'.[2] Nothing happened, however, and Kapitsa continued to be invited to meetings of the Special Committee. On 25 November Kapitsa sent Stalin a second, very detailed letter. Without having had any actual personal contact, Kapitsa nevertheless had a good understanding of Stalin's psychology, and no doubt every word was carefully chosen. He addressed Stalin as an equal, as the leader of science to the leader of the state, and Stalin had never received such a letter from anyone. Kapitsa made it obvious that he viewed the other government figures as second-rate functionaries who had no real understanding of the atomic question. It was particularly true of Beria.

> He has a conductor's baton in his hands ... but the conductor cannot simply wave the baton, he must also understand the score. This is Beria's weakness. ... Beria has a need to be always working, but to sit in the chairman's seat, crossing things out on draft resolutions – this hardly leads to the solution of problems. ... It simply does not work between me and Beria. ... I find his attitude towards scientists entirely unacceptable.[3]

After criticizing the work of the Special Committee and the Technical Council, Kapitsa went on to make a number of recommendations which were undoubtedly useful to Stalin. No one else could have informed Stalin about the state of affairs in such a direct manner. Then Kapitsa overtly – it was no longer a hint – expressed his desire to leave all atomic committees and councils. 'I cannot be a blind performer, it is a position that I have outgrown.'

Two weeks later Kapitsa was formally released from work on the bomb but was allowed to remain in all his academic positions. His letter to Stalin has been commented on repeatedly. Legends grew up around it. According to one account, Beria was so pleased at the departure of the obstinate Kapitsa that he arrived at the Institute of Physical Problems 'bringing a magnificent gift for Kapitsa – a richly inlaid double-barrelled hunting rifle'.[4]

According to another legend, Beria asked Stalin to sanction Kapitsa's arrest, but was unsuccessful. Both stories are extremely improbable. The vain, malicious Beria, well aware of Kapitsa's contempt, would hardly have sought to please him with a special present. Alternatively Beria would have understood that Kapitsa's arrest would not be in his own interest. All the work of Soviet Intelligence on the atomic bomb was based on the voluntary collaboration of several American and British scientists who had an extremely positive attitude towards the Soviet Union and towards Stalin personally. In view of his enormous moral and scientific authority among physicists throughout the world, if Kapitsa was arrested it could discredit the Soviet leadership and undermine the effectiveness of the intelligence service. Furthermore Stalin knew quite well that Beria was no angel and that Kapitsa's criticism was well founded.

The departure of Kapitsa from the project was also, apparently, a relief for Kurchatov. It was now easier for him to play the role of 'super-genius', quickly resolving complex problems of atomic physics without equations or calculations or even experiments. Kapitsa was left in peace. At the beginning of 1946 he was still regularly writing to Stalin. On 4 April 1946, for the first time in many years, Stalin sent a reply:

> Comrade Kapitsa!
> I have received all your letters. They contain much that is instructive
> – I am thinking about somehow meeting you to discuss them.
>
> About L. Gumilevsky's book, *Russian Engineers*, it is indeed interesting and will soon be published.
>
> J. Stalin[5]

Lev Gumilevsky's manuscript, which Kapitsa had sent to Stalin, was published in 1947. It was part of a popular series called 'Let us restore Russian priority', focusing on various areas of science and technology.

For some time it seemed as if Kapitsa's rather risky resignation from military atomic projects would have no adverse personal consequences. But unexpectedly, on 17 August 1946, Stalin signed a resolution of the Council of Ministers relieving Kapitsa of all state and scientific posts. Anatoly Aleksandrov, one of Kurchatov's collaborators and also a member of the Academy of Sciences, was appointed director of the Institute of Physical Problems founded by Kapitsa. This appointment was ratified by the Presidium of the Academy on 20 September. Kapitsa fell into disgrace. He and his family were living in a cottage in the grounds of the institute, but since this was now a top-security location, they had to abandon their home in the city and move to an Academy dacha on Nikolina Hill in a picturesque district near Moscow. Kapitsa's ignominious status continued for almost nine years and came to an end only after all the major questions relating to the construction of a thermonuclear weapon had been resolved. He was allowed to return to his research and was reinstated as the director of his institute. A few years later he was awarded the Nobel Prize.

The hydrogen bomb: early mistakes and the mobilization of scientists

In a modern atomic bomb the transition of the charge to the stage of critical mass that sets off an explosive chain reaction – the fission of atomic nuclei – takes place as a result of a massive compression (several hundred thousands of atmospheres) of plutonium or uranium-235 leading to an increase in their densities. As the metal is condensed its atoms move closer together and a critical mass is established. This super-pressure is provided by conventional explosive substances, i.e. by a great number of synchronized electrically detonated explosions directed inwards and positioned spherically at equal distances from the plutonium or uranium 'beads'. The beads are the size of a large apple. The outer pressure of the focused blast wave reduces the size of the bead almost twofold, and the neutron detonator at the centre of the bead starts the chain reaction of an atomic explosion. In the first bombs only 7–10 per cent of the plutonium or uranium was functional – the remaining mass evaporated in the explosion. Later modifications increased the fission co-efficient, which correspondingly increased the power of the blast.

In order to explode a hydrogen bomb by fusion – the fusion of deuterium nuclei at temperatures of millions of degrees, generated by an atomic explosion – pressure was required on an enormous scale. According to Teller's original theory pressure at hundreds of thousands of atmospheres, which could be created by conventional explosive materials, could also set off the chain reaction of thermonuclear synthesis. In order to prove this theory it would be necessary to do an inordinately large number of calculations, and the absence of fast computers meant that it would be an extremely slow process. Theoretical work both in the Soviet Union and the United States faced the same problem. The Soviet Union at that time was significantly behind the United States in the development of computers, which in the USSR were called 'electronic calculating machines'. But this handicap was largely overcome by manpower: a huge number of mathematicians were enlisted to work on the calculations. Each person was assigned to a specific problem, and often there was no apparent link to any larger goal. Universities increased their intake of students admitted to physics, mathematics and theoretical physics faculties. By 1950 the Soviet Union led the world in the number of its mathematicians.

The problems of the atomic bomb had been largely worked out by physicists from the scientific school of Academician Abram Joffe, who founded the Leningrad Physics-Technical Institute. They were mainly experimental physicists rather than theoreticians. However, theoretical physics and mathematics were crucial for initial research on the hydrogen bomb. Here the key figures were Igor Tamm, head of the theoretical department of the Physics Institute of the Academy of Sciences (FIAN); Lev Landau, head of the theoretical department of the Institute of Physical Problems (IFP); and Yakov Zeldovich, youngest of the theoreticians and head of the theoretical department of the Institute of Chemical Physics (IKF).

The best mathematicians at this time were working in the Institute of Applied Mathematics of the Academy of Sciences, headed by Academician Mstislav Keldysh. There were also leading mathematics schools at the Universities of Moscow and Leningrad, and, up to the war, also at Kharkov. During 1946 and 1947 the Council of Ministers issued orders signed by Stalin that incorporated these and other academic centres into the project to build a thermonuclear weapon and placed them under a regime of strict secrecy. It was Kurchatov's responsibility to co-ordinate the entire effort. However, during this period, and particularly in 1948 and 1949, Kurchatov was heavily involved with building industrial reactors and the production of plutonium for the first atomic bomb in the new atomic cities near Chelyabinsk and Sverdlovsk. The focus of work on the hydrogen bomb shifted to a secret centre in the Gorky region on the border with Mordovia, first known as KB-11 and later as Arzamas-16. The scientific head was the then virtually unknown Yuli Khariton. In 1947 Yakov Zeldovich was transferred to KB-11. By 1948, despite a vast number of calculations and a great deal of theoretical research, work was still not yet under way on the actual construction of a hydrogen weapon. As we now know, this was also the case in the United States. Soviet Intelligence had no 'sources' in the Teller group, however, and had no means of following the rate of American progress.

According to the theoretical model, after the beginning of the thermonuclear reaction in one of the ends of the cylinder containing liquid deuterium, the energy released in the nuclear synthesis would spread along the cylinder to detonate the thermonuclear reaction in the entire mass of deuterium. The explosion, although it would last for only part of a microsecond, took place in two stages. But would the thermonuclear reaction (synthesis) that started in the deuterium spread spontaneously or would it for some reason die out? The calculations were still not convincing. At Los Alamos they ordered new, more sophisticated computers with dedicated special programs to speed things up. Work on a number of questions had to be suspended until the new supercomputers arrived, since the American government did not have the luxury of compelling mathematicians from various universities to come and help Teller solve his problems.

In the Soviet Union, on the other hand, where Stalin's signature was tantamount to law for the Academy of Sciences, it was rather easy to mobilize scientists for any project of importance to the state. Towards the middle of 1948 neither Zeldovich nor Teller could find proof for a spontaneous thermonuclear reaction in liquid deuterium. It was time for fresh ideas and a different approach, which meant that new people had to be involved in the project. Kurchatov decided to enlist Tamm's group – at the time Tamm was the most qualified theoretical physicist in the Soviet Union. One of Tamm's young collaborators was the 27-year-old Andrei Sakharov, who described how he first heard about the project in his memoirs:

> Towards the end of June 1948, Tamm, in a rather furtive manner, asked me, along with another of his charges, Semyon Belenky, to remain behind after his Friday in-house seminar. As soon as we were alone, Tamm shut his office door and announced his startling news: by decision of the Council of Ministers and the Party Central Committee, a special research group had been created at FIAN. Tamm had been appointed to lead the group, and Belenky and I were to be among its members. Our task would be to investigate the possibility of building a hydrogen bomb.[6]

A third participant was Tamm's student, Vitaly Ginsburg. Soon, several more young physicists were added to the group. No one refused to take part in the research. Young scientists at that time were usually extremely poor and lived in very basic accommodation. Along with access to top-secret work, inclusion in the atomic project would mean a much better salary, higher status and a good apartment in Moscow. The recipients of these 'elite' apartments did not then know that from 1943 each of them was being bugged by the NKVD.[7]

Beria assigned the task of analysing the atomic scientists' private conversations to Department 'S' of the NKVD, headed by General Pavel Sudoplatov. The biggest problem for the security service was deciphering the conversations of Lev Landau, who to the end of his days never suspected that his every word was recorded on tape. He often branded the Soviet state structure as fascism and complained about being reduced to the level of a 'scientific slave'.[8] But there never was even the slightest leak of sensitive scientific information.

The American challenge

The new high-speed computers that arrived at Los Alamos in the middle of 1949 immediately accelerated the work of the American hydrogen bomb researchers. However, Teller and his collaborators were to be profoundly disappointed. It turned out that their original model for the super-bomb was based on a misconception. Their calculations showed that the spontaneous reaction in deuterium took place not at pressures of hundred of thousands but at tens of millions of atmospheres. Conventional focused explosions could never provide pressure of such magnitude. Teller had come to a dead end. The figures suggested that it would be possible to reduce the level of necessary pressure if the deuterium was mixed with tritium, a still-heavier isotope of hydrogen. But unlike deuterium, tritium does not exist in a natural state. It is a radioactive isotope with a half-life of about 12 years and could be produced in special reactors, but the process would be slow and too expensive. Zeldovich's group, which had followed Teller down the same path, found itself in the same quandary: only a large quantity of tritium combined with deuterium could ensure a self-sustaining thermonuclear reaction. But a tritium bomb would be too expensive and was not a realistic possibility.

These failures provided a favourable moment to end the hydrogen bomb project once and for all. Nuclear weaponry could have been limited to the considerable destructive power of the atomic bomb. The United States still had a monopoly, and by the summer of 1949 had acquired an arsenal of 300 atomic bombs, which, according the projections of the military, was enough to destroy approximately 100 Soviet cities and industrial centres and to remove 30–40 per cent of the economic infrastructure of the country. But American strategists considered this atomic arsenal to be insufficient to ensure a decisive defeat of the Soviet Union in case of war. The American government decided to accumulate at least 1,000 bombs by 1953.

In the middle of September 1949, when the Americans discovered that the Soviet Union had successfully tested an atomic weapon, they faced a choice. Was it an opportunity to stop the nuclear arms race and start negotiations? Or was it now even more urgent to acquire a new super-weapon – the hydrogen bomb? The international situation favoured the first alternative. The Berlin crisis had come to an end in May 1949, when Stalin abandoned the blockade of West Berlin without achieving his objectives. In China the Civil War was over. Although the proclamation of the new People's Republic of China on 1 October 1949 signalled a strategic defeat for the United States in Asia, nevertheless the conflict was finally over. It was an ideal time to undertake new initiatives to create stability instead of escalating the arms race.

In the United States several committees and commissions were set up to work out a new strategy. The prevailing view emerging from these consultations was clear: the advent of nuclear weapons in the Soviet Union combined with the victory of the communists in China constituted a threat to the security of the United States. On 31 January 1950 President Truman publicly announced that he had directed the Atomic Energy Commission 'to continue working on all types of atomic weapons, including the so-called hydrogen or super-bomb'.[9] The next day Truman's decision was all over the front pages of the American newspapers, with editorial comment largely favourable. Having taken his decision and announcing it publicly, Truman was convinced that the scientists would be successful. The entire effort would now be directed towards practical realization, and the project to build a hydrogen bomb would receive the essential financial and logistical support.

Truman's decision represented a triumph for Edward Teller, yet at the same time it caused him great distress. He had invented the idea of the super-bomb, although no one else saw the need for it. The whole project was the product of one man's megalomania, and now that he had finally won acceptance for his plan, he was unable to come up with the necessary proof that a hydrogen bomb could actually be built. Several months after Truman's announcement, calculations from the super-computer made it clear that the temperature and pressure generated by an atomic explosion were insufficient to start the deuterium chain reaction. Only tritium, an isotope of hydrogen with two neutrons in the nucleus, making these nuclei less stable, was suitable. But according to calculations made at Los Alamos, obtaining one kilogram of tritium would be the equivalent of obtaining 70 kilograms of plutonium, enough to produce 10–12 conventional atomic bombs. And there was still no guarantee that tritium would work.

According to historians of the American nuclear programme, Teller was in a state of despair. The most expensive military project in American history had been started on his initiative, but it turned out that his basic assumptions were wrong. After Truman's announcement the laboratory at Los Alamos as well as several other atomic installations spent 14 months seeking alternative solutions, but the vital new idea did not emerge. There was only one consolation for Teller and his colleagues: if the Soviet Union was following the same path on the basis of information gleaned from discussions at the 1946 Los Alamos seminar (Klaus Fuchs had been arrested in England in January 1950), then Soviet scientists were also wasting an enormous amount of time and effort on a futile quest. This assumption, however, was mistaken. The hydrogen bomb project had also been stepped up in the Soviet Union after Truman's announcement, with a similar focus on practical realization rather than theory. But the work had departed from Teller's original concept, since Zeldovich had checked and rejected his approach earlier than Teller himself. By the end of 1949 the efforts of the Soviet physicists were already concentrated on perfecting the Sakharov–Ginsburg model for a hydrogen bomb.

The Americans were striving to build a weapon that would be thousands of times more powerful than a standard atomic bomb. The Sakharov–Ginsburg model had several limitations. The calculations did show its absolute feasibility. The processes of plutonium fission and deuterium fusion would take place not in two stages, but simultaneously. But the hydrogen component of the bomb could not be increased beyond a certain limit, and this meant a restriction on the power of the explosion. It could only be 20–40 times greater than the standard plutonium bomb, which of course was a great disappointment. In terms of production costs, the destructive potential of this weapon would be no greater than that of an improved and upgraded atomic bomb. After it was tested in 1953 no further research was done on this model and it was never put into serial production. Yet it would be difficult to exaggerate the moral and political effect of the successful test.

Sakharov's hydrogen bomb

Edward Teller, the theoretical inventor of the hydrogen bomb, significantly overestimated his own scientific ability. He was not a physicist of wide vision and he lacked the experience of working in several different areas of research. But he did have a talent for lobbying politicians. He was also fanatically anti-communist and was considered to be an extreme reactionary. Teller discredited himself among American physicists when he testified against Robert Oppenheimer at a special security hearing where Oppenheimer, the 'father' of the atomic bomb and former head of the Manhattan Project, was charged with disloyalty. Oppenheimer opposed the building of the hydrogen bomb and was deprived of access to military secrets as a result of the hearing. The whole affair attracted worldwide attention. Teller managed to convince the American administration that even if Soviet physicists finally managed to construct an atomic weapon, they would never be able to manage a hydrogen bomb. Because the physics involved was so complex, and the essential mathematical calculations were so vast in number, he was convinced that a thermonuclear weapon could only be developed in the United States. Truman also received reports from other experts who took the same view. Although there was no lack of appreciation of the abilities of Soviet physicists, the Americans believed that the Soviet Union did not possess the industrial or raw material base essential for the existence of an atomic industry. According to US experts, the main factor limiting Soviet possibilities was the absence of uranium and a uranium industry. In addition there was a lack of computers.

Teller's inflated opinion of himself had little justification. A large number of Soviet physicists, even within the younger generation, could claim to have a broader scientific outlook and clearly were more talented. Igor Tamm, the leading Soviet theoretical physicist, had a wider experience of research than Teller, embracing thermodynamics, quantum mechanics, physical optics and other fields as well as nuclear physics. Lev Landau was also considerably more gifted. The profound mathematical intelligence of the young Yakov Zeldovich, honed precisely because he lacked access to sophisticated computers, enabled him to detect the hopelessness of the original model earlier than Teller. According to Sakharov, by the time Tamm's department was included in the research in 1948, he had already become extremely sceptical about Teller's approach and his group started looking for new solutions.

Towards the end of 1948, with rather surprising speed, Sakharov and Ginsburg worked out a new model for a hydrogen bomb, which immediately was recognized to be convincing and potentially feasible. In this model, the details of which have never been disclosed and are still classified, the problem of pressure was somehow resolved by the distribution of the deuterium in layers within the actual plutonium charge, rather than in a cylinder (hence the nickname 'layer cake' in discussions of the model among physicists). The atomic explosion would provide the temperature and pressure needed for the beginning of a thermonuclear reaction. In place of tritium, which was too expensive and would have had to be artificially produced, Ginsburg suggested using the light isotope of lithium, a natural element. It is the lightest of the hard elements of the earth's core and is easily accessible. Notwithstanding the need to separate lithium-6 from the other isotopes, the production of lithium-6 was thousands of times cheaper than the production of tritium. The process of isolating lithium-6 (it amounts to 7.4 per cent of natural lithium) is also much easier than separating deuterium from natural hydrogen. Moreover, it was possible to amalgamate lithium with deuterium to form a new compound, lithium deuteride, which had advantages over a basic mixture of the two elements. When the nucleus of lithium-6 absorbs one neutron at the moment of atomic explosion, it splits into two nuclei, tritium and helium-4. This releases more energy than the merging of two nuclei of deuterium, but less energy than the merging of deuterium and tritium nuclei. The formula for the reaction is:

$$^{6}\text{Li} + \text{n} = {}^{3}\text{H} + {}^{4}\text{He} + 4.6 \text{ MeV}$$

The tritium produced in the first reaction then sets off the subsequent reaction with deuterium.

The problem with this model lies in the fact that the mass of material for the thermonuclear explosion has to be in a certain proportion to the mass of plutonium in the charge. The light and heavy elements are distributed in layers. It is impossible therefore to increase the dimensions of the charge except at the expense of the deuterium. The advantage, however, is that the limited size of such a bomb makes it possible to test the bomb itself rather than first having to test more complex intermediate systems. This project was approved by the Special Committee on atomic energy in 1949. It was also decided to set up a special department for Tamm's group at Yuli Khariton's secret facility in the Gorky region. Just at the time when Tamm and Sakharov first arrived there in the summer of 1949, final preparations were being made to test the Soviet atomic bomb. The successful test took place on 29 August 1949, after which all the principal participants were given leave for the first time in several years.

When the members of the Special Committee and the Technical Council returned from the special Black Sea resort which also was part of the atomic administrative set-up (physicists swam in the sea accompanied by bodyguards), important decisions were taken about future work on the hydrogen bomb. The installation KB-11 would be significantly expanded and given a new name: Arzamas-16. Military versions of the atomic bomb would be built and produced there. Work on the hydrogen bomb would proceed on the basis of both existing designs, one by Sakharov and the other by Teller in modified form. Zeldovich had already been at the installation for more than two years, and from 1950 Tamm's entire group moved permanently to Arzamas-16. As extensive new construction got under way, Arzamas-16 became a closed atomic city. Comfortable cottages were designed for the new inhabitants of the installation. The young scientists were expected to remain there for many years: at atomic installations, there was no possibility of simply deciding to leave or resign.

Arzamas-16

After two missions to Arzamas-16 in 1949 Tamm's group settled there permanently in 1950, not only to continue theoretical research but also to implement construction decisions. Complex new facilities were needed – a special reactor for the production of tritium as well as a unit to separate the light isotope of lithium from the natural element. The technology for producing deuterium had already been worked out at the Institute of Physical Problems under the leadership of Anatoly Aleksandrov. But it was necessary to construct a special facility to produce the large quantities of deuterium that were required. There were a number of other difficulties, since the materials needed to build a thermonuclear weapon were different from those used to assemble an atomic bomb.

The decision to dispatch Tamm's group to Arzamas-16 was taken in the form of a Resolution of the Council of Ministers, signed by Stalin. Nevertheless, despite such a weighty endorsement, the security service refused to allow a most important member of the group, Vitaly Ginsburg, to have access to the secret installation. Ginsburg was Tamm's deputy in the theoretical department and, with Sakharov, was the inventor of the 'layer cake' design. He was older and more experienced than Sakharov but, unlike him, was a member of the Party. However, Ginsburg's wife, Nina, had been in trouble when she was a student at Moscow University in 1945. She was arrested with a group of other students, accused of 'counter-revolutionary activity', and after nine months in prison was sent into exile (she was allowed to return to Moscow only in 1953 after Stalin's death). Ginsburg was therefore considered to be 'unreliable'. This deprived him of the glory of becoming known along with Sakharov as a 'father' of the first Soviet hydrogen bomb, but on the whole it worked to his advantage. He continued to do effective research at FIAN and in 1956 was elected to be a full member of the Academy of Sciences. On their visits to Moscow Tamm and Sakharov continued to consult him and occasionally relied on him for certain calculations. Now 86 years old, Ginsburg is still working and recently published two books, one of which is a scientific autobiography.[10]

Sakharov flew to Arzamas-16 with other members of Tamm's group in March 1950. Tamm arrived in April with rucksack and skis, hoping, apparently, to go walking in the surrounding forest. However, on the first attempt, according to Sakharov, even before they reached the nearest woods, 'all of a sudden someone behind us shouted: "Stop, don't move!".'

> We turned around and saw a squad of soldiers and an officer of the Border Guards pointing their Kalashnikovs directly at us: they meant business. We were taken to a truck and ordered to sit on the floor with our legs stretched out in front of us. Four soldiers sat on a bench across from us brandishing submachine guns. We were told that if anyone tried to escape or pulled up his legs, they would shoot without warning.[11]

The extremely tough regime at Arzamas-16 is explained by the fact that most of its construction workers were prisoners. The town, as Sakharov wrote in his memoirs, published in 1990,

> embodied a curious symbiosis between an ultra-modern research institute, with its experimental workshops and proving grounds – and a large labour camp. ... The workshops, the proving grounds, the roads, and even the housing for the Installation's employees had been built by prisoners. They themselves lived in barracks and were escorted to work by guard dogs. ... Every morning long grey lines of men in quilted jackets, guard dogs at their heels, passed by our curtained windows.[12]

As Sakharov found out soon after beginning his work, prisoners sent to Arzamas-16, even those serving a short sentence, had virtually no chance of ever being free.

> The authorities were faced with an awkward problem: what to do with prisoners when their terms were up. They might reveal the location of the Installation, still regarded as top secret. ... The authorities found a solution to their problem that was simple, ruthless, and absolutely illegal: released prisoners were permanently exiled to Magadan and other places where they couldn't tell any tales. There were two or three such deportations, one in the summer of 1950.[13]

This was also standard practice at Chelyabinsk-40. Sakharov found out about the exile of prisoners to Magadan completely by chance, three months after his arrival at the installation. One of the prisoners, Olga Shiryaeva, whom Sakharov had often met together with Zeldovich, was part of a group about to be sent to Magadan. An artist and architect by profession, she had originally been arrested for 'anti-Soviet slander'. At the installation she was assigned to paint the ceilings and walls of the bosses' houses as well as the clubhouse where the sociable Zeldovich quickly befriended her. Sakharov recalls in his memoirs:

> Zeldovich woke me in the middle of the night ... he was agitated. Could I lend him some money? Fortunately I had just been paid, and I gave him everything I had. A few days later I learned that Shiryaeva's

term had expired and that she was being sent to Magadan, far to the east, for 'permanent resettlement'. Zeldovich managed to get the money to her, and after some months I learned from him that Shiryaeva had given birth to their daughter in a building where the floor was covered in ice an inch thick.[14]

The child born in Magadan survived. Twenty years later, in 1970, Sakharov met her with her father in Kiev. But at Arzamas-16 the two leading theoreticians on whom the fate of the Soviet thermonuclear weapon depended and with it the foreign policy of the country, had been unable to deal with what would seem to be a rather less difficult problem: how to protect a pregnant woman from total lawlessness and possible death.

Although like Teller, Zeldovich had (earlier) understood that the first design for a two-stage hydrogen bomb was unworkable, theoretical work continued on variants of this model. The task was to find a method of compressing deuterium and tritium, or deuterium and lithium, providing not hundreds of thousands, but millions of atmospheres. Someone suggested using powerful laser beams concentrated at one spot. In the United States Stanislav Ulam, a talented physicist who had emigrated from Poland, came up with a possible solution for Teller. The details of this solution are still classified, but the first American hydrogen bomb came to be called the 'Ulam–Teller' model. What we do know is that in this model, very high pressure was achieved by the use of X-rays from fission explosions to compress the thermonuclear fuel; this was the concept of radiation implosion. It required a large amount of tritium, and new reactors were built to produce what was needed. The preparation of a special structure for a test proceeded at great pace, despite the fact that there was still no bomb. Work continued on Saturdays (in the USSR Saturday was still an ordinary working day, but this was normally not the case in the United States). The test was scheduled for 1 November 1952 on a small atoll in the southern part of the Pacific Ocean. They did manage to meet the deadline and the test went off successfully. The atoll was completely destroyed and the crater from the explosion (covered by water) was more than a mile in diameter. Measurements indicated that the force of the explosion was equivalent to ten megatons of TNT. This exceeded the power of the bomb dropped on Hiroshima a thousand-fold.

When the American government announced the results of their test, there were reactions of shock and dismay in other parts of the world. It was obvious that such an extraordinarily powerful bomb could never be used against military targets. If it was not a weapon of war, it could only be a weapon of genocide or political blackmail.

Sakharov's hydrogen bomb, rather more modest in terms of its explosive power, was prepared for testing without any special haste.

Stalin received a report about the American test in the middle of November, and this only served to confirm his conviction that the United States was seriously preparing for war with the Soviet Union. In November 1952 Dwight D. Eisenhower was elected president of the United States. The extreme haste of Teller and his colleagues in testing prematurely a rather crude construction weighing more than 60 tonnes only days before the election, reflected their unease about Truman's imminent departure from the White House. There was a mood of uncertainty. Would Eisenhower decide to stop the test? As an experienced general, he might well have had doubts about the usefulness of such an excessively powerful weapon.

At the beginning of 1953 it was reported to Stalin that work on the Soviet hydrogen bomb, 20 times more powerful than an atomic weapon, was close to completion.[15] However, Stalin did not live long enough to see the bomb tested. The test took place on 12 August 1953. The Americans referred to it as 'Joe-4', in honour of 'Uncle Joe', the nickname given to Stalin in the United States during the war.

Epilogue

After the successful test of the hydrogen bomb, all the main participants in the project were given a long holiday. When they returned from the south, almost all the key figures were generously rewarded, in accordance with a secret decree by the Presidium of the Supreme Soviet. Tamm, Sakharov, Aleksandrov, Zeldovich, Landau and the head of Arzamas-16, General Zernov, were all made Heroes of Socialist Labour. Younger scientists were promptly elected to the Academy of Sciences. Kurchatov and Khariton received the title of Hero of Socialist Labour for the third time. The scientists each received a special enhanced Stalin Prize of 500,000 roubles as well. Even Vitaly Ginsburg was not forgotten – he was awarded the Order of Lenin.

When the first Soviet atomic bomb was tested in 1949 a number of security service officers and heads of labour camps attached to the atomic installations were given the title Hero of Socialist Labour. But as a result of Beria's arrest, fewer were honoured in 1953. Lieutenant-General Pavel Meshik, Beria's deputy, had been responsible for security in all the industrial and scientific nuclear installations and was one of the organizers of 'permanent exile' in Magadan for prisoners who had completed their sentence. He had been arrested and shot together with Beria. The 'special exiles' did not begin returning to central regions of the country until after 1955, with more than 10,000 people coming from Magadan alone. But they were still not allowed to live in large cities or close to a border.

After the test of the first Soviet hydrogen bomb, the efforts of Sakharov, Zeldovich and others were directed towards building a more powerful two-stage hydrogen bomb, similar to the one created by the Americans. It did not take them much time. The bomb was not tested until two years later, on 22 November 1955, although it could have been exploded earlier. The bomb itself had been prepared straightaway, but it was to be tested by being dropped from a plane, rather than on the ground. This required considerable modification of the atomic testing ground at Semipalatinsk and the resettlement of tens of thousands of inhabitants in the adjoining regions. A new Arctic testing ground at Novaya Zemlya was equipped to test the next generation of even more powerful hydrogen bombs.

CHAPTER 7

Stalin and the Atomic Gulag

Zhores Medvedev

The first uranium gulag

The Soviet atomic era can be said to have begun on 27 November 1942, the date of a top-secret GKO Resolution No. 2542SS 'On the Mining of Uranium' ('SS' meant 'top secret'). At that time there were still no uranium mines in the USSR, although since the beginning of the century it had been known that uranium ore was present in the Taboshar region of Tadjikistan. This was to be the location of the first uranium mining complex. The task of producing uranium was assigned to the Commissariat for Non-Ferrous Metals, which already had other enterprises in Central Asia. An existing factory was re-equipped, and by May 1943 it was already supplying four tonnes of 40 per cent uranium concentrate a year. It was expected that production would increase three-fold by the end of 1943.[1] On 30 July 1943, dissatisfied with the lack of real progress in mining and enrichment, the GKO (Resolution No. 3834SS) enlisted the services of several more commissariats and departments to ensure that all necessary equipment and cadres would be provided. The State Geology Committee and the commissariats for ferrous metals, machine construction, coal and ammunition were directed to contribute to the effort. The State Committee on Higher Education was charged with providing 18 physicists and chemists to assist with uranium production as well as 450 students to work during the academic holidays.

But the latest GKO directive turned out to be rather unrealistic. It was first necessary to dig the new mines, then extract the ore and transport it along mountain tracks on donkeys and camels to the central enrichment plant at Leninabad. This was hardly work for students during their holidays. Molotov was Deputy Chairman of the GKO, and his staff was responsible for devising the means of carrying out GKO resolutions.

Igor Kurchatov, who had by this time been appointed to be scientific head of the entire atomic project, was demanding 200 tonnes of pure uranium in order to begin work on the bomb – 50 tonnes for the experimental model and 150 tonnes for the industrial reactor. At that point he had only 700 grams of pre-war uranium powder. They seemed to be facing an insoluble impasse. The United States had had the foresight to gain control of uranium mines in the Congo, South Africa and Canada after the normal export possibilities afforded by Europe had disappeared. In Europe uranium was mined in Saxony, in the former Czechoslovakia and in France, and there were also deposits in Bulgaria. The American administration knew that there were no uranium mines in the Soviet Union, and this was the main source of their hope that they could maintain a nuclear monopoly, particularly after 1943. Towards the end of 1943 the United States and Britain received the good news that the uranium project in Germany had virtually come to a halt following an Allied bombardment that destroyed the factories producing heavy water in Norway. The German project was based on reactors that used heavy water (D_2O) to slow the neutrons in the chain reaction, since this required significantly smaller amounts of uranium. By the end of 1944 it was clear that the war in Europe would come to an end without the use of atomic weapons. But there was no question of halting the Manhattan Project. The possession of an atomic weapon would soon begin to have a different function.

Two years after the original GKO resolution, there was still no supply of pure metal uranium in the Soviet Union. No one was willing to work in mines in the wilderness of Central Asia, and at the end of 1944 only 500 people were employed in the entire uranium industry. There were no proper living facilities or any kind of technical support structure. Then geologists discovered more uranium deposits on the border between Tadjikistan and the Uzbek and Kirghiz Republics. But these deposits were located at a distance of between 100 and 450 kilometres from the enrichment plant at Leninabad. The transportation capacity of donkeys was not very high – each could only carry 75–100 kilos of ore along the mountain tracks. For each tonne of 40 per cent uranium concentrate, approximately 2,000 tonnes of ore had to be brought to the plant. Even in high-quality ore, the actual metal component amounted to only one-tenth of 1 per cent.

Given the Soviet conditions of those days, it would not be difficult to predict how the problem was solved. On 8 December 1944 Stalin signed GKO Resolution No. 7102SS which ordered the whole programme for mining and processing uranium to be transferred from the Commissariat for Non-Ferrous Metals to the Commissariat for Internal Affairs and put under Beria's control. This would solve the personnel problem. According to the next GKO Resolution, signed by Stalin on 15 May 1945, a unified plant complex (Kombinat No. 6) was established for mining and processing uranium ore throughout the Central Asian region. A colonel of the NKVD, Boris Chirkov, was appointed to be the first director.[2]

Once they were put in charge of the uranium mines, the leaders of the NKVD wasted little time in making appropriate arrangements. In February it was decided that 'special exiles' – deported Crimean Tartars who had been working on other projects – would be sent to the uranium complex along with prisoners who had some useful skill: mining specialists, geologists, chemists, mechanics and energy workers who would be selected from various labour camps.[3] By August 1945 Colonel Chirkov, soon to become a general, commanded a workforce of 2,295 prisoners. These were hardly ordinary *zeks,* as convicts were commonly called in Russian, given their previous experience of minerals, mining, chemicals and technical work, and they included men repatriated from Germany who had worked in German enterprises. There were also Vlasovites; however, after special intercession by the NKVD, the government decided to exclude them from PGU construction work in Leninabad.[4]

Uranium production was transformed. By the end of 1945 Kombinat No. 6 had processed approximately 10,000 tonnes of uranium ore which yielded seven tonnes of uranium concentrate, and 35,000 tonnes of uranium were processed during 1946. By the end of 1947 Kombinat No. 6 consisted of seven uranium enrichment plants that were supplied with ore from 18 mines; 66 tonnes of 40 per cent uranium concentrate were extracted from 176,000 tonnes of uranium ore, which meant almost 25 tonnes of metal.

In 1948 the production of uranium concentrate doubled. But this still was not enough to accommodate the needs of the industrial reactor that had been built near Kyshtym. A large part of the uranium fuel loaded into this reactor was either 'trophy' uranium, seized in 1945, or uranium from mines in Czechoslovakia and Germany. The decisive role of imports only began to decline in 1950, when more than 600,000 tonnes of ore per year were mined at Leninabad. There were 18,000 workers at Kombinat No. 6 at that time, of whom 7,210 were prisoners.[5] At the beginning of 1953, however, almost half of all the uranium loaded into the new generation of reactors was still coming from mines in Czechoslovakia and East Germany. Until 1952 these enterprises were controlled by the NKVD/MVD. The main workforce was made up of German prisoners of war or Germans who had been interned in Hungary and Czechoslovakia. In 1948 almost 50,000 prisoners of war were working in these mines, but from the beginning of 1950, this source of labour virtually disappeared when the government made arrangements for their release and repatriation.

The expansion of the uranium gulag

In 1950 the uranium mines of Central Asia were producing 80 per cent of all the uranium ore mined in the Soviet Union. In addition to more than 7,000 prisoners who had to be kept under guard, there were also several thousand workers from deported nationalities – Crimean Tartars and Moldavians. The Moldavians, who were mostly from Bessarabia, were legally given the right to return to their homeland in 1948. However, those who were working at Kombinat No. 6 were arbitrarily retained 'for reasons of state security'.[6] Uranium mining was one of the most closely guarded state secrets, and there may have been a leak if the Moldavians were permitted to return to Bessarabia. The authorities did make one concession: in 1950 they began transferring Moldavian workers from the face of the mine or from other life-threatening jobs to less dangerous positions elsewhere in the complex.

In 1946 uranium deposits were discovered in the rocks of Kolyma, which were known to be rich in rare metals. There had been a fall in the numbers of prisoners in the Magadan region during the war, partly because of the high death rate and also because of the decision by the GKO and the commander of the Far Eastern Army, General Apanasenko, to mobilize prisoners for service in the Red Army. The camps had contained a large number of military men who had fallen victim to the waves of terror in 1937–38. But in 1946 the labour camps in the Far East were filling up again, this time with deported nationalists from the western Ukraine and the Baltic. They began to build new uranium mines in 1947 that became part of the vast Dalstroi camp system in the remote northeastern part of the country (Magadan was the capital). Here there were prisoners who almost certainly would never be released. Their number included Trotskyists, Mensheviks, SRs and anarchists as well as members of nationalist, terrorist and other 'anti-Soviet' groups. The sending of ordinary convicts to these special camps was prohibited. The regime was exceptionally harsh, but perhaps for conspiratorial reasons the camps, rather than being assigned numbers, were given picturesque names evoking the natural beauty of mountains, lakes or trees. Similarly the pits and mines dispersed across this infinite territory were called 'Hope', 'Victory', 'Desire', etc.

The Kolyma uranium ore was rather inferior to that of Central Asia. But although the quality was poor, extraction took place on a very large scale. A large enrichment plant was built to obtain uranium concentrate using a centrifugal technique. The process was simple. Uranium ore was crushed by huge millstones, turned into a water suspension pulp and put into the centrifuge. The particles of ore with a higher concentration of uranium, which is the heaviest substance to be found on the earth's surface, precipitate more rapidly. The process is repeated several times, and the uranium concentrate undergoes a drying process. This enrichment plant was built in Butugychag, a camp of the 'Beregovoi Group'. Most of the inmates of this camp were from the western Ukraine which had been 'cleansed' of nationalists during the period 1945–47. There were more than 30,000 prisoners in the Beregovoi camp system in 1951.[8] It was made up of several separate units. Nickel, cobalt, coal and gold were also mined, as well as uranium. In the previous chapter I described the practice in Arzamas-16 of sending prisoners who had completed their sentences to 'permanent exile' in Magadan. In the documents of Glavpromstroi of the MVD, Arzamas-16 was give the codename 'Construction 880'. The relevant instruction was found recently in the archives of the MVD. Dated 7 December 1948, Order No. 001441 directs that 'All 2000 prisoners released from work at Construction 880 are to be sent to special camp No. 5'.[9] The camp was within the Dalstroi system. This practice was also referred to by Sakharov in his memoirs.[10]

The atomic centre at Sarovo, known as Arzamas-16, a settlement 75 kilometres from Arzamas town, was an ultra-secret location, for it was here that atomic bombs, both for testing and for military use, were to be constructed. This atomic city, known at the time as KB-11, was built by prisoners. However, on 2 and 31 May 1948 the Presidium of the Supreme Soviet decreed an amnesty for all prisoners serving short sentences. A recent history of Arzamas-16 states that 'on 30th August 1948, 2,292 prisoners in the camp were released.' Officials wanted to keep most of them at Arzamas-16 as free workers, since for reasons of state security, the MVD would not allow them to leave the territory. But the account goes on to say that 'the prisoners released from the camp had no clothes, their attitude to work was negative. ... Many openly declared that, having served their time, they did not want to be in prison again.'[11] And here the account stops. The author, L. Goleusova, gives no further information about the ultimate fate of these people. Only the text of MVD Order No. 001441, referred to previously, suggests how the problem was solved, with the two zeros before the number signifying that the order had been signed by Stalin.[12]

In 1951–53 new deposits of uranium ore were found in more accessible places – the Krivorozhsk region of the Ukraine, near Pyatigorsk in the Northern Caucasus, the Chita region, and also close to the city of Shevchenko on the eastern shore of the Caspian Sea. In each of these potential mining sites the first thing that happened was the construction of labour camps and the enclosure of vast stretches of land, which then became restricted territory. Concentration camp labour continued to be used for mining uranium long after 1953. Only in the 1960s, when blasting techniques replaced manual labour at the face of the mine and Khrushchev had inaugurated a policy of general rehabilitations and amnesties, was this practice finally curtailed. The 'uranium cities', however, remained 'closed' until the beginning of 1991.

The birth of the atomic gulag

An atomic gulag was rather different from a uranium gulag, since the building of atomic reactors, radiochemical factories and isotope separation plants required much more highly skilled workers than the mining of uranium. There was also the question of staffing a large number of secret scientific institutes and laboratories.

In 1989, on the 40th anniversary of the first testing of the Soviet atomic bomb, Kurchatov's deputy at Laboratory No. 2 and later his first biographer, Professor Igor Golovin, was asked in an interview for *Moscow News*: 'Was prison labour used on the atomic project?' He replied very candidly:

> On the widest scale! All the establishments, mines, atomic cities, even our institute in Moscow [then Laboratory No. 2, now the Kurchatov Institute of Atomic Energy – Zh.M.], prisoners worked in all these places. Have you seen our club? In that building, there was a prison. It was surrounded by a thick, high wall with machine gun turrets at each corner. The structure that contained the first atomic reactor – we called it 'the boiler' – all the buildings next to it, they were all put up by the hands of prisoners. And our modern, international centre for research at Dubna – here too, its first builders were prisoners. ... There were many thousands of them. All the specialists saw it and knew all about it.[13]

Obtaining and purifying uranium was only the preliminary stage, the easiest one, on the path to constructing an atomic bomb. The second stage, already obvious by 1940, was the process of separating natural uranium into the isotopes 238 and 235. Only isotope 235, comprising just 0.7 per cent of the isotopes in natural uranium, is suitable for the preparation of an atomic bomb. When a neutron strikes the nucleus of uranium-235, this causes it to split, leading to the release of two, sometimes three, free neutrons, and the whole process takes on the character of an accelerating, explosive chain reaction. But critical mass is necessary, because where there is only a small quantity of uranium, a large number of the neutrons released at the disintegration of the nucleus escape into the surrounding space and do not collide with new nuclei. The design of the first uranium bomb is therefore relatively simple: an explosive wave is used to create an instantaneous merging of two or three 'sub-critical' amounts of uranium-235 in order to produce one 'critical' or 'super-critical' mass, which contains at its centre a source of neutrons – an initiator. Calculations showed that the 'critical mass' of uranium-235 was roughly equal to 25–40 kilograms. In order to isolate this amount of uranium-235, a process of uranium hexafluoride gas diffusion was invented; given that it was a complex and multi-stage procedure, there was a probability that some gas would be lost in the process. It was therefore necessary to have several tonnes of pure natural uranium.

The critical mass of plutonium is much lower. However, plutonium is produced by an extremely complex and lengthy process that involves the controlled disintegration of uranium-235 in a special reactor. The neutrons that are then released are 'absorbed' into the nucleus of uranium-238 to form, via the appearance of neptune-239 in an intermediate reaction, the nucleus of plutonium-239 with a tinge of plutonium-240. In order to start a chain reaction, an industrial reactor using graphite as a neutron moderator would require, at a minimum, approximately 150 tonnes of natural uranium. Nevertheless Kurchatov decided to begin the Soviet nuclear weapons programme with a plutonium rather than a uranium bomb. Because of the shortage of uranium, this seemed to be a more economical approach. When 'spent' uranium is unloaded from the reactor, the uranium-235 content (after the isolation of plutonium) is only slightly lower than at the beginning of the process, decreasing from 0.71 per cent to 0.69 per cent. Therefore such uranium, once it has been regenerated in a radiochemical plant, can still serve as the raw material for uranium bombs. The plant that had already been built at Verkh-Neivinsk in the Sverdlovsk region to produce bomb-quality uranium-235 would be using regenerated rather than natural uranium. Unfortunately regenerated uranium contains a large number of radioactive contaminants which makes working with it a much more hazardous undertaking.

Construction work began at both atomic centres, Verkh-Neivinsk (Sverdlovsk-44) and Kyshtym (Chelyabinsk-40), in accordance with a resolution of the Sovnarkom dated 23 March 1946 and signed by Stalin. Although Kurchatov, Vannikov, Beria and other bosses of the atomic industry often took initiatives on a variety of questions, it was standard practice to have all final decisions personally approved by Stalin. This would ensure the support of other ministries and departments. Even where a seemingly trivial question was concerned, the appearance of Stalin's signature underscored the point that the atomic projects had to have absolute priority.

The construction of Chelyabinsk-40 got under way long before a sufficient quantity of uranium had been accumulated. A 100,000-kilowatt underground reactor had to be built in the industrial zone. There also had to be a large radiochemical plant for the separation of plutonium, a factory to produce plutonium metal, waste disposal facilities for products with high and medium levels of radioactivity and also a large number of other subsidiary factories and plants. It was planned to build housing for 25–30,000 inhabitants some ten kilometres from the industrial zone with an electric power station and other facilities. Almost adjacent to the industrial zone, there would be camps for prisoners and barracks for army construction units. The prisoners and conscripts were the first to arrive in the region, accompanied by the MVD troops who were guarding the convoys. Within the MVD, Chelyabinsk-40 was given the code name 'Construction-859', while the reactor and radiochemical plant, built at the same time, were known as 'Kombinat No. 817'.

The nearest reserves of prisoners and special deportees were located in the industrial districts of Chelyabinsk. It was from here that the first 10,000 prisoners were transferred to Kyshtym, on Beria's orders, in July 1946.[14] In October the prison camp at Chelyanbinsk-40 was given proper status. By the end of 1947 it held 20,376 prisoners under the supervision of a general in the MVD engineers, Mikhail Tsarevsky.[15] In 1948, as pressure increased to speed up the work, the overall number of construction workers, prisoners and soldiers from the MVD engineering regiments reached 45,000 people. Tsarevsky was in charge of the camp, now divided into 11 sections, and also of all the construction activities taking place in the industrial complex.

There was no real differences between prisoners and soldiers in the army construction units. They were both controlled by the same MVD department – Industrial Construction (Glavpromstroi). Both contingents were largely made up of former Soviet prisoners of war or repatriated workers who had some experience of mining and construction from their time in German camps. One of the men who helped build Kombinat No. 817, Anatoly Vyshimirsky, testified 40 years later:

> I served in the army in Sverdlovsk in a tank training regiment. ... In 1946 a battalion was formed from soldiers on the course and sent to Kyshtym in the Chelyabinsk region. Basically, it was those who had lived in occupied territory during the war, including some who had fought. To put it bluntly, we were all, so to say, sub-human, disgraced by the irremovable stain of German occupation. ... When we got to Kyshtym, we found other battalions of army construction workers who had arrived earlier. There were also former prisoners of war who had not been allowed to go home after they were freed from German camps. Many of them were no longer young; they had fought at Khasan and Khalkhin-Gol, in the Finnish campaign and even in the Civil War. One thing united them – they had all passed through the circles of the fascist hell. And this was the sum total of their guilt ... there were also ordinary prisoners. ... But our conditions were not

very different from the labour camps. It was as if we were all in one big camp.[16]

This picture was confirmed by another witness, Anatoly Osipov, from the Kalinin region:

On the 13th May 1946, our military unit (346 OPAB) was disbanded, and we youngsters, born in 1925–26, were sent on a troop train to Kyshtym in the Urals ... companies and battalions were formed at the station. All the military units were codified. Our regiment was called V/Unit 05/08. ... We army construction workers were the first to start digging a huge foundation pit under what was to be 'Unit No. 1', a building with an undisclosed function. Afterwards, prisoners built the structure and also the stuff inside. ... Frontline soldiers who had been taken prisoner were classified according to which army had liberated them. There were four categories: those who had been liberated by the Americans, by the British, or by Soviet troops and those who had never lived under occupation. Soldiers freed by the Americans were considered to be the most suspect; less so if it was the British or even better, the Russians, and finally there were the 'clean' ones. Conditions in the barracks as well as food and clothing corresponded to these categories.[17]

Accounts by prisoners who worked at the installation during this period paint a similar picture. According to I.P. Samokhvalov:

I was still at school, living in Chelyabinsk. They arrested me when I was in the 8th class and not yet 16. I was tried under Article 58 paragraph 10 and given five years for 'anti-Soviet' behaviour. To begin with I was taken to the 'death colony' at Karabash. At the end of 1946 we were sent to Kyshtym. ... I was allocated to camp section No. 9 in the working zone, where units A, B and Ts were being built. ... When the buildings were finished, we installed huge, round containers. ... It was there that I was freed from imprisonment ... but, in September 1949, they began to dismiss free workers, both single and family men. They deported us in cattle cars equipped with searchlights and an escort. ... When we arrived at the port of Nakhodka, the whole trainload was transferred to the steamer, *Soviet Latvia*, and we sailed across the Sea of Okhotsk to Magadan. ... We were distributed among the different mines. I ended up in a mine called 'Desire'.[18]

Most other camps in the atomic gulag were also established in 1946. The first camp for prisoners, at KB-11, was set up in May 1946 on land near the little town and monastery of Sarovo – the local population had been evicted during the war to make way for a factory producing shells for Katyushas. The prisoners had been taken from nearby Mordovian camps. This was to be the site of the most secret of all atomic cities, later known as Arzamas-16. By the end of 1947 there were more than 10,000 prisoners in the camp.[19]

They began building the atomic town Verkh-Neivinsk (Sverdlovsk-44) in 1946, although work on the industrial separation of uranium isotopes 235 and 238 did not start until after the first Soviet atomic bomb had been tested successfully in August 1949. Around that time a new camp was set up holding approximately 10,000 inmates. During the period of active work at this centre, 1950–51, the number of prisoners increased to more than 18,000.

Sacrifices

Every nuclear reactor has a tall ventilation stack to disperse the gaseous products of nuclear fission into the atmosphere. Some of these gases, such as iodine-131, are successfully reduced by the filters. But even to this day, no way has been found of filtering inert radioactive gases such as krypton-85 or xenon-133 with absorbents of any kind, precisely because they are inert. They are simply dispersed over a wide area via the high ventilation stacks, and, thanks to a short period of disintegration, there is no accumulation in the atmosphere. But at Chelyabinsk-40 the tallest ventilation stack, which was at the radiochemical plant and 151 metres high, emitted gases, aerosols and dust from a number of radionuclides, including uranium and plutonium. There was almost always yellow smoke billowing out of the chimney. This smoke contained nitric acid, which is used during the first stage of processing 'burned' uranium blocks from the reactor, and it killed the trees for many kilometres around the industrial zone. Only prison labourers were used to build what was then the highest chimney in the Soviet Union – 11 metres in diameter at the bottom and 6 metres at the top. Anatoly Osipov worked at Chelyabinsk-40 and explains:

> Only 'condemned men' were sent to work there, men with sentences of 10 to 15 years. Why 'condemned'? There were no safeguards. The chimney was rocking by two to three metres, and there were frequent accidents as every day workers crashed to their deaths.[21]

But the main dangers throughout Chelyabinsk-40 were linked to radiation. At the time the harmful effects of radiation were heavily underestimated, and almost nothing was known of its genetic and carcinogenic effects. The long-term consequences of radiation were also unknown. People were not even aware of the symptoms of radiation sickness. During the first months of operation, there was virtually no measurement or control of dosages at the industrial reactor or the radiochemical plant. 'Nobody knew the degree of irradiation being suffered by workers and engineers.'[22] In later years they began to use photo dosimeters – the dose of radiation was measured by the degree of darkness on the film. Such dosimeters were imprecise, and the extent of the dose was determined only after the event, at the end of the working day, or even once a week. Only high-energy external gamma radiation was monitored. Respirator 'petals' to protect the lungs from radioactive dust finally appeared in 1952. Special regulations on the control of conditions affecting workers' health had been introduced in 1949 following several instances of lethal irradiation. But even in 1951 workers in the radiochemical plant were exposed to average doses of 113 *ber* (biological equivalent of Roentgen) a year. This was 30 times higher than the maximum permitted dose.[23]

Everyone suffered irradiation: prisoners, civilian workers and senior personnel. According to one of the first doctors to work in Chelyabinsk-40, A.K. Guskova, the local museum contains film from Kurchatov's dosimeter reading that showed a single-day dose of radiation of 42 r.[24] A dose of 100 Roentgens could cause radiation sickness.

The contamination of the entire territory around the radiochemical complex was so severe that even people working on the land were endangered. According to Guskova:

> In 1951, Dr. G.D. Baisogolov and I treated 13 prisoners in the camp barracks who had been irradiated. Three of them were suffering from acute radiation sickness, and one had received a fatal dose. They had been exposed while digging a trench next to the building that contained the radiochemical plant. The basic active factor was external gamma-beta radiation from soil contaminated with nuclides.[25]

During the start-up of the reactor and the first weeks of operation, there were many small accidents and unanticipated problems. In order to solve these problems workers were casually exposed to fatal doses of radiation.[26] There was a considerable amount of exposure to radiation during the separation of plutonium in the radiochemical plant. According to official data '2,089 workers were diagnosed with radiation sickness during the period of organizing the start of plutonium production at the complex.'[27] A recent article by Vladislav Larin discusses the reasons for a good number of these cases.[28] However, there are no statistics that distinguish between the radiation problems affecting prisoners or soldiers as opposed to civilian personnel. Prisoners were never given their own dosimeters, and in any case there were no norms to limit a maximum degree of exposure. Nor was there any dosimeter control among the people who were living along the Techa River, despite the fact that fluid emissions from the radiochemical plant were pouring into the water. The population living near the high fence of the industrial zone had no idea what was going on. The whole question attracted attention only after a massive outbreak of radiation sickness among the inhabitants of villages close to the plant. As stated in a recent official report:

Some 124,000 people living in the flood lands of the Techa river in the Chelyabinsk and Kurgansk regions suffered from the radioactive pollution of the river and its banks. 28,000 people suffered from high doses of radiation (up to 170 ber). 935 cases of radiation sickness were recorded. About 8,000 inhabitants from 21 locations were resettled.[29]

This resettlement, however, did not take place until 1955. During the years 1948–53, top priority was given to the maintenance of absolute secrecy about the atomic complex, and this meant that tens of thousands of inhabitants of the flood plain of the Techa River continued using the river water for everyday purposes – for food, livestock, kitchen gardens, etc. The health of the local population was sacrificed for the sake of what was viewed as state security.

Dealing with the first catastrophe

The first really serious accident at Chelyabinsk-40 took place in January 1949. It turned into a radioactive catastrophe only because of a decision taken by the leaders of the Soviet atomic project. Details of the event remained secret until 1995, and the number of victims remains unknown to this day. But it is possible that even more people died here than at Chernobyl.

Approximately 150 tonnes of uranium had been loaded into the first industrial reactor. On 8 June 1948 it was brought to the 'critical' stage and on 22 June it reached its designed power of 100,000 kilowatts. Reactors intended for the production of plutonium were simpler in construction than the reactors of the next generation, which were built to produce electricity. In energy reactors the generation of steam takes place under high pressure while military reactors need only water to cool the uranium blocks. The small, cylindrical uranium blocks, 37 mm in diameter and 102.5 mm high, were covered by a thin aluminium casing. They were loaded into aluminium tubes, which had an internal diameter of a little over 40 mm and a height of about ten metres. These in turn were placed in a graphite cladding. The function of the graphite was to slow down the neutrons during the chain reaction, but this only worked in dry conditions. The uranium-235 fission chain reaction begins when the reactor has been loaded with approximately 150 tonnes of natural uranium. Water circulating inside the aluminium tubes prevents the uranium blocks from overheating as a result of the fission process or the accumulation of hot radionuclides. There were 1,124 tubes in the first reactor, containing about 40,000 uranium blocks. During the uranium-235 fission chain reaction, the neutrons, slowed by the graphite, generate plutonium-239 from uranium-238. Depending on the operating conditions of the reactor, the process of accumulating plutonium can go on for more than a year. The construction of the reactor allows it to 'unload' the uranium blocks from the aluminium tubes into a pool of water below. After immersion in water for several weeks in order to ensure the disintegration of the highly radioactive and gaseous short-lived nuclides, the blocks can then be transferred to the radiochemical plant.

In those days, there had not yet been any long-term research into the behaviour of metals, particularly aluminium, in conditions of powerful neutron irradiation and high temperatures. Therefore it came as a total surprise when the aluminium tubes began to leak, wetting the graphite. Powerful irradiation together with the constant contact with water and graphite at high temperatures had severely corroded the aluminium. After the reactor had been running for five months it became obvious that it could not continue to operate. This was no longer a local mishap – it was a major blow to the whole programme. On 20 January 1949 the reactor was stopped, and Stalin was informed.

For those in charge of the atomic project, there were two ways out of the situation: they could choose a safe option or embark on a course of action that would demand considerable human sacrifice. The first possibility would have been relatively easy. It would have meant unloading the uranium blocks along the emergency technical channels into the pool of water below and then gradually moving them to the radiochemical plant where any accumulated plutonium could be isolated. But this approach was problematic for a number of reasons. At the time of ejection from the reactor, occasionally with an active 'push', there was a danger that the thin aluminium casing of the blocks could be damaged, and such blocks would no longer be fit for secondary use. No one could calculate precisely whether enough plutonium had accumulated in the uranium load in order to make at least one nuclear bomb. It was also not known how much plutonium would be lost in the radiochemical separation process. It was important to have some reserves of plutonium. But there were not enough stocks of fresh uranium to provide a second new load for the reactor. It would also be essential to replace all the aluminium tubes. The new tubes would be given a strong, anodal, anti-corrosive covering in one of the aircraft factories.

The second, highly dangerous option was as follows: they could either carefully extract all the uranium blocks from the top of the tube by means of a special sucking apparatus or remove them, together with the tubes, up into the central operating hall of the reactor. After this it would be necessary to sort out the undamaged blocks by hand for possible secondary use. The graphite cladding, which was made up of large graphite bricks, could be dismantled by hand, dried out and used again. When the new aluminium tubes with anti-corrosive covering arrived, it would be possible to re-load the reactor and bring it up to capacity power.

After five months in the reactor, the uranium blocks were highly radioactive – it was a question of millions of curies. A considerable accumulation of radionuclides made the blocks extremely hot – temperatures exceeded 100 degrees centigrade – and there was gamma radiation from various isotopes, including caesium, iodine and barium. A.K. Kruglov, who was working at Chelyabinsk-40 at the time, admitted that 'it was impossible to extract the blocks without irradiating those doing the work.'[30] Kurchatov certainly understood this as well. They would have to make a choice: 'should they protect people or save the uranium load and reduce losses in the production of plutonium? ... It was the second course that was chosen by the PGU authorities and also by the scientific leadership.'[31] In other words, it was a decision taken jointly by Beria, Vannikov (the head of the PGU), his deputy Zavenyagin and Kurchatov himself.

Vannikov, Zavenyagin and Kurchatov supervised the work and were almost continuously present at the installation. Beria received regular reports and put pressure on the Ministry of Aviation Industry to made sure that the new aluminium tubes were delivered on time. It took 39 days to extract 39,000 uranium blocks – 150 tonnes of uranium – from the reactor. Each block had to be inspected individually. Yefim Slavsky, who was the chief engineer and subsequently in charge of the entire Soviet nuclear industry for many years, witnessed the whole operation. In memoirs, published in 1997, several years after his death, he wrote:

> It was decided to save the uranium load (and the production of plutonium) at a very high price – the inevitable irradiation of the personnel involved.

> From that moment on, the entire male workforce of the installation, including thousands of prisoners, took part in the operation to remove the tubes and extract the partially damaged blocks; all together 39,000 uranium blocks were extracted and processed by hand.

Kurchatov personally took part in the work. He was the only one at the time who knew how to recognize defective blocks through his experience of working on the experimental reactor at Laboratory No. 2 in Moscow. Slavsky continues:

> No words could have replaced the force of his personal example. Kurchatov was the first to step into the nuclear hell, into the central hall of the damaged reactor full of radioactive gases. He supervised the dismantling of the damaged channels and personally examined defects on the uranium blocks, piece by piece. Nobody thought about the dangers then – we, of course, simply didn't know anything. But Igor Vasilevich did know, yet he refused to retreat before the terrible force

of the atom. ... For him, erasing the failure turned out to be fatal. He
paid a cruel price for our atomic bomb. ... It was fortunate that he did
not continue sorting out the blocks to the end; if he had stayed in the
hall any longer, we would have lost him then and there.[32]

It remains unclear from Slavsky's account how long Kurchatov
remained in the central hall of the reactor. The work of sorting out
the highly radioactive uranium blocks went on around the clock in
six-hour shifts. There is no available record of dosimeter readings in
various parts of the central hall above the reactor, possibly because
the dosimeters were often not operating. Kurchatov probably worked
no more than two or three shifts because the radioactive danger was
so great. But as Slavsky wrote, even this turned out to be fatal.
Kurchatov suffered medium-intensity radiation sickness, which does
not automatically lead to cancer or acute radiation sickness but it
does harm the entire organism and brings about premature ageing.
In the first weeks after this kind of sub-lethal dose, the basic immune
system (the bone marrow) and intestinal functions are damaged. It is
difficult to say how long Kurchatov was ill after his courageous, even
desperate action. On the whole, biographies of Kurchatov do not
discuss the events at the beginning of 1949. The accidents at the
industrial reactor are referred to rather cryptically: 'Everything did
not always go smoothly, as often happens with something new.'[33]
Undoubtedly it was the exposure to radiation on at least several
occasions that drastically shortened his life. In the 1950s Kurchatov
rapidly became physically much weaker, was often ill, and died in
1960 at the age of 57.

MVD General Avrami Zavenyagin, Beria's deputy, was also irra-
diated while supervising the work of the prisoners and suffered
irreparable damage to his health. He died in 1958 at the age of 55.
Professor Boris Nikitin, the head of the radiochemical plant who also
took part in the identification of defective uranium blocks, suffered
more seriously. The defective blocks had been brought directly to his
sector of the installation. He fell victim to a more acute form of
radiation sickness which became chronic, and he died of it in 1952 at
the age of 46.[34] There are other known cases of early deaths linked to
radiation exposure among the scientists and engineers involved in
dealing with this accident, although it would be more accurate to
say, 'involved in saving the uranium load'. As for the thousands of
prisoners who for five weeks of uninterrupted labour, working in
shifts, unloaded and sorted the 39,000 blocks to save 150 tonnes of
uranium – how, when or where did they fall ill and die? No one
seems to know. These were the people who did the crucial physical
work that made the whole operation possible.

The forced labour camp at Chelyabinsk-40, known as ITL Construction 859, was reorganized on the orders of the MVD on 31

January 1949. It was given a new designation: ITL Construction 247. Tsarevsky remained as head of the camp. During 1949 the number of prisoners fell by 3,000.[35] There could have been various reasons for this reduction in the camp population. In any case the basic construction work was over.

'Released' to Magadan

Andrei Sakharov described how prisoners working at Arzamas-16 were sent into permanent exile after completing their sentences, to Magadan and elsewhere, in order to preserve secrecy.[36] This sometimes happened at other atomic sites as well, although it was not universal practice. Some of the best-qualified builders were offered the chance to stay on as 'free workers'. The transfer of workers from one installation to another was categorically forbidden – only senior scientific and administrative personnel were allowed to know about the existence of other sites. On 11 August 1948 Stalin signed a resolution of the Council of Ministers 'On the temporary special regime for former prisoners, who remain as free workers at plants nos. 817, 813, 550, 814'.[37] According to MVD classification, these numbers referred to Chelyabinsk-40 (there were two sections), Verkh-Neivinsk (Sverdlovsk-44) and Arzamas-16. It was less complicated to deal with the military construction units. The Council of Ministers simply decided to postpone their demobilization. A new resolution was issued along with a secret directive of the Presidium of the Supreme Soviet 'On the relocation of working contingents to special sites established by the MVD'.[38]

The main rationale for these resolutions was the determination to ensure that the existence of the atomic installations was kept secret. This is borne out by the testimony of I.P. Samokhvalov, quoted previously. Some of the military construction workers, especially those who had been former prisoners of war, fell into the category of 'relocation'. According to Tamara L., who worked at Chelyabinsk-40 where she married a soldier-builder,

> They were soldiers, but what kind? It became clear only when the building work was over. We found out then that my husband and I and our three-month-old son could not go where we wanted but only where we were sent. In August 1949 we were put on a freight train to Soviet Gavan and then in the hold of the steamer *Nogin* on plank beds to Kolyma. ... In Magadan they explained about demobilization, but forced the soldiers to agree to a three-year contract. We were sent to a mine called 'Desire', which before us had been worked by convicts, and we lived in common barracks – mud huts – men, women and children all together.[39]

Samokhvalov was sent to Magadan some months later, although through a different port and on another steamer. But he turned up at the same mine as Tamara L. and her husband, in accordance with one of the most important rules at that time: special settlers from the various atomic installations must be kept apart from each other. All arrangements were thought through in detail in order to ensure that secret knowledge was restricted to an isolated locality. Sergei Melnikov, a head teacher at the Magadan branch of the Khabarovsk State Technical University, studied the fate of the prisoners of Dalstroi. In an article published in 1995 he wrote that:

> The concept 'special contingent' appeared in official documents of the Ministry of Internal Affairs in 1949. MVD directive No. 00708 was issued in July 1949, concerning special contingent persons within the MVD system. In September, the head of Dalstroi issued instructions, carrying out this order.
>
> The first special contingent group arrived at Kolyma in the second half of September 1949, in conditions of total segregation. They travelled on the steamers *Soviet Latvia* (2,370 people) and *Nogin* (2,285 people) and also in October, on the *Dzhurma* (604 people). Altogether, 5,665 people arrived in 1949 until navigation came to an end for the winter.
>
> Two essential criteria were used to determine the ultimate destination of these new arrivals: the enterprise had to be in an isolated location, far from any other populated spot; the enterprise had to be at a place where the road came to an end.[40]

Although the two zeros prefixing the MVD order indicated that Stalin's personal authority was behind it, in fact all the leaders of the atomic project were involved in the implementation of this cruel practice. Documents in the MVD archive make it clear that the decisions of the Council of Ministers that were signed by Stalin and subsequently ratified as decrees of the Supreme Soviet were based on reports and drafts coming from Vannikov, Serov, Pervukhin, Zavenyagin and Komarovsky.[41] Material would be sent to Beria, and from him to Stalin. Vannikov was the head of the First Main Directorate (PGU) that handled all atomic matters. The others were his deputies.

The whole question of the future of the workers, once top-secret projects were completed, was discussed by the special committee on atomic problems on 23 May 1949. It was resolved that 'in order to ensure that secrecy is preserved with regard to the most important construction projects of the First Main Directorate, it is considered advisable to move former prisoners, repatriated soldiers and special settlers to Dalstroi.'[42] A government resolution was prepared and an appropriate MVD directive soon followed. There is also the possibility – it certainly cannot be ruled out – that people in the 'special contingent' who were chronically ill or who had lost the capacity to work because of age or injury or some other cause would have been 'liquidated'. Although 'special liquidation' did take place before and after the war, there is no evidence of it in the archives, since it was almost always a question of oral instruction. In the rare cases of a written order, there would only be one copy, which was acted upon and then immediately destroyed. Special coded departments and liquidation teams existed within the NKVD, the MVD and the MGB.[42]

Sergei Melnikov's work in the Magadan MVD archives confirms the accounts given by Samokhvalov and Tamara L. in 1989. He wrote:

> People in the first special contingent party were sent to the most distant settlements, such as the 'October' (687 km from Magadan) and 'Desire' (671 km from Magadan) mines, under the Western Mining Industry Directorate (now the Susuman district of the Magadan region); mines called 'Victory' (1042 km) and 'Hope' (1175 km) under the Indiga Industrial Mining Directorate (now the Oymyakonsk district of Yakutia); the 'Raskova' mine (522 km) under the Tenkinsk Industrial Mining Directorate; and to the Arkagalinsk building site (730 km), where they were constructing the Arkagalinsk hydroelectric power station and sought people from the special contingent with relevant professional experience.

> Later, in 1950, special contingent deportees were sent to other mines in the region.

> In accordance with order No. 00708 and related instructions, former prisoners who were subsequently transferred to the special contingent were people who had served their sentences in special regime sites of the MVD, i.e. in camps that were part of secret military installations, including places where chemical and atomic weapons were produced. Former prisoners who had worked at Chelyabinsk-40, Sverdlovsk-22 or Sverdlovsk-44 were sent to Magadan. From there, in order to maintain the secrecy of the atomic installations, they were transported to the most remote areas of the country, including far-flung Dalstroi enterprises.[43]

According to Dalstroi archives, on 1 January 1952 there were 10,348 'special contingent' workers on three-year 'contracts'. They were kept under guard and did not have the right to leave their assigned workplace or domicile. Somehow Western intelligence agencies learned that workers from the Soviet nuclear industry were arriving in Magadan. However, the information was misinterpreted and they came to the conclusion that the territory of Magadan was to be the site of a nuclear power station.[44]

After Stalin's death and Beria's arrest, the brutal practice of 'protecting secrecy' in this manner came to an end. People from the 'special contingent' began to be released in 1954–55. But their freedom of residence was still restricted. They were allowed to live only in the Urals, Siberia, the Far East or several parts of central Russia and were forbidden to settle near any border. Local KGB offices continued to keep them under observation. They also had to sign a permanent undertaking not to divulge information about their former work. Breaking this pledge would result in immediate arrest and imprisonment. Even normal employees of the atomic installations who left because of illness in 1957–58 or later were subject to these restrictions. Fragmentary recollections by people who had worked on the nuclear construction projects began to appear in the press only after 1991. But by then few of the participants were still alive.

The Siberian atomic gulag

In 1949, even before the successful test of the first bomb, Stalin decided to build a second set of atomic plants, structures that would be better hidden and protected from any possible nuclear attack. It would boost the security of the country enormously if there was a parallel system for producing atomic weapons, a system that would include reactors, radiochemical plants and bomb-making facilities. The existence of two independent systems would also stimulate competition and encourage technical progress. A series of Council of Ministers resolutions confirmed the decision to build the new centres. In the summer of 1949 the first of these resolutions approved the construction of an underground nuclear facility in the Krasnoyarsk area. A special geological expedition had identified a suitable rocky terrain on the banks of the Yenisei, approximately 80 kilometres north of Krasnoyarsk. In the autumn of that year a forced-labour camp was set up to build a railway link from the site to the city. The first battalion of military construction workers had arrived earlier on the steamer *Maria Ulyanova*. The new centre would be called Krasnoyarsk-26. Here, 400 metres under the rocks, there were plans to construct several reactors as well as a plant to produce plutonium. To begin with, even the living quarters were built in the mountain tunnels. Later, with the growth of the town, they were moved to the surface. Tunnels and chambers were drilled, 300–400 metres beneath the surface; in order to accommodate the whole industrial infrastructure, more rock was excavated here than in the construction of the entire Moscow metro. Unsurprisingly the prison camp kept expanding. The number of prisoners reached its highest point on 1 January 1953 – there were 27,314 inmates including 4,030 women. Called 'Granite ITL' by the MVD, it was classified as a 'special hard labour' camp because of the work, breaking rocks. A short account of the history of Krasnoyarsk-26 states that the camp section remained until 1963.[45]

The second atomic city in Siberia, Tomsk-7, was also founded in 1949 and was situated only 15 kilometres from the regional centre on the banks of the River Tom. Here too, there were plans for several reactors to produce plutonium, a radiochemical plant and a factory for separating out uranium isotopes 235 and 238. Sometime later a new factory for separating isotopes was built in the Krasnoyarsk region, approximately 50 kilometres east of Krasnoyarsk-26. This new facility was called Krasnoyarsk-45. Here, however, gas diffusion, the method used to separate isotopes for the first Soviet uranium bomb, was replaced by a gas centrifuge system. The Soviet Union was the first country to develop this method with the help of German scientists who came to the USSR after 1945. There was no need to organize a prison camp in order to begin building at Krasnoyarsk-45, as there was already a camp nearby. Indeed, the site was chosen because of the existence of an adjacent 'labour supply'. A history of Krasnoyarsk-45 gives a brief account of the start of construction:

> The building site was already operating like some kind of military unit. All available 'troops' were assigned to the site bosses ... there was a company of army builders – 200 men – and prisoners from several camps ... this was the basic workforce that built the town and all the industrial components. It was a mixed contingent – petty thieves, hard criminals, politicals ... all the politicals had a maximum sentence. ... The camp was disbanded in 1960.

> A maximum sentence meant 25 years; after the war, it was only handed down to Vlasovites or 'followers' of Bandera and other nationalists. It was considered to be 'real torture' to work with common criminals while 'the 'fifty eighters' could be trusted, they worked well, and among them there were many professionals.[46] [Article 58 of the Criminal Code dealt with political crimes against the state.]

Science and the gulag

In 1949 it was decided to set up new atomic physics centres combining both fundamental and military research. It was the scientists themselves who insisted on the need to expand existing institutes. Their work required more experimental reactors of various types, accelerators, radiochemical laboratories and other facilities, and it would have been difficult to find space in the already overloaded institutes of Moscow. But even where the initiative came from scientists, whenever a new facility was to be constructed, the first step was always the same: the establishment of a prison labour camp. It was standard procedure and regarded as normal for the Academy of Sciences to request a labour supply from the MVD. The new buildings of the Physics Institute, the Institute of Geochemistry and the

Institute of Biophysics of the Ministry of Health as well as extensions of other institutes in Moscow and Leningrad were all built by prisoners. In 1949 a small camp appeared on the banks of the Volga to the north of the Moscow region as part of the development of the small scientific town, later to become well known as Dubna. Work began with the construction of a powerful elementary particle accelerator and a synchrophasotron, in order to test a current theory that particle accelerators could generate trans-uranium elements that could be used to make considerably smaller atomic weapons.

Also in 1949 two prison camps were built in the Kaluga region on the banks of the Protva, not far from Maloyaroslavets. Here they began to erect a new physics-energy institute that would include the world's first small nuclear power station. The new centre was first called Maloyaroslavets-10 but later became Obninsk after the nearby village of Obninskoye. The new institute was devoted to research on small reactors using highly enriched uranium-235. Reactors of this kind could at some time in the future be adapted to power submarines. The new facilities were secret, but not top secret, which would have made it impossible for employees to leave or work elsewhere, while prisoners would have had to be deported to distant parts of the country after construction was completed.

It is said that appetite comes with eating; during the course of 1949 the Academy was making demands on the workforce of the MVD that began to exceed the capacity of the Construction Directorate to deliver. On 29 September the President of the Academy, Sergei Vavilov, asked Beria for a detail of prisoners to build a garage for the Academy and also living quarters for employees of the Physics Institute. Beria sent the request to the deputy head of the Construction Directorate, Nikolai Volgin, with a question about 'available resources'. Volgin's reply on 17 October declared that such tasks were inappropriate for the MVD Construction Directorate and that the Academy should turn to its own capital construction department.[47]

Epilogue

The recent opening of the archives has allowed us to have access to much of the hidden history of the development of nuclear weapons in the USSR, but certainly not everything. There are still secrets that have never been disclosed. The whole Soviet atomic industry certainly got off the ground at a truly astonishing pace. How did they manage it? Who should get the credit? The latter question has long been a source of controversy. Was it the intelligence service, or the scientists or the leaders of the country with their inimitable organizational skills? One thing, however, is clear: there can be no doubt that the gulag played a major role, making it possible to deal with problems at enormous speed, whether it was a question of constructing reactors, plants and testing ranges or building the entire infrastructure of each facility. It was the existence of this unique, enormous reserve of totally mobile and often highly skilled workers – essentially slave labour – that was crucial to the success of the whole project.

Does this justify the existence of the gulag? Certainly not! If the Stalinist political and economic model had avoided the gulag and other forms of forced labour, there would not have been such an urgent need to possess atomic and hydrogen bombs. It was the terror and the gulag that aroused so much apprehension in the rest of the world and caused other countries to feel threatened by the USSR. Today, after the transformation of Russia's political system and in a very different political climate, Russia and the United States face the colossal task of disposing of tens of thousands of atomic and hydrogen weapons. There has been an immense accumulation of radioactive waste. Billions of dollars and roubles will have to be spent in order to bury it safely and ensure that it will not leak into the environment for tens of thousands of years.

PART III. STALIN AND SCIENCE

CHAPTER 8

Generalissimo Stalin, General Clausewitz and Colonel Razin

Roy Medvedev

When the wave of terror hit the Red Army at the end of the 1930s, the world of military science was not exempt. Hundreds of teachers in every field of specialization were arrested and many were shot. Faculties of military history also sustained enormous losses. Disputes about the role played by military leaders or by one army or another in the Civil War could end up being settled in the basement of the Lubyanka. Of course work in the military academies continued, with teachers drafted from military colleges to replace the professors who had perished. Among them was the 37-year-old Yevgeny Razin, who became an assistant professor in the Department of the Art of War at the Frunze Academy. He had fought in the Civil War and in the 1920s was the commander of a regiment. When military titles were re-introduced he was given the rank of colonel.

Even in the best of times it was never an easy task to teach the history of war in Soviet military academies, but suddenly interference from above took on a new dimension. Scores of former Red Army leaders could no longer be mentioned by name; conceptions needed to be revised and facts distorted so that new heroes could come into being. Any book written wholly or in part by an 'enemy of the people' was withdrawn from libraries. There were no textbooks for the students in a number of important military subjects. Despite these difficult circumstances, Colonel Razin exhibited a surprising degree of energy and efficiency. At the beginning of 1939 he submitted a substantial manuscript to the military publishing house (Voenizdat) – a four-volume work entitled *A History of the Art of War from the Middle Ages to the First Imperialist War of 1914–1918.* It was largely a compilation. Razin turned to a number of nineteenth-century Russian military historians as well as to the work of French and German scholars; at the end of each volume he provided an extensive bibliography. He relied heavily on the ideas of Clausewitz, who will be discussed later. It was Razin's achievement to write about his subject in a way that made it accessible and interesting,

174

and his text included maps, graphs and illustrations. There was an urgent need for such a textbook, and by the end of 1939 the first two volumes of the *History* were published and distributed to military-educational institutions as well as to army and navy units. Razin became a professor and chairman of his department. He also joined the editorial board of the *Military-Historical Journal.*

At the end of the 1930s any personal success was always accompanied by an inevitable element of danger. Ill-disposed adversaries would suddenly make their appearance. A commission sent to the Frunze Academy by Lev Mekhlis, the head of the army's Political Directorate, found a number of mistakes in Razin's work, and in particular criticized his 'underestimation of Stalinist principles of strategy and tactics, based on a Marxist understanding of war'. Nevertheless Razin was not arrested nor was his book withdrawn from circulation. By special order of the Commissar of Defence, Semyon Timoshenko, it was decided that the textbook would be re-published in a new edition under the supervision of an editorial committee headed by Marshal Shaposhnikov, assisted by four generals and Academician Yuri Gotye, a specialist on the history of agriculture and local government in Russia.

The editors were instructed to complete their work by 1 December 1940 and they managed to meet the deadline. The first three volumes were at the printers in the spring of 1941, but at that point publication was held up by the war. During the war years Razin worked in the military history section of the General Staff. He was never promoted, and in the course of four years only received four medals. The colonel behaved cautiously at the General Staff but could not refrain from occasionally making critical remarks about military strategy during the first two years of the war, which provided additional material for his dossier in the Special Section.

Razin returned to work on his textbook after the war. Timoshenko's order was forgotten. Academician Gotye had died in 1943 and Marshal Shaposhnikov in March 1945. Razin began to prepare the first volume for the printers, having added an additional chapter on warfare in ancient India and China. Danger, however, was lurking in a quite unexpected quarter.

In the summer of 1945 a controversial debate flared up among Soviet military historians about the celebrated German military theorist Karl Clausewitz, whose book *On War* was regarded as a classic text by military historians in almost every country of the world. His personal history, as a scholar but also as a soldier who took part in almost all the major wars of his time, is rather interesting.

The future Prussian general joined the army at the age of 12 and became an officer when he was only 15. After Napoleon defeated

Prussia in the war of 1806–7, Clausewitz began teaching tactics and strategy at the War College in Berlin and was also one of his country's leading military reformers. He favoured an alliance between Prussia and Russia, and when the French emperor forced the Prussian king to support his preparations for a campaign against Russia, Clausewitz entered Russian service. He fought at Ostrovno and Smolensk and then in the famous battle of Borodino. In 1813 Clausewitz served as chief-of-staff of one of the Russian armies and in the following year joined the Russian–Prussian Silesian army commanded by Fieldmarshal Blücher. After Waterloo Clausewitz returned to teaching at the War College but spent much of his time studying the history and theory of military affairs. He considered himself to be a philosopher. A passionate Hegelian, he used the dialectical method in an attempt to link the main categories of military science in order to understand the characteristics, causes and essential nature of war. Many of his formulations later appeared in virtually all military encyclopaedias, the most famous of which was the aphorism that 'war is nothing more than a continuation of politics by other means', i.e. the military should always be subordinate to the political leadership. The Polish insurrection of 1830–31 forced Clausewitz to abandon his scholar's armchair; he commanded the Prussian forces on the Polish border, where he fell ill and shortly after died of cholera at the age of 50.

Not everything that Clausewitz wrote appeared in print, as he regarded many of his manuscripts as unfinished. After his death his widow, Maria von Clausewitz, prepared and published a substantial part of his theoretical and historical works in ten volumes, including the book for which he is most famous, *On War*. When he was in the process of writing it, Clausewitz told his friends that he wanted to produce a book that would still be read years later. He could hardly have imagined at the time that his books would continue to be admired for so long. His main works have been translated into scores of languages and are part of required reading lists in all the military academies of the world. This may seem surprising in view of the fact that Clausewitz was studying the wars of the eighteenth century and the Napoleonic period. His views were influenced by the war of 1812 and the campaigns of 1813–15. Nevertheless his profound reflections and rich analyses continued to influence later strategic concepts; all subsequent study of the history and theory of war inevitably had to take his ideas into account.

Friedrich Engels frequently wrote about war, military tactics and strategy. The second half of the nineteenth century had more than its share of battles and conflicts, and Engels analysed the nature of these conflicts, commented on the course of military operations and ventured prognoses about final outcomes. He also attempted to trace the evolution of military technology and discussed the role of different types of forces. Many of the articles in the *New American Encyclopaedia* on military themes were written by Engels. In one of his letters to Marx he wrote about the pleasure he got from reading Clausewitz's *On War,* praising it as an example of dialectical reasoning. Marx replied that he too had 'looked through Clausewitz. The fellow has common sense.'[1] In one of his letters to Wedemeyer, Engels called Clausewitz 'an original genius'.[2]

Lenin read *On War* when he was in Switzerland at the time of the outbreak of the First World War. He filled many notebook pages with quotations from Clausewitz and his own comments on them. These were preserved and published as 'Lenin's Military Notebooks' in the 12th volume of the *Lenin Collection.* They also appeared as separate pamphlets in 1933 and 1939. Lenin frequently quoted Clausewitz, 'one of the great and most profound writers on military affairs. ... Even in our time, any thinking person would benefit from an acquaintance with his ideas.'[3] It is hardly surprising, therefore, that all books on the history and theory of war published in the Soviet Union in the 1920s treated Clausewitz with great respect. *On War* was published in Moscow in 1934 and within two years there was a second edition. I have among my own collection the fifth edition, signed off to the printer on 4 March 1941.

The Second World War in effect became a testing ground for accepted political and military doctrine. As early as 1944 the military academies began to fill up with front-line officers. Every textbook and syllabus was now subject to fundamental revision. But as might be expected, as soon as the war came to an end several military historians began to question the authority of the *German* Clausewitz. The sharpest attack appeared in the No. 6–7 1945 issue of *Voennaya Mysl* (Military Thought). It is more than likely that the author of the attack, one Colonel Meshcheryakov, was prompted to write the article by someone higher up. Razin responded with indignation: he declared the article to be an 'anti-Leninist onslaught', that 'revises the judgement of Lenin and Engels'. When he received no support for his defence of Clausewitz, Razin sent a detailed letter to Stalin on 30 January 1946, along with his own theses on war and the art of war.

Stalin replied to Razin's letter rather quickly and in no uncertain terms. 'Lenin did not consider himself to be an expert on military affairs,' wrote Stalin. 'Lenin praised Clausewitz above all because, highly regarded in his time as an authority on military questions, Clausewitz, a non-Marxist, confirmed the well-known Marxist position that war is a continuation of politics by violent means.' These words were underlined by Stalin, although it is not quite clear how Clausewitz, who died in 1831, could have been able to confirm any kind of Marxist position, given that Marxism as an ideology only made its appearance 20 years later. 'From the standpoint of our own interests and of military science,' continued Stalin, 'we are obliged to expose not only Clausewitz but also Moltke, Schlieffen, Ludendorff, and Keitel along with other bearers of German military ideology.' Not only were the generals and field marshals listed by Stalin advocates of German militarism, but they were also the top military leaders of Germany from the time of the Franco-Prussian War until the Second World War. It was certainly not appropriate to place Clausewitz in this company. 'It is time to put an end to undeserved respect for German military authorities,' wrote Stalin. 'As for Clausewitz in particular, he, of course, has become obsolete. It is absurd to think of taking lessons from Clausewitz today.' It is not absurd, however, to learn from people who have knowledge and experience, and during the years of the Second World War Soviet colonels learned a lot from their adversaries. Stalin quite casually referred to Engels, whose mistaken judgements were foolishly 'argued with such passion'. Stalin also rejected Razin's theses on war: 'there is too much philosophy and abstraction. Clausewitz's terminology relating to the grammar and logic of war grates on the ear. Many of the theses are primitive. The tributes to Stalin also grate on the ear – it is simply embarrassing to read.'

It was a devastating reply, but not many people knew about it. Dated 23 February 1946, it was not published in *Bolshevik* until March 1947, when it marked the beginning of a debunking campaign. Clausewitz could now only be written about as a 'reactionary ideologue of German militarism'. As for the general who endured all the retreats and battles of 1812–13 in the Russian army, he was now described as an 'ignorant adventurer'. Colonel Razin attempted to dispute some of the cruder assaults on his hero, but this had unfortunate results. He was discharged from the army and arrested. The arrests of generals, which were common enough in the first post-war years, had to be personally approved by Stalin. But this did not apply to a colonel.

The Razin case was conducted by an investigator for 'especially important cases', Andrei Sverdlov, also a colonel but from a different agency. He was the son of the prominent Bolshevik who had been close to Lenin, Yakov Sverdlov. Early on Andrei Sverdlov linked his own fate with the organs of the NKVD. Well educated and able to speak several foreign languages, the younger Sverdlov gave lectures in the training institutions of the NKVD in addition to working as an investigator. He put together textbooks for the NKVD with titles such as *Special Course for Work as a Chekist* or *The Origins of the Right-Trotskyist Underground in the USSR and its Annihilation.* He also wrote thrillers for children and young people under the pseudonym A.Ya. Yakovlev, exalting the glorious deeds of Soviet Chekists. Considered to be an intellectual, Sverdlov was frequently assigned to cases involving well-known members of the intelligentsia. For example, he conducted the case of the writer Elizabeth Drabkina, who had once been his father's personal secretary. He interrogated Anna Larina, the widow of Bukharin. He did not beat women, but the situation was quite different in the interrogation of Pyotr Petrovsky, the editor-in-chief of *Leningrad Pravda*, a Civil War hero and the son of the Bolshevik Grigory Petrovsky, who had been part of Lenin's entourage. Petrovsky was shot after many days of torture. Sverdlov often beat prisoners himself or slammed the door against their fingers. During one of the interrogation sessions he knocked out six of Razin's teeth. Razin was broken, but sentences were not too harsh in those days – he was given only ten years in a labour camp.

All books by the 'enemy of the people' Razin were withdrawn from libraries and offices in the military academies. They were not, however, removed from Stalin's private library, containing more than 20,000 volumes. As has been mentioned previously, Stalin throughout his life was an avid collector of books. As he read, he would underline passages or make notes in the margin, usually with coloured pencils. His office kept a record of all his requests for books, amounting to hundreds of titles a year. With his unusually good memory Stalin enjoyed demonstrating his erudition. In January 1950 he needed to obtain some specific information about military history in preparation for a meeting with Mao Zedong, who considered himself to be an expert on 'people's war'. He began to leaf through a number of books including Razin's work. Appreciating its straightforward presentation, he remembered his harsh reply to the author's letter and asked Poskrebyshev to find out where Razin was and what he was doing. Possibly Stalin wanted to consult him about something.

Stalin's sudden interest in the fate of Razin aroused panic among all those who had played a role in his arrest. Even Beria was worried. Razin was extricated from his camp and flown to Moscow. The recent *zek* was not only made to look relatively decent, but a general's uniform was picked out for him! Razin had suddenly been promoted to the rank of major-general. Beria received the brand-new general personally and asked him to forget everything that had happened to him. It had all been a 'misunderstanding'.

Although the meeting between Razin and Stalin never took place, he was allowed to return to the Frunze Academy and once again became head of the Department of the Art of War. He resumed work on his textbook and the first volume appeared in 1955. Stalin was already dead but the Twentieth Party Congress was still to come, which explains why the preface was full of enthusiastic acclaim for Stalin while Clausewitz was subjected to derision. Even in the chapter on war between tribes in primitive society, Clausewitz is referred to as the 'ideologue of the aggressive policies of Prussian militarists'. By the time the second volume appeared in 1957 the author no longer referred either to Stalin or to Clausewitz. The third volume, published in 1960, was devoted to the history of war and the art of war in the seventeenth century. Razin had studied numerous archives and had been able to visit some 35 battlefields of the twelfth to the nineteenth centuries. But the years of imprisonment and torture had their effect and serious illness prevented him from completing his work. Razin died in 1964, leaving behind only rough drafts for the fourth and fifth volumes of his *History*.

Razin's books cannot be described as classic works, although they still are of some interest. In 1994 the St Petersburg publishing house Polygon brought out a third edition of Razin's three-volume *History of the Art of War*, without any changes to the text. A fourth volume on the wars of the eighteenth and nineteenth centuries was appended, but it was written by others. In 1997 the Logos publishing corporation together with the international publishing company Nauka (Science) started to prepare a new edition of Clausewitz's *On War*. Only the first volume appeared, however, as the publishers ran out of funds.

Many might find it surprising to learn that in the 1960s the publication of Stalin's collected works was completed by the Hoover Institute at Stanford University; the Soviet edition had only got as far as Volume 13 (the writings and speeches of 1934) and came to a halt when Stalin died. The American publishers assembled all the material they could find, from 1935 to 1952, and published the subsequent volumes in exactly the same typeface and format that had been used in the Soviet Union. The additional volumes appeared in a limited edition in 1966–67. One can find Stalin's 'Reply to Comrade Razin' in Volume 16, pages 28–34.

Andrei Sverdlov was transferred to the reserve in 1953 on grounds of ill health. He suffered three heart attacks and could no longer work for the state security organs. He was given a new position at the Institute of Marxism-Leninism where he wrote articles and pamphlets on the history of the Party and on the problems of Latin America. He helped edit a book about Ordzhonikidze as well as a biography of his father, Yakov Sverdlov. With his assistance the former commandant of the Kremlin, P.D. Malkov, wrote and published his successful *Memoirs of a Kremlin Commandant*. Although the Party organs received many statements from rehabilitated communists who had suffered at the hands of Andrei Sverdlov, neither the Institute nor the Ideological Department of the Central Committee were able to part with such a valuable colleague. He died in the middle of the 1970s at the age of 65 after his eighth heart attack.

CHAPTER 9

Stalin and Lysenko

Zhores Medvedev

The meeting at the Academy of Agricultural Sciences

On 27 July 1948 Stalin arrived at his Kremlin office late in the evening in accordance with his usual routine, but this time it was after an absence of ten days because of some undisclosed illness. His first visitors appeared at 10:10 pm – Malenkov and Trofim Lysenko.[1] They had come to get Stalin's approval of a draft report, 'On the Situation in Soviet Biological Science', written by Lysenko and sent to the Kuntsevo dacha on 23 July by Malenkov, who read it without changing anything in the text. They were both rather surprised to find that Stalin had made corrections in a number of places as well as critical comments in the margins. During the next hour Lysenko later recalled, 'Stalin gave me detailed explanations of his editorial changes and made recommendations on how better to present particular parts of my report.'[2] They were then joined by Beria, Bulganin, Mikoyan, Voznesensky and Kaganovich. For the next hour they discussed their concerns about the forthcoming meeting of the Lenin All-Union Academy of Agricultural Sciences (VASKhNIL) for which Lysenko had prepared his report. Stalin instructed Lysenko to inform participants at the final session of the assembly that his report had been read and approved by the Central Committee, i.e. to announce something that in fact had not occurred.

For more than 15 years there had been an ongoing dispute among scientists about the question of heredity. Stalin knew that Lysenko's position as President of VASKhNIL had become increasingly precarious since the end of the war, and this is what motivated his intervention. By 1940 Lysenko's theories had come to dominate Soviet genetics, but only because Stalin's active support included repressive measures against a large number of biologists. Lysenko's theories denied the existence of genes and attempted to prove that acquired characteristics could be inherited, a concept known as 'neo-Lamarckism'. There was a renewed interest in the problems of genetics in 1945, partly as a result of advances in biology in the United States, but mainly because Lysenko had begun to promote a new theory that contradicted Darwin's ideas on the origins of the species.

Any discussion of evolution inevitably raised questions about the mechanism of heredity. Lysenko's opponents maintained that his Lamarckian approach was not only unsound in theory but also futile in practice and a threat to the development of biology. The argument largely took place within the confines of the Moscow University and the Timiryazev Agricultural Academy in Moscow. However, the dispute reached a crisis point when Yuri Zhdanov openly criticized Lysenko at a seminar organized for regional Party cadres by the science section of the Central Committee on 10 April 1948. In his speech, 'Issues of contemporary Darwinism', Zhdanov made it clear that the views he was expressing were his own and not a new line set down by the Party. The younger Zhdanov, whose father was a member of the Politburo, had a degree in chemistry and, although only 29, occupied a rather senior position as head of the Central Committee's science section. This was certainly not a reflection of either his scientific prowess or his status in the Party. He had been given this post not only thanks to the patronage of his father, the Central Committee Secretary responsible for science and culture, but also on the recommendation of Stalin himself, who had given Zhdanov his daughter Svetlana as well. Stalin liked Yuri Zhdanov and hoped that the young couple would live in his large apartment in the Kremlin or at the Kuntsevo dacha. Living on his own without any members of his family, Stalin began to suffer from loneliness as he got older, and Svetlana was the only person to whom he felt close.

Lysenko received the full text of Zhdanov's speech from one of his supporters, the philosopher Mark Mitin. He became alarmed after reading it, understanding all too well that ideological workers throughout the country would come to the conclusion that Yuri Zhdanov's words amounted to an official directive. On 17 April he complained to Stalin by letter. After a month went by without a response, he wrote to the Minister of Agriculture, Ivan Benediktov, resigning as President of the Academy of Agricultural Sciences.[3]

Although VASKhNIL was formally subordinate to the Ministry of Agriculture, its president occupied a Central Committee *nomenkla-tura* post. Therefore Benediktov was not in a position to accept Lysenko's resignation, and inevitably the whole affair would have to be decided by the Politburo and most likely by Stalin himself. The science section of the Central Committee was part of the Department of Agitation and Propaganda, headed by Suslov. His deputy, Dmitri Shepilov, was the Party official who would have had to approve Zhdanov's speech. According to Shepilov's recently published memoirs, he enthusiastically supported what Zhdanov intended to say, since he had long been convinced that Lysenko's theories 'were a joke among real scientists throughout the world, including those who were well-disposed to the Soviet Union'.[4]

Both Shepilov and Zhdanov began to feel rather uneasy at the end of April, when they heard that Malenkov had asked for a steno-graphic report of the speech and specified that he wanted to be sent an uncorrected version. Since they knew that Malenkov had no direct interest in scientific questions, they assumed that he intended to show it to Stalin. It was a time of fierce rivalry between Malenkov and Andrei Zhdanov, and any blunder on Zhdanov's part worked to the advantage of Malenkov, who was striving to re-establish his influence in the Secretariat. The Lysenko question was discussed at a meeting of the Politburo towards the end of May. It was Shepilov who explained what had happened, and according to his memoirs he criticized Lysenko and spoke in defence of Zhdanov. But Shepilov, Zhdanov and Malenkov all misunderstood the situation: it was not in fact about Lysenko at all. What really was at stake was an ap-proach to science that Stalin himself supported passionately. He did have a certain amount of knowledge of the field, and on the question of heredity he was a Lamarckian. As far as the theory of genes was concerned, along with many others at this time, Stalin associated it with the completely unacceptable doctrines of eugenics and racism.

According to Shepilov, Stalin paid no attention to the attempt to defend Yuri Zhdanov:

> He went up to his desk, took a cigarette, shook out the tobacco out into his pipe and slowly walked along the table where everyone was sitting. Then he said very quietly, but I could hear the ominous tone in his voice: 'No, it can't be left like this. There has to be a special commission to look into it. The guilty must be punished as an exam-ple. Not Yuri Zhdanov – he's still young and inexperienced. It's necessary to punish the "fathers": Zhdanov,' (he pointed the stem of his pipe at Andrei Andreevich) 'and Shepilov. The Central Committee must draw up a detailed resolution. It all must be made clear to the scientists. We have to support Lysenko and demolish our home-bred Morganists.' Stalin began to name the members of the Politburo and other officials who would be members of the commission. Malenkov was chosen to head it. Andrei Zhdanov did not utter a single word during the whole meeting. Taking everything into consideration, it must have been quite a traumatic occasion for him.[5]

Stalin returned to the conflict between Yuri Zhdanov and Lysenko on 31 May when the Politburo met to consider candidates to be awarded Stalin prizes for science and invention. By this time it had become traditional for Stalin personally to recommend the recipients of the top awards. Those present at the meeting, in addition to the Politburo, included Sergei Kaftanov (Minister of Higher Education), Academician Aleksander Nesmeyanov (Chairman of the Stalin Prize Committee) and Vyacheslav Malyshev (Deputy Chairman of the Council of Ministers). Malyshev left a record of this meeting in his diary, recently discovered in the Party archive and published in full:

Before turning to the awards, Comrade Stalin called attention to the fact that Yuri Zhdanov (son of A.A.) had delivered a lecture condemning Lysenko, during which he stressed the fact that he was expressing his own personal opinion. Comrade Stalin said that there was no place for personal opinions or a personal point of view in the Party. There could only be the views of the Party. It was Yuri Zhdanov's goal to smash and destroy Lysenko. This was wrong. 'We must not forget,' said Comrade Stalin, 'that Lysenko is the Michurin of today in agrotechnology. ... Lysenko has his faults and has made mistakes as a scientist and as a man, and he has to be controlled, but to attempt to destroy Lysenko as a scientist is playing into the hands of the Zhebrakians.'[6]

Stalin's scornful reference to 'Zhebrakians' was unfair. A penitent Yuri Zhdanov, apologizing to his father-in-law, explained that he had consulted A.R. Zhebrak about genetics and went on to blame him for the whole blunder. Professor Anton Zhebrak had been head of the science section of the Central Committee in 1946. He left that post to become President of the Belorussian Academy of Sciences. Zhebrak was a prominent geneticist and a specialist in selection, and he headed the Department of Genetics and Plant Selection at the Timiryazev Academy of Agriculture. He was well known for developing certain new forms of polyploid wheat (with double sets of chromosomes) which were just in the process of being tested for their suitability to be introduced into selection practice.

Stalin's editorial contributions to Lysenko's report

In May 1948 Malenkov was no longer a Secretary of the Central Committee. He had lost this influential position in 1946 after an investigation into troubles within the military aviation industry – his role on the Politburo as well as his membership of the State Defence Committee gave him overall responsibility for this branch of industry. The Commissar for the Aviation Industry, A.I. Shakhurin, was arrested, while Malenkov received a reprimand and was given the job of supervising the communist parties of the Soviet Central Asian republics. Although he continued to be a Deputy Chairman of the Sovnarkom and spent more of his time in Moscow than in Tashkent, he would not have been able to set up any kind of commission on the problems of biology without consulting the Ideological Department of the Central Committee, which, in addition to its agitprop functions, had sections dealing with science. Andrei Zhdanov was then the head of the Ideological Department and was considered to be number two in the Party hierarchy after Stalin. Working independently, Zhdanov also began to prepare material for a Party directive on biology. He intended the directive to be approved at the end of a meeting of leading scientists, biologists and philosophers, organized by the Ideological Department. Preparation of the main report for the meeting was assigned to Shepilov and Mitin. The report was completed on 7 July, edited by Zhdanov and sent to Stalin. Many years later a copy of the original document was found in the Party archives. Entitled 'On the Situation in Soviet Biology', it had been sent to other members of the Politburo as well. A draft resolution was also drawn up for the Central Committee.

Stalin, however, turned out to be against restricting the discussion to an inner Party circle. He decided that any report on the situation in biology had to be made by Lysenko himself and not by Shepilov or Mitin, and at a scientific rather than a Party conference. The Central Committee meeting planned by Zhdanov would have given Lysenko a relatively strong hand against his critics, but if he were to read his own report to a scientific audience at the forthcoming VASKhNIL conference, a report that overtly had been approved by Stalin, this would put him on a pedestal and make him the virtual dictator of Soviet science.

Stalin was convinced at that time that every branch of science, like every sector of the economy, had to have one leading authority. Apparently he reckoned that if Lysenko were to be given extraordinary powers, he would be able to produce the kind of success for Soviet biology and agriculture that Kurchatov had achieved in Soviet physics, raising it to world-standard level. Stalin took it upon himself to organize the session of VASKhNIL where Lysenko's report would be discussed. Thus the question of genetics had unexpectedly become an issue of major state importance. Stalin was also in the process of removing Zhdanov from his position as the overall leader of the creative intelligentsia. Before the war Stalin had exercised personal control over all spheres of culture: literature, science and the arts. It had always been his ambition to be an intellectual leader as well as the boss of the Party, although during the war he had to concentrate on military issues. In this period all aspects of culture gradually came to be controlled by Zhdanov, who was even more conservative and dogmatic in his views than Stalin.

For several years Lysenko kept his report with Stalin's handwritten corrections in his office and would sometimes show it to visitors. After Stalin's death Lysenko sent the original text to the Party archives, keeping only a copy for himself. In 1991–93 two researchers from the Institute of History and the Institute of the History of Natural Science and Technology, V. Yesakov and K.O. Rossiyanov, found the original document in the archives and published an analysis of what Stalin had written.[7] It should be noted that Stalin did a good job as an editor, improving Lysenko's text, modifying the stridency and softening the anti-Western tone, and he also removed the false dichotomy between Soviet and Western science. At the same time, however, he fully approved Lysenko's adherence to Lamarckian theory.

Stalin removed the word 'Soviet' from the title of the report; in his view, 'On the Situation in the Biological Sciences' was a more correct formulation of the subject in question. All 49 pages had been examined meticulously. He struck out the second section of the report, 'The False Basis of Bourgeois Biology', and where Lysenko had claimed that 'any science is based on class', Stalin wrote: 'Ha, ha, ha ... and mathematics? and Darwin?' In one section where Lysenko criticized the views of T.H. Morgan and W.L. Johannsen, Stalin wrote in the margin: 'And what about Weissman?' Lysenko and his aides promptly added 12 paragraphs to the report, attacking Weissman.

Throughout the text, Stalin crossed out the term 'bourgeois'. For example, 'bourgeois world view' became 'idealist world view'; 'bourgeois genetics' became 'reactionary genetics'. In another section, Stalin added an entire paragraph, which made it clear that he had retained the Lamarckian convictions of his youth, exemplified in his 1906 essay 'Anarchism or Socialism'. Where Lysenko insisted on the absolute scientific basis of Lamarck's theory of the inheritance of acquired characteristics, Stalin added an additional sentence: 'One cannot deny that in the increasingly heated debate in the first quarter of the twentieth century between Weissmanists and Lamarckians, the latter were closer to the truth since they upheld the interests of science, while the Weissmanists abandoned science and became addicted to mysticism.'

Stalin's changes and additions to the text signalled a decisive departure from the doctrine that had dominated all the debates during the 1920s and 1930s – that science was based on class. He clearly had been influenced by the enormous advances in nuclear physics in the United States and Britain as well as the subsequent creation of the atomic bomb. By the end of the war Stalin had come to realize that progress in science and technology was less a matter of ideology than a question of substantial material support for scientists. Not everyone appreciated the significance of Stalin's speech in the Bolshoi Theatre on 9 February 1946 at a Supreme Soviet pre-election meeting for voters from the Stalin election district of Moscow. He said, 'I'm confident that if we give our scientists the help they need, they will soon catch up with and even surpass the achievements of science abroad.'[8] This statement was not just an empty declaration. By March 1946 the national budget's allocation for science had tripled, and the salaries of scientists were substantially increased.

Yet despite the rejection of the class basis of science, including the natural sciences, there was still no recognition of a 'world scientific community'. Scientific theories or trends were still divided into 'materialistic' and 'idealistic' categories. 'Soviet science' came to mean 'science of the motherland' in order to stress a continuity between the Soviet period and pre-revolutionary Russia. 'Anti-patriotic' now became, along with 'anti-Soviet', a term of abuse; anyone accused of 'anti-patriotic' behaviour would be subject to severe criticism or punishment. Soviet scientists were strictly forbidden to publish the results of their work abroad.

Malenkov, Zhdanov and Lysenko

Unlike Malenkov, Andrei Zhdanov was not merely a Party *apparatchik*. Until 1934 he had been the head of the Party in Nizhny Novgorod. After the murder of Kirov, Stalin sent him to Leningrad as Party leader, where he unleashed the terror campaigns of 1935–36. After the war the extraordinary fortitude shown by Leningraders during the almost three years of German blockade enhanced the special symbolic importance of the city as the 'cradle of the Revolution'. Zhdanov had remained in Leningrad for the duration of the war. In 1945 he was transferred to Moscow, became a Secretary of the Central Committee and straightaway found himself at the top of the Party hierarchy, second only to Stalin. All ideological departments of the Central Committee came under his control – earlier in his career he had supervised the Writers' Union as well as other arts organizations – and it was also part of his portfolio to deal with a number of international issues, including the fate of the territories occupied by the Soviet army.

Until 1946 Malenkov was in charge of almost all internal Party affairs. On the government side, Stalin mainly relied on Molotov. When various officials or commissariats sent important documents to Stalin for information or approval, copies were also provided for Malenkov and Molotov. Thus in effect this triumvirate was governing the country. If Stalin was on holiday, ill or too busy with other things, resolutions of the Sovnarkom or the GKO were signed by Molotov, while Central Committee resolutions were signed by Malenkov. At the end of 1945 Beria also became a Deputy Chairman of the Sovnarkom and was given a new office in the Kremlin. However, his Sovnarkom responsibilities were limited to two crucial programmes: atomic weapons and rockets. Beria's authority over the activities of the NKVD and the NKGB (which became ministries in 1946) proceeded from his portfolio on the Politburo. During the war Molotov was largely occupied with diplomatic affairs while the Supreme Commander-in-Chief, Stalin, directed military operations on both the western and eastern fronts. When it came to domestic state and Party issues, the two most influential figures in the leadership were Beria and Malenkov. Khrushchev's influence was restricted to the Ukraine.

Arriving in Moscow in 1946 Zhdanov energetically set about taking charge of the ideological sphere. He was responsible for a number of extremely conservative initiatives which later came to be known as the *zhdanovshchina*. Censorship was reinforced and a campaign set in motion to eliminate 'toadying before the West'; scientists were deprived of access to most foreign publications and the practice of translating certain Soviet academic journals into English was stopped. 'Courts of honour' were established, a rather original innovation, to try scientists accused of anti-patriotic behaviour (e.g. the case of Klyueva and Roskin, biologists who were working on cancer drugs); writers were condemned for 'defaming Soviet reality' (Zoshchenko and Akhmatova) while Shostokovich and Prokofiev were criticized for composing 'formalist' works that were 'incomprehensible' to the people. Stalin thoroughly approved of these campaigns – they were all very much part of the new Cold War with the West. The general public, however, associated the avalanche of restrictive ideological measures with Zhdanov rather than Stalin. Yet despite his many anti-Western projects, Zhdanov never was an admirer of Lysenko. He viewed the genetics conflict as a practical question rather than an ideological one. Soviet agriculture was in dire straits after the war, but all Lysenko's assurances about new agrarian successes and high-yield species apparently came to nothing.

Malenkov's unexpected disgrace and his removal from the Secretariat in May 1946 considerably strengthened Zhdanov's position. Simultaneously the 'Leningrad cadres' were promoted to the highest reaches of the leadership: Nikolai Voznesensky became a member of the Politburo in 1947, Aleksei Kosygin in 1948 and Aleksei Kuznetsov was made Secretary of the Central Committee responsible for the MVD and the MGB. There was also a change of leadership at the MGB. Beria's loyal protégé, Vsevolod Merkulov, was replaced by Viktor Abakumov, who from then on would take orders directly from Stalin. Zhdanov became the head of the Central Committee Secretariat, and from May 1946 all papers from various ministries that previously had been sent to Stalin and Malenkov were now sent to Stalin and Zhdanov.

With a seat on the Politburo and an office in the Kremlin, Beria also was becoming more powerful. Instead of the triumvirate there were now four men governing the country: Stalin, Molotov, Beria and Zhdanov, and of these four it was Zhdanov who played the main role in Party decisions and, in particular, the question of cadres. But when Yuri Zhdanov's unexpected intervention ignited the conflict between Andrei Zhdanov and Lysenko, this gave Malenkov and Beria the opportunity to begin their intrigue against Zhdanov and the entire 'Leningrad group'. It was not just the usual case of rivalry between factions seeking to gain Stalin's favour. Stalin's health had been visibly deteriorating and the struggle for power after his death had already begun. The participants in the controversy over genetics observed Stalin's fury at the attempt by 'Morganists' to subvert the predominating 'Lamarckians', but they failed to understand why he seemed to be more concerned with this issue than the erupting Berlin crisis that was threatening to bring the USSR and NATO to the brink of war. They were simply unaware of the fact that Stalin himself was an absolutely dedicated Lamarckian; he was fascinated by the idea that it might be possible to 'alter the nature of plants', and he was spending an increasing amount of time on this, his only hobby.

When Stalin decided that Lysenko would be the main speaker at the session on genetics, it was clear to Zhdanov that he had lost. According to Shepilov, in the middle of July, 'rumours were spreading that A.A. Zhdanov would be shifted "to other work" and that the leadership of the Secretariat would be restored to Malenkov. Anyone who was savvy about such matters understood that Beria and Malenkov had used the "Lysenko affair" in order to get rid of Zhdanov.'[9]

The VASKhNIL conference took place in Moscow from 31 July to 7 August 1948. Lysenko let it be known that his paper had been approved by the Central Committee. All the tensions of the preceding weeks had had an unfortunate effect on Zhdanov's health; he left Moscow for treatment, but it was not exactly a voluntary departure. Shepilov tells us: 'One sunny morning, Andrei Aleksandrovich rang me up and said: "I've been told to have medical care and take a rest. I won't be far from Moscow, at Valdai. They tell me it's easy to breathe there. … I don't think I'll be away for very long."'[10] While Zhadanov was recuperating at the Central Committee sanatorium at Valdai, Malenkov once again became a Secretary of the Central Committee, second only to Stalin. All important reports requiring Central Committee action were now sent to Malenkov instead of Zhdanov.

On 28 August 1948 a cardiologist from the Kremlin Hospital, Lydia Timashuk, flew to Valdai after Zhadanov had suffered a heart attack. She did an immediate electrocardiogram and diagnosed a heart attack in the region of the left ventricle. For some reason which still remains puzzling, the chief doctors of the Kremlin Hospital, Professors Vladimir Vinogradov, Pyotr Yegorov and Gavriil Mayorov, refused to accept this diagnosis, and in the case notes wrote: 'functional disorder due to sclerosis'. Therefore Zhadanov was not ordered to stay in bed. On 29 August Timashuk sent an urgent message to General Nikolai Vlasik, the head of Stalin's personal bodyguard (and also of the whole MGB Guards Directorate). She claimed that the consultants and Mayorov, the doctor in charge of treatment, had underestimated the seriousness of Zhdanov's condition and were allowing him to get out of bed, walk in the park, go to the cinema, and that the result of all this was bound to be fatal.[11] Timashuk's comments were passed on to Major A.M. Belov, the head of Zhdanov's guard, on 29 August. But on the same day, Zhdanov had a second heart attack and within 48 hours was dead.

There is much that remains unclear about this whole story, which four years later was to serve as the starting point for the infamous 'Doctors' Plot'. According to one version, General Vlasik immediately showed Timashuk's letter to Stalin. According to another, Vlasik was dismissed in 1952 and subsequently arrested because he had concealed Timashuk's letter and improperly had sent it to the head of the Kremlin Hospital, Professor Yegorov. The second version may be the more likely story, given the fact that Timashuk was dismissed and that she continued to write letters to various authorities, although there were other reasons for Vlasik's removal, as discussed previously. In August 1948 the key figures in this particular 'doctors' plot' were Russians: Vinogradov, Yegorov, Mayorov and Vladimir Vasilenko. But in some mysterious fashion, several years later the whole affair was transformed into a 'Zionist conspiracy' which Stalin intended to use as a pretext for removing Malenkov and Beria from their positions. As can be seen from the personnel changes at the Nineteenth Party Congress, Stalin had decided that his successors should come from a younger generation.

Stalin as a Lamarckian: transforming nature

In many Soviet and Western articles about Lysenko, it has been suggested that he possessed special psychological or hypnotic powers, rather like Rasputin, and that this explained his ability to impose his completely unfounded, often crazy theories on Soviet leaders, first Stalin and then Khrushchev. In reality Lysenko possessed no Rasputin-like qualities. It was not a question of Lysenko foisting his own bizarre theories on the leaders of the country and somehow managing to convince them of the validity of his arguments. On the contrary, it was he who got caught up in a game of trying to please his leaders, inventing pseudo-scientific proofs (often by falsifying his own experimental results) to confirm absurd ideas that they, themselves, had expressed. Stalin was a convinced Lamarckian while for Khrushchev it was more of an impulsive attraction. In any case Lamarckian theory would have had an obvious natural appeal for Bolsheviks, given their conviction that anything could be changed under the right conditions. Even Lenin, who wrote that any worker could run the state, could be called a social Lamarckian.

We all remember how Khrushchev thought he could grow corn near Archangel and Leningrad, and even hoped to 'adapt' it to the Urals and Siberia. But the story of the origins of the genetics debate that ultimately led to the 1948 conference is virtually unknown. The original conflict between the selection-geneticists led by Academician Nikolai Vavilov and the young Lysenko with his small group of followers began in 1931 in response to a ridiculous Party and government resolution 'On selection and seed growing'. Under the terms of this resolution, the full range of cultivated low-yield crops were to be replaced by high-yield varieties throughout the country within two years.[12] Stalin's 'revolution from above', collectivization, did not exactly improve Soviet agriculture at the beginning of the 1930s. On the contrary most rural districts faced the threat of famine, and famine did indeed ravish the southern regions of the country in 1932–33. It was this situation that prompted Stalin to make impossible demands on agricultural science. The resolution on selection and seed growing required the creation of new varieties of wheat that could replace rye in the northern and eastern parts of the country. The southern regions were to have new species of potato. The time limit for producing the new varieties was reduced from 10–12 years to four or five. It was expected that within this shorter period, Soviet wheat would be transformed into a high-yield variety with a high protein content, resistant to cold, drought, pests and blight.

Nikolai Vavilov and the majority of geneticists regarded these totally unrealizable goals as ludicrous. However, Lysenko and his still small group of followers gave assurances that it could be done. It was just at this time that Lysenko's lavish promises at various gatherings of collective farm 'shock-workers' caught Stalin's attention. When they were subsequently unable to deliver what they promised, Lysenko and his friends blamed their failure on a lack of co-operation from the adherents of 'bourgeois' genetics. Many of the prominent scientists who spoke out and criticized Lysenko in the 1930s were arrested in 1937–39 and perished in the camps and prisons, including Academicians Meister, Muralov and Tulaikov, Professors Levitsky, Karpetchenko, Govorov and Kovalev, as well as a number of others. And finally, in 1940, Academician Nikolai Vavilov was also arrested.

Until the end of his life, Stalin continued to believe that adaptations and 'miracle varieties' of one kind or another could solve the problems of Soviet agriculture. In 1946 he received sheaves of a special kind of branched wheat as a gift from Georgia. This particular variety of wheat, already known in ancient Egypt, produced large spikes and a greater number of seeds than usual. However, it could only be sown in rich soil and at a much lower density, while at the same time it produced an over abundance of leaves (too many leaves meant less grain), which ultimately meant that the final harvest did not bring improved results. And if the branched wheat was sown in the normal way, the results were again unacceptable. It would have a low protein content and poor resistance to disease. Nor would it be possible to make bread from its flour – the gluten content was insufficient. Nevertheless Stalin was impressed by the size of the spikes and he decided to instruct Lysenko to experiment.

On 30 December 1946 Stalin summoned Lysenko to the Kremlin and after a brief conversation, gave him a sack of branched wheat seeds and some sample specimens and asked him try it out. Lysenko immediately got several more sacks from Georgia and in the spring of 1947 sowed an experimental area with branched wheat. Soon after that, long before the harvest, Lysenko began proclaiming the unusual advantages of branched wheat in newspapers and journals, stressing the fact that Comrade Stalin had taken a personal interest in its cultivation. This was also a way of informing Stalin about his work. However, on 27 October Lysenko sent Stalin a detailed report on the results of the harvest, which unfortunately had not been a success. The branched wheat, which Lysenko called 'Cahetian wheat' (after the Georgian district where it was cultivated), only had a yield of 500 kilograms per hectare on the experimental field of an Odessa institute specializing in selection, which was two times lower than the average harvest in the region. In the Omsk region the entire crop was killed off by frost. At Lysenko's own experimental base in the Moscow region the harvest varied in different plots, from 400 to 3,000 kilograms per hectare. Stalin sent Lysenko a quick response. His letter showed an understanding of the problems of agro-technology but revealed total ignorance of the questions of selection and breeding:

> Dear Trofim Denisovich,
> It is very good that at last you have paid proper attention to the question of branched wheat. Undoubtedly, if we want to substantially increase the wheat harvest, branched wheat is of major interest since it contains the greatest potential to achieve this goal.
>
> It is unfortunate that you have not tried to grow this wheat in an environment 'convenient' for the wheat but rather in an environment that was convenient for yourself, the experimenter. This wheat is a southern variety, it needs a certain amount of sunlight and the provision of moisture. If these conditions are not present, it is difficult to realize the full potential of this wheat. If I were you, I would not have experimented with branched wheat in the Odessa district (too arid!) or near Moscow (too little sun!) but, for example, near Kiev or in the western Ukraine, where there is enough sun and guaranteed moisture. Nevertheless, I congratulate you on your experiment in the

districts outside Moscow. You can count on the government to support your undertaking.

I also welcome your initiative on the hybridization of wheat. It is certainly a most promising idea. There can be no doubt that the prospects for the present varieties of wheat are not very good, and hybridization could be some help.

We will talk soon in Moscow about rubber-bearing plants and the sowing of winter wheat.

About the theoretical situation in biology, I believe that the Michurin position is the only correct scientific approach. Weissmanists and their followers, who deny the inheritance of acquired characteristics, do not deserve to be discussed. The future belongs to Michurin.

With regards, J. Stalin
31.X.47[13]

Lysenko made maximum use of this letter, claiming an intimacy with Stalin that in reality did not exist. They never met each other, except officially. Nor had Lysenko ever been invited to Stalin's dacha. But the fact that Stalin was such an overt Lamarckian provided the main source of Lysenko's invulnerability. In 1948 there was a more extensive sowing of branched wheat, but this time it was not reported in the press since it was unsuccessful. In fact the attempt to introduce this species of wheat into Soviet agriculture was a total failure.

Having given Lysenko some very reasonable advice about regions that might be more hospitable to the growth of branched wheat, Stalin suddenly got excited about the possibility of using this wheat in order to improve the still meagre post-war harvests on collective and state farms. On 25 November, via his own office, he sent copies of Lysenko's report on branched wheat to all members of the Politburo, secretaries of the Central Committee and certain other senior officials with an accompanying letter saying that the questions raised by Lysenko would be discussed by the Politburo. The original of this letter, marked 'strictly secret' and 'to be returned to the Special Department of the Central Committee', was discovered in the Stalin fond of the Presidential Archive by Yuri Vavilov when he was looking for documents that might shed light on the arrest of his father in 1940.

Lysenko promised Stalin that there would be harvests of branched wheat of 10,000 kilograms per hectare by 1948 and that 100,000 hectares would be sown by 1951. Of course neither commitment turned out to be realizable. But Stalin's great enthusiasm for branched wheat would not have surprised the relatively small number of people in his inner circle who knew how keen he was to have new varieties and species of plant life grown in the USSR, plants that were normally only found in southern climates. At Stalin's dachas near Moscow and in the south, there were always large greenhouses that were usually positioned so as to allow him to enter directly from the house, day or night. There were always gardeners on his staff. Stalin loved to have exotic plants in his greenhouses, and pruning shrubs and plants was the only way he got physical exercise. In 1946 he was particularly keen on lemons. Molotov wrote about this in his memoirs with a certain irony:

> A special greenhouse for lemon trees was built at his dacha. A large one. ... And the way he pottered about there ... although I didn't see it. From everyone: oh! ah! And I – I can honestly say that there were fewer ohs and ahs from me than from the others, what I really thought was – to hell with it! A lemon tree in Moscow! What use could it have, what was so interesting, I had no idea. As if he was carrying out some kind of experiments. But if so, then first of all he should have known what he was doing.

> Akaky Mgeladze, the former First Secretary of the Central Committee in Georgia told me about these lemon trees. Stalin invited him to the dacha, cut off a bit of lemon and gave it to him. 'A good lemon?' 'Good, Comrade Stalin.' 'I grew it myself.'

> They walked about, chatted. Stalin cut another bit off: 'You have to try it.' So he had to eat it, praise it. 'I grew it myself. And where? In Moscow!' said Stalin. They walked a little more, and again he offered it: 'Look at it, it grows even in Moscow!'[14]

After the encounter with Mgeladze, Stalin obliged the Georgians to grow more lemons. In this republic lemon trees could grow on the sea-coast in the south. Stalin also insisted that lemon trees be grown in the Crimea, where unfortunately they were destroyed by winter frost. After that they planted lemon trees in trenches and covered them over in the winter. Thus the attempt to adapt lemons to the Russian climate was not very successful.

The well-known Soviet writer Pyotr Pavlenko, who lived in Yalta, was invited to see Stalin whenever he visited the Crimea. In his novel *Happiness*, published in 1947, he recreated a dialogue between Stalin and a gardener. The conversation was not entirely fictional, in the sense that it reflected views Stalin had actually expressed at various times. The novel takes place in the Crimea in the winter of 1945 when Stalin came for the meeting of the three Allied powers at the Yalta conference. One of the heroes of the novel, a former front-line soldier, Voropaev, was invited to visit Stalin:

> Wearing a light-coloured spring tunic and service cap, Stalin stood next to the old gardener by the grapevines. Glancing at Voropaev, he continued showing something to the gardener, which clearly was of serious interest to them both.

'Go ahead and try this method, don't be afraid,' said Stalin. 'I've tested it myself, it won't let you down.'

But the gardener, embarrassed and at the same time looking at Stalin with childlike admiration, made a helpless gesture: 'It's a little frightening to go against science, Josif Vissarionovich. There were some specialists here in the days of the tsar, but they were cautious.'

'They had no reason to be otherwise,' replied Stalin. 'Under the tsar, people were ignorant, it has nothing to do with us today. It's time for daring experiments! We need to have grapes and lemons in other regions besides here.'

'Climate, Josif Vissarionovich, puts a limit.' The gardener pointed to the grapevines: 'Look how fragile they are, how delicate ... how could they survive a frost?'

'Train them to accept harsh conditions, don't be afraid! You and I are southerners, but we also feel quite good in the north.' Stalin stopped speaking and took a few steps towards Voropaev.

'Here's a gardener, he's been working for forty-five years and he's afraid of science. This, he says, won't work, and that won't work either. In Pushkin's time, they brought eggplants to Odessa from Greece as a curiosity and now only fifteen years ago we started growing tomatoes in Murmansk. We wanted it to work and it did. We have to push for grapes, lemons and figs in the north. We were told that cotton wouldn't grow in the Kuban or in the Ukraine, but now it does. The point is to want something badly enough and get it done.'[15]

A number of agricultural innovations were introduced by Stalin, some more successful than others. Attempts were made to cultivate cotton in the Ukraine and the North Caucasus during the 1930s but later abandoned. More successful was the introduction of tea in Georgia, Azerbaijan and the Krasnodar region. The Soviet Union was therefore able to reduce its dependence on imported tea. It proved possible to grow peanuts in the southern part of the Ukraine. Australian eucalyptus trees, which supported drainage of the marshy soil, appeared on the Black Sea coast of the Caucasus. But Stalin's famous project to build the Great Turkmen Canal across the desert in the hope of turning Turkmenia into a country of olive plantations did not succeed. Construction work on the canal began in 1949, but it was still unfinished at the time of Stalin's death. The whole project was dropped in April 1953. Another of Stalin's ambitions was to end the USSR's dependence on imported natural rubber, but the attempt to cultivate wild rubber plants (*kok-sagyz*) ended in failure. When Stalin's dacha complex near Lake Ritsa was specially built for him in 1949, they also constructed a large greenhouse where he tried to raise cacao and coffee trees.

The 'Stalin Plan for the Transformation of Nature', announced in October 1948 without any preliminary discussion, was perhaps the most grandiose of all his agricultural projects. The 30-year plan envisaged the creation of forest belts across a huge territory in the south of the country which would hold back and tame the arid winds from the steppes of Kazakhstan and the deserts of Central Asia. These forests would protect the fields. Additionally there would be seven 'state' forest belts, each one thousands of kilometres long extending from north to south across the dry steppes of the Volga basin. Stalin's confidence that oak or other leafy trees of the forest zones of Russia could flourish in the dry Volga steppe country or in the salty, semi-arid areas near the Caspian Sea was not based on any experimental data but simply on the expectation that the new trees and plants would adapt to their new environment if they had been planted from seeds in arid conditions rather than transplanted as seedlings. A special state directorate was established with vast resources at its disposal to implement this project. After Stalin's death the attempt to plant trees in the steppes came to an end. In 1948, when the agriculture of the country had not yet recovered from the war, when there were almost no young, healthy men in the countryside, grandiose projects with no foreseeable results for 25 or 30 years, like the Turkmen Canal or the forest belts, were simply absurd.

Stalin, Lysenko and Sergei Vavilov

Classical genetics had pretty much been suppressed by 1939. When Nikolai Vavilov, the director of two institutes (plant breeding and genetics), was arrested in August 1940, he was one of the last victims. There had been no lack of denunciations against him, but for some time he was allowed to survive because of his international reputation. His arrest would have had to be sanctioned at the very highest level. According to recently declassified information, the Politburo twice considered denunciations against Vavilov but did not take a decision. By 1940 the great wave of terror was subsiding and there was reason to hope that the danger was over and the storm had passed him by. But with war engulfing Europe, the fact that some scientist or other had been acclaimed abroad became a less important consideration.

Complicated arrangements were made for his arrest. He was sent on an official field trip to the western Ukraine, now ceded to the Soviet Union under the terms of the Molotov–Ribbentrop Pact and the actual arrest took place in open country, almost entirely without witnesses. In the 1930s only ordinary people experienced a knock on the door in the middle of the night. Those who were prominent, including generals and marshals, were arrested according to carefully scripted scenarios in order to create an element of surprise and avoid publicity or the possibility of resistance. There are documents in Vavilov's investigation file that show how carefully they had planned his arrest. On 18 July the Commissar of Agriculture signed an order sending Vavilov to the western Ukraine to collect samples of cultured plants. Immediately after his departure from Leningrad, on 22 July, Beria sent a letter to Molotov in his capacity as Chairman of the Sovnarkom, requesting permission to arrest Vavilov. Neither Stalin nor Lysenko signed any of the relevant papers; the scenario was devised to conceal their involvement.

The arrest was hardly noticed abroad, and only in 1944 did questions start arriving from Britain and the United States. By 1945 there were an increasing number of queries about Vavilov's whereabouts. A large number of letters were addressed to the Academy of Sciences, including an official communication from the Royal Society of Great Britain – they had elected Vavilov to membership in 1942, just at the time when he was dying of starvation in the prison of Saratov. In June 1945 the Academy of Sciences celebrated the 220th anniversary of its founding, and more than 100 foreign scientists were invited to the celebrations. It was only then that Vavilov's friends from abroad found out what had happened to him. His younger brother, Academician Sergei Vavilov, a physicist who also had an international reputation in the field of light, fluorescence and optics, was present at the jubilee occasion. Lysenko did not participate. The President of the Academy, the elderly botanist Vladimir Komarov, was due to retire, and elections for the new president were set for 17 July. When Sergei Vavilov was chosen, his election was greeted with enthusiasm in the scientific community and was viewed as a sign that persecution and repression in the field of genetics had come to an end. Vavilov's election to the top scientific post in the country came as a serious blow to Lysenko, whose influence in the Academy was already diminishing. His opponents in the Academy and the universities now initiated a new, far-ranging discussion that caused a stir in several agricultural institutes. Thus Yuri Zhdanov's speech in April 1948 was part of a debate that began to threaten the existence of the entire school of 'Michurin biology'.

It should be said that the election of Sergei Vavilov as President of the Academy most certainly did not mean that genetics had become a legitimate discipline or that repression in general was over. Everyone understood that the final decision had been up to Stalin, as has been confirmed by recently published archive documents.[16] By choosing Sergei Vavilov from a list of 22 prospective candidates sent to the Kremlin on 7 July (with documentation on each one drawn up by the NKGB), Stalin above all wanted to create the impression that he had not been involved in the arrest of the elder brother. He had only recently become aware of the true extent of the deceased scientist's international prestige and he was determined to deflect any blame for the whole affair. Sergei Vavilov's 'reference' from the NKGB gave Stalin no reason to reject him, apart from the fact that his brother had been arrested and died in prison. It confirmed his 'political loyalty' and noted his huge scientific authority as well as his organizational abilities. 'His manner is straight-forward, his way of life modest', added the authors of the report, which was signed by the head of the Second Section of the NKGB, Lieutenant-General N.F. Fedotov. Copies of the candidate's profiles were also sent to Molotov and Malenkov. Other outstanding scientists on the list did not fare so well in the evaluation of their personal characteristics. Ivan Bardin, the Vice President of the Academy, did not 'associate with other scientists because of the excessive snobbery of his wife'. Academician Aleksandr Zavaritzky was 'quarrelsome and reserved'. The Academician and mathematician Ivan Vinogradov was 'unsociable and ignorant about other fields of science … single and a heavy drinker'. Even Igor Kurchatov, a Stalin favourite, had his faults: 'secretive, cautious, cunning and a real diplomat'. But needless to say, for someone in charge of atomic projects, these traits could hardly be seen as anything less than favourable.

State pseudoscience

In the summer of 1948, when I was still a student at the Timiryazev Academy of Agriculture, I was in the Crimea working on a project in the Nikitsky Botanical Gardens near Yalta as part of my degree requirements. I followed the proceedings of the VASKhNIL conference in *Pravda*. I was delighted to see that my scientific mentor Pyotr Zhukovsky, a VASKhNIL Academician and Chairman of the Botany Department at the Timiryazev Academy, made a very strong and ironic speech on 3 August criticizing Lysenko's basic theories. But at the final session of the conference, after Lysenko had let it be known that his report had been approved by the Central Committee, Zhukovsky spoke again, and this time his remarks were full of apology and self-criticism. Apparently the organizers of the session needed those who had been beaten to admit publicly the error of their ways. Zhukovsky arrived at the Nikitsky Botanical Gardens in mid-August. He was supervising a few projects and hoped to recuperate from what he had been through. As soon as we were alone he said to me: 'I concluded a Brest–Litovsk peace with Lysenko.'

By the time I returned to Moscow in early October, the demolition job was already over. Genetics research throughout the country had been destroyed, with all of Lysenko's critics dismissed from their posts. Once they were given emergency powers, Lysenko and his 'general staff' had worked relentlessly. In October the chain reaction began. On the basis of what happened at the VASKhNIL conference, pseudo-scientific concepts gained pre-eminence in other spheres of science as well. In physiology, microbiology, chemistry and cybernetics, work was pushed back by decades. The 'Brest–Litovsk peace' with Lysenko continued for far too long, lasting until 1965–66. The negative effects of this extended reign of pseudo-science in the USSR continued for an even longer period. A full overcoming of the consequences has yet to be achieved even to this day. The diminished authority of Soviet science, the delayed development of biotechnology, and the gigantic, extravagant, over-complex projects in nuclear physics and space have made Russian science too dependent on state coffers, which today are almost empty. In the USSR science never became the main force behind technological and economic progress. Although there has been a continual process of 'revival' and catching-up in science, technological and economic advances have largely come about as a result of imitation – the adoption of what has already been achieved in other countries.

Nikolai Vavilov was fully rehabilitated in 1956 and posthumously restored to his status as an Academician. After his arrest in 1940 he had been expelled from the Academy of Sciences and his name had been expunged from the list of former Academicians. His brother Sergei died of a heart attack in 1951. Yuri Zhdanov, who in 1950 became the father of Stalin's granddaughter Katya, remained in his Central Committee position until the end of 1953 and actively participated in all the destructive campaigns that did so much harm to Soviet science. Lysenko died in 1976. To the end of his life he continued to be an active member of the Academy of Sciences and the scientific head of an experimental station of the Academy not far from Moscow where he went on doing research on temperature, humidity and other factors as he continued his attempts to alter the heredity of local plants and animals.

CHAPTER 10

Stalin and Linguistics: An Episode from the History of Soviet Science

Roy Medvedev

Whenever Stalin intervened in a scientific or scholarly debate, the results were usually predictable: arrests, the suppression of ideas, and the promotion of careerists, fanatics or blatant charlatans. But there are exceptions to every rule and what took place in the field of linguistics proved to be one of them.

The science of language, or linguistics, was never considered to be one of our leading academic subjects. It was taught in a few faculties, but the number of specialists in the field was never very great. Nevertheless at the end of the 1920s passions were seething and a rather ungentlemanly battle was fought by one particular faction in order to gain supremacy within this narrow discipline. It had become an accepted principle, much to the detriment of scientific progress, that each branch of science or scholarship had to have a single undisputed leader, supported by a hierarchy of power and influence. In linguistics it was Nikolai Marr who aspired to this role with his 'new teaching' on language.

Marr, who was half-Scottish and half-Georgian, grew up in a Georgian environment in Kutaisi, where from an early age he exhibited extraordinary linguistic ability. He was able to speak 20 foreign languages and as a student was already writing articles about the special peculiarities of Georgian. Later he studied the origins of Armenian and led an excavation project in Armenia, which produced significant scientific results. At the beginning of the century Marr was not only regarded as one of the leading philologists in Russia, but was also a prominent archaeologist, an authority on the Caucasus and an orientalist. In 1912 he was elected to membership of the Russian Academy of Sciences.

Marr's best work had no connection with linguistics – he was thought to be something of a dilettante by the major scholars in the field. After 1910, however, linguistics became his main interest and central activity. His ideas were always extravagantly outrageous, but it was this quality that brought him considerable notoriety. To give a few examples: it was Marr's view that Georgian and Armenian were cognate languages; he believed that Russian was closer to Georgian

than to Ukrainian; he argued that the Svan language of the mountain people in the Caucasus living in Svanetia had its origins in
Germany; and he insisted that languages with different roots could
'cross breed' to create a new language. Marr's texts were difficult to
read, full of examples from languages that were obscure or extinct as
well as arguments that were incomprehensible. Many who were
determined to master the 'new teaching' soon gave up, finding it
'interesting, but impossible to understand'.

Several factors contributed to the public attention surrounding
Marr in the 1920s. His colleagues, of course, played a role. He was
also taken up by Lunacharsky, the Commissar of Education, who
had studied natural science and philosophy at the University of
Zurich and thought of himself as something of a philosopher.
Lunacharsky publicly called Marr 'our greatest Soviet philologist'
and even 'the world's greatest living philologist'. I find it hard to
imagine that Lunacharsky could have understood Marr's 'Japhetic
theory' (Japheth was a son of the Biblical Noah), according to which
the Indo-European and Semitic languages represented a later stage in
the development of the Caucasian language. But Marr had been one
of a small number of major scholars who had supported the Bolsheviks in 1917. He had even been a member of the Petrograd Soviet and
for a time chaired the Central Council of Scientists.

Before the end of the 1920s Marr did not possess the degree of
authority that would allow him to limit the development of other
trends in linguistics. Then in 1928 citations from Marx and Engels
began to appear in his articles and the terms 'bourgeois' and 'proletarian' were applied to linguistics. Academician Marr declared that he
had embarked on intensive study of the works of Marx, Engels and
Lenin. As might be expected, the extension of Marxism into the field
of linguistics allowed Marr to make one discovery after another. He
now claimed, for example, that language is nothing more than a part
of the superstructure arising out of the economic base, and therefore,
he asserted, all language can only be understood in terms of its class
character. Social revolutions lead to a qualitative leap in the development of languages and new social forms create a new language.
Influential party ideologists of the time readily welcomed Marr's
theory as part of the 'cast-iron inventory of the materialist understanding of history'(M.N. Pokrovsky); according to V.M. Friche 'the
dialectical constructs of Marr manifestly reflect the communist ideal'.
Marr also came to Stalin's attention. At the Sixteenth Party Congress
in 1930 Marr was chosen to speak on behalf of Soviet scientists:

> I carry out my scientific work, developing my theoretical studies of
> language, under the conditions of total freedom that Soviet power has
> brought to science. ... At a time when the class struggle is intensify-
> ing, it has become clear to me that an apolitical approach is false, and

I have discarded it. I am determined to use all my rejuvenated revolutionary creativity to be a warrior on the scientific front for the unequivocal general line of proletarian scientific theory and for the general line of the Communist Party.[1]

At the end of his speech, instead of the usual homage to Stalin, the Academician paid tribute to world revolution. However, Marr had delivered part of his speech in Georgian, which received an ovation in the hall. Many of the delegates may not have understood what he actually said in that language, but of course they understood to whom his words were addressed. Immediately after the Congress Marr was accepted as a member of the Party and within a year he became a member of the Central Executive Committee (VTsIK), one of the leading organs of Soviet power at the time.

If the 'new teaching' was declared to be 'Marxism in linguistics', those who rejected his theories would no longer simply be critics of Marr – among themselves they called it *marazmom* (a pun on the term 'marasmus' meaning senile decay) – they would become opponents of Marxism-Leninism, which even at the beginning of the 1930s was not without its dangers. When Marr was awarded the Order of Lenin, the most prestigious decoration one could receive at that time, it signalled official acceptance of his theory as the only correct line in the field of linguistics. Books and articles expressing alternative points of view were dismissed as 'idealism' and were condemned as 'scientific contraband', 'hostile constructions', 'wrecking in science', 'social-fascism' and even 'Trotskyism in linguistics'. But then in 1934, at the very height of this 'pogrom' type campaign, Academician Marr suddenly died.

The repressions of 1937–38 led to the arrest and murder of many who had been Marr's opponents. The death of one of his most daring critics, Professor E.D. Polivanov, was a great loss to science. In contemporary encyclopaedias he is referred to as one of the most prominent experts on eastern languages. But in 1937 he was described as a 'black-hundreds linguistics-idealist' and 'a kulak wolf hiding in the skin of a Soviet professor'. Another outstanding linguistics scholar who was arrested and died in the camps was N.A. Nevsky, who had deciphered Tungus hieroglyphics. (Fortunately his great work, *Tungus Philology,* was preserved in the archives of the Academy of Sciences and was published in 1960. In 1962 it was awarded the Lenin Prize.) Certain of Marr's influential supporters also fell victim to the terror, in several cases accused of links with Bukharin, and many of his powerful patrons were discredited.

The climate in linguistics began to change in 1939 when the prominent Soviet scholar Professor Viktor Vinogradov returned to Moscow from exile. The author of many academic textbooks and one of the contributors to the *Dictionary of the Russian Language,* he had been arrested at the beginning of the 1930s and sent to Vyatka (later, Kirov). After completing his term of exile he was given the right to live anywhere beyond a 100-kilometre zone around Moscow, and he chose to settle in Mozhaisk. At the beginning of February 1939 Vinogradov sent a letter to Stalin, asking for his trust and requesting permission to return to work and to live in the apartment of his wife in Moscow. 'I am considered to be an outstanding specialist,' he wrote, 'but I do not have the professional rights of any Soviet scholar.' Letters like this were written to Stalin all the time, although they rarely reached the addressee. But Vinogradov's letter was sent via Stalin's personal assistant, Poskrebyshev, and it did reach his desk along with a short reference from the NKVD. On the letter, in red pencil, Stalin wrote: 'Grant Professor Vinogradov's request. J. Stalin.' Molotov, Kaganovich, Khrushchev, Voroshilov and Zhdanov also appended their signatures below.[2] In such cases, Poskrebyshev would then inform all interested parties about the decision. Vinogradov would no longer have to fear further repression.

In 1946 Vinogradov was elected to the Academy of Sciences. It was known that he did not countenance the revelations of the 'new teaching'; he considered himself to be a pupil of the illustrious Russian linguistic scholar and historian Aleksei Shakhmatov, who died in 1920.

During the years 1939–48, scholars in the field of linguistics could work in relative peace, although formally they were still required to acknowledge the postulates of the 'great' Marr. The main proponent of the 'new teaching' and interpreter of the Japhetic school was now Ivan Meshchaninov, who possessed neither the authority nor the connections nor even the ambition of his teacher. The new leader of Soviet linguistics had not become an Academician until 1932, and he was compelled to be cautious and observe moderation. The whole situation changed, however, in 1948. Unfortunately the infamous VASKhNIL session initiated the beginning of pogrom campaigns throughout the sciences and not just in biology. A struggle got under way against bourgeois idealism, cosmopolitanism and 'kowtowing to the West'.

At that time I was a university student in Leningrad, where the 'Leningrad affair' was taking its toll within the academic community as well as among Party cadres. Many prominent scholars were dismissed from their jobs, expelled from the Party, deprived of their titles and even arrested. Mature students in their final year – army veterans – suddenly became teachers and assistant deans. In these circumstances many of the Marrists began to push Meshchaninov towards a conflict with the opponents of Marr, urging him to re-establish a monopoly position for the 'new teaching'.

The first attack on the 'anti-Marrists' took place at a meeting of the academic council of the Marr Institute of Languages and the Leningrad branch of the Russian language section of the Academy of Sciences. Meshchaninov gave the keynote address. He pounced on the reactionary academics who continued to uphold 'the obsolete traditions of pre-revolutionary liberal-bourgeois linguistics'. Many harsh words were directed against Vinogradov and his school. A number of major scholars from Leningrad and Moscow, such as A.A. Reformatsky, found themselves branded as 'idealists', but the list also contained the names of many Caucasian linguists, including Arnold Chikobava.

There was virtually no resistance to this onslaught in Leningrad, which had always been the centre of the 'new teaching' and where Meshchaninov controlled all senior positions in faculties and institutes. He also headed the Languages and Literature section of the Academy of Sciences. But in Moscow there was a strong contingent of linguistics specialists and philologists determined to make a stand. The most powerful resistance, however, arose in the Caucasus among an extremely talented group for whom the primitive theories of Marr had little relevance.

In Armenia the most prominent scholar in the field was Rachia Acharyan, who was considered to be the founder of Armenian linguistics. When he was young he had been acquainted with Marr and even enjoyed his patronage. However, once he embarked on his own independent research, he began to criticize the dogmas of Japhetic theory, and in 1915 Marr crudely dismissed his work as 'having no place in serious scientific discourse'. It should be said that Acharyan had been educated in two European universities and was a member of the Czech as well as the Armenian Academy of Sciences. His voluminous output included a number of distinguished publications: the *Armenian Etymological Dictionary*, the *Dictionary of Armenian Dialects*, the *Armenian Dictionary of Grammar* and *The History of Armenian Literature.* His unique achievement, unrivalled in its scope, was the *Comprehensive Grammar of the Armenian Language in Comparison with 562 Other Languages.* This four-volume work had to be published by lithograph, since the author used words and expressions from languages that could not be set in type by any printer in the Caucasus. At the end of the 1940s Acharyan had a greater reputation within the international community of linguistics scholars than either Marr or Meshchaninov. But Acharyan was elderly and unwell. It was his students and colleagues who were now playing the leading role in Armenian faculties, among whom there was an outstanding scholar and member of the Armenian Academy of Sciences, Grikor Kapantsyan.

The offensive by the Marrists in Armenia proved to be relatively successful. Although their professional authority was minimal in the republic, their pretensions were supported by the Ideological Section of the Central Committee in Moscow, which was the decisive weapon of the First Secretary of the Armenian Central Committee, Georgy Arutinov. Acharyan and Kapantsyan were removed from their posts and their supporters were expelled from the University of Yerevan and the Armenian Institute of Languages.

Things went differently in Georgia, where Arnold Chikobava, a member of the Georgian Academy of Sciences, was regarded as Georgia's leading linguistics scholar. He was the author of a series of Georgian dictionaries and an outstanding specialist on the structure and history of Caucasian languages. And he was certainly not a follower of Marr. Chikobava was an energetic and talented 52-year-old, a successful teacher at the University of Tbilisi who had many friends among the Party activists of the republic as well as in the academic community. He was on cordial terms with the First Secretary of the Georgian Central Committee, Kandid Charkviani. In addition to protecting Chikobava in Georgia, Charkviani persuaded him to send a complaint to Stalin. Needless to say, thousands of complaints and reports were sent to Stalin from all parts of the country, and most of them, unanswered, sank without trace into the recesses of the Central Committee. However, in this instance Charkviani was able to ensure that the letter actually reached Stalin's desk.

Chikobava had sent a straightforward and convincing account of the situation in linguistics, which Stalin read with great interest. Although he had no particular involvement in the whole question, he was astonished that major changes had taken place in an entire branch of scholarship without his knowledge. It was outrageous that the Academy of Sciences had announced the 'new teaching' to be the 'sole materialist Marxist theory of language' without his agreement and approval. It had been some time since Stalin, the supreme theorist and *coryphaeus* of Marxism, had publicly expressed theoretical views. Other serious questions were claiming his attention: economic problems, the world communist movement, the new socialist countries and, as always, international affairs. Other members of the Politburo publicly addressed these various issues – Zhdanov, Malenkov and Voznesensky – and their speeches and reports were cited everywhere, always with quotations from some 10- or 15-year-old statement by Stalin. Of course everyone knew that Stalin had approved Lysenko's speech at the VASKhNIL conference, but that was biology, and it was understood that Stalin would be reluctant to make a personal statement about such a specialized topic. Linguistics, however, was a subject much closer to his heart. In the past he had written about language as one of the most important symbols of the nation. A new public pronouncement in this field would enhance Stalin's reputation as a 'classic' of Marxism–Leninism. In any case he was genuinely curious about the question of the origin and development of language.

Stalin asked his secretary to gather together a selection of books on linguistics; some he read, others he just leafed through. Judging from his notes in the margins the book that apparently pleased him most was the popular *Introduction to Linguistics* written by D.N. Kudryavsky and published in 1912 in Yuryev (later, Tartu). As Stalin was such a quick reader, almost daily there was a new pile of books on linguistics in his study at the Kuntsevo dacha. 'You can't imagine what Comrade Stalin has to read!' exclaimed one of Stalin's visitors to his friends afterwards. It was Ivan Isakov, Admiral of the Fleet and head of the Navy General Staff at the Ministry of the Navy, who had come to report to Stalin at the end of March 1950 and was astonished to find that the Supreme Commander-in-Chief had so many books on his desk about the origins of language. As we have seen, Stalin tended to prepare himself before meeting new people and then astonished them with unexpectedly precise observations or questions about their work.

At the beginning of April 1950 Chikobava was notified that he was to meet the Secretaries of the Central Committee in Moscow on 10 April. But on the evening before, he was taken to the Kuntsevo dacha along with Charkviani and three other Georgian leaders where Stalin himself was waiting for them. The conversation began at nine o'clock in the evening. Stalin spoke first, commenting on and then making a few suggestions about the first volume of the *Dictionary of the Georgian Language*, edited by Chikobava, which had only just appeared. The book was there on Stalin's desk and it was obvious that he had looked at it rather carefully. They then turned to the 'new teaching' on language. Chikobava expected to limit himself to 20 or 30 minutes, but Stalin interrupted him, insisting that there was no need to rush. He listened with concentration, jotting things down in his large notebook and occasionally asking questions. He wanted to know which of the scholars in Moscow and Leningrad were opponents of Marr's theories. Chikobava told him about Academician Vinogradov, who was at the time coming under enormous pressure. From time to time tea and snacks were brought into the study. On hearing that Academicians Acharyan and Kapantsyan had been removed from their positions in Armenia, Stalin interrupted Chikobava and asked for a phone connection to Yerevan. Ministers and obkom secretaries knew that Stalin worked at night and therefore they themselves never went to bed before morning. The following exchange took place on the phone:

Stalin: Comrade Arutinov, do two men called Acharyan and Kapantsyan work in your republic?

Arutinov: Yes, Comrade Stalin, they do live here, but they are not working, they were removed from their posts.

Stalin: And who exactly are they?

Arutinov: They're scholars, academicians ...

Stalin: And I thought they were accountants, who can lose their position in one place and then be employed in another. You were too much in a hurry, Comrade Arutinov, too much in a hurry.

And with that Stalin put down the receiver without saying goodbye. The terrified Arutinov summoned his aides and the head of the science department of the Armenian Central Committee. They decided not to disturb Acharyan, who was ill, but a car was sent to fetch Kapantsyan. He was awakened, reassured (he might have thought he was being arrested) and brought to Central Committee headquarters. Arutinov informed the disgraced professor that he had been appointed director of the Armenian Institute of Languages. Kapantsyan replied: 'Could this news really not have waited until morning?'

Meanwhile at Kuntsevo, Stalin's conversation with Chikobava was coming to an end. It was seven o'clock in the morning. To Chikobava's surprise, Stalin suggested that he write an article for *Pravda* on the question of linguistics. 'But will they publish it?' he asked, still not fully understanding the situation. 'You write it, and we'll see. If it's suitable, it will be published,' replied Stalin.

Within a week the article was on Stalin's desk. Chikobava had two more long conversations with Stalin, each time for two or three hours. Evidently Stalin was continuing to absorb information about linguistics. Of course, those in his closest circle would not have remained unaware of his new interest in the subject. Malenkov, who had partially taken charge of Zhdanov's functions in the ideological leadership of the country after Zhdanov's death, invited Academician Vinogradov to come to see him; they had a long conversation, the contents of which have never been divulged.

On 9 May 1950 Chikobava's long article appeared in *Pravda* along with an editorial note: 'published as a matter for discussion'. Since the article harshly criticized the 'new teaching' on language and attacked Meshchanov personally, the latter was invited to reply. Thus began a public debate which did not carry on for very long. The articles appeared exclusively in *Pravda*; other papers had not been given permission to participate in the 'discussion'. During these days one of my friends expressed admiration for Chikobava, remarking how courageous he had been to challenge Marr's theories directly. But another, more subtle acquaintance suggested that the truly courageous one was Meshchanov, who still dared to question Chikobava's criticism. Meanwhile Stalin was preparing his own contribution with the help of Vinogradov, Chikobava and several other specialists, although it can be seen from the vocabulary and style that he wrote the final article himself. It was generally his custom to consult outside experts, who were always warned by Poskrebyshev that their conversations with Stalin were to be kept absolutely confidential.

Stalin's article 'On Marxism and Linguistics' appeared in *Pravda* on 20 June 1950. I still remember the day. Suddenly the examinations that were taking place at the university were interrupted, and teachers and students were told to go down to the entrance hall of the building where two loudspeakers had been set up. Stalin's article was read aloud by the most famous announcer in the country, Levitan, who had broadcast all the orders of the Supreme Commander-in-Chief during the war. Students from the philosophy, history and economics faculties listened in total silence, straining to remember as much as possible. It astonished us to hear Stalin say that language was not and never could be part of the superstructure arising out of the economic base, since language exists in a variety of different social and economic contexts without changing all that much over time. Questioning the suitability of a class approach to language, we were amused when he asked: 'Do these comrades believe that English feudal lords communicated with English peasants through a translator, did they not both use the English language?' It was astonishing to hear Stalin refer to the 'caste of leaders whom Meshchaninov calls the pupils of Marr'. 'If,' Stalin said, 'I had not been convinced of the honesty of Comrade Meshchaninov and his colleagues, I would say that their behaviour amounted to "wrecking".' What he said about Marr was unforgettable: he had never been able to become a real Marxist and in fact 'was only a simplifier and vulgarizer of Marxism'. We started glancing at each other with a sense of elation when Stalin declared that 'no science can progress without a clash of opinions, without freedom of criticism' and that 'an "Arakcheyev regime" had been set up in linguistics that cultivated irresponsibility and encouraged excesses.' It was a regime that had to be liquidated.

At this point the public debate came to an end, although Stalin did publish four more pieces in *Pravda* in response to some of the questions raised in the very many letters he received from linguistics specialists over the days and weeks following his original intervention. Meshchaninov lost all his positions, but his students and colleagues were spared, having repented with alacrity, and they immediately embarked on a process of re-education 'in the light of Comrade Stalin's work'. Repressions within the discipline had successfully been avoided, although attempts to settle old scores went on for some time. Vinogradov became the director of the Institute of Languages, which of course was no longer named after Marr. He was also put in charge of the Language and Literature section of the Academy Sciences as well as the journal *Voprosy Yazikoznaniya* (Questions of Linguistics). From the autumn of 1950 a new course was introduced as part of the social science syllabus in all institutions of higher education: 'Stalin's Teaching on Linguistics'. A simplified version of the course was taught in Party schools – even in the most remote rural districts. The following dialogue between two ordinary *kolkhozniks* (collective farmers) appears in a novel by Fyodor Abramov:

> 'Ivan Dmitrievich,' said Filya, 'they say that wreckers have again appeared?'
> 'What kind of wreckers?'
> 'Some sort of academicians. They want to destroy the Russian language.'
> 'Language?' asks the astonished Arkady, 'What do you mean – language?'
> 'Yes, yes,' insisted Ignaty, 'that's what I heard. And they say that Josef Vissarionovich himself fixed their brains. It was in *Pravda.*'
> 'Oh well', sighed the old watchman, 'we'll survive it. Last year some sort of cosmopolitans sold out to foreign capitalists, and this year it's academicians. I don't know, what will they think up next? Why can't they get rid of all those scum?'

Nevertheless it must be admitted that Stalin's contribution to the linguistics debate had on the whole a positive effect. Moreover, a discipline that had always occupied a rather modest position in the world of social science for a time acquired an unprecedented degree of prestige.

CHAPTER 11

Stalin and the Blitzkrieg

Zhores and Roy Medvedev

Operation Barbarossa

Hitler approved the plan for war with Russia on 18 December 1940; it was called 'Operation Barbarossa', a reference to the twelfth-century German king and Holy Roman Emperor. The date for the invasion was set at 15 May 1941. By January 1941 Stalin was familiar with the basic details of the plan, thanks to the precise reports he was receiving from Soviet Intelligence. A telegram of 24 March 1941 from one of the most reliable Soviet agents in Germany, Arvid Harnack (alias 'Corsican'), who worked for the German Minister of Economics, explained that the middle of May had been chosen because 'the Germans assumed that the retreating Soviet troops would not have time to burn the unripe grain; therefore they could gather in the harvest themselves.'[1] The Commissar for State Security, Vsevolod Merkulov, distributed this information to Stalin, Molotov, Beria and Semyon Timoshenko, the Commissar of Defence. There is no reason to think that the Soviet leadership questioned this date for the start of the war, particularly as it was confirmed by another reliable agent, Richard Sorge. From Tokyo, he too reported that according to information received from both the naval attaché and German ambassador (Eugen Ott) the date for the attack was related to 'the completion of sowing in the USSR. The war can start at any moment after that, and Germany then merely has to gather the harvest.'[2] Sorge's message reached Moscow at the beginning of May, when the month for the invasion of the USSR had already been shifted to June as a result of unexpected developments in the Balkans. Letters dispatched via secret diplomatic post to the German ambassador in Tokyo were now taking much longer to arrive because, since April 1941, diplomatic post bound for Japan was no longer sent through the USSR on the Trans-Siberian Railway. In the USSR it certainly was noted that Germany had stopped using the

Trans-Siberian Railway, even for the import of strategically crucial rubber from South-East Asia.

Stalin and his military leaders also were aware of the concentration of German troops along the whole western perimeter of the Soviet Union. By the end of March 1941 more than 100 divisions of the Wehrmacht were stationed on Polish, Romanian and Finnish territory, concentrated on the borders with the USSR. The armed forces of Romania, Hungary, Finland and even Slovakia had been brought to a state of military readiness. The Soviet Union also strengthened its own forces in the western border districts, but as yet there were no apparent signs of anxiety within the military or political leadership.

In order to guarantee a successful campaign against the Soviet Union, Hitler had to secure his southern flank, where a dangerous situation had arisen at the end of 1940. Greece was an ally of Britain, and her airfields could be used for the bombardment of the oil refineries of Ploiesti in Romania, at that time the main source of fuel for the German military machine. As Germany had no borders with Greece, the first attempt at occupation came from Italy, after the subjugation of Albania. But the Italian army was totally vanquished when it invaded Greece in October 1940. As well as driving the Italians out of their country, the Greeks managed to seize a bridgehead in Albania. This was the first serious defeat for what was known as the 'Tripartite Pact' or 'Berlin–Rome–Tokyo Axis'. Britain immediately came to Greece's assistance. With a powerful fleet in the Mediterranean, Britain was able to land its army on Crete and send an expeditionary force made up of three divisions and a tank brigade. The airports around Athens became a base for British planes. Given this situation, Hitler was unable to take a final decision about Barbarossa until Greece and its British ally were crushed.

In order to invade Greece the German army would have to pass through the territory of Romania, Hungary, Yugoslavia and Bulgaria, and it would take time to secure military alliances with these countries. Romania and Hungary quickly agreed to join the Tripartite Pact at the end of 1940; however, after Italy's defeat, Bulgaria and Yugoslavia declared their neutrality. This compelled Hitler to plan a possible occupation of the entire Balkan peninsula, which would have inevitable repercussions for the start of the eastern campaign.

Under intense pressure from Germany, Bulgaria agreed to join the Tripartite Pact on 1 March 1941. For three weeks the Yugoslavs defied Hitler's threats but finally gave in on 18 March and informed Hitler that they were prepared to join the Pact. The formal signing of the treaty was to take place in 25 March in Vienna. The attack on Greece was planned for 1 April, which left only a week to prepare the operation, and Hitler was in a hurry. But once again his plan had to be postponed as a result of a dawn coup in Belgrade on 27 March which brought a pro-Soviet, pro-British government to power. Exultant crowds came out on the streets shouting 'Down with Hitler', 'Alliance with the USSR', 'Three Cheers for Stalin and Molotov', 'Power to the Soviets'.

The German ambassador to Belgrade was convinced that the overturn in Belgrade (which involved only Serbs) had been orchestrated by the Russian and British special services. The Croats were against the coup, and former members of the government tried to save themselves from arrest, seeking refuge in Zagreb. When he received the telegram from Belgrade, Hitler flew into a rage and straightaway summoned his generals and military commanders from the General Staff. There was no discussion. Hitler ordered immediate preparations for an operation against Yugoslavia, to be combined with already existing plans for the seizure of Greece. 'Speed was of the essence ... to crush Yugoslavia with merciless harshness.' Hitler also announced that the beginning of Operation Barbarossa would be postponed for four weeks.[3]

The Balkan 'gift' for Stalin

All special operations of the Soviet secret service were usually planned by Stalin personally, or at least required his approval. In March 1941 the Yugoslav ambassador to Moscow, Milan Gavrilović, participated in secret negotiations for a possible friendship and mutual assistance pact between Yugoslavia and the USSR. Gavrilović also informed the Soviet leadership about developments within his own government. According to General Sudoplatov, at that time the deputy head of the intelligence section of the NKVD and responsible for special operations, Gavrilović had formally become a Soviet Intelligence source, controlled by the head of counter-intelligence, General Pavel Fedotov, as well as by Sudoplatov himself. An operations group was immediately dispatched to Belgrade, headed by Major-General Solomon Milshtein along with two experienced secret agents, Vasily Zarubin and A.M. Alakhverdov.[4] Until the end of 1938 Milshtein had been Beria's assistant in Georgia, and they moved together to Moscow in December 1938. In February 1941 Milshtein was appointed head of the newly created Third Directorate of the NKVD. In order to keep Milshtein's mission to Belgrade secret, his absence from the NKVD was camouflaged by a fictitious transfer to the post of Deputy Commissar of Forestry. The date of this 'transfer', 11 March 1941, was also the day of his arrival in Belgrade. Stalin had total confidence in Milshtein, and during the war years made him the head of counter-intelligence in the Red Army, also putting him in charge of the political supervision of army units.

Yugoslavia at that time was a monarchy with the king's dictatorial powers guaranteeing a balance between the different ethnic and religious groups of the population, each with their own territory and diverse historical experience. The heir to the throne, Peter II, was under age in 1941 and Yugoslavia was ruled by a regent, Prince Paul, whose brother, King Alexander I, had been assassinated in 1934 when his son was only 11 years old. In Vienna on 25 March the Prime Minister of Yugoslavia, Dragiša Cvetković, together with Prince Paul, signed the treaty linking their country to the Tripartite Pact. Mass demonstrations of young people protesting against the alliance with Germany began in Belgrade the next day. The streets were full of placards proclaiming 'Better war than the Pact', 'Better the grave, than slavery'.[5] General of the Air Force, Dušan Simović, led the opposition to the Pact, and it was he who was behind the 'palace revolution' in the early hours of 27 March.

On 28 March a special report by the army secret service landed on Stalin's desk, entitled 'On the Coup in Yugoslavia', signed by Lieutenant General Filipp Golikov. Copies were also received by Molotov, Timoshenko and Zhukov, at that time head of the General Staff. It stated that:

> The Regent Paul seized the throne with Hitler's agreement, and on the night of 27th March, Prince Peter was sent to Romania. Peter was intercepted *en route* by General Simović's people and brought back to Belgrade. In the morning Paul tried to escape to Zagreb but was seized. Cvetković and other ministers also were arrested. The Guards and units of the Belgrade garrison occupied all major institutions of the city. Peter II proclaimed himself king. ... General Simović was charged with forming a new government. ... Demonstrations took place throughout the country. ... Confusion reigned in German circles. The demonstrators overturned every vehicle bearing a swastika, the aide of the German attaché was wounded, and the German Embassy to Belgrade evacuated. ... The Yugoslav army is in a state of alert. At present its strength consists of 48–50 divisions and 10 brigades.[6]

Certain Western historians have attributed the organization of the coup in Yugoslavia to the station chief of the American secret service, Bill Donovan, while Churchill stressed the contribution of his own agents. It is most likely that the secret services of the USSR, the US and Britain, although not working in concert, all played a role towards achieving their common goal. But what really made the coup succeed was the resolute indignation of the Serb population at Prince Paul's capitulation to Hitler's pressure. In addition the Yugoslav army was extremely reluctant to accept the idea of German troops on Yugoslav soil and had no desire to participate in the war against Greece. Moscow quickly proposed a friendship pact to the new government. It was signed on 5 April and published in *Pravda* the following day. On the same day, Wehrmacht tank and infantry divisions were dispatched from their positions on the southern borders of the USSR to invade Yugoslavia. A defenceless Belgrade was subjected to massive bombing by the German air force. More than 17,000 people died and the city was almost totally destroyed.

In addition to the postponement of Operation Barbarossa, the events in Yugoslavia had an effect on the situation in Japan. News of the coup in Belgrade reached Berlin on the same day that the German Foreign Minister, von Ribbentrop, was having talks with his Japanese colleague, Matsuoka, who had just arrived in Berlin via Moscow. Negotiations had to be interrupted for several hours when a furious Hitler summoned Ribbentrop to the Chancellery. Matsuoka had been invited to Berlin to discuss further involvement by Japan in the war in the Far East. After his visit to Berlin he spent about a week in Rome, and on his way home found himself in Moscow the day after the German invasion of Yugoslavia. It was obvious by then that there was a long way to go before the 'new order' could be firmly established in Europe. Matsuoka's stay in Moscow lasted more than a week and included a long conversation with Stalin at the Kuntsevo dacha on 12 April 1941, followed by the conclusion of a neutrality pact between Japan and the USSR the following day, an event that took Germany by surprise. In his conversation with Stalin, Matsuoka called the pact a 'diplomatic blitzkrieg'. He tried to persuade Stalin to sell Japan the northern half of Sakhalin in exchange for Japanese neutrality in any conflict with Germany. He also offered to transfer the port of Karachi to the Soviet Union at some future date. Stalin, needless to say, was not interested in such an exchange.[7]

Blitzkrieg in the Balkans

Forty divisions of the Wehrmacht along with 24 divisions from Romania and Hungary took part in the operation against Yugoslavia and Greece, commanded by Field Marshal von Brauchitsch, who had been in charge of planning Operation Barbarossa. 1,200 tanks and approximately 2,000 planes were also transferred to the new Balkan front in order to ensure the rapid annihilation of the Yugoslav and Greek armies. Approximately a third of the entire tank armada that had formerly been concentrated in the east was transferred to the south, while of the 2,700 planes based along the border with the USSR, almost all the bombers were thrown into the Balkan operation. The seizure of Crete presupposed the use of airborne troops. The Germans had lost their air superiority over Britain by the spring of 1941, having sacrificed an enormous number of planes in the process, and this left the aviation industry of Germany and the occupied countries barely able to keep up with needed replacements. The

Soviet Union had significantly more tanks and planes in the western districts than Germany (approximately 10,000 and 8,000 respectively), which was the main reason why Stalin and the General Staff were convinced that the Balkan war would considerably delay any attack on the Soviet Union. They calculated that it would take Hitler at least three months to restore the offensive capacity of the Wehrmacht, and so Germany would be unable to mount an attack before the end of July. Therefore military action would have to be postponed for a year because the German army was unprepared for an autumn war and certainly not for war in the winter.

The Wehrmacht were masters of the blitzkrieg, the destruction of an enemy in one sudden blow using their entire military might without any reserves. Hitler had never planned an all-out war lasting several years. The German military industry had not increased its capacity since 1939, and the army replenished its technical equipment and transportation resources in Poland, France, Norway, Denmark, Holland and Belgium, seizing whatever it needed. The Germans could also take advantage of equipment left behind in France by the British. Military production in Germany had already contracted by the summer of 1941, as Hitler believed that after victory in the east he would no longer need a very large army.

The Balkan campaign turned out to be Hitler's greatest military success. Massive bombing demoralized the Yugoslav and Greek units on the ground, while more than 300 Yugoslav tanks together with their crews were destroyed by German tanks and armoured vehicles using flame throwers. The Yugoslav air force was also demolished, although some planes were able to get away and land in Soviet Moldavia. The government of Simović and King Peter II escaped first to Bosnia and then through Greece and Cyprus to Britain. The Yugoslav army did not offer any serious resistance, and by the 17 April the Yugoslavs had surrendered. Hundreds of thousands of Yugoslav soldiers were taken prisoner. The Greek army held out for a few more days and surrendered on 22 April, but the British expeditionary forces avoided engaging in battle and were evacuated. On 27 April 1941 the German army entered Athens, and the Greek capital was declared an 'open city'.

The capture of Crete was tackled as an independent operation. The first airborne troops were landed on 20 May and by 1 June the resistance of the British and Greek armies was over. However, this time the Wehrmacht did sustain serious losses. Although only about 200 German soldiers died in the process of occupying the whole of Yugoslavia, in the battle for Crete 3,986 German soldiers and officers were killed and 2,594 wounded. In addition Germany lost 350 planes, mainly bombers and transport Junkers – almost half of the transport aircraft used in the operation.[8] These were not replaced until 1943, and their loss certainly limited the possibilities of operations on Soviet territory in the summer of 1941.

In May and the beginning of June German divisions and technical support units returned to their positions along the Soviet border. The troops and officers were in high spirits, although considerable damage had been done to their equipment. The stony roads of Yugoslavia and Greece had taken their toll on the tanks and lorries, and the planes had also been seriously affected. When the Wehrmacht finally had to cope with Russian roads, more tanks were lost due to technical problems than as a result of enemy shells. At the end of July 1941 Germany only had 1,400 planes left on the Eastern Front. According to the Barbarossa plan, military industrial production in Moscow, Leningrad and Kharkov was to be wiped out from the air, but this proved impossible to accomplish.

Could a blitzkrieg have succeeded against the USSR?

Stuck in his bunker in Berlin in the spring of 1945, Hitler often remarked to his companions that it was the five-week delay at the beginning of the eastern campaign that prevented him from achieving victory before the onset of winter. Churchill expressed the same view in his memoirs of the Second World War, and a number of Western historians have come to the same conclusion. But discussions along these lines are rather pointless, since ultimately whether the attack began in May or in June 1941 would have had no effect on the outcome. In either case, Hitler had no real possibility of carrying on a lightning war for more than four or five weeks. The strategy of blitzkrieg rests on the assumption that after the first major defeat, the enemy army is compelled to surrender. The relatively open concentration of Wehrmacht forces along the Soviet border, the violations of Soviet airspace and numerous other provocations had only a single purpose: to draw the main forces of the Red Army as close to the border as possible. Hitler wanted to win the war in one gigantic battle. According to the new timetable for Operation Barbarossa worked out after the occupation of Yugoslavia and Greece, Germany anticipated 'bitter fighting along the border for about four weeks, after which there could be nothing more than weak resistance to any further operations'.[9]

These expectations, however, turned out to be mistaken. The blitzkrieg plans had already been wrecked by the middle of July during the dry, warm days of summer and not in the autumn or winter of 1941. The bitter battle that began in July on the approaches to Odessa continued for more than two months. Also in July the German army was stopped near Smolensk for almost a month while fierce fighting continued until the middle of August. In the northwest the serious clashes began only in August. Not one of the goals of Barbarossa for the first eight weeks of war was achieved, while the Wehrmacht losses were much higher than expected. By the end of July Hitler had almost no reserves at his disposal and was forced to re-deploy his divisions from one section of the front to another in order to continue his attack. But even if the war had begun in May, it still could never have been over before winter. Although in 1941 Stalin managed the immediate military operations on the front rather badly, his overriding concern was to make sure that there were maximum forces in reserve.

In direct contrast to the General Staff and Red Army commanders who were concentrating on the situation on the border, Stalin's efforts were directed towards international developments using all means at his disposal to avert war. It was obvious at the time that both Hitler and the German General Staff were seriously underestimating the real power and strategic potential of the Soviet Union.

Right at the end of April, after the defeat of Yugoslavia and Greece, Stalin invited the German military attaché along with other military experts on a trip to the Urals and Western Siberia in order to have a look at several military factories producing new model tanks and planes.[10] At that time the new T-34 tank, superior to any type possessed by the Germans, had gone into major industrial production. A new bomber with a speed and range that out-classed the German Junkers was also on the production line. Berlin received several accounts of this trip, and according to information received from Soviet agents in Germany it was the aviation factory in Rybinsk that made the greatest impression on the German experts. A Soviet agent with the code alias 'Starshina' (Lieutenant Schulze-Boysen), working in Germany in the external relations department of the General Staff of the Luftwaffe, reported to Moscow that:

> The Germans never expected to find industry developed and functioning on such a scale. A number of things they were shown came as a complete surprise. The Germans were very positively impressed by the 1200 horsepower engine – they had no idea that such an engine existed. They were also astonished that the Russians had managed to accumulate more than 300 I-18 airplanes. ... They never imagined the USSR could produce these planes in such large numbers.[11]

However, Göring's aide, who informed him of the German visit, suggested that the Russians had cleverly assembled all their planes together in one factory in order to create a false impression.

Soviet Intelligence reports from Germany, which give us a much fuller understanding of basic Soviet tactics in April–June 1941, remained classified until a short time ago. The real names of the agents known as 'the Corsican' and 'Starshina', who provided information that was so highly regarded by the Berlin resident of the NKVD, have only recently been revealed. (Both agents were exposed by the Ge-stapo in 1942 and executed.)

Stalin becomes head of government

Dictators tend to run their countries through personal instructions or orders, and this was certainly true of Hitler, but until 1941 Stalin governed the Soviet Union via the Politburo. Politburo decisions were then transmitted and implemented through a system of Party com-mittees and bureaux at various levels or were converted into law as decrees of the Presidium of the Supreme Soviet. Almost all enact-ments of the Council of People's Commissars also had their origin as drafts approved by the Politburo. This system may have been cum-bersome, but it ensured that the Party and not the government was at the pinnacle of power. In the unprecedented situation of May 1941, however, as the country prepared for war, it was crucial to be able to take decisions more rapidly.

On 4 May the Politburo approved a resolution naming Stalin Chairman of the Council of People's Commissars in view of the need to 'ensure absolute unity in the work of the leadership' and 'given the present tensions of the international situation, to raise the authority of Soviet organs (i.e. government or executive bodies) and provide them with every conceivable reinforcement in order to sup-port their task of defending the country.'[12] Molotov, who had been Chairman of the SNK since 1930, now became Stalin's deputy and 'the leader of USSR foreign policy'. Zhdanov would be Stalin's deputy on the Central Committee Secretariat. Stalin's new title was formal-ized on 6 May 1941 by a decree of the Presidium of the Supreme Soviet and was interpreted in the USSR and also abroad as a means of concentrating absolute power in Stalin's hands.

Assuming his new post as head of government, Stalin thought it was important to make a 'public' statement on the subject of mili-tary policy and defence against the threat of aggression. His speech, later referred to as 'Stalin's speech of 5 May 1941', has long been the subject of discussion and speculation among Russian and other histo-rians. It was delivered to an audience of military academy graduates without a written text, and although at the time it was considered to be secret its contents were reconstructed after Stalin's death from the recollections and notes of those who had been present at the occasion in the Great Hall of the Kremlin.

Stalin's speech of 5 May

The graduation ceremony for students of the military academy traditionally took place in the Kremlin, but it was not customary for

Stalin to speak. As the audience arrived for the ceremony on 5 May 1941, only the particularly thorough checks on all those invited indicated something unusual was about to happen. Approximately 1,500 people gathered in the hall of the Great Kremlin Palace, about half of whom were new graduates of the academy. Their professors and teachers were also invited, along with personnel from the Commissariat of Defence and the General Staff, members of the government and Presidium of the Supreme Soviet, leading Comintern figures and staff from the Commissariats of Internal Affairs and State Security. The whole event was chaired by Marshal Timoshenko, the Commissar for Defence. After several scheduled speakers had addressed the audience, Timoshenko unexpectedly gave the floor to Stalin, whose speech went on for 40 minutes. The full text has never been published, but despite the fact that it is usually considered to have been confidential the audience was never given any formal warning not to divulge its contents. On 6 May 1941 the central press announced the appointment of Stalin as Chairman of the Sovnarkom and published a brief note about his speech, including the statement that 'Stalin noted the profound changes that have taken place in the Red Army during the last years, and he stressed the fact that the Red Army had been reformed and substantially re-equipped in accordance with the demands of contemporary warfare.'

Vyacheslav Malyshev, the Commissar for Machine Construction, whose responsibilities at that time included the production of tanks, made an entry in his diary as soon as he returned from the Kremlin:

> Comrade Stalin spoke for about an hour and dwelt on two questions: the training of commanders and the 'invincibility' of the German army. With regard to the first question, Comrade Stalin said: 'You left the army three to four years ago. Our army today is very different from the way it was at that time – it's much larger and better equipped. It has grown from 120 to 300 divisions. One third are mechanized, armoured divisions. ... Our artillery has been transformed, with more cannon and fewer howitzers. ... We didn't have mortar and now we do; until recently we lacked anti-aircraft artillery and now we have a decent amount.'

Malyshev then turned to the 'German' part of the speech, which seemed to him to be its most sensational aspect. Stalin harshly condemned Germany as a country that had shifted from a process of reversing the 1919 Versailles Treaty to a policy of waging aggressive war. 'The Germans have become conquerors. ... That's something quite different. ... There have been similar cases in the past – for example – Napoleon.'[13] Such overt criticism of Hitler's actions was astonishing, since all publications at that time strictly adhered to the principles of the 'friendship and borders' treaty with Germany. When

Yugoslavia was attacked, the Soviet government sent a note of protest to Hungary, but not to Germany.

A 'short record of Stalin's speech' was discovered in the archives after 1991 and published in *Istorichesky Arkhiv* in 1995. Subsequently the historian Lev Bezymensky reconstructed the speech using the 'short record' as well as the recollections of military personnel who were present during that evening in the Kremlin, and in 2000 published a fuller version. According to Bezymensky, 'Stalin provided top-secret data about Red Army numbers which any foreign agent would have paid a lot of money to get hold of.' But in his view none of this secret information ever got abroad. The crucial part of Stalin's speech was not so much the question of the number of divisions but his account of their size: 'The divisions themselves have become a little smaller, more mobile. Divisions now contain 15,000 soldiers, whereas in the past it used to be 18–20,000.'[14] This certainly was secret information, but it did not actually correspond to reality. Stalin indulged in considerable exaggeration when describing Soviet air and tank formations. The majority of the Red Army's tanks and planes had been built in 1935–36 and were now rather obsolete, with new models added to the force only at the beginning of 1941. According to the plans for January to May 1941, the army was to be supplied with 955 T-34 tanks – serial production had begun at the start of the year at the Stalingrad and Mariupol tractor factories.[15]

It was just in this period during April and May that Timoshenko and Zhukov were constantly urging Stalin to bring the divisions in the western districts up to full strength. According to Zhukov, 'only at the end of March did Stalin finally authorize 500,000 soldiers and sergeants to be called up and sent to the border areas, but even these reinforcements only meant that infantry divisions became some 8,000 men strong. ... As a result, on the eve of the war, out of 170 divisions in the border districts, 19 divisions were made up of 5–6,000 men, seven cavalry divisions numbered on average 6,000, and 144 divisions had 8–9,000 men.' In interior regions of the country the majority of divisions had suffered 'staff reductions', or had only just begun the process of military training and the formation of divisions. On 15 June 1941 Zhukov reported to Stalin that Soviet divisions, 'even those with a numerical strength of 8,000 men were practically two times weaker than their German equivalents.'[16] Each German division stationed along the Soviet border contained approximately 14–15,000 soldiers.

As the graduates of the military academy assumed command posts in the army, they found out soon enough that there was not one division in the Soviet army with 15,000 men. Nor were Soviet divisions as mobile as Stalin had declared them to be. The redistribution of troops during this period took place mainly at night, on the whole either on foot or by horse-drawn vehicles.

By announcing fictitious information about the strength of the Red Army, Stalin could have had only one goal in mind: the spread of disinformation to Hitler and his General Staff. Judging by archive material, despite enormous efforts, the German ambassador in Moscow never succeeded in discovering the contents of Stalin's speech. But German Intelligence would undoubtedly have had a number of other sources of information besides the ambassador, and Stalin's speech could not have remained secret. It clearly had been prepared for export, since any truly confidential speech would never have been delivered to an audience of 1,500 people. Stalin was almost certainly attempting to convince the German generals that their plan for a blitzkrieg was unrealistic. They were facing not only an enemy of equal strength, but one that was technically better equipped and ready for war.

The real position on the western borders

From the beginning of 1941 the Main Intelligence Administration of the General Staff, the Commissariat for State Security and the Intelligence Administration of the NKVD were almost daily sending summaries about the build-up of German forces along the western border to Stalin, the Ministry of Defence and the General Staff. There were large numbers of Soviet Intelligence agents in the territory of what had formerly been Poland, as well as in Romania, Hungary and Bulgaria, who not only reported the movement of German divisions to the border but also details of the transport of military equipment, the building of new airfields, ammunition and fuel depots and the expansion of the road network.

In April and May 1941 Stalin received almost daily visits in the Kremlin from Timoshenko (Commissar for Defence), Zhukov (head of the General Staff), Zhigarev (commander of the Air Force) and Kuznetsov (chief of the naval forces) along with the commissars for military industry, state security and other government and military officials crucial to the defence of the country. Undoubtedly the over-riding question at all these meetings and at all Politburo sessions was the problem of defence. Thanks to the work of Soviet secret agents in Germany, the Soviet government was well aware of the operational plans of the German General Staff, knew what was discussed at Göring's meetings and even had access to the precise bombing plans for the first days of the war. According to 'Starshina', German military preparations were carried out so openly precisely in order to demonstrate their superior strength and thus intimidate the Russians psychologically. Almost weekly Stalin, Molotov, Voroshilov, Timoshenko, Zhukov, Beria, Kuznetsov and Zhdanov received special reports from the General Staff intelligence administration with detailed information about the deployment of German forces along the front and within the theatre of military operations. These special reports were signed by Lieutenant-General Golikov and were a composite of data received from a variety of intelligence sources. The position on 25 April was that Germany had 95–100 divisions along the border with the USSR; 55–58 divisions were stationed in Yugoslavia, Greece and Egypt; 72 divisions were in the occupied countries of Europe and nine divisions were in Italy; 30 divisions were in the front reserves and 12 divisions were in the reserves of the High Command. On 25 April the German army contained 296 divisions overall with about 40 further divisions in the process of formation.

Ten days later, the next special report informed government and military leaders that a regrouping of German forces had increased the contingent on the Soviet border to 107 divisions, the addition largely made up of tank and motorized divisions. Simultaneously from the Baltic to Hungary, civilian populations were being removed from border districts. Hungarian and Romanian troop formations were concentrating along the Soviet border, taking the total number of divisions there to 130. Other divisions arrived, largely from Yugoslavia and Greece. By 15 May, ten days later, General Staff intelligence reported that 'the overall strength of the German forces amassed against the USSR has reached 114–119 divisions' and attached charts showing their deployment in various directions.[17] The newly arrived divisions were concentrated in southern border districts. This special report was distributed to all members of the Military Council, the Ministry of Defence and to all members of the Politburo. However, the biggest German troop transport to the east got under way on the 25 May: '47 German divisions, including 28 tank and motorized divisions, were transferred closer to the Soviet border from 25 May to the middle of June.'[18] Stalin, however, was still not convinced that war was inevitable.

On 15 June 1941, after Timoshenko and Zhukov insisted on the urgent need to transfer more units to the USSR's borders, arguing convincingly that given the existing correlations of forces, 'we will certainly not be capable of confronting or repulsing the thrust of the German army in a disciplined fashion', Stalin still tried to assure them that their fears were unfounded. 'Hitler is not such a fool that he's unable to understand that there is a difference between the Soviet Union and Poland or France or even England or indeed, all of them put together.'[19] However, Stalin did give his consent to the recommendation of the Ministry of Defence and the General Staff to strengthen the Soviet forces on the Western Front. During April and May scores of infantry and motorized divisions had been secretly transported to the west from military districts in the interior of the country. According to the plan presented to Stalin on 13 June by the General Staff, 186 divisions were deployed along the four Western Fronts, out of which 97 divisions were stationed on the South Western Front and 44 divisions on the Western Front. The Northern and the North Western Fronts contained 45 divisions. Five armies, made up of 51 divisions, remained in the reserves of the High Command. There were still 66 divisions remaining in the interior of the country, largely in the Far Eastern, the Transcaucasian, Crimean, Moscow and Leningrad military districts.[20]

At this point, convinced that the beginning of war was imminent, the Ministry of Defence and the General Staff implored Stalin to transfer a larger number of divisions from the reserves to the western borders and to create a more solid, concentrated disposition of forces in the regions near the front. Stalin categorically rejected this demand, insisting on the need to maintain large-scale reserves at a considerable distance from any conceivable front line. After the war, studying all the General Staff maps in the archives when working on the first volume of his memoirs, Zhukov came to the conclusion that the advice he had given in the spring of 1941 was possibly mistaken:

> It is common to criticize Stalin for failing to move the main forces of our army from the interior of the country in time to meet and repulse the enemy attack. I am hesitant to be dogmatic about what might have happened if he had done so – whether the outcome would have been better or worse. It is certainly possible that our army, inadequately provided with anti-tank and anti-aircraft defences and less mobile than the forces of the enemy, would not have been able to withstand the slashing, powerful blows of the armoured force of the enemy assault and would have found itself in exactly the same dire situation as the forces who actually were in the border districts during the first days of the war. And in that case, who knows what the result might have been for Moscow, Leningrad or the south of the country.[21]

At the time of writing his memoirs, Zhukov also had access to the strategic plans of the creators of Operation Barbarossa. He became convinced that the numerous violations of the Soviet border in April–June 1941 by the German army and air force and the overt transfer of military units to the border were intentionally provocative: 'Hitler's command was counting on us bringing our main forces up to the border with the intention of surrounding and destroying them.'[22]

There is the well-known saying that war is waged 'not with numbers, but with skill'. Stalin, as we now see, was much less convinced than his generals and marshals about the real strength of the Red Army. He certainly understood that the repressions that decimated the Red Army command in 1937–38 during his own terror campaign substantially weakened the military strength of the USSR.

It was indeed the weakness of the Red Army, deprived of its best commanders, that motivated Stalin to make his pact with Hitler in 1939.

Was there justification for concluding the 1939 German–Soviet Pact?

After the occupation of Czechoslovakia in September 1938 and the subsequent Munich agreement that in effect consented to what had taken place, Germany began to prepare for war with Poland. But given that Poland was protected by French and British military guarantees, this could easily turn into war on two fronts. The Soviet Union had genuine territorial claims on Poland since the period of the Civil War when Poland took advantage of the weakness of the Russian Federation and in 1920 attacked the newly formed Ukrainian and Belorussian republics as well as Lithuania. As a result of the defeat of the Russian Soviet Federated Socialist Republic (RSFSR) in this war, Poland annexed the western regions of the Ukraine, Belorussia and Lithuania, including the cities of Lvov, Brest, Grodno and Vilnius. Clearly if Germany were to attack Poland, the Soviet Union could not allow the German army to occupy land that had historically been part of Russia and that would leave German troops much too close to Kiev, Minsk and Leningrad. If the Red Army invaded Poland from the east in order to defend Western Ukraine and Belorussia, Germany could end up fighting a war not only with Poland but also with France, Britain and the USSR simultaneously. In 1939 the Wehrmacht only had 80 divisions and was in no position to take on so many strong opponents. It was this situation that made it necessary for Hitler to come to an agreement with Stalin.

For entirely different reasons, Stalin too was not ready for a major war. The Red Army, with 150 divisions numbering approximately 2 million men, was quite well equipped. Its weakness lay not in an inadequate number of tanks and planes but in a serious lack of experienced commanders after the purging of the officer corps during 1937–38. Within 15 months, 36,000 army officers and 4,000 naval officers had been arrested. In the autumn of 1938, 13 out of 15 Red Army commanders and 154 out of 195 commanders of divisions were shot on the basis of false accusations. They were replaced by new personnel from the lower ranks, but the quality of the new officer corps was on a quite different level. The fighting capacity of an army always depends upon the talent and experience of its commanders. Hitler quite rightly believed that his officer corps was more experienced and generally superior to that of the Soviets. However, in 1939 the German armed forces still had not yet had any real exposure to battle.

As we know, the initiative for the non-aggression pact between Germany and the USSR came from Hitler. At first Stalin wavered, but not for very long. The strategic advantages of such a pact were all too obvious. Only the political aspects were problematical. An alliance with the aggressive Nazi regime was extremely unpopular within the Soviet Union and was received with horror by communists throughout the world. When Germany began to increase the size of its army in 1935 in violation of the Versailles Treaty, Stalin and a large number of Soviet military experts came to the conclusion that war with Germany was ultimately inevitable. Soviet military doctrine had previously viewed Japan, Turkey and Poland as the main potential enemies of the USSR. Germany and Italy were also seen as adversaries, but only on foreign soil, as in Spain; therefore they were viewed as presenting no immediate military threat to the Soviet Union. The position changed after Germany's occupation of Austria and Czechoslovakia. Clearly Poland would be the next victim. After the Munich agreement Stalin was convinced that the creation of the 'impenetrable' Maginot Line by countries of the Entente would drive Hitler's aggression to the east. There was no certainty that France and Britain would declare war if Germany attacked Poland. These countries were capable of sacrificing Poland in the same way that they had sacrificed Czechoslovakia. By concluding a pact with Hitler, Stalin made it inevitable that the Entente countries would embark on war against Germany, which meant that France and Britain would be the first to test Germany's renewed military strength.

Since Germany had only 20 divisions on the western border at the time of the Polish campaign against more than 100 French divisions and the British Expeditionary Force, no one could have predicted that France and Britain, with their enormous military superiority, would have put up such a feeble defence in the autumn of 1939 without even venturing to subject the German positions to artillery bombardment. It is not that the pact with Germany gained a great deal of time for the Soviet Union, because in any case Hitler would not have had an army large enough for war in the east before May 1941. However, the pact did give the Soviet Union an enormous strategic advantage in the inevitable war ahead. From the Black Sea to the White Sea, the USSR was able to shift its entire western boundary 200–300 kilometres further into the heart of Europe. And precisely in the vulnerable northwestern sector, the border became shorter by almost 600 kilometres. As a result Leningrad and Kronstadt were now located deep within Soviet territory, whether approached from the Baltic states or from Finland. The population of the USSR increased by almost 25 million. Stalin's personal authority within the country, somewhat shaken during the 1937–38 period of terror, now increased considerably.

When the war began on 22 June 1941 the western territories of the USSR played the role of buffer zone. Within five days the German army rapidly penetrated the 'old' border in Belorussia. It took them 12–15 days to reach that point in the Ukraine, and then only after very heavy fighting. The battles in the Baltic states continued for more than two months. The Red Army offered strong resistance, and Tallin was not abandoned until the end of August. This was a serious failure for the blitzkrieg. According to the Barbarossa plan, the German army should have taken Leningrad in August, freeing up divisions that would then head for Moscow and close off the environs of the city from the north.

Intelligence reports

It has been widely believed that despite the fact that Soviet Intelligence provided the Soviet leadership with accurate information about Hitler's plans, Stalin ignored these reports and even regarded some of them as disinformation. Many studies of Stalin and the German–Soviet war include an account of the following incident that did indeed take place: the Commissar for State Security, Vsevolod Merkulov, submitted an agent's report from Berlin on 17 June, warning that military action was about to begin; Stalin wrote: 'Comrade Merkulov. You can tell your "source" from Ger. air force headquarters to go f— his mother. This is not a "source" – it's someone spreading <u>disinformation</u>. J. St.'

The entire document, preserved in the Presidential Archive, has recently been published in full.[23] Looking at this 'Report from Berlin' in the context of the many other reports that were coming from Berlin in May–June 1941, there are grounds for believing that in this case Stalin was right. The report of 17 June was a composite of information from two different 'sources' and did not contain any useful information. The style of the cipher text was different from a typical, precise agent's report; it had been put together by the resident of Soviet Intelligence in Berlin, Amayak Kobulov, who never had any professional espionage training and occupied the post of First Counsellor at the USSR embassy. Kobulov and the ambassador, Vladimir Dekanozov, were friends of Beria and had worked in Georgia until 1938. The cipher contained only one bit of concrete information, a statement that 'the first air raid targets would be the "Svir-3" electric power station, Moscow factories producing airplane parts, and also automobile repair workshops.' It was also stated that Hungary would participate in the military action.

From detailed reports of the GRU General Staff as well as from information sent by agents in Hungary and Romania, Stalin was aware of the fact that preparations were under way in Hungary to take part in the war against the Soviet Union. But Moscow factories were situated beyond the range of German planes, and it would hardly have been possible for German pilots to identify and target specific enterprises. The Svir-3 power station, built on the tiny River Svir in the Mogilev region, had no military significance whatsoever. There were a great number of other more important military targets in Belorussia and hundreds of auto repair depots in the border regions. Railways, airports and a great many other potential objectives were considerably more important for defence. During the course of June 1941 Stalin was receiving scores of reports from agents and military intelligence with precise and detailed information, and he could easily distinguish between genuine messages and disinformation. During this period Soviet Intelligence had many reliable agents in Germany and other countries whose reports were taken very seriously by Stalin.

On 1 June 1941 military intelligence received a radiogram from 'Ramza' (Richard Sorge) in Tokyo. At the time, Sorge was working as the press attaché at the German Embassy and enjoyed the trust of the German ambassador, Eugen Ott. 'Berlin has informed Ott that the German attack on the Soviet Union will start in the second half of June. Ott was 95% certain that this would be the beginning of war.' Sorge also cited some indirect evidence corroborating this information. On 6 June Merkulov, the head of the NKGB, prepared a detailed report for Stalin and the Central Committee on military preparations being made by Germany on Polish territory. The report was based on verified messages from several agents. The following day Stalin was informed about military arrangements in Romania. Copies of these reports were sent to Molotov, Voroshilov, Timoshenko, Zhukov and Beria as well as to other political and military leaders. On 11 June 'Starshina' (Schulze-Boysen) passed on information from Berlin via Kobulov that Göring's headquarters had moved from Berlin to Romania, close to the Soviet border. There were also plans to transfer second-line planes from France to Poland, near Poznan. Intensive consultations were under way between the German, Finnish and Romanian general staffs. At the same time, detailed messages were coming in from agents in Poland who reported that a large number of German troops had arrived at the border and that air-raid shelters were being constructed. They were amassing supplies of petrol and diesel fuel as well as makeshift bridges that could be set up at river crossings.

All this information could hardly have been and indeed was not ignored. On USSR territory a large number of military units were

228 THE UNKNOWN STALIN

moved closer to the border. On 13 June Timoshenko and Zhukov ordered the Kiev military district 'to transfer all remote divisions and the command headquarters together with their units to new encampments nearer to the state border, as indicated in accompanying maps'.[24] The divisions were to be marched west at night in total secrecy. The date for carrying out this order, however, was 1 July. Similar instructions were sent to other military districts. The resident of Soviet Intelligence in Hungary, Colonel N.G. Lyakhterev, reported on 14 June that four new divisions had appeared in one of the Polish–Soviet border districts and that 'on 15 June the Germans will complete their strategic deployment against the USSR'.[25] On 15 June military intelligence informed Stalin, Molotov, Malenkov and other Politburo members about German divisions stationed on the Soviet–Finland border and of the arrival by sea of two new motorized divisions in Finland. Information about the concentration of German forces at the Soviet border was received from Switzerland and other countries. The Soviet Intelligence resident in Rome reported on 19 June that the beginning of military action against the Soviet Union was scheduled to take place between 20 and 25 June. On the same day, Timoshenko and Zhukov gave orders, approved by Stalin, to camouflage airfields and create dummy sites. However, once again the date for implementation was 1 July. During those same weeks at the beginning of June, NKVD units carried out a series of arrests and expulsions of 'anti-Soviet elements' from the border districts of Moldavia, Western Ukraine and the Baltics. Tens of thousands of families were sent to the interior of the country.

The Soviet Intelligence resident in Sophia, Pavel Shateyev, reported on 20 June that the attack would come on 21 or 22 June. On the same day, a radiogram came from Sorge, warning of the inevitability of war.

21 June 1941

The 'working date' for the beginning of the German attack was 22 June. In accordance with an order from the High Command of 10 June to the land forces of Germany, 'at 13:00 on 21 June the army would be given one of two signals: either "Dortmund", which meant that the offensive would start on 22 June as planned ... or "Altona", indicating a postponement.'[26]

At 13:00 on 21 June the units of the Wehrmacht received the signal 'Dortmund'. On the same day, Hitler informed Mussolini of the impending action against the USSR. He also wrote an address to the army and the German people, which was to be broadcast in the morning of 22 June. German units, which until then had been stationed at a distance of 25–30 kilometres from the border, began to take up their assault positions.

At 14:00 Stalin was handed a telegram from the Soviet ambassador in London, Ivan Maisky, informing him that according to information received from the British Foreign Office, the Germans would attack on the following day. By 1940 British Intelligence had managed to crack the secret German codes and was well informed about German preparations and intentions. On the same day, the General Secretary of the Comintern, Georgy Dimitrov, rang Molotov and asked him to tell Stalin that according to Zhou Enlai and Mao Zedong, Germany intended to attack the Soviet Union on 21 June.[27]

Many reports were arriving from the border districts about the movement of German troops in their direction. By the evening the sound of engines and the advance of German tanks could be heard at the border posts. According to Marshal Zhukov, German armoured units stationed at some considerable distance from the border were moved to their positions for attack during the night of 21–22 June.

On 21 June Stalin telephoned the commander of the Moscow military district, I.V. Tyulenev, ordering him to put the anti-aircraft defence of Moscow into a state of immediate alert.[28] Meanwhile the staff at the German embassy in Moscow were feverishly burning documents. Papers were burned in the courtyard as well as in fireplaces, and clouds of smoke could be seen rising above the embassy building. Stalin was informed of this by both the intelligence service and the Moscow fire brigade. At about 8 o'clock in the evening Zhukov told Stalin on the telephone that a German deserter, a lance-corporal, had turned up at the border post in the Ukraine with the information that the German forces were in position to mount an offensive on the morning of 22 June. Stalin responded: 'Come to the Kremlin with the Defence Commissar in 45 minutes.'[29] When Zhukov and Timoshenko arrived at the Kremlin at 20:50 they had already prepared a draft directive to be sent to all military districts, warning of a possible German surprise attack at dawn on 22 June and ordering all units to be brought to full military preparedness. Stalin shortened the text a little and approximately two hours later it was sent from General Staff headquarters to all border districts.

The directive was absolutely clear, stating that military action could begin on 22 June; it commanded that forward defence positions were to be occupied in all fortified border districts in the course of the night, that all units were to be brought to full military readiness, aircraft dispersed and camouflaged, and a black-out imposed on all cities and military objectives. There were only three or four hours left for the Soviet army deployed along the western border to prepare for the German offensive. But Stalin himself was still not absolutely convinced that Hitler had really decided to attack the USSR. He said to Zhukov: 'Perhaps there still can be a peaceful settlement.' The last person Stalin saw that day was Beria. After Beria left at 11 o'clock in the evening, Stalin rang the General Staff headquarters several times. At about 2 o'clock in the morning he finally left for the dacha where he always spent the night, but he was not allowed much time to sleep. At 3:40 he was woken by a telephone call from Zhukov informing him that the war had begun.

The information from the German corporal, a former communist, had been taken more seriously than normal intelligence reports, apparently because it came from such an extraordinary source. This was the first time a German soldier had voluntarily crossed over to the Soviet side. It could hardly have been an attempt to provoke some kind of Soviet preventive action that could then be labelled as 'aggression', since there was too little time left for anything except defensive preparations. The border troops maintained a constant state of military alert and the transition to full military readiness would not take more than one or two hours. This also applied to the border districts in general. It was more complicated to carry out the dispersal of front-line aircraft at night, and as a result a large number of planes were destroyed on the ground during the first days of the war. But this saved the lives of air force personnel, and in the first phase of the war experienced pilots were more crucial than outmoded aircraft.

The Lvov NKVD went on questioning the German deserter until morning, and by that time his information was conclusively confirmed. The Ukrainian NKVD reported to Moscow that the deserter, Alfred Liskow, was 30 years old, a joiner in a furniture factory in Bavaria and had served in the 221st Sapper Regiment of the 15th Division. He was a former communist. According to his statement, the commanding officer of his company informed the soldiers in the evening of 21 June that the unit would begin crossing the Bug River that night on rafts, boats and pontoons.[30]

A 'crisis in the Kremlin' at the beginning of the war?

It was Khrushchev in his February 1956 'secret speech' at the Twentieth Party Congress who first told the story of Stalin's sudden depression during the first days of the war, claiming that he had relinquished the leadership of the country. According to Khrushchev:

> After the first disastrous defeats at the front, Stalin thought that the end had come. ... For a long time after this he did not actually direct the military operations and ceased to do anything whatsoever. He returned to active leadership only when some members of the Politburo visited him and said that it was urgently necessary to take certain steps in order to improve the situation at the front.[31]

In his memoirs, which Khrushchev dictated after his removal from power in 1964 and which were recorded on tape by his son Sergei, he repeated this version of events, adding more detail with references to stories from Beria. Khrushchev himself was in Kiev at the beginning of the war and could have had little first-hand knowledge of what was actually taking place in the Kremlin. Khrushchev reports that Beria told him that:

> when the war began, Stalin gathered the members of the Politburo. ... Stalin was totally shattered and made the following declaration: 'A war has started and it will end in catastrophe. Lenin bequeathed to us a proletarian Soviet state, and we've screwed up.' This is literally what he said. 'And I am giving up the leadership' and he left. He left, got into his car and drove to the *blizhny* dacha.

Beria's version of what happened next is the same as Khrushchev's original account. After a week, members of the Politburo visited Stalin at the dacha.

> When we arrived, I saw from his face that Stalin was alarmed. I dare say that Stalin thought we had come to arrest him for abandoning his post and failing to do anything to repulse the German invasion.[32]

This story – that Stalin gave up the leadership during the first days of the war – has been repeated by quite a few reputable authors, citing Khrushchev as their source. The power crisis in the Kremlin during the first week of the war also became the subject of several works of fiction. Biographies of Stalin published in the West have repeated the tale, often with additional embellishment. In the well-illustrated biography of Stalin by Jonathan Lewis and Phillip White-head, published in Britain and the United States in 1990 and used as the basis for a television series, they describe events of 22 June 1941 as established fact without making any reference to Khrushchev or Beria:

> Stalin himself was prostrate. For a week he rarely emerged from his villa at Kuntsevo. His name disappeared from newspapers. For ten days the Soviet Union was leaderless. ... On 1 July Stalin pulled him-self together.[33]

Alan Bullock, in his dual biography of Hitler and Stalin published in 1991, also asserts as fact the allegation that Stalin 'suffered some kind of breakdown' and that there are 'no orders or other documents signed by Stalin from 23 to 30 June'.[34] Bullock also repeats the story that members of the Politburo discussed the possibility of arresting Stalin. Even though the whole episode is a complete fabrication, it nevertheless has appeared in encyclopaedias and even in such an authoritative work as the *Oxford Encyclopaedia of the Second World War*, published in 1995.[35] But one has only to read the memoirs of

Marshal Zhukov, where Stalin's activities, orders and directives during the first days of the war are well documented, in order to become convinced that the story is false.

At the beginning of the 1990s the visitors' book from Stalin's Kremlin office covering the years 1924–53 was discovered in the Politburo archive. These records were kept by Stalin's junior secretaries in Stalin's office. These rather dry documents are of enormous interest to students of Soviet history, and were published in chronological order with commentaries and explanatory notes by the journal *Istorichesky Arkhiv* during the years 1994–97.

The visitors' book makes it clear that on 22 June, the day that the war began, the first to appear in Stalin's office at 5:45 am were Molotov, Beria, Timoshenko, Mekhlis and Zhukov. About two hours later the gathering was joined by Malenkov, Mikoyan, Kaganovich, Voroshilov and Vyshinsky. In the course of the day a large number of senior military, state and Party figures came and went. Meetings went on without interruption for 11 hours. It is known that more than 20 different decrees and orders were issued that day, including the text of the appeal to the Soviet people, drafted collectively and read out on the radio by Molotov. Stalin, who had not slept the night before, left earlier in the evening to have a short rest at the Kuntsevo dacha, only 15 minutes' drive from the Kremlin. But he was unable to sleep and returned to the Kremlin at 3 am on 23 June in order to consult with military leaders and members of the Politburo. Meetings continued in the afternoon. Voroshilov, Merkulov, Beria and General Nikolai Vatutin (deputizing for Zhukov who had flown to the southern front) finally left Stalin's office at 1:45 am on 24 June.

Activity during the next days was just as strenuous. On 26 June Stalin worked in the Kremlin from midday to midnight and received 28 visitors, mainly military leaders and members of the government. The largest number of meetings took place on Friday 27 June with 30 people coming into the office. The following day, 28 June, was similar, with the final meetings coming to an end after midnight. Stalin did not go to his Kremlin office on the Sunday; however, the assertion by two biographers, Radzinsky and Volkogonov, that this was the day Stalin fled and shut himself up in the dacha hardly corresponds to what actually happened.[36] Both authors have rather unreliably based their conclusions on the fact there are no entries in the Kremlin office visitors' book for 29 and 30 June. But according to Marshal Zhukov, 'on the 29th Stalin came to the *Stavka* at the Commissariat for Defence twice and on both occasions was scathing about the strategic situation that was unfolding in the west.'[37] On 30 June Stalin convoked a meeting of the Politburo at the dacha at which it was decided to set up the State Defence Committee (GKO). According to Mikoyan's recollections – a collection of notes he made at various times, preserved in the archives and published as a book entitled *Tak Bylo* (How It Was) many years after his death – the idea of creating the GKO came from Molotov and Beria. Members of the Politburo had come to the dacha on their own initiative without any invitation, having prepared the GKO project in advance:

> Molotov, who spoke for us, said that it was crucial to concentrate power in order to be able to take decisions more rapidly and get the country back on its feet. The head of the new body of course would be Stalin. He looked at us with amazement, but offered no objection, saying only, 'All right.' Then Beria said that five members of the State Defence Committee would have to be named: 'You, Comrade Stalin, will be at the head of it, and the members will be Molotov, Vorshilov, Malenkov, and me (Beria).' ... On the same day they approved a decree creating the GKO, which was published in the press on 1st July.[38]

Khrushchev's stories about Stalin's depression and Mikoyan's account of how the GKO came to be set up on 30 June were reproduced in the very detailed biography of Stalin written by Dmitry Volkogonov in 1989 and translated into many languages. Nevertheless Mikoyan's version of events is extremely unconvincing.

Molotov was always known for his total submissiveness to Stalin. It is difficult to imagine that he would have taken the initiative to establish such an important organization, and it is also extremely unlikely that Beria would have dared present such a list. The concentration of power in the GKO was such that only Stalin could have proposed it. A supreme organ already did exist – it was called the Politburo – but during the war Stalin was reluctant to convene meetings of the Politburo, and, indeed, they did not take place. Stalin wanted to be in a position to take all decisions independently. Therefore besides Stalin, only two Politburo members were included in the GKO, Molotov and Voroshilov, both of whom came to his office virtually every day in any case and were considered to be old friends. They were the only ones in the inner circle to address him in the familiar form of 'you' and sometimes used his old Party nickname, 'Koba'. In 1941 Malenkov and Beria were still only candidate members of the Politburo. Zhdanov was based in Leningrad, while Khrushchev was in Kiev. Kalinin was by then an old man whose function was largely limited to signing decrees. For whatever reason, Stalin did not want to have to consult Mikoyan, Kaganovich or Andreev on military matters. For a certain time the GKO became a new, slimmed-down version of the Politburo. The existence of the GKO did not prevent Stalin from taking decisions on his own, but it meant that he could share responsibility for any consequences. Such a simple plan could not have been thought up by Molotov or Beria. Thus Stalin did not abandon the leadership of the country during the first days of the war, although he did push aside a large number of his Party colleagues, convinced that collective Party leadership would only have been a hindrance in wartime conditions.

Stalin's one-man dictatorship was consolidated considerably by the war. He was soon given the newly created title of Supreme Commander-in-Chief and also became the USSR Commissar for Defence, with Timoshenko and Zhukov as his deputies. The role and importance of the Politburo and the Central Committee declined and did not recover their importance until after Stalin's death in 1953.

If one looks at all Stalin's actions and the military decisions that were taken during the first days of the war, with hindsight it is perfectly possible to come to the conclusion that given the intensity and the power of the blow inflicted on the USSR by the German army and its allies, whose forces taken together amounted to almost 200 divisions, the tactical decision to keep the main forces of the Soviet army 200–300 kilometres from the border was absolutely correct. It was this that made it possible to carry out local counter-attacks and on 26 June, on Stalin's orders, to create a new reserve front using the 5th Army. Soon after that a new third defence line was established. The German army continued to advance but only at the price of very heavy losses.

It could be said that Stalin's major miscalculation, which was shared by his military commanders, was to base the whole defence plan on the assumption that the main focus of the German army's attack would not be directed towards Moscow and Leningrad but rather in the direction of the Ukraine and the Northern Caucasus. It was in these regions that major resources could be found – grain, coal and oil. Therefore the largest forces of the Red Army were stationed in the south, distributed deep within the interior of the country. The German command was able to deploy approximately 160 divisions straight away, which explains why the Germans were able to advance so rapidly in the first days of the war. According to the plan for the blitzkrieg, it was assumed that the main battles would take place during the first weeks, after which the Wehrmacht would move east with increasing speed. But things turned out quite differently. The German army advanced rapidly during the first days and weeks but then was increasingly held back by the stubborn, self-sacrificing resistance of the Red Army. Hitler's war against the USSR was lost long before the final attack on Moscow. The review of Red Army units in Red Square on 7 November 1941 marked the beginning of a new war, which the British historian John Erickson has called 'Stalin's War with Germany'.[39]

CHAPTER 12

Stalin and Apanasenko: The Far Eastern Front in the Second World War

Roy Medvedev

The new commander

Considerably more tension existed on the eastern frontier of the Soviet Union at the end of the 1930s than along the western borders. Having occupied Manchuria, the Japanese military began to seize the few other provinces of China one after another and was preparing to attack the USSR. The Japanese Kwantung Army, formed in the north of China, was carrying out continual reconnaissance sorties and in a variety of ways was regularly breaching the Soviet frontier. After several major military provocations, Stalin proposed reorganizing the Far Eastern Military District (DVO) and the Special Far Eastern Army (ODVA) into the Far Eastern Front (DVF), and this took place in 1938. By July–August 1938 this front had already had its baptism of fire in the vicinity of Lake Khasan, the scene of a large-scale battle that was much talked about at the time. But the outcome of this encounter left Stalin dismayed: although the Japanese army had been forced back, it had not been totally defeated despite very high losses on the Soviet side. In part this was what prompted mass arrests among the officers of the DVF in the autumn. Among the victims was Marshal Vasily Blyukher, the first commander of the front, who had been spared during the purge of the military leadership in 1937 but was shot on Stalin's orders on 9 November 1938. In May 1939 a large force from the Kwantung Army invaded allied Mongolian territory. A battle raged for several months along the Khalkin-Gol River and at the end of the day the Japanese units were surrounded and totally defeated. The military skirmishes in the region only came to an end in the autumn of 1939 at the request of the Japanese. War had broken out in western Europe, and Stalin wanted to avoid being drawn into a protracted confrontation in the east. Although in 1940 and the beginning of 1941 Stalin's attention had been focused on developments on the western borders, he did not neglect to take measures to strengthen the defences of the Far East. By the middle of 1941 the DVF consisted of several dozen well-trained, well-armed divisions, tank, artillery and air forces numbering approximately

704,000 men.[1] But the Japanese Kwantung Army was almost as large, with about 700,000 soldiers.

Along with the re-enforcement of the DVF, there were a number of personnel changes, some the result of repressions. General Zhukov, who had led the victory over the Japanese on the Khalkin-Gol, was appointed head of the General Staff and took up this post on 1 February 1941, while in January of that year Colonel-General Shtern, who had replaced Blyukher as commander of the Far Eastern Front and had participated in the battles of Lake Kasan and Khalkin-Gol, was arrested and shot. His replacement, General Joseph Apanasenko, had been known to Stalin since the days of the Civil War. Stalin summoned him from Tashkent, where he commanded the Central Asian Military District, in order to personally inform him about the appointment and send him off.

Apanasenko began his military career in 1914 at the fronts of the First World War. During the Civil War he quickly rose to be a divisional commander in the First Cavalry Army. In the 1920s and 1930s he served in different posts in the Leningrad, Belorussian and Kiev Military Districts. Stalin first met him during the battle for Tsaritsyn in 1918 but did not meet him again until Apanasenko was invited to the Kremlin before his assignment to Tashkent. They saw each other a number of times after that, and Stalin trusted him. Nevertheless Apanasenko remains virtually unknown outside his native Stavropol region.[2] When Soviet historians list the generals who distinguished themselves during the Second World War, Apanasenko is never mentioned. Nor does his name appear in the 12-volume *History of the Second World War* that was compiled in the 1970s. Yet this general was certainly one of the war's great heroes.

The commanding officers of the DVF, both at headquarters and in the field, reacted to the news of Apanasenko's appointment with a certain trepidation, as he had a reputation for being extremely rough. The well-known human-rights activist of the 1960s and 1970s, General Pyotr Grigorenko, was a lieutenant-colonel serving at the Far Eastern Front headquarters in 1941 and later wrote in his memoirs:

> General Joseph Apanasenko was named as commander of the Far Eastern Front several months before the war began. Even his physical appearance seemed unpleasant – he looked as if he had been hacked out of an oak log by an axe, not to mention his reputation as a petty tyrant of little education and intelligence. He had a powerful but somehow unpolished figure and his features were crude. His loud, hoarse voice lent everything he said a mocking tone. He swore profusely, usually in a humiliating fashion, and when he lost his temper, which he often did, the culprit could expect no mercy. His neck would begin to redden and even his eyes became bloodshot. And so we were hardly delighted by the change of command. However, those closest

to Apanasenko soon discovered his poor reputation to be in many respects unfounded. Above all, we soon noticed that he had a colossal
natural intelligence. And although uneducated, he read a great deal
and was skilled at evaluating his subordinates' proposals, selecting
whatever was most expedient in the circumstances. Secondly, he was
daring. If he decided to do something, he did it, assuming all responsibility. He never put the blame on a subordinate for carrying out his
orders. If a subordinate actually was at fault, Apanasenko would not
turn him over to the minister or to a court-martial, but would mete
out the punishment himself.[3]

Apanasenko chose a number of high-ranking officers to accompany
him to the front, almost all of whom turned out to be strong and
competent commanders.

As Apanasenko familiarized himself with the general situation and
studied existing strategic plans, he soon noticed that there was no
parallel transport route for motor vehicles along large sections of the
Trans-Siberian railway. Since the railway line passed quite close to
the border in a number of places, this made the army extremely
vulnerable. If the Japanese were to blow up a few of its numerous
bridges or tunnels, the army would no longer have freedom of manoeuvre or access to reliable supplies. Apanasenko immediately
ordered building to begin on a road that would stretch for almost
1,000 kilometres, using local workers as well as army construction
units. He set an almost impossibly short deadline for this huge task –
five months. Running ahead of our story, it can be said that
Apanasenko's orders were executed and that the road from
Khabarovsk to the Kuibyshevka-East station was completed in September 1941.

Tempting opportunities for Japan

During the first months of 1941, while Apanasenko was taking
urgent measures to strengthen the Far Eastern Front, secret consultations were taking place in Japan – within the government, the
General Staff and the circle around the emperor. A critical debate was
under way concerning the basic directions and goals of Japanese
military-colonial expansion. Although plans existed on a grandiose
scale, so far neither the details of implementation nor the order and
sequence of operations had been worked out. Militaristic groups had
become the prevailing force in the Japanese power structure of the
1930s; a massive, well-armed army had been established along with
a large navy and air force, with particular importance attached to
aircraft carriers. However, unlike Germany, Italy or the Soviet Union, Japan had no single, all-powerful ruler. The emperor and his
family, the commanders of the army and navy and the diplomatic
leadership did not always share a common view. Therefore all ques-

tions in Japan had to be decided collectively after discussion and consultation, which largely took place in the emperor's Privy Council of senior statesmen. In 1940 it was decided to include all former prime ministers in this body in order to establish a crucial continuity of power. However, this created a rather unwieldy decision-making process, particularly in complex situations.

The general direction of Japanese and German aggressive intentions was clear by the end of 1936, when they signed the 'Anti-Comintern Pact', joined by Italy a year later. The documents of this Tripartite Pact (as it was re-named in 1940) made it clear that its target was the USSR and the Communist International, with secret agreements stipulating different forms of co-operation and support 'in case war broke out between the USSR and any one of the signatories of the pact'. The intent of these expansionist designs suited the aspirations of the ruling circles in Britain and France, who put no obstacles in the way of the rearmament of Germany and even significantly contributed to the process. The policy of compromise and non-interference allowed Germany to annex Austria and the Sudetenland and led to the victory of Franco in Spain. Hitler was in no hurry to march east towards the USSR, but Japan was operating more actively: in addition to the Kwantung Army's bridgehead in Manchuria, the Japanese began to prepare a Kurile-Sakhalin base where, according to Soviet military intelligence, several divisions were being deployed.

The world was on the brink of war, and the general staffs and intelligence organizations of all the major powers were feverishly working out possible variants of how it might begin. One of the most likely aggressive moves for the Tripartite Pact was a German attack on Poland and the Baltic states, providing a passage to the borders of the USSR, to be followed by an attack on the Soviet Union in concert with a simultaneous attack by Japan in the east. In any case, this was what was being hoped for in Paris and London, and plans of this kind did exist in Berlin and Tokyo. However, in the course of a few days, everything changed. The non-aggression pact between Germany and the Soviet Union, signed in Moscow at the end of August, came as a complete surprise not only to Britain and France but also to Japan. Engaged in the extremely hurried negotiations in Moscow, Germany had neither the time nor the inclination to consult the Japanese, although this would have been obligatory under their earlier secret agreements. The Japanese government resigned but first sent a note of protest to Berlin complaining that the Soviet–German non-aggression treaty violated the secret protocols of the Anti-Comintern Pact. The Japanese leadership was in such a state of confusion that it took two more changes of cabinet before Prince Konoe was named head of government.

The rapid defeat and capitulation of France and the defeat suffered by the British Expeditionary Force in the summer of 1940 also took the Japanese by surprise. France's colonies in South-East Asia were now left 'ownerless', and this was particularly true of Indochina. Japan decided to appropriate the peninsula, occupying it at the beginning of 1941. But the administrations of the numerous British colonies in Asia – India and Burma, Singapore and Hong Kong, Malaysia and Ceylon – also found themselves in a very vulnerable position. For Japan, already waging a war against China and possessing a huge, extremely strong army as well as a large and powerful fleet, this new temptation would have been hard to resist; unlike the Soviet Far East, it appeared to be rather easy prey. The size and strength of the Soviet Union presented a formidable challenge, whereas Britain appeared to be on the edge of destruction, her fate apparently inevitable. It was only a logical next step, therefore, when the Japanese ambassador in Moscow transmitted a message from Prince Konoe to the Soviet government at the end of 1940 proposing the conclusion of a neutrality pact between Japan and the Soviet Union. Negotiations soon got under way, although at a more leisurely pace than the negotiations for the Molotov–Ribbentrop Pact.

Before taking a final decision the Japanese found it expedient to send their Minister of Foreign Affairs, Yosuke Matsuoka, to Europe to evaluate the situation and have talks with their allies. He was a politician and diplomat with considerable influence in the ruling circles of Japan. In 1933 he had represented Japan at the League of Nations and in 1936, by then Minister of Foreign Affairs, had signed the Anti-Comintern Pact. Matsuoka embarked on his trip on 12 March 1941, travelling through the Soviet Union. The Kremlin carefully followed his progress, and when he reached Moscow on 25 March he was invited to the Kremlin for a two-hour conversation with Stalin and Molotov. News of this meeting aroused disquiet in Berlin, but Matsuoka assured the German ambassador to Moscow, Count Schulenburg, that he would report all the details of his conversation with Stalin to Ribbentrop.

The Japanese Foreign Minister arrived in Berlin on 27 March, where he had several meetings with Ribbentrop and was received by Hitler. Without putting all their cards on the table, they told him a great deal about their plans. In March 1941 Germany was at the height of its power, in control of almost all of continental western Europe. A decision had already been taken to attack the Soviet Union and energetic preparations were under way in the east for the campaign that would signal a new triumph for the German armed forces and weapons. The blitzkrieg in preparation was intended to demolish the Red Army. Hitler and Ribbentrop were so confident of success that they asked for no help from Japan with regard to the USSR. But they did ask Japan to consider the question of war against Britain and particularly a quick attack on Singapore. Britain was too heavily engaged in Europe to be able to defend its colonies in Asia. If Japan were to deliver a blow in Asia, this would affect Britain's ability to hold out in Europe, and she could be defeated by the end of 1941.

The details of the German–Japanese negotiations in the spring of 1941 only became known after the war, during the trials of major Japanese war criminals as well as from the publication of secret Japanese documents by the US State Department. Right from the start Ribbentrop told Matsuoka that the non-aggression pact with the Soviet Union had been merely a tactical agreement, which Hitler could violate any time it suited him. 'Germany was confident,' said Ribbentrop, 'that the Russian campaign would end with the absolute victory of German arms and the total defeat of the Red army and the Russian state. The Führer was convinced that once military action against the Soviet Union got under way, within a few months nothing would be left of the great and powerful Russia.'[4] Matsuoka met Hitler and Ribbentrop again in April after a trip to Italy. He complained of the absence of a single, strong-willed leader in Japan, but he assured them that Japan would try not to lose this chance, the kind that came only once in a thousand years. When it was time, Japan would be resolute and prepared to attack. Ribbentrop advised Matsuoka not to stop in Moscow or have any negotiations in Russia on his return trip, but this went against his instructions.

A very warm reception awaited Matsuoka in Moscow where he spent a week, meeting Molotov several times and also Stalin. These talks were a source of alarm in Berlin and London. Only on the morning of 15 April did Matsuoka inform the German ambassador that at 2:00 pm Japan and the USSR would sign a pact of neutrality. Stalin was delighted with this outcome and decided to express his pleasure in an unusual manner, unusual in terms of diplomatic practice: the Foreign Minister's train was held back for an hour and suddenly Stalin and Molotov appeared at the Yaroslav Station. Stalin warmly greeted Matsuoka and his entourage and, after a short conversation, wished them a good trip. Afterwards Stalin beckoned to Count Schulenburg, put his arm around his shoulders and said: 'We must remain friends. You have to do all you can to make it possible.' Stalin greeted the German military attaché, Colonel Krebs, with equal warmth. Needless to say, the reports of all the diplomats present at the station contained a detailed account of the whole episode.

The Japanese leaders discussed all aspects of Matsuoka's mission at great length. Japan was quite prepared to attack Britain's colonies in Asia, but was uneasy about the attitude of the United States. Secret talks in Washington came to a dead end as the US made demands that were regarded as unacceptable by the Japanese. In Tokyo they began to think in terms of striking a sudden, powerful blow against the United States. In 1941 America was not regarded as a serious military power – the country did not even have a large-scale army. Of course the US had an enormous variety of potential resources at its disposal, but in 1941 everyone was thinking in terms of a blitzkrieg on land or sea. The United States did have a large navy with separate fleets on the Atlantic and the Pacific. Almost the entire Pacific fleet was based at Pearl Harbor in the Hawaiian Islands, which presented yet another temptation for the Japanese military. All Japan's twentieth-century wars began with a surprise attack.

The spread of war

The Japanese had received detailed information from a number of different sources about Germany's imminent invasion of the Soviet Union, and so the event itself did not come as a surprise. A special meeting of the government took place in Tokyo on 22 June at which they discussed and refined already existing plans for an attack on the USSR by the Kwantung Army. It was decided, however, to hold off taking action until the German army achieved final victory. Several weeks later, in the presence of the emperor, it was decided that Japan would adhere to the neutrality pact concluded with the Soviet Union but would continue active preparation for a move to the south. A few of those present at the meeting, including Matsuoka, favoured an immediate attack on the USSR, but most of the other leaders were against it.

The battles on the Soviet–German front during the summer could be regarded as presaging the defeat of the Soviet Union, as the German army captured a large part of the Ukraine, Belorussia, Moldavia and the Baltics. However, Hitler was unable to achieve his major goals: the battles around Odessa, Kiev and Smolensk smashed the German blitzkrieg and the German army was stopped at the gates of Leningrad and at the distant approaches to Moscow. The Germans then began to prepare for a new assault, intended to take place at the beginning of October.

Japan followed events on the Soviet–German front with intense interest, and more voices could be heard in favour of an immediate attack. However, another view prevailed. In October, just at the time of the height of the battle at the far reaches of Moscow, the government of Prince Konoe resigned and a new government came to power, led by General Tōjō Hideki, who without much difficulty convinced the emperor and princes of the need to attack Pearl Harbor as well as the British naval base at Singapore. They began to organize aircraft carriers and a large fleet as the main forward force, intending

the destruction of the American fleet to coincide with the capture of
Moscow and Leningrad. The Japanese, as we know, were completely
successful, which is more than can be said of Hitler.

General Apanasenko and the battle for Moscow

In July and August several infantry brigades were transferred from
the Far East to the Western Front. But this was only a small part of
the DVF forces. Stalin was alarmed at the thought of war on two
fronts, and according to intelligence reports the strength of the
Kwantung Army was growing continually in terms of both men and
armaments. The Japanese were preparing to send several thousand
experienced railway workers to Manchuria, which could mean only
one thing: the Japanese army was planning to take control of the
main line of the Trans-Siberian Railway.

The new German assault on Moscow came up against fierce opposition. However, the Germans succeeded in breaking through at a
number of points on the front and were advancing far to the east.
Many Soviet divisions were surrounded around Vyazma. The road to
Moscow was protected by badly armed and hurriedly assembled
units along with several divisions of the People's Volunteer Corps.
The evacuation of Moscow that began in the middle of October did
not always take place in an orderly fashion. A large number of ministries and other departments were moved to Kuibyshev on the
Volga. Although Richard Sorge's information from Tokyo made it
clear that Japan had no intention of attacking the Soviet Union for
the time being, the situation could rapidly change if Moscow were to
fall. The forces fighting on the Western Front already included divisions transferred from the Urals, Western Siberia, Central Asia and
Kazakhstan, but many of them sustained substantial losses, while in
the Far East there were scores of battle-ready divisions and a large
supply of military equipment.

The idea to move part of the DVF to the Western Front came up in
the Far East as well as in Moscow; many officers were requesting to
be transferred to an army that was engaged in action. On 10 October
1941 the First Secretary of the Khabarovsk regional Party committee,
G.A. Barkov, sent a long letter to Stalin proposing the immediate
transfer of not fewer than ten divisions of the DVF for the defence of
Moscow:

> Our far eastern borders are being defended by a very large army,
> amounting to a million well-trained fighting men. A large part of this
> army could be sent by special train to crucial sectors of the western
> and southern fronts, leaving only the minimum necessary cover in the
> Far East plus aircraft, part of the Pacific fleet and the Amur flotilla.
> The military leadership of the Far Eastern Front obviously will object
> to this proposal, and I, myself, understand perfectly well that this im-

plies a considerable risk – it could provoke Japan to take military action. But risks cannot be avoided in war, and if we suffer defeat on the Western Front, the Far East would never be able to resist on its own. In that situation we could be defeated on both sides.[5]

Even before receiving this letter Stalin sent for Apanasenko along with the commander of the Pacific fleet, I.S. Yumashev, and the First Secretary of the Primorsk kraikom, Nikolai Pegov. Their meeting took place in Stalin's Kremlin office on 12 October and went on for some time, but no decision was taken. However, the situation around Moscow continued to deteriorate and several days later Stalin rang Apanasenko to ask how many divisions he could transfer west by the end of October or the beginning of November. Apanasenko replied that up to 20 infantry divisions and seven or eight tank formations could be sent, provided of course that the railway service could produce the required number of trains.

The transfer of troops began almost immediately and the whole operation was personally supervised by Apanasenko. General A.P. Beloborodov, the commander of one of the divisions being moved to the west, later wrote in his memoirs:

> The railway men gave us the green light all the way. We stopped at the main stations for no more than 5–7 minutes. They uncoupled one engine and connected another, filled it up with water and coal – and off we went! As a result all thirty-six echelons of the division crossed the country from east to west at the speed of a courier train. The last echelon left Vladivostock on 17th October and by 28th October our units already were in the Moscow region and off the train at Istra and other nearby stations.[6]

In November the Far Eastern divisions were already either engaged in defensive action around Moscow or preparing for the attack that began on 6 December. Without these fresh, well-trained divisions it would almost certainly have been impossible to win the battle for Moscow in December 1941.

Apanasenko's daring initiative

Having sent division after division to the west, Apanasenko could not remain passive. His decision was one which any commander in his place would have been very hesitant to take: to form new regiments and divisions to replace those that had been sent to the west, while giving them the same names and numbers. It was a risky thing to do because independent military formations were strictly forbidden and no supplies of weapons, food or uniforms would be allotted to these new divisions of the DVF. Of course Moscow knew about this daring initiative but feigned ignorance, offering neither approval nor condemnation. According to the former head of the General Staff of the

Armed Forces of the USSR, General Moiseyev, neither the General Staff nor the Stavka had the resources to equip new military formations that had not been included in the central plan. Moscow's position could be described roughly as follows: we have no objection to Apanasenko's initiative, but let him find a way out of his difficulties himself.

At this point General Apanasenko embarked on a surge of frenzied activity. Training of recruits was expanded, with young men arriving even from Moscow to join units of the DVF. In the Far East and Siberia Apanasenko called up men aged 50–55, indeed, all those who were able to carry a weapon. In wartime the commander of the Far Eastern Front was the most powerful figure in all the adjacent regions. His orders had to be carried out by officials at every level, including obkom and kraikom (territorial Party committee) secretaries. Supported by economic enterprises and Party workers, Apanasenko organized new arms production in the Far East. Thousands of training rifles were put into full working order, weapons were repaired, and mortars, mines, shells, cartridges and radio transmitters were produced. He mobilized motor transport, had damaged vehicles put into working order and requisitioned local horses. According to Grigorenko, Apanasenko even sent his best subordinates to the prison camps of Kolyma and the whole of the Far East in order to seek out military officers and soldiers who had fallen victim to the purges of 1937–38 and put them back in the army. Indignant camp administrators and the leadership of Dalstroi objected and sent complaints to Beria and Stalin, but in these months Stalin was unwilling to interfere with Apanasenko's activities and was determined to protect him. Towards the end of 1941 Stalin's attitude towards front commanders began to change, but he continued to trust Apanasenko. A system of 'army sovkhozi' had been established in the Far East in Blyukher's time, and it was now expanded to help provide the army with provisions. There was an enormous amount of land in this part of the USSR but a shortage of labour, and these new farms helped to feed the soldiers.

It was not only because its forces were occupied elsewhere that Japan held back from attacking the Soviet Union in the winter of 1941–42. The Kwantung Army was stronger than ever. Although they may have been waiting for a decisive German victory, they were also expecting Soviet divisions in the Far East and Siberia to be reduced from 30 to 15, with aviation, armoured tank forces and artillery cut back by two-thirds. But the awaited reduction of Soviet forces in the region apparently never took place. According to German Intelligence, divisions from the Far East were already fighting on the Western Front. However, Japanese military intelligence reported to headquarters that all the divisions of the DVF were in their former positions, carrying out their regular training exercises. From documents that became available after the war, it is clear that the Kwantung Army was preparing for war with the Soviet Union and had plans to 'assimilate' Soviet territory. Thus, for example, in the 'Plan for the administration of territories and the common development of Great Western Asia', devised by the military and colonial ministries of Japan at the beginning of 1942, it is stated: 'The Primorie will be joined to Japan, regions adjoining the Manchurian Empire will become part of the sphere of influence of that country, and the Trans-Siberian Railway will be put under the full control of Germany and Japan with Omsk as the dividing point.'[7]

Japan's attack on the United States and Britain eased the position of Germany. For America and partly for Britain, the centre of gravity of military action shifted to the Pacific Ocean and to South-East Asia. Plans for a second front in Europe were set aside and Germany, no longer so worried about the rear, could roll out a great new offensive on the Eastern Front. German forces reached the Volga at Stalingrad and exploited their success in the North Caucasus. At the time the situation seemed catastrophic, and if Baku and Stalingrad were to fall, it would have the most serious consequences. The Stavka again turned to the Far East, and new regiments and divisions arrived from the Far Eastern Front. Altogether in the first two years of the war the Far East supplied 17 infantry, three tank and two cavalry divisions, two airborne landing and four infantry brigades, scores of bombardier and fighter regiments and a number of special units and subunits.[8] But amazingly the size of the DVF force remained the same. On 22 June 1941 there were 703,700 soldiers on the Eastern Front. On 1 July 1942 the force contained 1,446,000 military personnel while on 1 July 1943 the numbers were 1,156,000.[9] The most difficult problem was feeding so many people. Several years ago I received a letter from an old soldier, a veteran of the Far Eastern Front, K.N. Soloviev, living in Pyatigorsk. He wrote that in 1942–43 soldiers at the front were virtually starving, and some of them were so weak that they could not serve. When this happened they were sent to the regional collective farms or the 'military state farms' to recuperate. Nevertheless Soloviev testifies that the army as a whole 'had been very strong, with many old and experienced soldiers who had seen action in the First World War and the Civil War also'.

Germany did not seek Japan's intervention in the autumn and winter of 1941. But by the autumn of 1942, rather than asking for peripheral assistance, Germany was seeking direct help from the Kwantung Army. According to German Intelligence the Soviet Union no longer had battle-worthy divisions in the Far East. Germany had declared war on the United States and wherever possible was sinking American ships. But Japan was not attacking US ships carrying

Lend-Lease provisions since these ships sailed into Far Eastern ports under the Soviet flag. However, the Japanese were convinced that there had never been any reduction of Soviet forces in the Far East and that they were in fact stronger than ever. It was of course true that on the orders of Apanasenko and under his personal supervision, defences were being continually improved and engineering installations upgraded. In 1941 regional defence battalions occupied only 3–4 kilometres of territory parallel to the front at a depth of 1.5–2 kilometres, but by the end of 1942 a deep, multi-stage defence extended along the whole border zone with special attention given to anti-tank installations and the erection of fortifications at all likely enemy approaches. The defences of major Far Eastern cities also were re-enforced: Khabarovsk, Vladivostock and Blagoveshchensk. The Far East had truly been turned into a fortress, and there could no longer be any question of a Japanese surprise attack. The Kwantung Army, spread out for thousands of kilometres along the border, had neither enough troops nor reserves to carry the day in the Far East. Therefore even in the autumn of 1942, at the time of the most successful advance of the German army on the Eastern Front, Japan preferred to maintain armed neutrality. But it is important to point out that the Japanese militarists were certainly not held back by the treaty signed in April 1941; above all, they were deterred by Soviet military strength. They had many opportunities to convince themselves of this strength, as small units of the Kwantung Army frequently violated the Soviet border, thus providing authentic intelligence information gained in the process of direct combat.

Meanwhile, in the first months of 1943, Stalin and the General Staff continued to procure Apanasenko's second-string divisions from the Soviet–Chinese border. General Apanasenko was again determined not to expose his positions and he began to make efforts to form third-string divisions. Where it was impossible to form a division, he set up infantry brigades instead. But now the whole process became easier. The Stavka could hardly have two divisions in the west designated by identical numbers. This meant that official recognition finally had to be given to Apanasenko's 'independent activity'. All new Far Eastern divisions, brigades and regiments were assigned new numbers, given their own military flags and were now included within the centralized supply system.

The death of General Apanasenko

Joseph Apanasenko met Stalin in October 1942, and Stalin summoned him to Moscow again in January and February 1943. Apanasenko pleaded to be sent to a fighting army on one of the active fronts, and Stalin promised to think about it. But it took until

25 April for the order to come, freeing Apanasenko of his duties as commander in the Far East and ordering him to leave for Moscow where he would be at the disposal of the Stavka. The new assignment, however, was delayed, and the general decided to call attention to himself in a letter to Stalin:

> I am Your soldier, Comrade Stalin. You know that we sent quite a few extremely well trained and equipped infantry divisions, and also artillery and air regiments from the Far East to the west. To replace those divisions sent west, I immediately tried to form and train new ones. I can report that the forces I have left on the Far Eastern front are fighting fit. The economy is also in a good state. Industry and agriculture in the Primorsk and Khaborovsk regions are doing quite well. There will be no complaints.[10]

At the end of May 1943 Apanasenko was appointed Deputy Commander of the forces on the Voronezh front, under General Nikolai Vatutin. 'You must not be offended,' Stalin told him. 'You have no experience of contemporary battle situations. Spend a little time as deputy commander, and afterwards I will give you a front.' But fate decreed otherwise. Apanasenko was at his post for only three months. On 5 August 1943, at the height of the battle of Kursk, Joseph Apanasenko was mortally wounded and died without regaining consciousness. He was buried in his native Stavropol according to his expressed wish. During the war he did not distinguish himself in battle and did not participate in attacks or retreats. But what he did in the Far East made such an enormous contribution to the final victory that he certainly should be considered one of the outstanding military leaders of the Second World War.

PART V. THE UNKNOWN STALIN

CHAPTER 13

Stalin as a Russian Nationalist

Zhores Medvedev

Portrait of the generalissimo

After the Soviet victory in the Second World War all traces of Stalin's Georgian origins disappeared from his official portraits. The process actually started earlier, at the beginning of the 1930s, when they began to soften Joseph Vissarionovich Dzhugashvili's pronounced Caucasian features. But the Georgian element disappeared entirely in the post-war portraits of the generalissimo, whose majestic new image was devised appropriately to depict the leader of all times and of all peoples. The forehead was raised a little, the Georgian pointed nose made smaller and a little broader, the nostrils aligned with the upper lip, the arched left eyebrow lowered and the chin moved slightly forward. The face became a perfect oval. Only the eyes and moustache, Stalin's most characteristic features, remained unaltered. Karpov's portrait of Stalin in his full dress uniform replete with medals and decorations, painted in 1946, was modelled on a photograph of the illustrious Russian explorer and geographer, General Nikolai Przhevalsky. This subsequently led to rumours of a possible family connection between the great leader and the famous explorer, although no such tie actually existed.

The official biography of Stalin published after the war provided no details about his father, and there is still no information about when or where the latter died. This helps to account for the stories that began to circulate even during Stalin's lifetime, that the shoemaker Vissarion Dzhugashvili, hardly an appropriate parent for the exalted ruler, was not in fact his real father. Several alternative candidates were suggested, including one of the Georgian princes in Gori. The rumour that Stalin's father could have been the great Russian explorer Przhevalsky began to spread after the war and turned out be the most persistent of all the myths, no doubt because of the clear resemblance between the two in the famous 1946 portrait. Przhevalsky, it was claimed, had once paid a visit to Gori. The

story turned up again in the 1997 biography of Stalin by Edvard
Radzinsky: 'The Russian explorer Przhevalsky did indeed visit Gori.
His moustachioed face, in encyclopaedias published in Stalin's time, is
suspiciously like that of Stalin.'[1] One of Stalin's granddaughters,
Galina Dzhugashvili, recently wrote that Przhevalsky, 'returning
from one of his expeditions, passed through Gori and later sent
money to the mother of my grandfather'.[2] But the facts are very
different. Nikolai Przhevalsky not only never went to Gori, but never
even set foot in Georgia. As is customary for a professional traveller,
Przhevalsky always kept a detailed diary. From January 1878 until
the end of 1881 he was in the middle of extended travels in China
and Tibet, interrupted only once by a return trip to St Petersburg
when his mother died.[3] The route to China in those years passed
through the southern Urals and Central Asia, and a large part of the
trip east of Ufa had to be made by camel caravan. Georgia would
have been entirely out of the way. Since Moscow and St Petersburg
were not linked with Baky or Tiflis by railways at that time, it was
clearly impossible to 'pass through' Gori on the way from China to
St Petersburg.

Nevertheless the perceptible likeness between Stalin and Przhevalsky did not come about accidentally. Because Stalin never sat for
portraits, painters always had to work from photographs. It was
important to have a standard image as a model, an image that was
younger, nobler and above all more Russian than the actual subject,
and Przhevalsky's face was perfect. The Russian people, whom Stalin
had already proclaimed to be 'the most outstanding nation of all
nations within the Soviet Union',[4] needed to have a leader whose
appearance had no trace of 'alien' features. In post-war films such as
The Third Thrust and *The Battle of Stalingrad*, a Russian actor,
Aleksei Diky, was chosen to play the role of Stalin (replacing the
Georgian Mikhail Gelovani), and appeared on the screen without a
Georgian accent. Stalin personally approved this change, and Diky
was awarded the Stalin Prize for each of his films.

Towards the end of the 1980s, in order to put an end to speculation about Stalin's parentage, the Stalin museum in Gori
miraculously managed to find a photograph of Vissarion Dzhugashvili, aged 25 or 30. There was a clear resemblance between father and
son, but doubts have been expressed about the authenticity of this
recent discovery.[5] The print lacked certain qualities typical of nineteenth-century photographs, while the face of Vissarion
Dzhugashvili was partly covered by an army cap and beard, although beards were rarely seen in Georgia at that time. No
photographs have ever been found of Stalin's mother as a young
woman.

'One and indivisible' or 'a union of equals'

Stalin was a member of the first Soviet government formed immediately after the Revolution on 25 October 1917, as People's Commissar for Nationalities. In the published list of People's Commissars he appeared as Dzhugashvili, his real name, with his alias, Stalin, in brackets. Other members of the Council of People's Commissars were treated in a similar fashion – including Bronstein (Trotsky) and Ulyanov (Lenin). Stalin was the only member of the Central Committee of the RSDRP Bolshevik faction in Petrograd at this time who came from one of the key national minorities, and his Georgian name influenced Lenin's decision to select him for the nationalities post, although few people had ever heard of Dzhugashvili. Lenin was completely unaware of the fact that Stalin had distanced himself from his Georgian origins and had come to identify himself as a Russian – culturally, psychologically and politically. Stalin had never been a genuine internationalist nor was he inclined to be concerned about protecting the rights of the non-Russian minorities of the country. The other representative of the national periphery in the Bolshevik leadership, the legendary Stepan Shaumyan, found himself in Baku in October 1917 and was appointed to be the ambassador extraordinary of the Sovnarkom in Transcaucasia. Returning from Switzerland after 15 years in exile, Lenin barely knew those members of the Central Committee who arrived in Petrograd from Siberian exile in the spring of 1917.

According to Trotsky, Lenin was a poor judge of character. 'Lenin never allowed himself to form a general impression of a person. His eye was like a microscope. He enormously exaggerated whatever quality happened to come within his field of vision in given circumstances.'[6] Lenin regarded Stalin as 'that splendid Georgian', always ready to carry out any assignment. When they finally did clash at the end of 1922 over how to create a Soviet Union out of the ruins of the Russian empire, it was not because Stalin's views had altered in any way. What had in fact changed crucially by that time was Stalin's personal position in the Party. After Lenin's first stroke in May 1922 Stalin became the *de facto* head of the Central Committee and had become accustomed to taking independent decisions.

Historians have long been aware of the disagreement between Lenin and Stalin over the first constitution of the USSR, but the dispute needs to be freshly examined because recent events have made it possible for us to assess the details more objectively. Most previous accounts of this conflict have questioned Stalin's scepticism about the durability of a 'union' based on the 'solidarity of the workers' (i.e. Party discipline), and various authors have argued that his insistence on the need for tough central power to hold the entire structure together was wrong. Today, a decade after the surprisingly rapid collapse of the Soviet Union, it can be argued that Lenin was the one who was politically short sighted when he proposed a less restrictive first constitution for the Soviet Union.

The tsarist empire began to disintegrate shortly after the February Revolution. Once the imperial court disappeared, the empire began to totter, and the Provisional Government was unable to assert its power over all parts of the former regime. The Ukrainian Rada was established in Kiev in June 1917, a president chosen, and the newly formed separatist government started peace negotiations with Germany. Soon Finland and Georgia declared their independence. In Turkestan an ongoing insurrection, provoked in 1916 by the tsarist government's attempt to mobilize Muslim peasants for army service, showed no sign of coming to an end. The Brest–Litovsk armistice treaty with Germany, signed by the Bolsheviks in 1918, recognized Russia's defeat and provided for a dismemberment of Russia that tended to ignore ethnic boundaries. Under the provisions of the treaty, Russia had to recognize the independence of the Ukraine, which in addition to territory that historically had been Ukrainian also included the Crimea and four provinces – Kharkov, Yekaterinoslav, Kherson and Odessa – where a majority of the population was Russian. (Most of the territories around the Black Sea, once part of the Ottoman Empire, had been conquered during the reign of Catherine the Great.) Belorussia became a protectorate of Germany. The Brest–Litovsk agreement deprived Russia of coal from the Donbass and oil from Baku. This was the situation in July 1918 when the Fifth All-Russian Congress of Soviets met and adopted a constitution for the new country: the Russian Soviet Federated Socialist Republic. The national minorities of this mini-Russia were granted cultural autonomy but did not have the right to withdraw from the federation.

The Brest–Litovsk treaty was repudiated in November 1918, and by the time the Civil War came to an end in 1921 a large part of Russia's former territory had been recovered. However, since the independence of the Ukraine, Georgia and Armenia had been recognized by the rest of Europe, overt annexation imposed by the military superiority of the Red Army was out of the question; central political control from Moscow was established by the transfer of power to local Bolshevik organizations. Each of the republics, now proclaimed to be 'soviet' and 'socialist', proceeded to sign a treaty with the RSFSR. The union would be maintained by Party discipline, the army and the institution of special commissars endowed with extraordinary powers who received their instructions directly from Lenin. But the actual dictator of the whole Caucasus region at that time (Transcaucasia), Sergo Ordzhonikidze, was in fact taking orders from Stalin rather than Lenin. Stepan Shaumyan had been killed in

1918. There are conflicting stories about his death, but according to the official Soviet version, he was executed by British troops along with other Baku commissars.

By the middle of 1922, after the introduction of the New Economic Policy brought about a revival of the economy and the beginnings of a unified transport system, it seemed an appropriate time to adopt a new constitution in order to re-establish the political unity of the country. On 11 August 1922 the Orgburo set up a drafting commission, which in normal circumstances would certainly have been chaired by Lenin, but he had been seriously ill since May when a stroke left him partially paralysed and temporarily unable to speak. His condition had improved by the beginning of August, and he began to speak, dictate and annotate documents. With a little assistance he was also able to move about and go to the Kremlin, but the doctors imposed strict limitations on his working day, fearing a second stroke. Therefore Stalin, who by that time was the General Secretary of the Central Committee and head of two commissariats, also became the chairman of the Constitutional Commission. However, the person considered to occupy second place in the Party during this period was not Stalin but Trotsky, while Zinoviev and Kamenev came third and fourth. Since Lenin exercised power through the Sovnarkom rather than the Party apparatus, Trotsky, the Commissar for War, was regarded as Lenin's First Deputy within the government. Lev Kamenev also was a Deputy Chairman of the Sovnarkom and usually presided over sessions of the Politburo. Grigori Zinoviev headed the Petrograd Soviet and the Executive Committee of the Communist International. In 1922 these three men still had considerably more influence in the Party than Stalin, but they considered routine day-to-day work in various commissions and committees to be 'bureaucratic', and tried to avoid it whenever possible. The Constitutional Commission included four members of the Central Committee – Kuibyshev, Ordzhonikidze, Rakovsky and Sokolnikov – as well as Bolshevik leaders from the republics that were part of the Union. Molotov was included a month later. The only moderate nationalist within the group was the representative of Georgia, N.G. Mdivani, while the rest were either ethnic Russians or Russified Bolsheviks.

According to the proposed constitution, drafted with considerable input from Stalin, the Ukraine, Belorussia, Georgia, Armenia and several other republics would join the Russian Federation. Within the structure of the new RSFSR, each of these new entrants would receive exactly the same rights as the current members of the RSFSR such as the Tartar or Bashkir republics. There would be no need to create any additional 'union' institutions, since the powers of the Sovnarkom would be extended to the new members of the Union, but the Central

Executive Committee (TsIK) would be expanded in order to carry out its function as a legislative organ. Representatives of the autonomous republics were to be included on the TsIK in proportion to the size of the populations they represented. Military, diplomatic, transportation and communications commissariats would only exist at the level of central government. Commissariats of finance, production, labour and agriculture in the republics would be formally subordinate to the RSFSR commissariats in Moscow, as had already been the case for all 'organs of the struggle against counter-revolution'. However, commissariats of justice, education, internal affairs, land ownership, health and social security in the autonomous republics would have independent status.[7] Stalin was proposing to create a significantly more centralized, unified state than the model he had outlined in his speeches of 1921 or the first half of 1922 as the Commissar for Nationalities who was then fully supporting Lenin's approach.

Stalin's draft was sent to the Party Central Committees in the republics and was approved by all of them with the exception of Georgia. The Georgian Party comrades were in favour of economic amalgamation with the RSFSR but wished to retain all other attributes of independence. The sessions of the Constitutional Commission took place on 23 and 24 September 1922 under the chairmanship of Molotov. The Commission approved Stalin's draft as a basis for agreement, with one abstention coming from the representative of Georgia. A special note was appended to the draft, rejecting the resolution of the Georgian Central Committee. On the next day, 25 September, the Commission's materials were sent to Lenin at the Gorki estate near Moscow and simultaneously distributed to all members of the Central Committee, to be approved at the forthcoming Central Committee plenum on 5 October.

Lenin was indignant. He had envisaged the creation of an 'open union' of equal republics in the hope that once capitalism had been overthrown in other countries of Europe and Asia, they too might be inclined to join. In his view, Russian nationalism was the most dangerous obstacle to the future transformation of the Russian Revolution into a revolution of the world proletariat. On 26 September Lenin summoned Stalin to Gorki for explanations, but Stalin refused to accept Lenin's arguments or change his own position. On the next day they both sent their objections and mutual accusations to the Politburo, with Stalin attacking Lenin's position as 'national liberalism'. Lenin proposed a number of specific changes to the draft constitution, and in particular suggested that the new state be called 'The Union of Soviet Republics of Europe and Asia'.[8] He also wrote to Kamenev, telling him that the discussion of the draft constitution in the Politburo would be postponed until his arrival at the Kremlin on 2 October.

In 1922 the Politburo consisted of seven members including Lenin, and since only one member, Tomsky, would support Stalin in this dispute, there was no way that he could get approval for his draft at the Central Committee plenum set for 5 October. Therefore a revised draft was put together, signed by Stalin, Molotov, Ordzhonikidze and Myasnikov (the leader of the Armenian delegation) and distributed to all members of the Central Committee. However, Stalin refused to accept Lenin's preferred name for the new country and opted instead for a temporary 'Union of the Republics'. He also rejected another of Lenin's demands – that there be a revolving chairmanship of the Central Executive Committee with each republican leader holding the position in turn, in order to guarantee a basic equality between the republics.

The plenum that met two weeks later adopted a compromise name: the Union of Soviet Socialist Republics (USSR). Lenin was extremely displeased. He was not able to be present at the meetings of the plenum but on 6 October wrote to Kamenev stressing the need to fight against Russian great-power chauvinism and insisting once again that the representatives of all the republics must take the Central Executive Committee chairmanship in turn.[9] Although the plenum accepted his proposal, this and certain other amendments made by Lenin were not included in the final draft of the constitution, prepared for discussion and ratification at the First All-Union Congress of Soviets due to take place in Moscow on 30 December. By this time Lenin was no longer able to put up a struggle. On 16 December his health had taken a serious turn for the worse.

On 30 December 1922, once the Congress had approved the declaration and treaty signalling the formation of the USSR, Lenin, seriously ill in Gorki, dictated a memorandum entitled 'On the question of nationalities'. Along with his letter to the Politburo of September 1922, this memorandum lay hidden away in secret Party archives and remained unknown in the Soviet Union until the autumn of 1956. It was published only after Khrushchev's condemnation of the Stalin cult at the Twentieth Party Congress. However, Stalin's own contributions to the whole discussion have never been made public and still remain inaccessible in a secret Stalin fond in the Presidential Archive.[10] Particularly after 1991 there has apparently been a reluctance to reveal how well Stalin understood the potential danger of disintegration, given certain constitutional preconditions. He was less optimistic than others about the spread of revolution in the West, believing on the contrary that there was a need to make preparations in order to be in a position to repel aggression.

In his memorandum, dictated over two days with three interruptions for rest, Lenin included an apology to the proletariat:

I am, it appears, much at fault before the workers of Russia for not having intervened with sufficient energy and incisiveness in the notorious question of 'autonomization'. ... It is said that we need a unified apparatus. From where do these assertions originate? Is it not from that very same Russian apparatus which ... we adopted from tsarism and only barely managed to anoint with soviet chrism. ...

In such conditions it is quite likely that the 'freedom of secession from the union' with which we justify ourselves, will prove to be a mere scrap of paper, incapable of defending the other nationalities in Russia from inroads of that truly Russian type, the Great-Russian chauvinist who essentially is a scoundrel and a bully in the manner of a typical Russian bureaucrat. There can be no doubt that the insignificant percent of Soviet or Sovietised workers will drown in this sea of Russian chauvinist riffraff like a fly in milk.[11]

Lenin ridiculed the concept of the 'great nation', 'great only in respect of its acts of violence'. He derisively referred to Stalin as 'that Georgian ... who is not only a true "social-nationalist" himself but also a crude Great-Russian Derzhimorda, violating the interests of proletarian class solidarity'. Lenin was referring to Derzhimorda, a character in Gogol's *Inspector General* who came to symbolize brutal police methods and mentality. He went on to argue that it was hardly surprising to find Stalin and Dzerzhinsky at the forefront of a 'Great-Russian nationalist campaign', since it is well known that 'assimilated non-Russians always overdo things when it is a matter of truly Russian attitudes'.

Lenin proposed returning to this whole question at the next Congress of Soviets in order to make crucial changes to the constitution of the USSR. His memorandum was read out to leaders of delegations to the Twelfth Party Congress but was not disclosed to the delegates at large. The Congress adopted a resolution 'On the national question', but Lenin's recommendation for the 'equality of rights' was not adopted until the 'Stalin Constitution' of 1936. It was, however, decided to create a second chamber of the Supreme Soviet, to be called the Soviet of Nationalities, which would have equal representation from all the republics, although even here there was no question of an alternating chairmanship. In any case it was the Presidium of the Supreme Soviet that issued decrees, and debates in the chamber had little effect on legislation.

Analysing the events of the pre-war period today, it does seem clear that the strictly centralized economy, which played such a crucial role in the rapid industrialization of the country, would never have been possible if Lenin's model for the Union had been adopted. Lenin even went so far as to oppose a centrally directed general transport system. And if instead of the USSR with its 'autonomous' and 'union' republics (the latter distinguished by a formal right to secede), an extended Russian Federation had been established as originally envisaged by Stalin, this certainly would have led to an even more rapid economic, political and ethnic integration of the country. Along with an accelerated process of Russification, there could have been the genuine birth of a 'Soviet people' that paid much less heed to ethnicity, rather like the experience of the United States. What turned out to be a hybrid combination of two constitutional projects resulted in an extremely uneven economic and national integration of the country. Nevertheless, a 'Soviet people' did emerge, with the Russian language, mixed marriages and a harmonization of different national cultures as unifying factors. In the course of 70 years the process of ethnic integration was strongest in the central regions of the USSR, above all in Moscow and Leningrad. There was also a considerable degree of integration in Kiev, Minsk, Tbilisi, Baku, Tashkent and Kharkov. If the USSR had continued to exist for another 40–50 years, 'the Soviets' would have become as much a reality as 'the Americans'.

It was the dispute over the constitution that prompted Lenin to write his famous *Testament*, in which he suggested that Stalin should be transferred to another, less responsible post. The *Testament* was in fact a preliminary document. According to Trotsky, Lenin was planning to carry out a reorganization of the Central Committee apparatus at the Twelfth Party Congress in April 1923. In March of that year he began to take steps to remove Stalin from the leadership, as well as Ordzhonikidze and Dzerzhinsky. Trotsky's claim that Lenin had in fact chosen him as his heir has a certain credibility. According to Trotsky, it was Lenin's intention

> to create the most favourable conditions for me to work either alongside him, if he is able to recover, or in his place, if he is overcome by illness. But since the battle never reached a climax or even a middle stage, it brought about the opposite result. Lenin had only managed to reach the point of **declaring** war on Stalin and his allies; therefore only those who were directly involved knew about it, but not the Party.[12]

Lenin suffered a second, more massive stroke on 19 March 1923. Trotsky links Stalin's subsequent advancement to the fact that it was impossible for Lenin to play any kind of role at the Twelfth Party Congress. However, more objective sources suggest that Stalin triumphed largely because what almost the entire Party leadership feared above all was the possibility of Trotsky coming to power. Stalin was the only real alternative to Trotsky and his plans for world revolution.

The war and Russian nationalism

For the first ten years after Lenin's death official Party propaganda and the 'organs for the struggle against counter-revolution' fought against nationalism in all its forms and manifestations, including the Russian variety. There was a robust attempt to create a 'Soviet people', which had some success thanks to the rapid process of urbanization. However, from the middle of the 1930s traditional Russian nationalism began to be encouraged, inspired above all by an essential need to instil a sense of pride and patriotic spirit throughout country. A clear enough threat from the West had appeared in the shape of German fascism. Hitler's theory of race, proclaiming the inferiority of the Slavs and the necessity of *lebensraum* for the Germans at the expense of western Slav territory, inevitably provoked a response in the USSR. Counter-propaganda found its natural ingredients in the glories of Russian history, and the change was particularly noticeable in films. The themes of the most popular films at the end of the 1920s and the beginning of the 1930s were inspired by the Revolution: *The Battleship 'Potemkin'*, *Chapaev* (a Civil War commander), *Lenin in October*, *We from Kronstadt* etc, while in the second half of the 1930s historical Russian patriotism dominated the screens with films such as *Minin and Pozharsky* (Kuzma Minin was a merchant and *zemsky* elder of Nizhny Novgorod who organized the People's Army in 1611–12 and, together with Prince Pozharsky, freed Moscow from Polish rule; a monument to Minin and Pozharsky was erected on Red Square in Moscow in 1818), *Suvorov* (one of Russia's legendary generals) and *Aleksandr Nevsky* (Prince of Novgorod, Kiev, and later Grand Duke of Vladimir who destroyed the Swedish army in a famous battle at the Neva River in 1240). Stalin took a personal interest in Soviet cinematography and often sent for specific scenarios, read them, made changes and even followed the process of shooting and assembling the final film.

Nevertheless Stalin did not succeed in his attempt to prepare the people of the Soviet Union for war. Many factors must be taken into account in order to explain the heavy defeats suffered by the Red Army in 1941–42. Perhaps the absence of 'Soviet' patriotism among large sections of the population, particularly the peasants who made up the majority of rank-and-file soldiers, was one of them. Yet the fact that it was only possible to mount a truly heroic defence at the walls of cities that had been the scene of military triumphs in the past, cities that played an enduring symbolic role in Russian history – surely this must be relevant; this was true of Brest, Odessa, Smolensk, Sevastopol, Leningrad and Moscow, while Ukrainian, Belorussian, Lithuanian and Latvian cities surrendered almost without a fight.

The terrible defeats of the first days of the war convinced Stalin of the need to revitalize Russian patriotism. His speech on 3 July 1941, declaring that the country was fighting a 'patriotic war', proved to be a political turning point. The change became even more obvious in a second speech at a review of the troops of the Moscow garrison in Red Square on 7 November 1941. On this anniversary of the Russian Revolution, Stalin appealed to the army to be inspired by the 'courage of our great ancestors: Aleksandr Nevsky, Dmitry Donskoi, Kuzma Minin, Dmitry Pozharsky, Aleksandr Suvorov and Mikhail Kutuzov'[13] (Kutuzov was field marshal and commander-in-chief of the Russian army during the Napoleonic Wars).

Official propaganda operating through the system of political commissars was slower to change. Until the end of 1941 speeches and declarations in the press still referred to 'mortal combat' between fascism and communism. But by 1942 the political slogans disappeared, and the war was transformed into a battle between Germans and Russians, which essentially is what did take place in the defence of Stalingrad. It was just at the time of the Stalingrad campaign that Stalin abruptly introduced a whole range of new policies, focusing on an active restoration of Russian historical traditions, first of all in the army. 'White Guard' shoulder straps replaced 'Red Army' tabs on uniforms, 'commanders' became 'officers' and 'Red Army men' were once again referred to as 'soldiers'. Traditional Russian military ranks were restored: sergeant, lieutenant, captain, major and colonel. The institution of military commissars was downgraded, thus re-establishing a single command. Veterans of the First World War received permission to wear their tsarist medals and crosses for heroism, while new Russian decorations were established: the Order of the Patriotic War, orders of Aleksandr Nevsky, Suvorov, Kutuzov and Nakhimov. For Ukrainians there was the Order of Bogdan Khmelnitsky.

The most significant nationalist reform took place in September 1943 – the full legalization of the Russian Orthodox Church. Thousands of priests, languishing in prisons and camps, were amnestied, released and provided with parishes. The amnesty was not, however, extended to Catholic priests in the Baltics or Western Ukraine, nor were Muslim or Jewish clergymen set free. On 4 September 1943 Stalin invited the Metropolitan of the Russian Orthodox Church to the Kremlin and together they mapped out a series of measures for the revival of the Russian Church. It was decided to resurrect the Holy Synod (which had been dissolved in 1935), organize an election of the Patriarch, publish a journal of the Moscow Patriarchy and establish theological courses along with a number of other steps to support the new policy. Even the arrangements for producing candles for divine service were not forgotten. In order to improve his living conditions Stalin put the residence of the former German ambassador at the disposal of the Metropolitan. It was a luxurious, fully furnished detached house with a garden. Although their discussions came to an end only late at night, on the following day TASS announced that the meeting had taken place and *Izvestia* published an account of what had been decided; the details were also broadcast on the radio.

In May 1943 the Comintern was dissolved. The rationale behind this decision was explained in *Pravda* on 30 May 1943 in a piece entitled 'Stalin's Reply to Mr King' (a Reuters correspondent):

> The dissolution of the Communist International ... will make it easier to organize pressure by all peace-loving nations against the common foe, Hitlerism, and expose the Hitlerites' lie that Moscow intends to interfere in the life of other states or 'bolshevize' them.

However, there were aspects of Stalin's revival of Russian nationalism that were neither justified nor legitimate. When the Muslim peoples were expelled from the Northern Caucasus, the steppes of the Lower Volga and the Crimea in 1943–44, various accusations were used as a pretext for this grandiose 'ethnic cleansing', but in fact it was an act of forced Russification throughout the entire European part of the USSR. Those who were exiled were not only people whose land had at some point suffered German occupation (the Karachai, Kalmyks, Ingush, Chechens, Balkar and Crimean Tartars) but also Muslim ethnic groups living in Georgia and Armenia, the Turks (who lived in the Meskhetia border area of Georgia and Turkey), the Kurds and Muslim Armenians. In the case of the last group, exile to Uzbekistan and Kirgizia took place in the autumn of 1944 when the war had already moved on to German territory. Altogether about 2 million people were deported to the east. Belorussian and Ukrainian peasants from destroyed and burned-out Russian villages were resettled in the fertile districts seized from the Muslims, while mountain villages and hamlets remained empty.

In the autumn of 1943 Stalin decided to change the national anthem. Although by that time people had become accustomed to the sound of the 'International', it now would become exclusively the hymn of the Party. Stalin took great interest in the competition to write the words and music for the new anthem and edited the chosen text, inserting a number of reasonable revisions. The orchestration was also modified in accordance with his wishes.[14] On 1 January 1944 the new national anthem of the USSR, hailing Stalin and 'the great Rus', was played on the radio for the first time.

At the end of the war military schools were established very much in the style of the old Russian army, with the goal of training young men to be professional soldiers from childhood. The cadets wore the uniforms of the old Suvorov Military College or the Nakhimov Naval

College. Obviously these schools were no longer for the children of noblemen: priority was instead given to the sons of officers who died during the war. The final action of the war took place in the east rather than the west and led to the symbolic restoration of territory lost to Japan in 1905: Southern Sakhalin, the Kurile Islands and Port Arthur.

A Georgian in the role of Russian emperor

After the end of the war Moscow became the capital of a novel political empire that included several west European countries recast as 'people's democracies' within its sphere of direct administrative control. Several historians have suggested that Stalin intended to incorporate these countries into the USSR and give them the rights of the union republics, as envisaged by Lenin in 1922. But Stalin never entertained plans of this kind. He understood that it would hardly be possible to extend Russification to Hungary, Poland, Romania and Czechoslovakia. An extension of the western and eastern borders of the USSR beyond the historical boundaries of Russia would have meant ending the process of moulding a 'Soviet people'. The new 'people's democracies' were exhorted to 'learn how to build socialism from the example of the Soviet Union'. Russian was made a compulsory foreign language in the schools of these countries, and thousands of young members of the communist parties and Komsomols of the 'people's democracies', the future nomenklatura, were sent to study in Soviet institutions of higher education. For young people from Albania, Yugoslavia and, after 1949, China, the USSR seemed to be a rather developed country. But inevitably Hungarians, Poles, Czechs, Romanians and even Bulgarians found 'Soviet reality' much less attractive. Zdenek Mlynář, the young Czech communist who later became a colleague of Dubček and a hero of the 'Prague Spring', was sent to study at Moscow University in 1950. By chance he was assigned to the same group as Mikhail Gorbachev, and in his recollections of Moscow in the 1950s he wrote:

> Our faith was undermined above all by the absence in Soviet life of just those values that were proclaimed to be the necessary preconditions for the victory of communism. ... We were shocked by the low standard of living, the poverty and backwardness, the greyness of Soviet existence ... there was not enough food. Five years after the war people were still wearing old army uniforms, and the majority of families lived huddled together in one room. ... In a crowd they picked your pocket, there were drunks lying in the street, ignored by indifferent passers by, etc., etc.[15]

It is a familiar enough picture, but above all it reflects a Western psychology, a Western approach to life. For western and central Europe, 'civilization' meant material comfort.

In the post-war period Russification intensified significantly and began to assume the features of an official ideology. The history syllabus in schools and universities was revised, accompanied by an artificial inflation of past achievements in Russian culture, science and technology. Under the slogan: 'Let us restore the truth!' it was claimed without foundation that numerous scientific discoveries and technical inventions had been the work of Russian scientists and engineers. Russians were said to be the originators of the steam engine, bicycles, zeppelins, aeroplanes, electric lamps, etc. 'Kowtowing before the West' now became a punishable political deviation. Even in the 1930s Stalin had begun to advance the thesis that progressive figures had existed among the Russian tsars, an entirely heretical view for a Leninist. Pride of place was given to Peter the Great. Aleksei Tolstoy wrote his novel *Peter I* under Stalin's personal supervision and in March 1941 received the Stalin Prize as a reward. But because he had been a 'Westernizer', Peter the Great became less appropriate as a hero and lost his pre-eminence during the war. In 1943 Stalin asked Sergei Eisenstein to write a film scenario about Ivan the Terrible. He was pleased with the result and requested that the film be completed as quickly as possible. The first part was shown in cinemas in 1944 and judging by Stalin's interest, particularly in the second part of the film, he clearly was beginning to visualize his own role in Russian history as a continuer of Ivan's tradition as the creator of a powerful, centralized state. Contrived justifications for Ivan's cruelty could be used in future to legitimize Stalin's own use of terror.

Russification went on in all spheres of Soviet life, and a detailed study of all aspects of this process including a variety of post-war innovations would be a large undertaking. The school system was reformed in 1946; as in the old gymnasium, pupils now wore school uniforms with boys and girls instructed separately. A series of new laws were enacted designed to 'strengthen' the family, making divorce a more complicated procedure that could take place only through the courts. In addition to the political content of publications, censorship organs started to take an interest in the purity of the Russian language, removing foreign words from texts if there was a clear Russian equivalent. Thus if one was speaking about a driver, it became compulsory to use the word *voditel* rather than *shofer*, and similarly *vrach* rather than *doktor* and *samolyot* rather than *aeroplan*. In March 1946 the Council of People's Commissars was renamed the Council of Ministers, and commissars were transformed into ministers on Stalin's personal initiative. Trotsky described how the Sovnarkom came into being on 26 October 1917 in his autobiography:

> A quick session opened in a corner of the room ... [a meeting of members of the new government in the Smolny – Zh.M.]
>
> 'What shall we call them?' asks Lenin, thinking aloud. 'Anything but ministers – that's such a vile, worn out word.'
>
> 'What about commissars,' I suggest ... 'They could be people's commissars.'
>
> 'The Council of People's Commissars? That's splendid, it smacks of revolution.'[16]

The minutes of the Central Committee plenum held in March 1946, where Stalin briefly explained why it was necessary to change the name of the government, has recently been found in the archives:

> On the question of ministries. 'People's commissar', or 'commissar' in general, reflects the period of an unstable regime, the period of civil war, the period of revolutionary destruction. ... This period is over. ... It is time to drop 'people's commissars' and have 'ministers'. The people will understand very well, why the damned commissars had to go.[17]

In 1948 another traditional phenomenon of old Russia made its appearance – state anti-Semitism. The question of Stalin's anti-Semitism is a complex issue which has often been debated in articles as well as in special books devoted to the subject. Unlike Hitler his anti-Semitism was neither ethnic nor racist in origin, nor was it based on religious antipathy as in tsarist Russia. Although the USSR supported the creation of the state of Israel in 1948, anti-Semitism became official policy once it became clear that Israel was staunchly pro-American. Thus it would seem that Stalin's anti-Semitism was fundamentally 'political', although this can be no more than a supposition.

To this day the motivation behind so much of Stalin's behaviour remains a riddle. He often took decisions without offering any arguments or reasons, even when it came to vital issues such as the preparations for war in May–June 1941. It may have been part of a calculated design to create the cult. Stalin required unquestioning support without discussion, and many of his political shifts were never explained. A series of enigmas have been left as a legacy for future historians. To this day the question is still asked: was Stalin actually a communist? In his book *Conqueror of Communism*, published in New York in 1981, Valery Chalidze maintained that Stalin 'restored the Russian empire although in a more despotic form'.[18] Chalidze suggests that Stalin was carrying out a secret plan that had already been worked out by the beginning of the 1920s. This view is shared by the prominent American sovietologist Robert Daniels, who believes that Stalin embarked on a systematic counter-revolution, killing more communists than all the fascists put together. 'In terms of the classical revolutionary process, Stalin significantly surpassed Bonapartism. The end result of his counter-revolution was an imperial restoration.'[19]

This proposition has some plausibility. However, there can really be no doubt that Stalin was a convinced Marxist. Beyond the boundaries of strictly inner Party disputes, Lenin and Trotsky also favoured authoritarian political methods and both were quite prepared to rely on terror. During the period 1918–21, overt terror to a large extent originated as a tactic of the Sovnarkom rather than the Secretariat of the Central Committee. During the first years after the Revolution Lenin and Trotsky were out to destroy everything and everyone linked to the Russian empire and in particular to capitalism; it was their intention to make 25 October 1917 the starting date of a new civilization, a fresh beginning in the history of the world. But as things turned out the constructive stage of the revolution belonged to Stalin. Although he replaced old authoritarian Russia with a country that may have been new in terms of its social and economic structure, in the final analysis it was authoritarian Russia that prevailed.

CHAPTER 14

The Murder of Bukharin

Roy Medvedev

Stalin and Bukharin in 1930–33

On the night of 1 January 1930 there was a knock on the door of Stalin's apartment in the Kremlin. Stalin was celebrating the New Year with friends – Molotov, Voroshilov, Kaganovich and their wives – and he got up to open the door to the new, uninvited visitors. Standing on the threshold were Bukharin, Rykov and Tomsky, bearing bottles of wine. They had been Stalin's main opponents in 1928–29, and now the former leaders of the 'Right Opposition' had come to seek a friendly reconciliation. 'Come in, come in!' said Stalin after a short pause, and then said to the others, 'Look who has arrived!' But they never managed to have a frank conversation, and the late arrivals departed before the other guests, well before dawn.

In the mid-1920s Nikolai Bukharin's enormous influence within the Party was second only to that of Stalin; he was a leader of the Comintern and regarded by many to be the foremost communist theorist of his time. But Stalin was now in no hurry to restore Bukharin to the ranks of the leadership, despite the fact that he was prepared to acknowledge his 'mistakes' and to make a public recantation – a ritual that had already been tested out on leaders of the 'Left Opposition'. Bukharin was relegated to a minor post as director of research at the Supreme Economic Council. On 19 February 1930 *Pravda* published an article by Bukharin entitled 'The Great Reconstruction' containing a very superficial analysis of the 'current stage of the proletarian revolution'. The article received attention largely because of the renown of its author, with few people aware of the fact that it had been authorized and also carefully edited by Stalin.

Bukharin, normally a very active person, found it extremely difficult to endure disgrace and was simply not capable of conducting any kind of opposition within 'his' Party. He wrote several letters to Stalin (at the time, this was a normal method of communication between members of the Politburo), but they remained unanswered. Bukharin's isolation made him physically ill, unable to work and frequently tearful. He was overwhelmed by Mayakovsky's suicide. On 15 April 1930 he pushed his way through the crowd standing in front of the Writers' Club and stood for a long time at the poet's coffin in the entrance hall, a poet whose verse he had so often published during his ten-year stint as editor of *Pravda*. However, when the director of the club and friend of Mayakovsky, Boris Kireyev, suggested that he speak to the crowd from the balcony, Bukharin adamantly refused and crept out by a side door that opened directly onto Herzen Street, returning to his apartment in the Kremlin. Some time afterwards he admitted to having had thoughts of committing suicide himself in the spring of 1930. He went to the Crimea for rest and treatment later that spring and then on to Kirgizia and the Pamir. Although Bukharin was still a member of the Central Committee, he did not attend the Sixteenth Party Congress at the end of July, nor did he write anything about it in the press.

During the years 1930–33 the general situation in the country was getting worse and this was particularly true of the countryside. Forced collectivization and the exile of 'wealthy' peasants to the northern and eastern parts of the country, along with large numbers of 'middle' peasants as well, led to a mass slaughter of cattle and horses. Repressions were directed against 'bourgeois specialists', 'nepmen' and former Mensheviks; scores of labour camps were created and a general brutalization of the regime, in the Party and the country, was taking place. And finally, the famine of the winter of 1932–33 cost the lives of millions of peasants in the Ukraine, the Northern Caucasus and Kazakhstan. Bukharin did not react to any of these events, altogether refusing to discuss politics even with his closest friends, family or former students. He simply did not want to hear anything about what was actually happening around him, and when sent letters and accounts by others was reluctant to read them. This reflected a determination to remain aloof from the stirrings of discontent and protest that were beginning to emerge within the Party. However, total isolation from the real world was impossible, and on one of his trips home from the south, travelling through the Ukraine, he could not avoid seeing the crowds of women and children, even at small stations, with stomachs distended with hunger. At larger stations or near the towns, detachments of troops kept the hungry away. Telling his father about it later in Moscow, Bukharin exclaimed, 'If this is happening ten years after the revolution, how can one live!' and he collapsed, sobbing on the couch.

Bukharin reappeared at a Party forum for the first time in 1932 at the Seventeenth Party Conference. His speech, however, was strictly limited to a discussion of the technical problems in the development of industry and did not stray beyond that theme. In a talk at the Academy of Sciences – he had been made a member in December 1928 – Bukharin spoke only about the problems of 'contemporary capitalism'. In the course of three years, there had been no political or work-related conversation with Stalin, although Bukharin frequently met Stalin's wife, Nadezhda Alliluyeva, an old friend. He was sitting next to her at the large Kremlin banquet on 8 November 1932 to mark the 15th anniversary of the October Revolution, with Stalin opposite, when a sudden quarrel between Stalin and his wife erupted and spoiled the general mood, although no one imagined that it would lead to tragedy. Alliluyeva left the table, accompanied by her friend, Polina Zhemchuzhina, the wife of Molotov. They walked for a long time along the paths of the Kremlin, but apparently Nadezhda was unable to calm down. Stalin was devastated by the suicide of his wife and for several days was in such a terrible state that members of the Politburo and relatives feared to leave him alone. But despair and grief soon gave way to a rush of spiteful anger, most likely because of the contents of the letter left by his wife which were never disclosed to anyone.

After the funeral Stalin took the initiative for a meeting with Bukharin and asked him to exchange apartments, explaining that it was too difficult to continue living in the space he had shared with his wife. The exchange took place almost immediately; neither apartment was very large, only two or three rooms with a hall and a long corridor. Stalin did not receive his second apartment in section No. 1 of the Council of Ministers building until later, during the war. This second apartment was on the ground floor next to a specially guarded entrance with a direct connection to his office. It was much more spacious, fine enough even for receiving Winston Churchill, and today it is the site of the Presidential Archive. However, after Alliluyeva's death, conversations between Stalin and Bukharin never went beyond family subjects. According to the visitors' book in Stalin's Kremlin office Bukharin's first 'business' meeting with Stalin did not take place until 14 July 1933. His previous visit had been on 11 January 1929.[1]

In 1933 Bukharin began to participate more actively in Party and public life. He took part in a joint session of the Central Committee and the Central Control Commission in January, where the successful completion of the first Five Year Plan was announced. That year also marked the 50th anniversary of the death of Marx, and this occasion was observed throughout the communist movement. A long essay by Bukharin, 'Marx's Teaching and its Historical Influence', appeared in the Soviet press. In an attempt to sum up the basic features of the 'titanic, all-embracing ideology, devised by the monumental genius of Marx', it was only at the end of the 100-page work that Bukharin referred to Comrade Stalin, who 'had contributed a number of new theoretical generalizations which are now a guiding force in the complex practical work of the Party'.[2]

A screening campaign was organized at the end of 1933, in effect a purge of Party members who were insufficiently militant or loyal to the general Party line. For Bukharin it was a rather humiliating experience to be repeatedly called in for questioning. On each occasion he had to repudiate his recent 'right deviation' and sing the praises of the 'ideological Field-Marshal of the revolutionary forces – Comrade Stalin'. Although Bukharin passed the test, the purge commission did note in its report that he 'had not entirely overcome his alienation from the Party'. Before the decision of the purge commission was reported to the Party cell or Bukharin informed of its content, a draft was sent to Stalin for approval, and also to Molotov and Kaganovich (i.e. to the Central Committee and the Sovnarkom), and this was by no means a mere formality. The chairman of the Moscow regional Party purge commission, Knorin, wrote an unambiguous covering note: 'I request your instructions.'[3] Stalin approved the decision of the commission.

Stalin and Bukharin in 1934

The Seventeenth Party Congress assembled on 26 January 1934 in Moscow, and even as it met was called 'the Congress of Victors'. Bukharin had been chosen to be one of the delegates of the Moscow Party organization to the Congress, and he decided not only to participate but also to make a speech which of course would include self-criticism. After harsh condemnation of the 'right deviation' as 'anti-socialist' and 'anti-Leninist', he declared that 'Comrade Stalin was entirely correct, when, brilliantly applying Marxist-Leninist dialectics, he smashed a whole series of right deviationist theoretical propositions for which I, above all, bear responsibility.'[4] A large part of Bukharin's speech was devoted to attacking German fascism and Japanese militarism. Several historians have attempted to find disguised criticism of Stalin in the speech – even the flattering reference to Stalin as the 'field-marshal of the proletariat' has been interpreted as a hint in the direction of the German Chancellor, Field-Marshal von Hindenburg, who charged Hitler to form a government in 1933 and made Hitler his successor. But if indeed such hints were intended, they were so cleverly concealed as to remain unnoticed. It was Bukharin's conviction, expressed in his speech and in letters to Ordzhonikidze, that all members of the Party were obliged to set aside their quarrels and rally round Stalin and the Party leadership in order to confront the enormous external and internal dangers facing the country. The point here was that he, Bukharin, could still make a considerable contribution to the common cause.[5] This position suited Stalin perfectly, and supported by Ordzhonikidze he allowed Bukharin to extend his activities and return to the political stage.

Stalin permitted Bukharin to remain on the Central Committee, but only as a candidate member, and on 17 December Bukharin was appointed editor of *Izvestia*, the second most important Soviet daily. Bukharin was genuinely delighted with his new position, which opened the possibility for important work and would allow him, so he thought, to demonstrate his new dedication to the cause of the Party and socialism. Moreover, within the pages of the less official *Izvestia* it would be possible to publish things that could not have easily appeared in *Pravda*. It was his goal to turn *Izvestia* into an interesting paper and he managed to achieve this quite rapidly. By the middle of 1934 *Izvestia* had become the most popular and widely read Soviet newspaper. Bukharin frequently published his own articles and also commissioned essays from other recent members of the 'right' and 'left' oppositions, including Kamenev, Preobrazhensky, Rykov and Radek. Radek's articles were particularly successful. He also welcomed contributions from various literary figures – Gorky, Kassil, Chukovsky, the Tur brothers, Ehrenburg, and there were poems by Pasternak and Demyan Bedny. At the same time, the editorial staff and the editor-in-chief remained absolutely loyal to Stalin. The editor of *Izvestia* became an almost regular visitor to Stalin's Kremlin office.

Bukharin tried to avoid all political confrontations, but that was not always possible. Although he made no attempt to interfere when some of his younger disciples got into trouble for having not totally 'disarmed', it was extremely difficult to bear the arrest of Osip Mandelshtam, a poet whom he greatly admired. In the past Bukharin had often defended him against the authorities as well as the carping 'proletarian' critics. But at the end of 1933 Mandelshtam had begun to recite his verse about Stalin to his friends, sometimes with slight variations. The lines, which later were to become so famous, were never actually written down by the poet. According to Nadezhda Mandelshtam, his widow, no more than ten people knew about their existence. Here is the poem, in one of its variants, translated by the late Max Hayward:

We live, deaf to the land beneath us,
Ten steps away no one hears our speeches,

But where there's so much as half a conversation
The Kremlin's mountaineer will get his mention.

His fingers are fat as grubs
And the words, final as lead weights, fall from his lips,

His cockroach whiskers leer
And his boot tops gleam.

Around him a rabble of thin-necked leaders -
fawning half-men for him to play with.

They whinny, purr or whine
As he prates and points a finger,

One by one forging his laws, to be flung
Like horseshoes at the head, the eye or the groin

And every killing is a treat
For the broad-chested Ossete.[6]

The poet's wife turned to Bukharin for help when Mandelshtam was arrested. Bukharin was extremely upset when he heard about the arrest, jumped up from behind his desk and began to pace up and down his office. 'He hasn't written anything rash, has he?' 'No, just a few poems in his usual manner, nothing worse than you know already,' she replied. Bukharin began making an effort to get Mandelshtam released and sought the help of Pasternak and Anna Akhmatova, who turned to Avel Yenukidze, regarded as a close friend of Stalin. But no one could explain the reason for the arrest. Finally Bukharin wrote to Stalin. He never received a reply but was invited to come and see Genrikh Yagoda, the People's Commissar for Internal Affairs and the head of the secret police. Yagoda welcomed him rather affably, got up from behind his desk and recited from memory Mandelshtam's verse about Stalin. Bukharin was horrified: 'this so frightened him that he gave up his efforts,' wrote Nadezhda Mandelshtam years later in her memoirs. 'I never saw him again.' It is likely that as well as being frightened, it was clear to Bukharin that any effort would be useless under the circumstances. He was also outraged at having been intentionally deceived. 'I misled Bukharin quite deliberately,' acknowledged Nadezhda Mandelshtam, 'out of a calculated desire not to frighten off my only ally.'[7] Nevertheless Stalin displayed considerable leniency towards the poet. Mandelshtam escaped with the relatively light punishment of exile to Voronezh where he continued to write poetry, unaware of the suffering that lay ahead. According to several witnesses, as he decided Mandelshtam's fate Stalin said: 'Isolate him, but keep him alive.'[8]

The inaugural Congress of Soviet Writers opened in the Hall of Columns of the Trade Union House on 17 August 1934. Elaborate preparations were made as if for a major celebration, with music and welcome speeches to greet the delegates. The present-day Theatre Square was decked out with flowers and the walls of the hall were covered with huge portraits of Shakespeare, Molière, Tolstoy, Gogol, Cervantes, Heine, Pushkin, Balzac and other great figures of literature. It was an enormous, colourful spectacle, but not without its moments of drama. Gorky insisted that the keynote address on contemporary poetry be assigned to Bukharin, who was considered to be something of a connoisseur as well as an expert on the theory of poetics. When confirming the agenda and list of speakers at the

Congress, Stalin reluctantly agreed. As he later informed his audience, Bukharin of course knew that the text of his speech, 'On Poetry, Poetics, and the Tasks of the Poet in the USSR', would be sent to the Central Committee Secretariat and would be carefully examined by Stalin. It was a genuinely interesting speech, despite the fact that Bukharin described poetry as, above all, an important component of the ideological struggle and very much an affair of the Party. He appeared at the 19th session of the Congress, spoke exclusively about Russian poetry for more than three hours and was given a prolonged ovation at the end. Gorky, who made the first keynote speech, was the only other person who was applauded as enthusiastically. Foreign observers described the reception given to Bukharin as a sign of his immense popularity among broad circles of the Soviet intelligentsia, including the younger generation. In his memoirs, Joseph Berger, a former Comintern official, recalled a story told to him in 1937 by a disciple of Bukharin in one of the Solovki camps:

> He spoke on poetry at the first Writers' Congress. He was welcomed with a storm of applause, his speech was interrupted with outbursts of noisy acclaim and when he finished it seemed that the ovation would never stop. Bukharin stood on the platform, pale and looking as though he was frightened to death; as he was going out he said in a low voice to a few of his friends: 'What have you done? You have signed my death warrant.' And it was true. The ovation could not have escaped Stalin's attention.[9]

This account is perhaps not entirely accurate. Bukharin's speech had been vetted by Stalin, and he did not fail to say at the end that 'all your applause belongs not to me but to that great Party, of which I am a member, and which entrusted me with the honour of speaking at this meeting.'[10] Nor did Bukharin conceal the fact that Stalin, who had not graced the Congress with his presence but closely followed the proceedings, rang to congratulate him on his 'splendid speech'. But along with all the praise, Bukharin was bitterly attacked, mainly by former members of RAPP (the Russian Association of Proletarian Writers) and other radicals. As a skilful debater Bukharin had no trouble in responding to these denunciations at length at the end of the session, to the even greater delight of his audience. But this time his remarks had not been approved in advance. He avoided philosophical abstraction and pounced on his opponents, overwhelming them with a brilliant and convincing critical onslaught. According to the stenographic report of the meeting, Bukharin's final words were interrupted 27 times by 'applause' and 'storm of applause'. But it was this success that aroused disapproval in the Kremlin. Before the final closure of the Congress Bukharin was made to read a statement in which he apologized for the acrimonious tone of his final remarks. 'I can in no way defend the sharpness of my polemical style, which was inappropriate.' He went on to say that his speech should in no way be interpreted as a directive and that he had no desire to put pressure on the Congress.[11] Few participants could have had any illusions about the reasons for Bukharin's declaration.

The murder of Kirov put an end to the brief, superficial liberalization of the spring and summer of 1934. The repression of former oppositionists began, primarily among the 'left', and Zinoviev and Kamenev, who had been leaders of the 'Left Opposition', were arrested. At the beginning of December 1934 *Izvestia* was reminding its readers about events in Germany in 1933 connected with the burning of the Reichstag. At the same time, Bukharin wrote a series of articles for the paper on the illegality of opposition within the USSR, no matter whether 'right' or 'left'. He was simply repeating Stalin's thesis that opposition leads to counter-revolution. Well before the court's verdict was announced, Bukharin was describing Zinoviev and Kamenev as fascist degenerates.

Stalin and Bukharin in 1935

In the first months of 1935, terror against the former oppositionists was gaining momentum. Repression was also beginning to hit former Mensheviks, SRs, Kadets and other parties long absent from the political stage. 'Unproletarian elements' in Leningrad and Moscow were exiled to the provinces, including formerly prominent aristocratic families. Yet at the same time, Stalin tried to restore something of the liberal atmosphere of mid-1934. The economic situation in the country had improved a little. It was at a Kremlin party in 1935 that Stalin came out with his famous remark, 'Life has become better, Comrades, life has become gayer.' At the Kremlin there were receptions and various gatherings with lavish refreshments, one after another, for shock workers, *stakhanovites* and representatives from the republics. Stalin made more welcome speeches in the course of 1935 than in any other year before or after. There was a kind of holiday atmosphere in the Kremlin, with decorations raining down on Party and state workers at all levels including the Order of Lenin, the highest possible honour. Great celebrations were organized to mark the successive 15th anniversaries of Soviet triumphs in the Civil War, over Denikin, Wrangel and the Polish interventionists, with, needless to say, Stalin's role highlighted on each occasion. It seemed as if the most difficult times were over and a straight road to prosperity and socialism was in sight.

In this context it seemed appropriate to think about changes to the constitution of the USSR. When the Seventh Congress of Soviets met at the beginning of February 1935 a decision was taken to set up

a Constitutional Commission. Bukharin was elected as a member of
the Central Executive Committee at this Congress and was included
on the Constitutional Commission as head of the sub-commission
dealing with the most important aspect of the new constitution – the
rights and obligations of Soviet citizens. At a Kremlin reception on 4
May for graduates of the military academy Stalin suddenly came up
to Bukharin, who normally attended all such occasions. Raising his
glass, Stalin said, 'I want to propose a toast to Comrade Bukharin.
We all know and love our Bukharin, our Bukharchik. And "whoever
brings up the past – loses an eye".' That apparently relieved some of
the tension that was beginning to accumulate around former leaders
of the 'right deviation'.

Major changes were also taking place in Bukharin's personal life
at that time. His second marriage had ended in divorce in 1930, and
he now married for the third time and was happy. His new wife,
Anna Larina, was a beautiful 19-year-old and the daughter of a well-
known Party figure, Yuri Larin; from childhood she had been acquainted with all the prominent Party leaders, including Stalin.
When he heard about her marriage Stalin rang to congratulate
Larina. And soon after, meeting the couple at a Kremlin reception, he
jokingly said to Bukharin: 'Here, Nikolai, you have out-galloped me.'
After the suicide of Nadezhda Alliluyeva, Stalin lived a bachelor's
existence in his new dacha at Kuntsevo and saw almost no one so-
cially except for the large Alliluyev family.

Stalin and Bukharin in 1936

The question of purchasing part of the Marx–Engels archive from the
German Social Democrats came up at a Central Committee meeting
at the end of 1935. Once Hitler came to power in Germany the Social
Democrats went underground, and the leading figures who emigrated were now extremely short of funds. They were prepared to
sell a substantial portion of the manuscripts in their possession to the
Marx–Engels–Lenin Institute in Moscow. Stalin proposed that a
group, led by Bukharin, be sent to have a look at the documents with
the object of possibly buying them. The Politburo's decision included
a list of persons whom Bukharin was permitted to meet in connection with the negotiations. One of them was the French socialist
leader, Léon Blum, along with the German and Austrian social demo-
cratic leaders, Friedrich Adler and Otto Bauer. The Russian émigré
Mensheviks, Fyodor Dan and Boris Nicolaevsky, would play the role
of intermediaries; they had left the Soviet Union in the 1920s and
Bukharin knew them personally. Stalin took a particular interest in
the whole affair, and he and Bukharin had several conversations
about it. On 7 February 1936 Stalin invited Bukharin to the Kremlin,

and according to Larina he turned his attention to his guest's attire. 'Your suit is too shabby, Nikolai, you can't go that way, you have to be properly dressed.'[12] The next evening Bukharin received a call from the special atelier at the Commissariat of Foreign Affairs and within two or three days a new suit was ready for his trip.

Bukharin left Moscow at the end of February. He spent several days in Vienna and later visited Copenhagen, Amsterdam and Berlin, but the main part of his time was spent in Paris. He regularly wrote to Stalin about his meetings and conversations. 'Koba loves to get letters,' he said to his friend Ilya Ehrenburg, who was the special correspondent of *Izvestia* in France. Ehrenburg was also some kind of special representative of the USSR in western Europe, frequently visiting Spain and other countries, and he had personal access to Stalin when necessary.[13]

A great deal has been written about Bukharin's trip to France and his various encounters while he was there. Larina wrote about it in detail in her memoirs, as did the widow of Dan. The French papers and the Russian émigré press gave considerable space to Bukharin's itinerary and pronouncements, and Ehrenburg later described their meetings. All these accounts, however, frequently contradict one other. Thus, for example, Lydia Dan wrote that Bukharin called Stalin a devil when talking to her husband. 'He will destroy us all ... he's compelled to take revenge on people, and any communist who has performed great services for the Party arouses his fear and anger.' In contrast Boris Nicolaevsky said that Bukharin absolutely refused to take part in conversations about Stalin. Only on one occasion, when he saw Shota Rustaveli's poem, 'Hero in the Skin of a Tiger', on someone's desk, published by Georgian émigrés, did he say, 'I saw this book the last time I visited Stalin. He loves the poem and was pleased with the translation.' A Russian monograph devoted to Bukharin's meetings and conversations in Paris has recently been published in Moscow.[14]

In April Stalin allowed Anna Larina to join her husband abroad. She was pregnant, and her arrival in Paris convinced contemporary observers that it was part of a deal and that Bukharin would not return to the USSR. Several of his acquaintances discussed this possibility with Bukharin, but he was adamant that he could not live in exile and was determined to go back to Moscow. 'Stalin is now the symbol of socialism, that is reality, and we can do nothing about it. I have to return and drink my cup to the last.' Bukharin reportedly said this to Fyodor Dan.

The archives were never purchased because Stalin found the asking price too high. Thus Bukharin's mission arrived at a dead end, and he returned to Moscow at the end of April via Germany, where he bought a large number of books for his own library. At the end of

May Larina gave birth to a son whom they called Yuri. Bukharin reported personally to Stalin about the results of his trip and at the end of the conversation Stalin said, 'Don't be upset, Nikolai, we'll get the archive, they'll let us have it in the end.'[15] Bukharin returned to his work at *Izvestia* and the Constitutional Commission.

On 1 July 1936 Bukharin visited Stalin in his Kremlin office. It was to be their last meeting. Bukharin requested a leave of absence and received permission to spend almost two months away from Moscow. After two weeks at the *Izvestia* dacha on the outskirts of the city with his wife and young son, Bukharin decided to go as far away from Moscow as possible. Since the days of Lenin, hunting had been a favourite pastime for the majority of Bolshevik leaders, and Bukharin was no exception. He decided to fly to the Pamir mountains in Kirghizia, as he had done in 1930. The well-known Soviet poet and translator Semyon Lipkin, who was in Frunze working on a translation of the Kirghiz epic poem *Manas*, described his surprising encounter with Bukharin more than 50 years later in his essay, 'Bukharin, Stalin and *Manas*':

> I was struck by Bukharin's appearance – I never expected that he would seem so Russian. He looked like a Russian worker, like those I saw at the printers, with darkish fair hair, broad shoulders, premature baldness and a large forehead. And he spoke wonderful Russian. I had seen several Bolshevik leaders close up before Bukharin, but there was a distinct difference between Bukharin and his colleagues. His language was picturesque – free and cheery, and down-to-earth. I found out that he had come to rest and go hunting in the Kirghiz mountains. His Izvestia secretary, Semyon Lyandres, father of the now popular writer Yulian Semyonov, accompanied him.[16]

Bukharin and Lyandres soon left for the mountains with several guides. Since transistor radios did not yet exist, Bukharin was able to forget about his Moscow troubles for a while.

He was still in the mountains on 19 August 1936 when the new trial of Zinoviev, Kamenev and a group of their supporters got under way in Moscow. The proceedings took place in the Trade Union House in front of a carefully selected audience; it was the first 'public' show trial of former leaders of the opposition. The accused readily spoke of their crimes, acknowledged their evil intentions and informed the court of their 'criminal' association with Bukharin, Rykov, Tomsky and other former 'rightists'. Kamenev testified that his differences with Bukharin were tactical rather than political; Bukharin 'had chosen the tactic of infiltration within the Party and winning the personal trust of the leadership'. On 22 August Andrei Vyshinsky, the Chief Procurator of the USSR, announced in the press that he had begun an investigation into the affairs of Tomsky, Rykov, Bukharin and several other well-known figures of the opposition. Throughout the country a wave of mass meetings demanded not only severe punishment for the accused but also 'a full investigation of the connections of Bukharin, Rykov and Tomsky with the Trotskyist-Zinovievist criminal gang'. When he heard of these accusations, Tomsky committed suicide.

Bukharin came down from the mountain and arrived in Frunze on the last day of the Moscow trial, the day the verdict was announced. He found out about it all, listening to the radio and reading local papers, and was devastated. He sent urgent telegrams to Stalin and Yagoda asking them to postpone carrying out the sentence. He implored them to arrange a confrontation with Zinoviev and Kamenev so that he could refute their accusations, but a day later Bukharin heard that they had been executed. Bukharin assumed that he would be arrested in Frunze, or perhaps in Tashkent where he had to change planes, but when he arrived in Moscow only his wife and a car from *Izvestia* were waiting at the airport.

He tried to ring Stalin as soon as he got home but was told that Stalin was not in Moscow. He rang a second time and found out that Stalin had left for Sochi the day after Zinoviev and Kamenev were shot. He sent Stalin a long letter by state messenger and locked himself in his apartment, not that anyone was about to ring or visit him. Week after week went by as he waited in a state of increasing trepidation. People continued to be arrested in Moscow, including several who were close to Bukharin. At the end of September Yagoda was removed as Commissar for Internal Affairs and replaced by Nikolai Yezhov, a swiftly promoted, relatively young Secretary of the Central Committee. His appointment was regarded as a move towards accelerating the terror.

After the trial of Zinoviev and Kamenev, Stalin introduced a new procedure: significant statements made by prisoners under interrogation were to be duplicated, marked 'secret' and distributed to all members and candidate members of the Central Committee. This would include Bukharin, who read his packet of papers from the NKVD with horror and incredulity, but he still had no idea of the methods being used to extract such testimony. His disbelief was understandable, given the fact that he, Bukharin, was mentioned frequently in the interrogations as a leading organizer of terror and 'wrecking'. He had no idea what to do. He thought that he had friends among the members of the Politburo, but Ordzhonikidze never replied to his letter nor did Kalinin, who only recently had called Bukharin 'the greatest theoretician of our Party'. Voroshilov unexpectedly sent him a short note: 'I ask you, Comrade Bukharin, do not turn to me with any questions.' Stalin was his last hope, and Bukharin wrote to him almost daily, always beginning his letter or note with the salutation, 'Dear Koba!' Stalin did not reply but at the same time seemed to be trying to encourage Bukharin to keep up his hopes. According to Larina, whom I often met in the 1970s, she and her husband went together to Red Square on 7 November for the celebration of the 19th anniversary of the October Revolution. They had an *Izvestia* pass to be admitted to the stands near the platform on top of the mausoleum. Stalin noticed Bukharin. Suddenly Larina saw a guard pushing his way towards them through the crowd. She thought that they would be told to leave Red Square immediately, but the young Red Army soldier saluted and said: 'Comrade Bukharin, Comrade Stalin asked me to inform you that you are not in the right place and he requests that you come up to the platform.'[17]

But only days later Bukharin had to face a much more distressing ordeal. He was not summoned to the Lubyanka but taken straight to a room in the Kremlin where a confrontation took place between Bukharin and a number of prisoners who had incriminated him in their 'confessions' – former Trotskyists as well as several young academics and political figures who had been part of the 'Bukharin school'. He had to face, one after another, Sokolnikov, Radek, Serebryakov and others. They all spoke of their 'criminal links' with Bukharin and claimed that he was the head of yet another underground counter-revolutionary terrorist centre. Bukharin was stunned by his encounter with Yefim Tseitlin, who had been one of his favourite disciples. In the presence of the investigator of his case, Tseitlin declared that Bukharin had personally given him a revolver and positioned him on the street just where Stalin was due to drive by. Stalin took a different route that day, which prevented the assassination from taking place.

As soon as he returned home Bukharin took out his pistol. A gold disc was attached to the handle, engraved with the words, 'To the leader of the proletarian revolution N.I. Bukharin from Klim Voroshilov.' Bukharin had decided that there was nothing left to do but kill himself. He said goodbye to his wife, locked himself in his study, and for a long time held the pistol in his hand but was unable to pull the trigger. This scene was to be repeated several times. Sometimes Bukharin clutched the pistol in front of his wife, tossed it in the air and then once again hid it in his desk. Often these outbursts of despair ended in hysterics, after which he would retreat into himself for long, unhappy hours. Bukharin no longer did any work at *Izvestia*, although technically he was still editor-in-chief. He could still manage to write articles, but only on anti-fascist subjects, and even these remained in a drawer of his desk.

At the end of November a group of strangers arrived at his door from the housekeeping department of the Kremlin. Bukharin was sure that they had come to do a search, which in those months would not have been unusual, even in a Kremlin apartment. But in fact it was worse; they had brought Bukharin an order to vacate the Kremlin. He got extremely upset and was at a total loss to know what to do. He immediately started thinking about his enormous collection of books and personal papers. How could he transport them and where? At that moment the internal Kremlin telephone suddenly rang. It was Stalin. 'So, how are things with you, Nikolai?' as though everything were perfectly normal. Bukharin did not know how to reply, and after a pause said that he was being served an eviction notice. Without asking anything further, Stalin exclaimed in a loud voice, 'Tell them all to go to the devil.' Hearing that, the uninvited guests beat a hasty retreat.

In 1936 it was still the rule that the Central Committee had to sanction the arrest of any of its full or candidate members. On 4 December 1936 Stalin convened a plenum of the Central Committee in the Kremlin, prohibiting any mention of it in the press. There is still no reference to this meeting in any of the literature on the history of the CPSU. Fragments of the shorthand record of the December plenum were discovered only several years ago among Stalin's personal papers kept in the Presidential Archive. The plenum approved the final text of the USSR constitution and heard a report from Yezhov on the activities of the 'anti-Soviet Trotskyist and Right organizations'.[18] Yezhov, joined by several other speakers, demanded that Bukharin and Rykov be expelled from the Party and their case handed over to the NKVD. Bukharin tried to defend himself, categorically denying all the accusations that had been made against him. Stalin spoke cautiously, but said that although it was impossible simply to believe Bukharin, there had to be more substantial evidence. Arrangements were made for a confrontation to take place on 7 December during an interval between sessions of the plenum. On one side there were Pyatakov, Radek, Kulikov, Sosnovsky and several other prisoners, all of whom had implicated Bukharin. On the other there was Bukharin, who was given the opportunity to refute their accusations. Questions were asked by Stalin, Molotov, Voroshilov, Kaganovich, Andreev, Ordzhonikidze and Zhdanov. At the evening session of the plenum Stalin reported that he had not found the statements of all the accusers to be convincing. Therefore he proposed that they 'consider the question of Rykov and Bukharin to be unfinished and postpone a decision until the next plenum'. Stalin was playing with Rykov and Bukharin like a well-fed cat plays with a half-dead mouse.

Several days after the plenum Bukharin got a call from the Secretariat asking him to go to the *Izvestia* office to receive the famous German writer Lion Feuchtwanger who was visiting Moscow and had asked to meet him. Bukharin obeyed. For the last time in his life he sat in the spacious office of the editor-in-chief. However, Feucht-wanger, who apparently found something better to do, never turned up. According to Aleksei Snegov, who after his rehabilitation occu-pied a senior position in the MVD and participated in the investigation of secret materials from the 1930s, Feuchtwanger had suddenly been honoured with a rather important privilege that previously had only been offered to pro-Soviet or pro-communist Western writers. Stalin personally gave instructions for Feucht-wanger to be paid an honorarium *in dollars* for his books published in the USSR. It amounted to what was a huge sum at the time, approximately $100,000. The receipt of this honorarium apparently affected the inclinations of the great European writer, who discovered that he no longer had such a pressing need to meet Bukharin.

Another major political trial began in 1937, with former Trotsky-ists as the predominant group among the accused: Pyatikov, Sokolnikov, Serebryakov and Radek. This is not the place to provide an account of this fresh judicial frame-up. It is relevant to note, however, that the precision of the accusations levelled against Bukharin in the course of the trial made it clear that his days were numbered. In the middle of January he was officially removed from his position at *Izvestia*, although he continued to live in his Kremlin apartment in a state of voluntary house arrest. He went on writing letters to Stalin, always beginning them 'Dear Koba!'

The regular meeting of the Central Committee plenum took place in the second half of February. The first point on the agenda was 'the case of Comrades Bukharin and Rykov'.[19] When news of this reached Bukharin, he began to prepare a long statement containing a detailed analysis of all the accusations made against him in the January trial and also in the various face-to-face confrontations. He expressed no doubts about the guilt of his accusers, several of whom had been his friends and disciples. On 20 February, Bukharin sent his almost 100-page-long argument to the Secretariat, requesting that it be distrib-uted to the members of the Central Committee as the text of the speech he would have made at the plenum. In a short cover note Bukharin wrote:

> I am sending this statement of almost 100 pages to the CC Plenum in reply to the heap of slander contained in the testimonies. My nerves are at breaking point. The slander has put me in an intolerable posi-tion, I cannot bear it. ... I swear by the last breath of Ilyich, who died in my arms, that to suggest all this terror, wrecking, blocs with Trot-skyists has anything to do with me is base slander. I cannot live like this any longer. I am not in a physical or moral state to come to the Plenum: my legs won't take me, I cannot endure the atmosphere, I am unable to speak, I don't want to sob. ... In this extraordinary situation, from tomorrow, I will start a total hunger strike until the accusations of treason, wrecking, terrorism are withdrawn. I will not

live with such accusations. I warmly wish you success. ... Inform my wife of the plenum's decision on point number one, let me come to an end and die here, don't drag me anywhere, stop them from pestering me. Farewell. May you prevail. Your Bukharin.[20]

Stalin immediately made arrangements for the letter and the 100-page statement to be duplicated and distributed to all members of the Central Committee. At the same time the Politburo condemned Bukharin's hunger strike and his refusal to attend the plenum. Bukharin was informed about this by Stalin himself on the phone. 'Against whom are you declaring a hunger strike?' he asked. 'Against the Party?' 'But what can I do?' replied Bukharin. 'You intend to throw me out of the Party.' 'No one is intending to throw you out of the Party,' said Stalin and hung up. Bukharin grasped at the straw and decided to attend the plenum.

The infamous February–March plenum of the Central Committee convened on 23 February 1937 in the Kremlin opened the darkest pages in the history of the Party and the country as whole. Decisions taken here provided the ideological basis for a new wave of repressions and launched the bloody mass terror that then became the central focus of government policy. The first session was presided over by Molotov, who confirmed the agenda and then gave the floor to Yezhov, the Commissar for Internal Affairs. He accused Bukharin and Rykov of training various terrorist groups to carry out the assassination of Stalin, for whom they were said to bear a malevolent hatred. According to information held by the NKVD, the leaders of the 'right' had been involved with more than ten such groups, although none of them had been able to achieve their goal. Yezhov proposed therefore that Bukharin and Rykov be expelled from the Party. He was followed by Anastas Mikoyan, whose comments were petty, malicious but ultimately unpersuasive. He referred to various chance meetings, letters, statements and rumours but did not come up with anything real, neither deeds nor criminal activity. Mikoyan went so far as to deny that a warm relationship had existed between Bukharin and Lenin, insisting that Lenin had other, much closer disciples and colleagues. It was then Bukharin's turn to speak, but he only dealt with minor questions, mainly trying to refute Mikoyan's insinuations. Stalin frequently interrupted him, and their futile dialogue took up several pages in the stenographic report of the meeting:

Stalin: Why should Astrov lie?
Bukharin: I don't know ...
Stalin: You and he (Radek) babbled on and on and then you forgot.
Bukharin: Really and truly not, I didn't speak to him.
Stalin: You do tend to babble a lot.

> Bukharin: That's true, I babble a lot, but I did not babble about ter-
> rorism, that's absolute nonsense.
> Stalin: You're good at making speeches on anything.
> Bukharin: I am telling the truth here, no one can make me say mon-
> strous things about myself.
> Stalin: No one is asking you to slander yourself. That would be the
> worst crime.[21]

During the evening session on 24 February Molotov again gave the floor to Bukharin: 'Comrades, I have to make a very brief statement. I would like to apologize to the plenum of the Central Committee for my thoughtless and politically harmful act, declaring a hunger strike.' Stalin shouted, 'Not good enough! Not good enough!'[22] After this skirmish, which continued for a few minutes, it was time for Rykov to speak. He also limited himself to very trivial questions, made contradictory statements and clearly was trying to draw a boundary between himself and Bukharin, implying that he had not in any way been involved in the creation of the 'Bukharin school'. The meeting continued on 25 February, with all speakers denouncing Bukharin and Rykov in the strongest possible terms, even referring to incidents from the days of the Revolution and Civil War. Bukharin kept interrupting with shouts of 'Lies!' 'Slander!' 'Absolute rubbish!' Stalin also intervened often. Bukharin and Rykov were given the chance to say their 'last word' during the morning session of 26 February. It really did turn out to be the last time that Bukharin would address a Party audience. He spoke at length, attempting to refute the accusations made against him during the previous days. He was frequently interrupted, particularly by Molotov and Miko-yan. Khrushchev also made several hostile remarks. Among other points, Bukharin tried to explain why he had written so many letters not only to the Politburo but also to Stalin personally, as if 'trying to take advantage of his goodwill'. 'I do not complain,' shouted Stalin. 'I turned to Stalin', said Bukharin,

> as the highest authority in the Party. ... This practice was established
> even in Lenin's time. Whenever one of us wrote to Ilych, it was usu-
> ally about a question that would not go to the Politburo, we wrote
> about our doubts, our uncertainties, etc.

The discussion concluded with a final summing up by Yezhov, who repeated and even sharpened all the previous accusations. He declared that the investigation of the case would continue and that everyone could rely on its objectivity.[23]

The plenum set up a commission of 36 members to prepare its decision on the case of Bukharin and Rykov. All members of the Politburo were on the commission, along with a number of the most well-known members of the Central Committee, including Nadezhda Krupskaya, Maria Ulyanova, Maxim Litvinov, Nikita Khrushchev and Semyon Budenny. On the evening of 26 February and the morning of the 27th the plenum discussed questions relating to the coming elections to the Supreme Soviet under the new constitutional arrangements. Bukharin was at home, writing his letter 'To a future generation of Party leaders', which he asked his wife to memorize. He said to her, 'You're young, you will live long enough to see other people leading the Party.' He tested her several times, and when he was convinced that she had memorized every word, he burned the text. Two decades later, having constantly repeated the words to herself during years of prison, camp and exile, she finally returned to Moscow and was able to write the letter down and send it to Khrushchev. Later she sent it in turn to Brezhnev, Andropov, Chernenko and Gorbachev. Bukharin's letter has often been published and reactions have varied. But almost all commentators have quoted Bukharin's description of the NKVD as an organization that had turned into 'a poisonous machine using the methods of the middle ages' to do its foul work in order to 'cater to Stalin's morbid suspiciousness, I am afraid to say any more'. Yet Bukharin goes on to assure the 'future leaders of the Party' that over the last seven years he had not had 'even a shade of disagreement with the Party' and that he had 'never plotted against Stalin'.

Mikoyan chaired the meeting of the plenum's commission. The first to speak was Yezhov, who demanded that Bukharin and Rykov be expelled from the Party, handed over to a military tribunal and shot. Postyshev agreed that the accused had to be expelled from the Party and brought to trial, but without application of the death penalty. Stalin, who was the fourth person to speak, proposed the following formula: 'expel them from candidate membership of the Central Committee, but instead of committing them for trial, turn the case over to the NKVD', i.e. for further investigation. After that only Manuilsky, Kosarev, Shvernik and Yakir continued to advocate a trial and execution. All the rest, according to the record, expressed support for Stalin's proposal. The final decision was unanimous.[24]

At the evening session of the Central Committee plenum, unusually it was Stalin rather than Mikoyan who reported on the decisions taken by the commission. He made a point of saying that 'it would be wrong to lump Bukharin and Rykov together with the group of Trotskyists and Zinovievists, since there is a difference between them, a difference that speaks in favour of Bukharin and Rykov.' The plenum voted in favour of adopting the resolution of the commission, with two abstentions – by Bukharin and Rykov – who had listened in silence as Stalin presented his brief report.[25] On the same day, Bukharin and Rykov, who had left the session earlier than the others, were arrested in the hall and taken to the Lubyanka.

Bukharin in prison

Bukharin and Rykov were brought straight to the secret-political section of the NKVD, the same unit that had only just completed preparations for the trial of the 'parallel centre', allegedly headed by Pyatakov and Radek. It was around nine o'clock in the evening. The first interrogation of Bukharin was assigned to a commissar of the NKVD, Viktor Ilin, who was considered to be the Lubyanka's 'specialist on the Mensheviks'.

The 'good cop/bad cop' routine is a familiar method of interrogation and common in all countries. In the Lubyanka Ilin played the role of 'good' interrogator and was never asked to apply what was called 'special pressure' on prisoners. In the 1960s Ilin worked as business manager of the Union of Writers, having spent eight years in prison himself during the post-war period. He had good relations with almost all the writers, helping them to sort out problems to do with dachas, vacations and medical treatment. He never concealed the fact that he had worked for the NKVD in the 1930s and 1940s, and after the Twenty-Second Party Congress talked more freely about certain aspects of his experience. Inevitably his stories were recorded by some of the writers to whom he spoke, but there is no way of reliably checking their accuracy.

According to Ilin, Bukharin walked into the interrogation room as if he were entering his new office. He looked around, extended his hand to the interrogator but then quickly withdrew it and said, 'It's a long time since I was here.' His looked tired and confused but also somehow cheerful. Ilin did not understand his remark and cautiously asked, 'You have been in this room before?' 'No,' replied Bukharin, 'but I have been in your organization as a member of the board.' It was in fact true that at the end of 1918 Lenin had appointed Bukharin as Party representative on the board of the Cheka with the right of veto after he had complained about the excesses of the 'red terror'. And on several occasions Bukharin did use this right. 'I believe that we've met at the House of Scientists,' continued the prisoner to his jailer. Ilin replied that he had been there on several occasions, and then sent for tea and sandwiches. They continued chatting for more than an hour with Bukharin leading the conversation, as if he had forgotten where he was or why he was there. Then suddenly Bukharin was silent, obviously exhausted. Ilin suggested that he lie down on the couch, and Bukharin covered himself with his leather coat, put his head and arm on the bolster and fell asleep. At one o'clock in the morning, he was finally taken to his cell.

To this day very little is known about the interrogation of Bukharin or about his behaviour during his time in the Lubyanka's special NKVD section. Mikoyan, whom I met several times in 1962–63, told me that Bukharin was never tortured and that in the first months he resisted all pressure, refusing to admit any of the charges against him. The pressure was then intensified. His interrogators were well aware of Bukharin's anxiety about his young wife, Anna Larina, and their infant son, and this proved to be a useful tool. Bukharin was also very troubled about his father, who had been living in their Kremlin apartment. His first wife, Nadezhda Lukina, now ill and confined to bed, lived there as well. Bukharin knew of cases where the arrest of an important figure led to the repression of other adult family members. He was told that his own family continued to live in the Kremlin, but it was made perfectly clear that their future was dependent on his behaviour and the degree to which he was prepared to co-operate, to 'disarm' himself before the Party. They made it possible for Bukharin to work in prison, and he was provided with paper, a typewriter and all his personal belongings. He asked for books from his own library, which only Anna could select. 'Bring me the books which we bought in Germany,' he wrote. She was given permission to break the seals on the study door, and the books arrived quite quickly. He asked for letters from Anna, but she refused to write the investigator's dictated texts. Nevertheless Bukharin was able to see that the parcels really did come from his wife, as she was the only person who was familiar with his affairs during the months before his arrest.

Although Bukharin started giving evidence almost at once, the interrogator found his testimony inadequate, a view that was shared by Stalin who was following the questioning of Bukharin and Rykov with great interest. The pressure got stronger. Voroshilov came to the Lubyanka several times for 'negotiations' with Bukharin. We have no details of their conversations, but it is known that in June 1937 Bukharin finally did sign the text of the official indictment. Voroshilov had pointed out corrections on the document, which clearly had been made in Stalin's familiar handwriting. It was a near total capitulation and Stalin was satisfied. The prisoner was able to return to reading and writing, ignorant of the fact that his wife and son were immediately arrested and sent to a prison in Astrakhan. Later the child was put into a children's home in the Urals and Larina dispatched to ALZhIR, the infamous Akmolinsk camp for wives of traitors to the fatherland. Bukharin, however, was still under the illusion that his family was living in Moscow as before and that one day he would be able to see them.

The prison manuscripts

Prison writing, whether literary, political or scientific, has become a genre in its own right all over the world. It is particularly true in the history of socialist thought – many of its key texts were written in prison. The Italian monk Tommaso Campanella (1568–1639) spent 27 years in prison and during this period wrote all of his major works, including the celebrated *City of the Sun.* The gifted Marxist theorist who founded the Italian communist party, Antonio Gramsci, spent the last ten years of his life in a fascist prison in Turin. It was there that he wrote his most famous work, smuggled out by friends, the seven-volume *Prison Notebooks,* which has had a major influence on socialist thought throughout Europe as well as in Italy and is still being studied to this day. The Czech communist writer, Julius Fučik, wrote his widely known *Reporting with a Noose around One's Neck* behind the walls of the Prague prison, shortly before being executed by the Nazis. Turning to Russia, one immediately thinks of Chernyshevsky, whose novel *What is to be Done* was written in the first months of 1863 in the Petropavlovsk Fortress and published by Nekrasov later that year. Nikolai Morozov, a member of *Narodnaya Volya* (the People's Will) spent 25 years in solitary confinement in the Schlüsselburg Fortress yet was somehow able to write numerous works on history, theology, physics, chemistry and astronomy. A fellow revolutionary, Nikolai Kibalchich, an engineer and chemist who made explosives for the revolutionaries, gave a packet of papers to his lawyer several days before his execution for attempting to assassinate Tsar Alexander II in 1881, but instead of the usual plea for mercy, it contained an astonishing 'Design for an Aeronautic Device' – a description and plans for a flying machine based on rocket design. Today Nikolai Kibalchich is considered to be one of the pioneers of rocket engineering.

During his year of preliminary detention in one of the St Petersburg prisons, Lenin wrote a large part of his *Development of Capitalism in Russia*, published legally in 1899. Friends and relatives kept him supplied with whatever books and journals he needed. The leading Russian economist Nikolai Kondratiev (1892–1938) wrote two major books in Vladimir prison, but only one of them survived, rescued by his wife, his *Economic Statics and Dynamics.* It was published in Russia for the first time in 1992 and is considered by many economists to be a classic. Although it would hardly have been possible to write books in Stalin's labour camps, poetry was different and could be memorized. Solzhenitsyn wrote his 'Feast of Victors' at the beginning of the 1950s, and before the war Yelena Vladimirova wrote her long poem 'Kolyma', as well as a number of other verses. Varlam Shalamov also wrote poetry in the camps.

In recent years there have been almost no political prisoners in the Soviet Union or Russia, but the few who did exist were free to write as much as they liked. The former Chairman of the KGB, Vladimir Kryuchkov, arrested in 1991, wrote a long book of memoirs entitled *A Personal Affair.* An inmate in the same prison, Anatoly Lukyanov, former member of the Politburo and Speaker of the first Soviet parliament, produced a number of poems.

Many authors have done their best work in prison. Musa Dzhalil's *Moabitsky Notebooks* is a perfect example. Perhaps it is the emotional tension of the situation, a striving to express what might be one's final words. As the Polish satirist Yezhi Lets wrote,'certain thoughts come to us best of all under escort'.

Bukharin's prison manuscripts, however, cannot be regarded as his best work. Nor is it appropriate to regard them as 'the last battle between Bukharin and Stalin', as some commentators have done. What makes these manuscripts special is not so much the content as the circumstances in which they were written.

Bukharin was able to continue working until the preparations for his trial came to an end in the middle of January 1938; at this point the procurator's office joined the interrogation, with Andrei Vyshinsky participating personally. They had provided him with a writing table in his cell and permitted him to send papers to his wife (so he thought), via the investigator. Apparently he believed, or desperately wanted to believe, that he was being shown genuine kindness. He never found out anything about the fate of his family.

On 15 January, he wrote a long letter to his wife:

> I am writing to you on the eve of my trial for only one reason. ...
> Whatever you read, whatever you hear, whatever terrible things are
> said about me or indeed, whatever I say myself – try and remain calm
> and courageous. They will be giving you three manuscripts: a) a long
> philosophical work of 310 pages called A Philosophical Arabesque; b)
> a volume of poems; c) the seven first chapters of a novel. They have to
> be typed in three copies. The poems and the novel can be edited by my
> father ... above all, the philosophical piece must not be lost. I worked
> so hard and put so much into it and compared to some of my earlier
> writing, it is fully developed and DIALECTICAL from beginning to end.
> There is yet ANOTHER book, *The Crisis of Capital, Culture and Social-
> ism* – I wrote the first half of it when I was still home. Try and
> RESCUE it. I don't have any of it, and it would be a great pity if it was
> lost. ... In any case, whatever happens at the trial, afterwards I will be
> able to see you and kiss your hands.[26]

Anna Larina finally did get to read this letter at the end of 1992, 55 years after it was written. It was sent to her from the Presidential Archive after the intervention of friends and particularly the efforts of the American academic Professor Stephen Cohen. At the time, Sergei Shakhrai, a member of Yeltsin's immediate circle, was in charge of the hurried and chaotic search for different kinds of documents relevant to the 'case of the CPSU' before the Constitutional Court, and he gave instructions that copies of Bukharin's letters and manuscripts be handed over to his widow. In 1915 a young British soldier on the way to the German front threw a bottle with a note into the sea, addressed to his newborn daughter. The soldier was killed shortly afterwards, and the bottle remained in the water until it was discovered by chance in 1995. The soldier's daughter was still alive and lived in Austria. It was an extraordinarily emotional moment when this 80-year-old woman read the letter from her 20-year-old father. It was even less likely that Anna Larina would ever read the letters written to her by her husband or actually receive his manuscripts. And yet it happened.

This is not the place to discuss Bukharin's 'little volume of poetry', particularly since only a few of the verses were intended for publication. Bukharin was a connoisseur of poetry and was even considered to be an expert in the theory of poetics, but he was not a poet, and his own efforts lacked that magic – Akhmatova called it the 'hidden magic' – that is a feature of true poetry. The journalist Otto Latsis called Bukharin's poems 'a rhyming political calendar' and not without reason, while the inclusion of several odes to Stalin showed that the author of the verses was by no means addressing his work exclusively to 'future generations'.

A major part of Bukharin's prison manuscripts were published in 1996 by the Bukharin Fund, set up by his son along with several historians. The first volume contained Bukharin's *Socialism and Culture*, which continues his many previous explorations of the question of culture. Undoubtedly what Bukharin wrote during the 1930s on socialism and culture exemplified the best of what was being written on that subject in the Soviet Union at the time. Nevertheless it would be difficult to describe Bukharin's book as a work of great significance. Writing in his prison cell Bukharin was doubly a prisoner. He was trapped within the confines of Marxist dogmas or, rather, the even narrower Soviet–Marxist dogmas, and even if it were possible under the circumstances, he had neither the inclination nor the capacity to break free. He did have a longstanding interest in cultural problems and was one of the leading specialists in this field, although he was elected to the Academy of Sciences in 1928 as an economist. But even within the context of his previous work on culture, the prison manuscripts have nothing particularly new to offer apart from the frequent endorsements of Stalinist policies and praise for Stalin himself.

Of course Bukharin was not writing for publication. He understood that for some time to come this would be out of the question, and the most he could hope for (and this was promised by one of the investigators, Lev Sheinin) was that the manuscript of his new book would be given to his wife for safekeeping. No doubt either the investigator or the Commissar, Yezhov, would have a look at his manuscript and evaluate it, but the main and perhaps the only real reader would be Stalin. Thus an enormous number of pages were written for the benefit of just one person. This is confirmed by B. Frezinsky in his introduction to *The Prison Manuscripts*. It was clear to Bukharin that his own life and the fate of his family depended on Stalin's decision alone and that it was Stalin who would decide whether his manuscripts should be saved or destroyed. 'Therefore Bukharin's book, perhaps even unintentionally, became another long letter to Stalin, although this time without the usual "Dear Koba!"'[27]

Given this combination of motive and circumstance, it would hardly be possible to produce a serious scholarly work. Rather than exhibit his intellectual potential, Bukharin's first concern was to prove his own reliability and make it clear that he was not an 'enemy of the people' or a spy or a terrorist but in fact a loyal, dedicated adherent of Stalin and pupil of Lenin. Therefore it would be absurd to expect a serious, honest or objective evaluation of the situation of culture in the USSR. Although Bukharin's book does attack fascism, there is not a trace, nor could there have been, of the slightest hint of criticism of the cultural policies of the Soviet state or the Party. His book is an apologia for the Party, the Soviet regime, for Stalin and the dictatorship of the proletariat. Soviet society, according to Bukharin, had already become a good society, successfully built according to a scientific plan, thanks to the 'genius of the founder of Marxism' and the 'mastery of the Stalinist leadership'. Needless to say, he went on to argue that the dictatorship of the proletariat is the only authentic democracy, that state and co-operative property were the only appropriate forms of ownership under socialism and that all private property must be abolished.

This was more or less the line of all Party theoreticians at the time, and it was not simply a question of dogmatism or fear of repression. The reality of the situation in the 1930s provided little material for a more informed understanding of capitalism and socialism. With difficulty the capitalist world was attempting to recover from the crash of 1929–33 and had not yet shown any convincing capacity for economic development. Many predicted that Roosevelt's New Deal would be a failure, and the prospect of a scientific-technological revolution was not yet on the horizon, certainly not in the capitalist world. Indeed the spread of fascism seemed the most likely prospect for the future. The colonial world had not yet begun its struggle, and a new world war for international hegemony appeared to be inevitable and not far off. In these circumstances internal disputes within the Party were not merely undesirable, but were out of the question. It is worth remembering that even Western intellectuals rejoiced at the strengthening of the USSR and were reluctant to acknowledge, or even to perceive the faults of the Soviet political system. The critics of Soviet socialism were few and far between; Bukharin was not even prepared to argue with opponents such as Nikolai Berdyaev and André Gide.

For almost all socialists, dogmatism became an inevitable if illusory defence. Trotsky was no exception, and his primitive conceptions were of little interest to anyone in the Soviet Union. Neither Trotskyism nor the ideas of the Fourth International provided an acceptable intellectual alternative for the left. Therefore it is pointless today to attempt an analysis, and certainly not a critical analysis, of the books written by Bukharin in prison; it also makes little sense to eulogize them. What could Bukharin write, sitting in prison, in the long section of his book entitled 'Socialism and Freedom'? Yes, of course he wrote that all aspects of freedom had been extended in the Soviet Union except the freedom to propagate harmful, virtually extinct religious ideology. From behind the walls of the Lubyanka, Bukharin tried to show that there was no conflict between the individual and society in the USSR, that the rights of the individual were never sacrificed to the needs of society, that the great idea of equality had been translated into reality. In other words he was echoing prevailing Soviet ideology.

Several contemporary commentators claim to have found hidden criticism of Stalin and Stalinism in Bukharin's books. Bukharin's daughter, Svetlana Gurvich, is convinced that when her father sketched the features of the 'new man' of the future, a person free of envy, spite, dishonesty, vanity or love of power, he was pointing to Stalin, since the qualities named were those of a 'Bolshevik in the negative variant and were absolutely characteristic of the "leader of all peoples"'.[28] Thus, she argues, Bukharin was able to deceive the tyrant and his censors. I find this interpretation rather unconvincing. In addition to the usual formulas, such as 'Leninist-Stalinist national policy', one can find a number of extremely abstract arguments in Bukharin's book that are difficult to comprehend. Thus, defining the main features of socialist culture, the author wrote: 'The spiritual culture of socialist society has no place for sublimated forms of commodity fetishism and empty metaphysical abstractions nor for sublimated forms of categories of hierarchy connected with some type of religious consciousness.'[29] It could well be the case that this statement contained something resembling veiled criticism of the 'cult of personality', but if so it is not criticism that Stalin would have had to fear.

Bukharin considered his *Philosophical Arabesques* to be the most important of his prison writings.[30] Philosophy had never been a central subject for Bukharin, and his prison manuscripts may well have been his best work in this field. In the history of Marxist philosophy, however, they are no more than a work of exposition.

When contemporaries or future generations attach the name of a major philosopher to his teaching or doctrine, e.g. Kantian, Hegelian or Marxist, it means that certain principles have been established that can then be studied or expanded, explained or popularized. Often there is also a final stage: vulgarization. In Russia it was Plekhanov and Lenin who studied Marx and went on to develop his theories, while Bukharin tended to be no more than an interpreter or popularizer of Marxism. And what about Stalin? He was the author of the section 'On Dialectical and Historical Materialism' for a history of the Party, also written in 1937. It is fair to say that he was a mixture: in part a popularizer but undoubtedly also a vulgarizer of Marxist philosophy.

After Lenin's death Bukharin deservedly was regarded to be the Party's most competent theorist, but mainly with reference to four subjects: general economics, the theory of NEP, the international communist movement and the new culture. He seldom addressed questions of 'pure' philosophy and had something of an inferiority complex vis à vis the superior erudition of many of the authoritative Soviet philosophers of the 1920s and 1930s. Bukharin was also inhibited by the verdict of Lenin's 'Testament', which although never made public at the time, was known to all the Party leaders. Lenin wrote:

> Bukharin is not only a most valuable and major theorist of our Party, he is also rightly considered to be the favourite of the whole Party, but it is doubtful whether his theoretical views can be classified as fully Marxist, for there is something scholastic about him (he has never made a study of dialectics and, I think, never fully understood it).

During his battle with the 'right deviation' at the end of the 1920s, Stalin often publicly repeated Lenin's words, calling Bukharin a 'doubtful Marxist'. The press regarded Bukharin's work as mechanistic and anti-dialectical. In prison Bukharin decided to prove this judgement false. Although he called his new work 'Arabesques', in reality it was an essay on Lenin's *Philosophical Notebooks*. It was the equivalent of a diploma exercise or at best a dissertation, in which the writer hopes to convince his teachers or professors that he has fully mastered the subject under discussion. The *Philosophical Notebooks* was published in 1929–30 in *Collected Lenin* Nos. IX and XII, and also as a single volume in 1933 and 1935. But by 1925 the work was already available to Party theorists who were engaged in the process of compiling and studying the theoretical legacy of the deceased leader.

Lenin had been thinking about writing another book on the philosophy of Marxism that would be a follow-up to his *Materialism and Empiriocriticism*. The *Philosophical Notebooks* were ten exercise

books containing synopses of the work of various major philosophers including Marx, Engels, Hegel, Feuerbach, Aristotle, Lassalle
and Plekhanov along with notes, drafts and observations that Lenin
recorded in the course of 1914–16 in Switzerland and never intended
for publication as such. However, Lenin's main interest at the time
was Hegel. He had read *The Science of Logic* in Siberia and was now
ready to study the texts more seriously. In one of the exercise books
he wrote that it was impossible really to understand Marx or *Capital*
without knowing Hegel. These words put the leaders of the Party in
a difficult position: almost all professed to have a good knowledge of
Marxism and had made a considerable effort to study *Capital,* but
now they were suddenly faced with the need to master Hegel.

Stalin also began to study Hegel. He had nourished philosophical
ambitions ever since he had been a young man, as can be seen from
his early series of articles *Anarchism and Socialism.* But he had never
attempted to come to terms with Hegel. It was a difficult task, and he
asked a leading philosopher, Jan Sten, to give him private lessons on
the dialectic. Stalin found it difficult to master even some of the basic
ideas and grew increasingly irritated. The lessons took place twice a
week, but after a few months they came to an end, leaving Stalin
with an enduring hostility towards German idealistic philosophy
which later, after the war, he called 'an aristocratic reaction to the
French Revolution'. Bukharin was more successful, no doubt helped
by the fact that he spoke and read German fluently. Thus in prison,
Bukharin once again turned to Hegel, using books that were brought
to his cell but also citing many works from memory.

Bukharin dealt with a large number of questions in his *Philosophical Arabesques*, exhibiting an enviable if superficial erudition.
Like Lenin, Bukharin's main interest lay in questions relating to the
theory of knowledge and the role of practice as a criterion of truth.
He wrote at length about the problem that Engels termed the main
question of philosophy: the relationship between the material and the
ideal, between matter and consciousness, and the distinction between
subjective and objective idealism, mechanistic and dialectical materialism.

Several commentators on the *Philosophical Arabesques* have
detected a hidden polemic against Stalin in the text and believe it to
be a condemnation of the Stalinist regime. They cite a particular
passage in which the author harshly criticizes subjective idealism and
'the solipsism of the devil' as an extreme manifestation of that idealism. I rather think this exemplifies a trick of the imagination,
influenced by wishful thinking.

A whole set of problems are discussed in Bukharin's book, problems that are dealt with in all basic textbooks on dialectical
materialism: space and time, consciousness and matter, the abstract

and the concrete, consciousness of the world, the 'thing in itself', thought and sensation, conceptions of freedom and necessity, and so on. Bukharin criticized mechanistic notions of materialism where even thought is considered to be in some sense material. But he was also critical of 'psycho-physical parallelism', that is, the idea that the spiritual is as primary and eternal as matter. Consciousness and soul are only a special attribute or state of matter and not separately substantiated forms of being. Bukharin denied the existence of any kind of life force, or entelechy, animating nature. Repeating several of Lenin's formulations on the theory of knowledge, Bukharin maintained the view that all matter contains a certain spiritual aspect, although this idea is little understood. Spirit arises out of matter, since thinking matter, or man, in the final analysis arose and developed out of inorganic matter. Thus spirit is another form of matter, and the main difference between materialism and idealism consists in the fact that idealists consider matter to be another form of spirit. But why is it necessary to come to such extreme conclusions?

The work contains many rather confused and muddled statements. He writes, for example: 'The hypostasis and isolation of pure "free will" is the lynchpin of the "cultural-ethical" waffle of the Kantian epigones' (p 161). Many sections of the book are hard to read because the author jumps from one theme or idea to another. He writes in parentheses, 'Let fools forgive me, the clever will catch on.' Bukharin was not attempting to create new theories or express original ideas; his aim was to clarify Lenin and sometimes Marx and Engels as well.

He repeatedly inveighed against those who consider spirit, or entelechy, as having perceptible, separate spiritual substance, although Bukharin's conclusions here are patently unconvincing, and it would be more productive to regard a human being as a whole, body and soul. Bukharin gets caught up in internal contradictions. He tries to show that the world is not only infinite but is also characterized by infinite diversity. But at the same time he declares that there is only one substance at the basis of the world – matter, which develops from one form to another, acquiring an endless stream of new qualities in the process.

Here is one more phrase from the book: 'Goethe was an aesthetic pantheist with a considerable leaning towards sensationalist materialism' (p 263). Such language is hardly appropriate for a popular work. Even Marx's innovative economic views were generally less influential than they might have been because of their excessive complexity; this is particularly true in the first chapter of *Capital,* where even educated Marxists had difficulty groping their way through the formulas and technicalities of Marx's argument. Above all, Bukharin was concerned to praise Lenin, with the last (40th) chapter devoted to Lenin as a philosopher. And only at the very end of the text did he refer to Stalin as the successor of Lenin. 'The genius of Lenin lit up the world. But every age finds the people it needs, and history, moving forward, put Stalin in his place, whose thoughts and actions have been at the centre of the next historical phase, and under his leadership, socialism has triumphed forever.'[31] His final words were about 'the great Stalinist five-year plans'. Bukharin completed his work, as he himself pointed out, on '7–8 November 1937, the anniversary days of the great victory'.

If one compares Bukharin's texts with the work of Soviet philosophers at the end of the 1930s and the beginning of the 1940s, of course Bukharin exhibits a greater degree of originality. As a student in the philosophy faculty of the LGU in 1946–51, I certainly would have learnt more if I had been able to use the books of Bukharin instead of articles by Mitin, Yudin, Chagin and Aleksandrov. However, even if Bukharin's books had been published at the end of the 1930s, they would not have had much influence on the accepted dogmatic approach to the general problems of existence.

One or two weeks after completing his *Philosophical Arabesques*, Bukharin began to write an autobiographical novel called *Vremena* (Times Past), containing scenes from his childhood and youth in Moscow with portraits of parents, teachers and friends. Various major public events also featured in the story. The novel remained unfinished and was published in Moscow in 1994. In his own notes to the book, Bukharin compared it to Tolstoy's *Childhood* and *Youth* and Gorky's *Childhood* and *University*, but the claim is an exaggeration. Only a thousand copies of Bukharin's novel were published and it did not excite much interest among critics or the general public. This is not the place to discuss its literary merits.

The last act of the drama

Did Stalin have a detailed plan to discredit and destroy all former opposition leaders? Many authors believe that this was indeed the case and that from the first months of 1935 he was carrying out his plan, step by step. Certainly there must have been some kind of working scenario for punitive-political action. The last act of Stalin's bloody drama took place in the first half of March 1938 in the October Hall of the Trade Union House, with the whole world watching. Much has been written about the show trials in Moscow and particularly about the main one, the trial of the 'anti-Soviet Rightist-Trotskyist Bloc'. The first books appeared fairly soon, by Lion Feuchtwanger, George Davis and Arthur Koestler.[32] Aleksandr Solzhenitsyn devoted a few pages to the trials in his *Gulag Archipelago*, and it must be said that the facts in his account are accurate, particularly with regard to Bukharin. However, the reader might be rather taken aback by the strange malicious pleasure with which Solzhenitsyn writes about Bukharin and the other accused. The author, who cannot hide his satisfaction at the reprisals meted out by Stalin to his former opponents, shows greater respect for Stalin than for his victims, whom he calls 'dismal obedient goats'.

I have written at length about the show trials of the 1930s and do not want to repeat myself here.[33] But with regard to the last trial involving Bukharin, in addition to new documents that have become available, I also have had access to three participants in the drama, the first of whom was involved quite reluctantly. Ilya Ehrenburg, whom I got to know in 1965, has himself written about what he witnessed. He sat in the October Hall as one of the 'representatives of the public' on Stalin's orders: 'Get a pass for Ehrenburg and let him have a look at his pals.' My second informant was the former correspondent of the *Manchester Guardian*, Ed Stevens, who was reporting on the trial for his paper. He returned to Moscow after the war, working as a correspondent for papers from several different countries. He received permission to buy a comfortable detached house on Ryleyev Street, a privilege that was unheard of at that time. A rather motley crowd often gathered at Stevens' house – one could find Yuri Zhukov, a *Pravda* columnist, the dissident Vladimir Bukovsky, and certain diplomats. Yevgeny Gnedin, my third informant, was head of the press department of the NKVD in 1938. It was his job to supervise the foreign correspondents accredited to the Moscow courtroom. Gnedin himself was arrested in 1939 but managed to survive 17 years of prison, camp and exile.[34]

The first session of the Military Collegium of the Supreme Court of the USSR began on the morning of 2 March 1938. There were approximately 500 people in the hall. The first five rows were occupied by members of the NKVD, with many other NKVD men spread among the spectators. The state prosecutor was Andrei Vyshinsky, the Chief Prosecutor of the USSR. The President of the Judicial Collegium was Vasili Ulrikh. Among the 21 prisoners in the dock, it was Bukharin who was the focus of universal attention. An American historian later wrote:

> This man was the main accused, he was the most important of all the defendants in the sensational Moscow show trials. A favourite of Lenin and of the whole Party, a prominent theorist of the international communist movement and the leading figure in the Comintern, Bukharin was undoubtedly the most well-known publicist of the communist revolution. But now he was a pitiful shadow of the person who used to be able to inspire wild enthusiasm at crowded mass meetings, whenever he appeared on the platform. Now he was being accused of secret links with internal and external enemies of the Soviet

people, of attempting to restore capitalism in Russia, of plotting the murder of the most important Soviet leaders and of seeking to overthrow the communist regime in order to bring about the dismemberment of the Soviet state, with the intention of turning Russia over to the fascist aggressor.[35]

Commentators have expressed contradictory opinions about Bukharin's behaviour at the trial and his final plea, which he read out from a prepared text. Solzhenitsyn wrote that Bukharin and his colleagues 'bleated out everything they had been ordered to say, slavishly abased themselves and their convictions, confessed to crimes that they could never have committed and drenched themselves in their own urine'.[36] On the other hand the American scholar Stephen Cohen is inclined to agree with the American correspondent Harold Denny, who, in his reports from Moscow, wrote of Bukharin's courageous and fitting behaviour:

> Mr Bukharin alone, who all too obviously from his last words, fully expected to die, was manly, proud and almost defiant. He is the first of the fifty-four men who have faced the court in the last three public treason trials who has not abased himself in the last hours of the proceedings.[37]

This view is not entirely shared by the British diplomat, Fitzroy MacLean, who also was present at the trial and many years later wrote:

> Among all the accused, it was the last words of Bukharin that stand out. It was impossible not to feel that standing there before us was a representative of a vanishing cohort – the cohort of people who made the revolution, who all their lives struggled for their ideals and now, unwilling to betray these ideals, found themselves being crushed by their own creation. Bukharin once again denied that he had ever been a spy or a saboteur or that he had plotted the murder of Lenin. However, this did not mean, he continued, that he was not guilty or did not deserve to be shot ten times over. Once they had deviated from Bolshevism, from the line of the Party, he and his friends inevitably turned into counter-revolutionary bandits.[38]

Summing up the controversy about Bukharin's behaviour at the trial, Robert Conquest wrote the following in his famous book, *The Great Terror*:

> Bukharin's calculation that his tactics would adequately expose the falsity of the charge against him seems to have been too subtle. It was, of course, plain that he denied all overt acts of terrorism and espionage. But who was affected by this? Serious independent observers in any case did not credit the charges, and would not have done so even if he had confessed to all of them – any more than they did in the case of Zinoviev. But, to the greater political audience for whom the

trials were enacted, the impression received was simply that 'Bukharin had confessed.'[39]

Bukharin's testimony was full of striking contradictions, and this was true of his 'last word' as well. He admitted the facts of terror and sabotage, but at the same time insisted that he had given only the most general instructions:

> I was a leader and not a cog in these counter-revolutionary affairs. ... The monstrousness of my crimes is immeasurable. ... I admit that I am responsible, both politically and legally, for the defeatist orientation and for wrecking activities, although I personally was not involved. ... On bended knee before the Party and the country, I await your verdict.[40]

There are those who believe that the text of Bukharin's final plea was written in advance and had been shown to Vishinsky and also to Stalin. It was of course hardly a negotiation between equals. Certainly Stalin needed Bukharin's testimony at the trial, which is why there may have been a certain degree of accommodation. But at the trial itself, what appeared to be a battle between Bukharin and Vyshinsky was in fact a stage-managed encounter scripted so as to strengthen the appearance of authenticity. The complete, unedited stenographic record of the trial of the 'Right-Trotskyist bloc' was discovered in 1995 in the Presidential Archive. The text contains some unknown editor's correction marks and also alterations made by Stalin, who crossed out whole sentences with coloured pencils. Interestingly Stalin left many phrases in the text that were later interpreted as courageous declarations by the accused, but he removed a variety of unimportant details.[41] Bukharin's widow is convinced that he was promised that his life would be spared, perhaps that he would be sent to a remote place of exile.

Late in the evening of 12 March the court recessed for deliberations that went on for six hours. The session reconvened at four o'clock in the morning. The tired spectators, guards and accused took their places. Moscow was still asleep, and the streets around the Trade Union House were empty. The legend that thousands of Muscovites were standing outside the trial building waiting to hear the sentence has no basis in fact. With everyone standing, the President of the court took about half an hour to read out the verdict. Eighteen of the accused, including Bukharin, were sentenced to 'the supreme penalty – to be shot'.

On 14 March only four of the condemned prisoners appealed to the Presidium of the Supreme Soviet for a pardon. Rykov and Yagoda submitted short statements. Krestinsky's plea was calm, even business-like. But Bukharin's letter was full of despair and extremely emotional:

> There is not a single word of protest in my heart. I deserve to be shot ten times over for my crimes. ... But I want to assure the Presidium of the Supreme Soviet that spending more than a year in prison has given me the chance to reconsider my past, which I now regard with contempt and indignation. It is not fear of death that makes me seek pardon and mercy. I have been inwardly disarmed and restored in a new socialist way. The former Bukharin is already dead, he no longer exists. If I were to be granted physical life, that life would be devoted to working for the socialist fatherland in whatever conditions I found myself, whether isolated in a prison cell, in a concentration camp, at the North pole, in Kolyma, wherever. ... In prison I wrote a number of works which bear witness to my full transformation. Therefore I dare to appeal for mercy, appealing to revolutionary expediency. Give me the chance to nurture a new, second Bukharin – let him be as PETER – this new man will be a total contrast to the one who is already dead. I am absolutely confident: the years will go by and great historical thresholds will be crossed under the leadership of STALIN; you would not regret the act of charity and mercy for which I beg. I would make every effort to prove this gesture of proletarian magnanimity to be justified.[42]

There was no sign of pride or daring in Bukharin's plea. We can only imagine Stalin's considerable pleasure as he read Bukharin's words, but a pardon was not granted. Bukharin was shot on 15 March 1938. According to Aleksei Snegov, who got to see documents relating to Bukharin's final days, the prisoner asked for pencil and paper just before his execution in order to write a last letter to Stalin. His wish was granted. The short note began with the words, 'Koba, why do you need me to die?' Stalin kept this pre-execution letter in one of the drawers of his desk for the rest of his life.

CHAPTER 15

Stalin's Mother

Roy Medvedev

Yekaterina Georgievna Dzhugashvili never occupied a very large place in the thoughts or feelings of her son, Joseph Stalin. According to the historian Vladimir Antonov-Ovseenko, author of *Stalin and his Time*, Stalin was coarse and cynical about his mother and gave orders for her to be constantly watched, assigning that task to two trusted female communists. Although he refers to the testimony of several Georgian Bolsheviks and their relatives,[1] this is nevertheless a perfect example of pure invention. It is true, however, that Stalin paid little attention to his mother, and there is no evidence to suggest that he ever felt any affection for her. Svetlana Alliluyeva wrote:

> He was a bad and neglectful son, as he was father and husband. He devoted his whole being to something else, to politics and struggle. And so people who weren't personally close were always more important to him than those who were.[2]

In the spring of 1904 Stalin stayed with his mother for a few weeks in the small Georgian town of Gori after escaping from his first period of exile in Siberia. They would never again spend an extended period of time together. The Revolution was approaching, and Stalin, who already had become a conspicuous figure among the Caucasian Bolsheviks, was constantly on the move. He was working one day in Tiflis (renamed Tbilisi in 1936), the next in Baku. He then moved from Batumi to Kutaisi and also travelled to St Petersburg and Finland in order to supervise the transportation of a consignment of weapons.

In 1905 Stalin married. According to one version, it was his mother who found the bride, but this in fact was not the case. Stalin met Yekaterina Svanidze through her brother, who had been a close friend at the Tiflis seminary. Later a well-known figure in Georgia and Moscow, Alyosha Svanidze was arrested, sentenced to death, and shot on 20 August 1941. Beria personally reported his execution to Stalin on the very day it took place.

In 1907 Stalin, his wife and their small son Yakov went to live in Baku. Stalin was in prison when Yekaterina Svanidze died of pneumonia, although he was allowed by the prison authorities to attend the funeral. Stalin went back to Party work in Georgia after his wife's death but had little opportunity or desire to see his mother. After two more arrests and periods of exile he left the Caucasus without making any attempt to contact her. For more than ten years, Yekaterina Dzhugashvili had no information about her son. Her life was extremely remote from politics, and she could only pray for the welfare of her Soso while continuing as before, doing laundry, sewing and cleaning for her wealthier neighbours.

In May 1921 when the Civil War was over, Stalin travelled to Nalchik for rest and treatment. At the end of June he went from there to Tiflis, where the Bolsheviks had taken power some months before. As People's Commissar for Nationalities and member of the Politburo, Stalin participated in a plenum of the Georgian Central Committee and spent time with republican Party leaders, many of whom were acquaintances from the past. He also visited the Svanidzes and took his son, Yakov, back with him to his new family in Moscow. He never saw his mother, although he asked the new Georgian leaders to look after her. In his biography of Stalin, Dmitry Volkogonov wrote that Stalin's mother stayed with her son in Moscow in 1922,[3] but there seems to be no evidence to confirm that this visit ever took place. In April 1922 Stalin's second wife, Nadezhda Alliluyeva, spent several weeks in Georgia with her young son Vassily. She met Stalin's mother, to whom her husband had written his first letter:

> 16 April 1922. Mama dear! Greetings! Be well, don't let sorrow enter your heart. You know the saying: 'While I live, I'll enjoy my violets, when I die the graveyard worms can rejoice'. This woman – she's my wife. Take good care of her. Your Soso.

Stalin's next letter was not written until 1 January 1923 and was even shorter:

> Mama dear! Greetings! May you live ten thousand years. I kiss you. Your Soso.[4]

From the autumn of 1922 Yekaterina Georgievna began to receive more detailed letters from Nadezhda Alliluyeva. News of her son's life always came to her from others. As the mother of Stalin, this woman, who did not speak Russian and could neither read nor write in Georgian, was now receiving a considerable amount of attention. But Stalin himself took little interest in her and when on holiday in Georgia, never invited her to join him. Nor did he ever visit Gori, where the modest home of the Dzhugashvili family had been transformed into a Stalin museum surrounded by a large marble pavilion. (The museum has been shut several times over the years, but after recent renovations it reopened with no shortage of visitors. It contains many photographs and portraits of the young Stalin and his mother, and several years ago a portrait of Stalin's father suddenly appeared as well. Vissarion Dzhugashvili had been a shoemaker who died in unknown circumstances at the end of the nineteenth century. Later, Stalin never referred to his father, and even the date of his death does not appear in any of the official Stalin chronologies. The portrait was only 'found' in 1989, and there is a clear resemblance between father and son, but several of Stalin's biographers consider the portrait to be a fake.)

The Georgian authorities could hardly ignore the mother of the man whose power had grown continuously and whose brutality could be felt in every corner of the country. They insisted that she come to Tiflis where they installed her in a wing of a small palace in the centre of the city, which in the past had been the residence of the Russian viceroy in the Caucasus. Stalin's mother moved to the capital with all her worldly goods and chose to settle in just one room of the palace. Whenever anyone from the Georgian leadership travelled to Moscow, she would dictate a letter to her son. She also sent him parcels containing jam and local sweets. In return she received small amounts of money along with short notes, which she carefully put away – in the course of 16 years (1922–37) there were 18 letters all told. Later they were preserved as secret documents in one of the Stalin fonds at the Marx–Engels–Lenin Institute (the name of this institute was repeatedly changed). The historian Shota Chivadze was employed by the Central Committee to translate Stalin's letters into Russian, and he kept the draft copies of his work. Not long before his death, Chivadze handed these drafts over to his colleague, Professor Leonid Spirin, who was the first to disclose their existence.[5] Today the letters sent to Yekaterina Dzhugashvili by Stalin and his wife can be found in the Presidential Archive, located in Stalin's former Kremlin apartment. Edvard Radzinsky, who describes the letters almost as if they had been his own original discovery, was one of the people able to have a look at them in this archive.[6]

It was not only Stalin's many preoccupations that made it difficult for him to write to his mother. Although he spoke Georgian well and occasionally read Georgian texts, he never had any need to write in the language and was out of practice. For many years Stalin's family had included the son of a professional revolutionary, Artem (Fyodor Sergeyev), who had died in an accident in 1921. Stalin regarded Artem as a friend and took his small son, also called Artem, to live with his family, sharing a room with the young Vasily. When asked in an interview 70 years later, 'Did Stalin's mother ever come to Moscow?', Artem Sergeyev replied:

> She never left Tbilisi. I remember one time he sat with a blue pencil, writing her a letter. One of the relatives of Nadezhda Sergeevna asked, 'Joseph, you're a Georgian, of course you're writing to your mother in Georgian?' Do you know what he said? ... 'What kind of Georgian

am I, when it takes me more than two hours to write a letter to my
mother. I have to think about every word I write.'[7]

The longest letter Stalin ever wrote to his mother was dated
March 1934, half a year after the suicide of Nadezhda Alliluyeva:

> Greetings, dear mother! I received your letter. I also got the jam, the
> ginger and the sweets. The children were very happy and send you
> their greetings and thanks. It's good to hear that you're well and
> cheerful. I am in good health, don't worry about me. I can bear my
> lot. I do not know whether you need money. In any case, I'm sending
> you five hundred roubles. I'm also sending photos – of myself and the
> children. Keep well dear mama, do not lose your cheerful spirits. I kiss
> you. Your son Soso.
>
> 24/III – 34. – The children send you their best regards. My personal
> life is hard since Nadya's death. But never mind, a strong man must
> always remain strong.[8]

Only very few members of the Party leadership knew about the
suicide of Nadezhda Alliluyeva. The official announcement of her
death and the numerous obituaries referred to her 'end', her 'un-
timely death', her 'poor state of health', followed by 'death snatched
her away', 'death mowed her down'. No medical report on the cause
of death was ever published. The body was examined by the Chief
Doctor of the Kremlin Hospital, A. Kanel, with two other doctors in
attendance, L. Levin and D. Pletnev. Attempts were made to convince
them to sign a medical report that she died of appendicitis, but all
three refused.[9] In 1932 this would not have automatically entailed
unfortunate consequences. Rumours began to circulate, but they
would not have reached Stalin's mother, who was given the semi-
official version of events, that Nadezhda died of acute appendicitis.

Stalin's mother was well looked after. She was cared for by the
best doctors, and her modest needs were supplied by the state. The
old woman who had served others for a large part of her life now
had two servants herself. But she never abused her new situation;
she kept to almost all her old habits and refused to accept most of the
privileges that were offered. She was given a permanent pass to a box
at the Georgian opera but much preferred going to church.

Stalin was not the first son born to Yekaterina Georgievna. She
was 15 when she gave birth to Mikhail, who died within a year. Her
second son, Georgi, also died in infancy. Soso, or Joseph, was her
third child. Only in 1990 were historians able to obtain access to
documents from church archives and other local sources. They were
quite surprised to discover that Stalin was not born on 21 December
1879, as stated in all the biographies, but in fact a year earlier. In the
first part of the register of births, marriages and deaths of the Uspen-
sky church in Gori, it is recorded that on 6 December 1878 a son,

Joseph, was born to the Orthodox Christian peasant Vissarion Ivano-
vich Dzhugashvili and his lawful wife Yekaterina Gavrilovna,
residents of Gori. The baby was christened on 17 December by the
Archpriest Khakhanov, assisted by the sub-deacon, Kvinikadze. The
same date of birth is on the school leaving certificate, issued by the
Gori Junior Seminary when the young Dzhugashvili graduated with
honours in June 1894.[10] Stalin's mother would hardly have been able
to recall the exact day and year of his birth. But she did indeed remember all her sons. At the end of each year, when the Georgian
leaders came to congratulate her on the birthday of the 'great Stalin',
the independent, sharp-tongued Yekaterina Dzhugashvili would
often remark that her first born, Mikhail, was the most clever, the
most beautiful of the three.

Her health began to deteriorate at the beginning of the 1930s; she
was frequently ill and seldom left her room. In June 1935 Stalin
decided to send his children to Tiflis to visit their grandmother. In a
letter of 11 June he informed his mother:

> I'm sending my children to see you. Kiss them and make them wel-
> come. They are good children. If I can manage it, I'll try to come and
> see you.

Many years later Svetlana Alliluyeva recalled the experience:

> I thought back to the time when Yakov, Vasily and I were sent to call
> on my grandmother in Tbilisi when she was ill. ... We spent about a
> week ... in Tbilisi and only about half an hour with my grandmother.

> She actually lived in a beautiful old palace with a park. Her room was
> small and dark with a low ceiling and little windows facing on a
> courtyard. There was an iron cot and screen in one corner. The room
> was full of old women wearing black, as old women do in Georgia,
> and a little old lady was half-seated on the narrow iron cot. We were
> led up to her. Awkwardly, she embraced us with hands that were
> knotted and bony. She kissed us and spoke a few words in Georgian.
> Yakov was the only one who understood. He answered while we
> stood quietly by. ...

> All the old women in the room were friends of hers. They took turns
> kissing us and they all said I looked very much like my grandmother.
> She offered us hard candies on a plate. The tears were rolling down
> her cheeks. ...

> We left quickly and didn't pay any more visits to the 'palace'. Though
> I was only about nine at the time I wondered why Grandmother
> seemed so poor. I'd never seen such an awful-looking black cot.[11]

Yekaterina Georgievna's health continued to deteriorate, and in
the autumn, after a separation of very many years, Stalin decided it
was time to pay her a visit. On 18 October, *Zarya Vostoka* (Dawn of
the East), the main newspaper of the republic, had a front-page story

in large print: 'Comrade Stalin in Tiflis. On the morning of 17 October, Comrade Stalin came to Tiflis to visit his mother. After spending the whole day with her, Comrade Stalin returned that evening to Moscow.' No further information about the encounter was provided. But three days later TASS correspondents were invited to interview Yekaterina Dzhugashvili. Their report, 'A Conversation with the Mother of Comrade Stalin', was published in *Zarya Vostoka* on 22 October and contained the usual stereotypes, current at the time. The following excerpt is characteristic:

> My meeting with Soso. ... I hadn't seem him for a long time. I haven't been well, I've been feeling weak. But being with him filled me with such joy, it was as if I had grown wings. My illness and weakness suddenly disappeared. ... I asked him about my grandchildren. I love them more than anything in the world, my Svetlana, Yasha and Vasya. ... The time passed without us noticing. We talked about the old days, about friends and family. He joked a lot, we were laughing. We sat together for a long time, and I was so happy, to have my own Soso with me.

'We listened with rapt attention,' wrote the journalists, 'to the slow speech of this frail old woman who had endowed the world with the greatest of men.' An analogous report appeared in *Pravda* on 23 October. For several days many papers published leading articles devoted to the 'new' subject of parents and children. It was pointed out that during the years of Civil War, collectivization and industrialization, many Bolsheviks lost touch with their relatives and often did not even know where their parents were or how they were doing. It was the duty of such Bolsheviks to take an interest in their parents, to look after them along with any other elderly relatives.

According to Professor Leonid Spirin, Yekaterina Dzhugashvili was warned about her son's impending arrival only an hour before he actually appeared. After a vacation in Gagra, Stalin decided to return to Moscow via Tiflis. He arrived, accompanied by his guard. Yekaterina Georgievna was aware that her son was some kind of powerful boss in the country but had little notion of his true position. She asked: 'Joseph, what exactly are you?' 'Secretary of the Central Committee of the Communist Party', he replied. But his mother had no idea what this meant. Therefore to make things clearer, Stalin said, 'Mama, do you remember our tsar?' 'Of course I do.' 'Well, I'm something like the tsar.'[12] According to Svetlana, Stalin was amused to recall some of the things his mother said. When he had asked her, 'Why did you beat me so often?' she replied, 'You seem to have turned out all right.' And when they were saying goodbye, her parting words were: 'All the same, it's a pity you didn't become a priest.'

Yekaterina Dzhugashvili's health did not improve. At the end of May 1937 she contracted pneumonia. The doctors did everything they could, but late in the evening of 4 June Stalin's mother died. Stalin was immediately informed in Moscow. He did not go to Tbilisi, but it was not, as has been suggested by Edvard Radzinsky, because he feared exposing himself to the anger of the local population, already badly affected by the terror. According to Radzinsky, 'He knew that Caucasians were skilled in vengeance and he did not dare to go to Georgia for her funeral. This was something else he would never forget: that his enemies had prevented him from saying farewell to his mother.'[13] But this is a most unlikely explanation. There were many visits to Georgia after 1937, but at the beginning of June Stalin was definitely not thinking about his mother.

By the end of May the wave of terror was sweeping the country with ever increasing brutality; in Moscow alone hundreds of people were being arrested daily – army officers, members of the Central Committee, top economic and industrial leaders, commissars, scientists and writers. The celebrated generals Tukhachevsky, Yakir, Uborevich, Feldman, Kork, Primakov and Putna were all arrested. The Supreme Military Council was convened in Moscow from 1 to 4 June, attended by hundreds of senior army personnel. The central theme under discussion was the activity of the 'traitors' and 'spies' who had managed to worm their way into the ranks of the Red Army. Stalin and Voroshilov both spoke. Several days later the Military Collegium of the USSR Supreme Court sentenced all the army commanders, with Tukhachevsky at the head of the list, to be shot. Preparations were being made for the June plenum of the Central Committee, at which the NKVD would be given emergency powers and made directly subordinate to Stalin. In Moscow alone, up to 1,000 people were being shot every day. The state was paralysed with fear. During these days, Stalin would hardly have given much thought to his mother. To avoid false rumours, he gave orders that there was to be no announcement of his mother's death in the central press. Therefore there were no obituaries or public condolences.

In Georgia, however, the death of Stalin's mother could not be left to pass 'unnoticed' in view of the special place that funeral rites had in Georgian tradition. On Saturday 5 June all Georgian papers published a photograph of Yekaterina Dzhugashvili along with the following notice:

The Central Committee of the Communist Party (Bolsheviks) of Georgia, the Central Executive Committee and the Council of People's Commissars of the Georgian SSR wish to inform the working people of Georgia that on the 4th of June at 23:05, the mother of Comrade Stalin, Yekaterina Dzhugashvili, has died after a long illness (pneumonia and paralysis of the heart).

The funeral commission, headed by G. Mgaloblishvili, the Chairman of the Georgian Sovnarkom, included several Old Bolsheviks: A. Kekelia, G. Sturua, M. Nioradze and G. Gochashvili. Although Stalin's mother had been a deeply religious woman all her life, it was decided to bury her according to a secular ritual that had been established for the funerals of prominent state and Party figures. On the following day the papers announced that the body of Ye.G. Dzhugashvili had been transported from her apartment at the palace to the House of the Red Army and Navy on Rustavelli Street. Three days were set aside for those who wished to bid farewell to the deceased, 6–8 June (until 10 o'clock in the evening on the first two days and on 8 June until 4 o'clock in the afternoon). Among the scores of wreaths on the coffin, prominence was given to two large arrangements with the following inscriptions in Georgian: 'For my dear and beloved mother from her son Joseph Dzhugashvili' and 'For our dear and never to be forgotten Yekaterina Georgievna Dzhugashvili from Nina and Lavrenty Beria'. During the next three days hundreds of people from all parts of Georgia as well as delegations from the neighbouring republics came to visit the open coffin of Stalin's mother. The newspapers reported that 'Endless lines of people, stretching for several blocks, came until late in the evening to pay their last respects to Ye.G. Dzhugashvili.' An obituary notice appeared in the press, signed by the entire Georgian leadership, along with a short biographical account of her life. Here one can read that the parents of Yekaterina Dzhugashvili were peasants from the village of Gambarsula; she was their only daughter, but there were several sons, all of whom managed to get an education. Within Georgian culture these men would be considered to be close relatives of Stalin, but none of them were present at the funeral. We have no information about the fate of this branch of Stalin's family.

On 8 June at 4 pm there was a short civil funeral. At 5:15 Beria, Mgaloblishvili, Makharadze, Bakradze, Musabekov and Goglidze lifted the coffin and carried it out of the House of the Red Army. As *Zarya Vostoka* reported:

> The funeral procession moved slowly along the streets towards Davidov Hill. A large crowd of people followed the coffin. The sounds of the funeral march could be heard along the hilly streets of the city as the procession approached the building of the Mtatsmindsky Writers' Museum, not far from where a new grave had been dug in the cemetery. Then, the minutes of the last silence.[14]

Short speeches were made by representatives of the Georgian government, by leaders from the neighbouring Azerbaijan and Armenia, by People's Artist of the USSR, Akaky Khorava, and representatives of the worker's collectives of the city. At 6:50 pm the body of Yekaterina Dzhugashvili was lowered into the grave. Thus the mother of Stalin, a simple peasant woman, who spent her life sewing and washing and who dreamed that one day her son would become a priest, was buried not far from the graves of Aleksandr Griboyedov and Ilia Chavchavadze, famous Russian and Georgian poets and writers of the previous century. She had never wished to see her son as a new god or tsar, bestowed on us by fate or revolution. She continued to believe in a God in the heavens above, but her coffin was lowered into the earth accompanied by the familiar tunes of the 'International'.

Notes

Chapter 1: Riddles Surrounding Stalin's Death

1   A. Avtorkhanov, *Zagadka smerti Stalina* (Frankfurt am Main: Posev, 1976).
2   Edvard Radzinsky, *Stalin* (London: Hodder and Stoughton, 1996; Moscow: Vagarius, 1997).
3   'Iz vospominnany A. I. Mikoyana', *Sovershenno sekretno*, No. 10 (1999), p 25.
4   I.V. Valedinsky, 'Vospominaniya o vstrechakh so Stalinym I. V.', *Istochnik*, No. 2 (1998), pp 68–73.
5   Lars T. Lih, Oleg V. Naumov and Oleg V. Khlevniuk (eds), *Stalin's Letters to Molotov 1925–36* (New Haven and London: Yale University Press, 1995), pp 175, 181, 202, 214, 239; *Pisma I. V. Stalina V. M. Molotovu. 1925–1936. Sbornik dokumentov* (Moscow: Rossiya Molodaya, 1995), pp 139, 156, 158, 197, 217, 257.
6   Valedinsky, 'Vospominaniya o vstrechakh so Stalinym I. V.', p 70.
7   Svetlana Alliluyeva, *Dvadtsat pisem k drugu* (Moscow: Izvestiya, 1990), p 114; *Twenty Letters to a Friend* (New York: Harper and Row, 1967; London: Hutchinson, 1967), p 199.
8   *Ibid.*, pp 20–1 (English edition, pp 29–30).
9   *Ibid.*, p 156.
10 Pavel Sudoplatov, *Razvedka i Kreml* (Moscow: Geya, 1996), p 389; Pavel Sudoplatov and Anatoly Sudoplatov, *Special Tasks* (London: Little Brown, 1994), p 334.
11 N.S. Khrushchev, *Vospominiya* (Moscow, 1999), pp 127, 389. This edition, in four volumes, contains a complete transcription of Khrushchev's reminiscences, recorded on tape in 1970. Abridged versions of this 'raw material' have been published in English (1971) and Russian (1997), with certain changes introduced by the translators and editors.
12 Sergei Khrushchev, *Nikita Khrushchev. Krizisy I rakety* (Moscow: Novosti, 1994), Vol. 1, p 24.
13 Radzinsky, *Stalin*, p 553 (Russian edition, pp 614–16).
14 Tape-recorded interview by Roy Medvedev.
15 A.T. Rybin, *Kto otravil Stalina? Zapiski telokhranitelya* (Moscow: Gudok, 1995).
16 Radzinsky, *Stalin*, p 553.
17 Dmitry Volkogonov, *Sem vozhdei* (Moscow: Novosti, 1996), Book 1, p 316.

18 Svetlana Alliluyeva, 'Dva poslednikh razgovora', *Moskovskiye novosti*, No. 42 (21 October 1990), pp 8–9.
19 Rybin, *Kto otravil Stalina?*, p 12.
20 *Ibid.*, p 13.
21 Nikita Khrushchev, *Vospominaniya*, p 264.
22 Rybin, *Kto otravil Stalina?*, p 13.
23 Alliluyeva, 'Dva poslednikh razgovora'.
24 Sergei Khrushchev, *Nikita Khrushchev*, pp 24–5.
25 Radzinsky, *Stalin*, p 556 (Russian edition, p 618).
26 N. Khrushchev, 'O kulte lichnosti i yevo posledstviyakh. Doklad na zakrytom zasedanii XX syezda KPSS 25 fevralya 1956 goda', *Izvestiya TsK KPSS*, No. 3 (1989).
27 V. Malkin and L. Lykova (comp), 'Tsel byla spasti zhizn bolnovo. Materialy doktora Timashuk', *Istochnik*, No. 1 (1997), pp 3–16.
28 Avtorkhanov, *Zagadka smerti Stalina*, pp 206–7.
29 Sudoplatov, *Razvedka i Kreml*, p 362.
30 A.N. Yakovlev (ed), *Sbornik dokumentov 'Lavrenty Beria'. 1953* (Moscow: Moskovsky mezhdunarodny fond 'Demokratiya', 1999).
31 *Politburo, Orgburo, Sekretariat TsK RKP(b), VKP(b) KPSS. Spravochnik* (Moscow: Gospolitizdat), p 115.
32 Alliluyeva, *Dvadtsat pisem k drugu*, p 22 (English edition, p 31).
33 Rybin, *Kto otravil Stalina?*, p 13.
34 *Ibid.*
35 A.L. Myasnikov, 'Konchina', *Literaturnaya gazeta*, 1 March 1989, p 13.
36 N. Barsukov, 'Mart 1953. Stranitsy istorii KPSS', *Pravda*, 27 October 1989, p 3.
37 'Protokol sovmestnovo soveshchaniya Plenuma TsK KPSS, Soveta Ministrov SSSR I Prezidiuma Verkhovnovo Soveta SSSR 5 marta 1953 g.', *Istochnik*, No. 1 (1994), pp 107–11.
38 Konstantin Simonov, *Glazami cheloveka moyevo pokoleniya. Rasmyshleniya o Staline* (Moscow: Kniga, 1989), p 228.

Chapter 2: Stalin's Secret Heir

1 'Posetiteli kremlevskovo kabineta I. V. Stalina', *Istorichesky Arkhiv*, Nos. 5–6 (1996) and No. 1 (1997).
2 N. Khrushchev, *Khrushchev Remembers* (New York: Little Brown, 1971), pp 243–4.
3 Konstantin Simonov, *Glazami cheloveka moyevo pokoleniya. Razmyshleniya o Staline* (Moscow: Kniga, 1990), pp 211–13.
4 D.T. Shepilov, 'Vospominaniya', *Voprosy istorii*, No. 7 (1998), p 30.
5 L.N. Yefremov, 'Neopublikovannaya rech I.V. Stalina na Plenum TsK KPSS 16 Oktyabrya 1952 g.', *Dosye 'Glasnosti'*, No. 3 (2000), p 9.
6 Khrushchev, *Vospominaniya*, p 286.
7 Simonov, Glazami cheloveka moyevo pokoleniya, p 214.
8 Khrushchev, *Khrushchev Remembers*, pp 246–7.
9 Svetlana Alliluyeva, *Dvadtsat pisem drugu*, p 114; *Twenty Letters to a Friend*, p 199.
10 *Istorichesky arkhiv*, No. 2 (1994), pp 51–2.
11 Shepilov, 'Vospominaniya', p 3.

12 *Natsionalnye repressii v SSSR. 1919–1952 gody* (Moscow: Insan, 1993), Vol. 1, pp 260–2.
13 Roy Medvedev and Dmitry Yermakov, *Sery kardinal* (Moscow: Respublika, 1992).
14 Serge Petroff, *The Red Eminence. A Biography of Mikhail A. Suslov* (Clifton, New Jersey: The Kingston Press, 1988).

Chapter 3: Stalin's Personal Archive

1 Dmitry Volkogonov, *Lenin* (Moscow: Novosti, 1994), 2 vols.; *Lenin: Life and Legacy* (London: HarperCollins, 1994). In 1996 Volkogonov published an additional short biography of Lenin, based on new archive materials: *Vozhd pervy: Vladimir Lenin. Sem vozhdei. Kniga I* (Moscow: Novosti, 1996), pp 21–162.
2 A.G. Latyshev, *Rassekrechenny Lenin* (Moscow: MART, 1996).
3 Richard Pipies (ed), *The Unknown Lenin* (New Haven and London: Yale University Press, 1996).
4 'Znaniya, broshennye v ogon', *Vestnik Rossiiskoi AN*, Vol. 66, No. 7 (1996), pp 625–35.
5 D. Shepilov, 'Vospominaniya', *Voprosy istorii*, No. 3 (1998), p 20.
6 Svetlana Alliluyeva, *Dvadtsat pisem k drugu*, p 22; *Twenty Letters to a Friend*, pp 30–1.
7 Dmitry Volkogonov, *Triumf i tragediya. I. V. Stalin. Politichesky portret. Kniga vtoraya* (Moscow: APN, 1989), part 2, p 45; see also *Stalin. Triumph and Tragedy* (London: Weidenfeld and Nicolson, 1991).
8 Dmitry Volkogonov, *Vozhd vtoroi: Iosif Stalin. Sem vozhdei. Kniga I* (Moscow: Novosti, 1996), p 260.
9 *Stalinskoe Politburo v 30-e gody. Sbornik dokumentov.* Seriya *Dokumenty sovetskoi istorii* (Moscow: AIRO-XX, 1995). 'The Politburo Protocols, 1919–40', *The Russian Review*, Vol. 55 (1996), pp 99–103. A survey of the collection of Politburo protocols is held in the RTsKhIDNI, fond 17, op. 3.
10 V.A. Kozlov and S.B. Mironenko (eds), *'Osobaya papka' I. V. Stalina. Arkhiv noveishei istorii Rossii. Iz materialov Sekretariata NKVD-MVD. Katalog dokumentov* (Moscow: Blagovest, 1994); *Stalin's 'Special Files'*, Archive of Contemporary Russian History. Vol. 1 (University of Pittsburgh: The Centre for the Study of Russia and the Soviet Union, 1994).
11 Ella Maksimova, 'Lichny fond Stalina stanovitsya obshchedostupnym. No pochemu lish chastichno?', *Izvestiya*, 30 October 1999.
12 Edvard Radzinsky, *Stalin*.
13 Yevgeny Gromov, *Stalin. Vlast i iskysstvo* (Moscow: Respublika, 1998).
14 V.A. Malyshev, 'Dnevnik narkoma', *Vestnik Arkhiva Prezidenta Rossiiskoi Federatsii*, No. 5 (1997), pp 103–47.
15 John Erickson, *The Road to Berlin* (London: Weidenfeld and Nicolson, 1983), pp 110–12.
16 I.V. Valedinsky, 'Vospominaniya o vstrechakh so Stalinym I. V.', *Istochnik*, No. 2 (1998), pp 68–73.
17 I.M. Gronsky, *Iz proshlovo* (Moscow, 1991), p 155, quoted in Yevgeny Gromov, *Stalin*, pp 165–6.

18 Lars T. Lih, Oleg V. Naumov and Oleg V. Khlevniuk (eds), *Stalin's Letters to Molotov 1925–1936*, p 233; *Pisma I. V. Stalina V. M. Molotovy. 1925–1936. Sbornik dokumentov*, p 247.
19 Lev Trotsky, 'Za stenami Kremlya', *Byulleten oppozitsii*, No. 72 (December 1938), pp 9–10.
20 *Ibid.*, p 12.
21 Boris Bazhanov, *Vospominaniya byvshevo sekretarya Stalina* (Moscow-St Petersburg: Vsemirnoe slovo, 1992); *Bazhanov and the Damnation of Stalin* (Athens: Ohio University Press, 1990).
22 Roy Medvedev, *K sudy istorii* (New York: A. Knopf, 1974), p 601; *Let History Judge. The Origin and Consequences of Stalinism* (New York: Columbia University Press, 1989), p 550.
23 Robert Tucker, *Stalin in Power* (New York and London: W.W. Norton, 1990), p 77.
24 A. Avtorkhanov, *Tekhnologiya vlasti* (Frankfurt/M: Posev, 1976), p 208.
25 Arkady Vaksberg, '"Delo" marshala Zhukova: Nerazorvavshayasya bomba', *Literaturnaya gazeta*, No. 32 (5 August 1992), p 12. (General Kryukov and the singer Ruslanova were released in July 1953.)
26 Mark Deich, 'Podpisano Stalinym. Dobycha tainy germanskikh reparatsii', *Stolitsa*, No. 29 (1994), p 21. Taken from the manuscript of the historian Pavel Knyshevsky, which was still unpublished as of 2002.
27 See note 18.
28 Lih, et al (eds), *Stalin's Letters to Molotov*, p 183 (Russian edition, p 169).
29 *Ibid.*, p vix (Russian edition, p 5).
30 *Stalinskoe Politburo*, p 122.
31 Gromov, *Stalin*, p 190.
32 P.L. Kapitsa, *Pisma o nauke* (Moscow: Moskovsky rabochy, 1989), p 174.
33 Volkogonov, *Triumf i Tragediya*, p 45.
34 Vokogonov, *Vozhd pervy*, pp 325–6.
35 'Posetiteli Kremlevskovo kabineta I. V. Stalina', *Istorichesky arkhiv*, No. 1 (1997), p 39.
36 'Poslednyaya "otstavka" Stalina', *Istochnik*, No. 1 (1994), p 110, edited and with a commentary by Anatoly Chernyaev. The protocol was signed by Khrushchev and is held in APRF, fond 2, op. 2, d. 196, l. 1–7.
37 Yu. G. Murin (comp), *Iosif Stalin v obyatyakh semi. Iz lichnovo arkhiva. Cbornik dokumentov* (Moscow: Rodina, 1993).
38 *Istorichesky arkhiv*, No. 2 (1994).
39 Vokogonov, *Vozhd pervy*, pp 260–1.
40 Viktor Pribytkov, *Apparat* (St Petersburg: VIS, 1995), pp 77–8.
41 Zolotukhina's account recorded on tape by Roy Medvedev.
42 Robert Tucker, *Stalin. Istoriya I lichnost* (Moscow, 1990), translated from the first volume of Tucker's trilogy, in English: *Stalin as a Revolutonary* (New York and London: W.W. Norton, 1990).
43 Gromov, *Stalin*, p 7.
44 L. Spirin, 'Glazami knig. Lichnaya biblioteka Stalina', *Nezavisimaya gazeta*, 25 May 1993.
45 Svetlana Alliluyeva, 'Dva poslednikh razgovora', *Moskovskiye novosti*, No. 42 (21 October 1990), p 9.
46 Rosamond Richardson, *The Long Shadow. Inside Stalin's Family* (London: Abacus, 1994).

47 Isaac Deutscher and David King, *The Great Purges* (Oxford and New York: Basil Blackwell, 1984). A photographic history of repression in the USSR from 1918 to 1953. Text by Deutscher, written in 1965. David King is thought to have amassed one of the best existing photograph collections of the history of the USSR.

48 Nigel Blundell, *A Pictorial History of Joseph Stalin* (London: Sunburst Books, 1996). Photographs of Stalin and his circle in various periods of Soviet history.

49 David King, *The Commissar Vanishes. The Falsification of Photographs and Art in Stalin's Russia* (Edinburgh: Canongate Books, 1997). The book contains the best-known photographs of Stalin and his circle, published at different times. In later publications, the images of Stalin's former colleagues who suffered repression have been removed.

50 Mikhail Lyubimov, 'Shinel No. 5', *Sovershenno sekretno*, No. 5 (1996), p 27. Article on the fate of Stalin's personal belongings, based on documents assembled by T.V. Domracheva and M. Yu. Prozumenchikova, members of the staff of the Centre for the Preservation of Contemporary Documentation.

Chapter 4: The Twentieth Party Congress

1 *Otechestvennaya istoriya*, No. 3 (1997), pp 43–4.

2 On the preparation of Khrushchev's speech at the Congress, see D.T. Shepilov, 'Vospominaniya', *Voprosy istorii*, Nos. 3–11 (1998); V.P. Naumov, 'K istorii sekretnovo doklada N.S. Khrushcheva na XX cyezde KPSS', *Novaya i noveishaya istoriya*, No. 4 (1996); N.A. Barsukov, 'XX cyezd v retrospective Khrushcheva', *Otechestvennaya istoriya*, No. 6 (1956).

3 From the archive of E. Yu. Maltsev (in the possession of Roy Medvedev).

Chapter 5: Stalin and the Atomic Bomb

1 *Pravda*, 13 October 1941, p 3.

2 W. Laurence, 'Vast Power Source in Atomic Energy Opened by Science', *New York Times*, 5 May 1940.

3 'U istokov sovetskovo atomnovo proyekta: Rol razvedki, 1941–1946 gg.', *Voprosy istorii yestestvoznaniya i tekhniki*, No. 3 (1992), pp 107–8.

4 G.K. Zhukov, *Vospominiya i razmyshleniya* (Moscow: Novosti, 1990), Vol. 1, p 341.

5 S.V. Kaftonov, 'Po trevoge', *Khimiya i zhizn*, No. 3 (1985), p 8 (a record of V. Stepanov's conversation with Kaftonov).

6 *Sto sorok besed s Molotovym. Iz dnevnika F. Chuyeva* (Moscow: Terra, 1991), p 81.

7 'U istokov sovetskovo atomnovo proyekta: Rol razvedki, 1941–1946 gg.', pp 115–16.

8 *Ibid.*, p 118.

9 I.N. Golovin, *I. V. Kurchatov* (Moscow: Atomizdat, 1967), p 63.

10 N. Riehl and F. Seitz, *Stalin's Captive. Nikolaus Riehl and the Soviet Race for the Bomb* (American Chemical Society, 1996), p 152. Riehl's book was first published in Germany in 1988 under the title *Ten Years in a Golden*

Cage. It was translated into English with notes and additional material by Fredrick Seitz, a participant in the Manhattan Project.

11 *Sistema ispravitelno-trudovykh lagerei v SSSR. 1923–1960. Spravochnik* (Moscow: Zvenya, 1998), pp 444–5.

12 I.S. Drovennikov and S.V. Romanov, 'Trofeiny uran, ili Istoriya odnoi komandirovki', *Istoriya sovetskovo atomnovo proyekta: Dokumenty, vospominaniya, issledovaniya. Vyp. I* (Moscow: Yanus-K, 1998), p 226.

13 M. Rebrov, 'Bez grifa "sekretno"', *Krasnaya Zvezda*, 24 August 1994.

14 *Sistema ispravitelno-trudovykh lagerei v SSSR. 1923–1960. Spravochnik*, pp 113–14.

15 'Posetiteli Kremlevskovo kabineta I. V. Stalina', *Istorichesky arkhiv*, No. 4 (1996), p 116.

16 'U istokov sovetskovo atomnovo proyekta. (Novye arkhivnye materialy)', *Voprosy istorii yestestvoznaniya I tekhniki*, No. 2 (1994), pp 128–9.

17 'Posetiteli Kremlevskovo kabineta I. V. Stalina', *Istorichesky arkhiv*, Nos. 5–6 (1996), p 4.

18 A.M. Pestrosyants, 'Reshenie yadernnoi problemy v 1943–1946 gg.', *Sozdanie pervoi sovetskoi yadernoi bomby* (Moscow: Energoatomizdat, 1995), p 59.

19 A.K. Kruglov, 'Ot opytnovo reaktora F-1 v Laboratorii No. 2 k pervomy promyshlennomu yadernomu reaktoru v Chelyabinske-40', *Sozdanie pervoi sovetskoi yadernonoi bomby* (Moscow: Energoatomizdat, 1995), p 84.

20 *Ibid.*, pp 85–6.

21 'Zhertvy plutoniya. Intervyu A. Guskovoi', *Obshchaya gazeta*, 19–25 August 1999, p 15.

Chapter 6: Stalin and the Hydrogen Bomb

1 *Atomny proyekt v SSSR. T. 1, Chast pervaya. Fizmatlit* (Moscow: Nauka, 1998), p 325.

2 P.L. Kapitsa, *Pisma o nauke 1930–1980* (Moscow: Moskovsky rabochii, 1989), p 234.

3 *Ibid.*, pp 240–6.

4 *Ibid.*, p 247 (note by the editor to Kapitsa's letter).

5 *Ibid.*, pp 257–8.

6 A.D. Sakharov, *Vospominaniya* (New York: Chekhov Press, 1990), p 129; see also Andrei Sakharov, *Memoirs* (New York: Knopf, 1990; London: Hutchinson, 1990) p 94.

7 P. Sudoplatov, *Razvedka i Kreml* (Moscow: TOO 'Geya', 1996), p 221.

8 A.N. Yakovlev, 'Istochnik iz okruzheniya Landau soobshchil...', *Obshchaya gazeta*, 25 November–1 December 1999.

9 David Holloway, *Stalin and the Bomb* (New Haven and London: Yale University Press, 1994), p 301.

10 V.L. Ginsburg, *O nauke, sebe i drugkikh* (Moscow: Nauka, 1997).

11 Sakharov, *Vospominaniya*, p 161 (Russian edition), p 119 (English edition).

12 *Ibid.*, pp 154–5 (Russian edition), pp 113–14 (English edition).

13 *Ibid.*, p 180 (Russian edition), p 114 (English edition).

14 A.A. Fursenko, 'Konets ery Stalina', *Zvezda*, No. 12 (1999), p 175.

Chapter 7: Stalin and the Atomic Gulag

1 L.D. Ryabev (ed), *Atomny proyekt SSSR. Dokumenty I materially. T. 1, 1938–45* (Moscow: Nauka, Fizmatlit, 1998), p 275.
2 V.I. Vetrov, V.V. Krotkov and V. V. Kunichenko, 'Sozdaniye predpriyatii po dobyche i pererabotke uranovykh rud', *Sozdaniye pervoi sovyetskoi yadernoi bomby* (Moscow: Energoizdat, 1995), pp 170–98.
3 *Sistema ispravitelno-trudovykh lagerei v SSSR. 1923–1960. Spravochnik.* Sostavitel M.B. Smirnov i obshchestvo 'Memorial' (Moscow: Zvenya, 1988), p 265.
4 V.A. Kozlov and S.V. Mironenko (eds), *'Osobaya papka' L. P. Berii. Arkhiv noveishei istorii Rossii.* T. 4. Iz materialov Sekretariata NKVD-MVD SSSR 1946–1949 gg. Katalog dokumentov (Moscow: Gosud. arkhiv Rossiiskoi Federatsii, 1996), p 31.
5 *Sistema ispravitelno-trudovykh lagerei v SSSR. 1923–1960. Spravochnik,* pp 433, 354.
6 Kozlov and Mironenko (eds), *'Osobaya papka' L. P. Berii,* p 457.
7 A. Kokurin and N. Petrov, 'MVD.Struktura, funktsiya, kadry', *Svobodnaya mysl,* No. 12 (1997), pp 110–11.
8 *Sistema ispravitelno-trudovykh lagerei v SSSR. 1923–1960. Spravochnik,* p 167.
9 *Ibid.*
10 A.D. Sakharov, *Vospominaniya.*
11 L. Goleusova, 'Kak vse nachinalos. K 50-letiyu pervovo yadernovo tsentra', *Mezhdunarodnaya zhizn,* No. 6 (1994), p 140.
12 *Zapolyarye* (gazeta), 18 September 1991. Statya sotrudnika KGB Komi ASSR V. M. Poleshchikova o lageryakh Vorkuty.
13 *Moskovskiye novosti,* No. 41, 8 October 1989.
14 Kozlov and Mironenko (eds), *'Osobaya papka' L. P. Berii,* p 68.
15 *Sistema ispravitelno-trudovykh lagerei v SSSR. 1923–1960. Spravochnik,* p 449.
16 A. Vyshemirsky, 'Pismo-otklik na statyu o Chelyabinsk-40 Pestova', *Argumenty i Fakty,* No. 16, 14–20 October 1989.
17 A.S. Osipov, 'Pismo-otklik na statyu o Chelyabinsk-40 Pestova', *Argumenty i Fakty,* No. 16, 14–20 October 1989.
18 I.P. Samokhvalov, 'Pismo-otklik na statyu o Chelyabinsk-40 Pestova', *Argumenty i Fakty,* No. 16, 14–20 October 1989.
19 *Sistema ispravitelno-trudovykh lagerei v SSSR. 1923–1960. Spravochnik,* p 451.
20 *Ibid.,* p 419.
21 Osipov, 'Pismo-otklik na statyu o Chelyabinsk-40 Pestova'.
22 A.K. Kruglov in V.N. Mikhailov (ed), *Sozdaniye pervoi sovyetskoi yadernoi bomby* (Moscow: Energoatomizdat, 1995), p 114.
23 *Ibid.,* p 115.
24 A.K. Gyskova, *ibid.,* p 162.
25 *Ibid.,* p 149.
26 Kruglov, in Mikhailov (ed), *Sozdaniye pervoi sovyetskoi yadernoi bomby,* p 87.
27 *Ibid.,* p 116.
28 V. Larin, 'Mayak's Walking Wounded', *The Bulletin of Atomic Scientists,* Vol. 55, No. 5 (1999), pp 20–7.

29 Kruglov in Mikhailov (ed), *Sozdaniye pervoi sovyetskoi yadernoi bomby*, p 116.
30 *Ibid.*, p 85.
31 *Ibid.*
32 'O radiatsionnoi opasnosti togda nikto ne dymal. Intervyu Ye. Slavskovo, zapicannoe M. Rudenko', *Delovoi Mir*, 19–22 December 1997, p 9.
33 P. Astashenkov, *Kurchatov* (Moscow: Molodaya Gvardiya, 1967), p 153.
34 Kruglov in Mikhailov (ed), *Sozdaniye pervoi sovyetskoi yadernoi bomby*, p 116.
35 *Sistema ispravitelno-trudovykh lagerei v SSSR. 1923–1960. Spravochnik*, p 416.
36 Sakharov, *Memoirs*, p 155 (Russian edition), p 134 (English edition).
37 Kozlov and Mironenko (eds), *'Osobaya papka' L. P. Berii*, p 431.
38 *Ibid.*, p 432.
39 Tamara L. Chast. Letters quoted in notes 16–18 are in the author's possession.
40 S.M. Melnikov, 'Atomny Gulag', *Rossiya*, 11–17 October 1995.
41 Kozlov and Mironenko (eds), *'Osobaya papka' L. P. Berii*, p 431.
42 A. Kokurin and Yu. Morukov, 'Gulag: Struktura i kadry', *Svobodnaya mysl*, No. 3 (2001), p 123.
43 Melnikov, 'Atomny Gulag'.
44 M. Solomon, *Magadan* (Toronto, 1971).
45 *Sovershenno otkryto* (Krasnoyarsk), No. 1 (1993), p 6.
46 *Ibid.*, No. 2 (1994), p 8.
47 Kozlov and Mironenko (eds), *'Osobaya papka' L. P. Berii*, p 606.

Chapter 8: Generalissimo Stalin, General Clausewitz and Colonel Razin

1 K. Marx and F. Engels, *Sochineniya*, 2nd edition, Vol. 29, pp 207, 210.
2 *Ibid.*, Vol. 28, p 487.
3 V.I. Lenin, *PSS* (Collected Works), Vol. 26, p 316; Vol. 32, p 79; Vol. 36, p 292.

Chapter 9: Stalin and Lysenko

1 'Posetiteli kremlevskovo kabineta I. V. Stalina (1947–1949 gg.)', *Istorichesky Arkhiv*, No. 5–6 (1996), p 41.
2 *Pravda*, 8 March 1953.
3 'Iz istorii borby s lysenkovshchinoi', *Izvestiya TsK KPSS*, No. 7 (1991), p 111.
4 D.T. Shepilov, 'Vospominaniya', *Voprosy istorii*, No. 6 (1998), p 9.
5 *Ibid.*, p 10.
6 V.A. Malyshev, 'Dnevnik narkoma', *Vestnik Arkhiva Prezidenta Rossiiskoi Federaatsii*, No. 5 (1997), p 135.
7 'Iz istorii borby s lysenkovshchinoi', pp 120–1; K. O. Rossiyanov, 'Stalin kak redactor Lysenko', *Voprosy filosofii*, No. 2 (1993), pp 56–9.
8 *Pravda*, 10 February 1946.
9 Shepilov, 'Vospominaniya', p 10.
10 *Ibid.*, p 11.

11 'Tsel byla spasti zhizn bolnovo. Pisma Lidii Timashuk', *Istochnik*, No. 1 (1997), pp 3–16.
12 *Pravda*, 3 August 1931.
13 Yu. Vavilov, 'Avgust 1948. Predystoriya', *Chelovek*, No. 4 (1998).
14 *Sto sorok besed s Molotovym. Iz dnevnik F. Chuyeva* (Moscow: Terra, 1991), p 252.
15 P. Pavlenko, *Schastye* (Moscow: Sovetsky pisatel, 1947), pp 164–5.
16 'Vybory ili vybor? K istorii izbraniya prezidenta Akademii nauk SSSR. Iyul 1945', *Istorichesky arkhiv*, No. 2 (1996), pp 142–51.

Chapter 10: Stalin and Linguistics

1   *XVI syezd VKP(b). Stenograficheskyy otchet* (Moscow, 1931), p 98.
2   *Vestnik Arkhiva Presidenta RF*, No. 1 (1998), pp 154–5.

Chapter 11: Stalin and the Blitzkrieg

1   V.P. Naumov (ed), *1941 god. Dokumenty, Kniga Pervaya* (Moscow: Mezhdunarodny fond 'Demokratiya', 1998). Arvid Harnack was a Soviet agent from 1932. He was recruited during a visit to Moscow on Comintern business. Harnack was uncovered by the Gestapo in 1942 and hanged in December of that year. His wife, Mildred, was also arrested and executed in 1943.
2   Naumov (ed), *1941 god. Dokymenty, Kniga Vtoraya*, p 175.
3   Jan Kershaw, *Hitler 1936–45* (London: Allen Lane, The Penguin Press, 2000), pp 362–3.
4   Pavel Sudoplatov, *Razvedka i Kreml* (Moscow, 1996), pp 136–7; Pavel Sudoplatov, *Special Tasks* (London and New York: Little Brown and Co., 1994), pp 118–19.
5   Misha Glenny, *The Balkans. 1804–1999. Nationalism, War and the Great Powers* (London: Granta Books, 2000), pp 468–74.
6   Naumov (ed), *1941 god, Kniga Pervaya*, pp 804–5.
7   Naumov (ed), *1941 god, Kniga Vtoraya*, pp 69–74.
8   Antony Beevor, *Crete. The Battle and the Resistance* (London: Penguin Books, 1991), p 230.
9   Naumov (ed), *1941 god, Kniga Vtoraya*, p 146.
10 Sudoplatov, *Razvedka i Kreml*, p 135; English edition, p 117.
11 Naumov (ed), *1941 god, Kniga Vtoraya*, pp 131–2. Harold Schulze-Boysen was part of a group reporting to the Soviet Intelligence resident in Berlin, Amayak Kobulov, who officially was employed as adviser to the Soviet ambassador. Kobulov, who was not a spy by profession, broke some of the basic rules by visiting agents in their apartments, assembling them together, etc. This led to the exposure of the entire network.
12 *Stalinskoe Politburo v 30-e gody. Sbornik dokumentov,* 'Dokument No. 17' (Moscow: AIRO-XX, 1995), pp 34–5.
13 V.A. Malyshev, 'Dnevnik narkoma', *Vestnik Arkhiva Prezidenta Rossiis-koi Federatsii*, No. 5 (1997), pp 115–16.
14 Lev Bezymensky, *Gitler i Stalin pered skhvatkoi* (Moscow: Veche, 2000), pp 427–33.
15 Naumov (ed), *1941 god, Kniga Vtoraya*, pp 163–4.

16 G.K. Zhukov, *Vospominaniya i razmyshleniya* (Moscow: Novosti, 1990), Vol. 1, p 323.
17 Naumov (ed), *1941 god, Kniga Vtoraya*, pp 213–15.
18 Zhukov, *Vospominaniya i razmyshleniya*, p 359.
19 *Ibid.*, p 384.
20 Naumov (ed), *1941 god, Kniga Vtoraya*, pp 359–61.
21 Zhukov, *Vospominaniya i razmyshleniya*, Vol. 2, pp 25–6.
22 *Ibid.*, p 27.
23 Naumov (ed), *1941 god, Kniga Vtoraya*, pp 382–3.
24 *Ibid.*, p 358.
25 *Ibid.*, p 365.
26 *Ibid.*, pp 340–1.
27 *Ibid.*, p 416.
28 I.V. Tyulenev, *Cherez tri voiny* (Moscow: Voenizdat, 1960).
29 Zhukov, *Vospominaniya i razmyshleniya*, Vol. 1, p 386.
30 Naumov (ed), *1941 god, Kniga Vtoraya*, p 422.
31 N.S. Khrushchev, 'O kulte lichnosti i yevo posledstviyakh. Doklad na XX syezde KPSS', *Isvestiya TsK KPSS*, No. 3 (1989), pp 128–70.
32 N.S. Khrushchev, *Vospominaniya*, pp 95–6.
33 Jonathan Lewis and Phillip Whitehead, *Stalin. A Time for Judgement* (New York: Pantheon Books, 1990), p 122.
34 Alan Bullock, *Hitler and Stalin. Parallel Lives* (London: HarperCollins, 1991), p 805.
35 'Stalin', *The Oxford Companion to the Second World War* (Oxford: Oxford University Press, 1995).
36 Dmitry Volkogonov, *Triumf i tragediya*, Book II, Part I; Radzinsky, *Stalin*.
37 Zhukov, *Vospominaniya i razmyshleniya*, Vol. 2, p 38.
38 A.I. Mikoyan, *Tak bylo. Razmyshleniya o minuvshem* (Moscow: Vagarius, 1999), p 291.
39 John Erickson, *The Road to Stalingrad. Stalin's War with Germany* (London: Weidenfeld and Nicolson, 1975), Vol. 1.

Chapter 12: Stalin and Apanasenko

1 *Istoriya Vtoroi mirovoi voiny. 1939–1945* (Moscow, 1980), Vol. 11, p 184.
2 A. Lysenko, *Iosif Apanasenko* (Stavropol: Stavropolskoye knizhnoye izdatelstvo, 1987).
3 Pyotr Grigorenko, *V podpolye mozhno vstretit tolko krys* (Moscow: Zvenya, 1997), p 192; Grigorenko, *Memoirs* (New York and London: W.W. Norton, 1982), p 127.
4 W. Churchill, *Vtoraya mirovaya voina. Kniga V* (New York: Izdatelstvo Chekova, 1956), p 201.
5 *Izvestiya TsK KPSS*, No. 12 (1990), p 213.
6 *Sovyetskaya Rossiya*, 20 October 1989.
7 M. Yu. Roginsky, S. Ya. Rozenblit, *Mezhdunarodny protsess glavnykh yaponskikh voennykh prestupnikov* (Moscow-Leningrad: Izdatelstvo yuridicheskoi literatury, 1950), p 246.
8 *Istoriya Vtoroi mirovoi voiny*, Vol. 11, p 184.

9   *Krasnoznamenny Dalnevostochny* (Khabarovsk, 1978), p 139.
10 Lysenko, *Iosif Apanasenko*, p 331.

Chapter 13: Stalin as a Russian Nationalist

1   Radzinsky, *Stalin*, p 27 (Russian edition); p 21 (English edition).
2   G. Dzhugashvili, 'Vse vspominayut ruku deda', *Mir za nedelyu*, 25 September–2 October 1999.
3   N.M. Przhevalsky, *Tretye puteshestviye v Tsentralnuyu Aziyu* (St Petersburg, 1883); S. Khmelnitsky, *Nikolai Mikhailovich Przhevalsky* (Moscow: Molodaya Gvardiya, 1950). Przhevalsky was in Zaisan, near Lake Issyk-Kul when he received news of his mother's death at the end of March 1878. He left Zaisan at the beginning of April by camel caravan and arrived in Petersburg on 23 May. According to church records Stalin was born on 6 December 1878. The railway line to Central Asia, reaching Ashkhabad and Samarkand, was constructed in 1888, the year of Przhevalsky's death.
4   *Pravda*, 25 May 1945.
5   J. Lewis and P. Whitehead, *Stalin. A Time for Judgement*, pp 6–7.
6   L. Trotsky, *Moya zhizn. Opyt avtobiografii* (Berlin: Granit, 1930), p 61.
7   V.I. Lenin, *PSS* (Collected Works), Vol. 45, pp 556–7.
8   *Ibid.*, pp 211–13.
9   *Ibid.*, p 214.
10 APRF, fond 45, op. 1, d. 25. Volkogonov refers to this fond in his *Sem vozhdei* (Moscow, 1996).
11 *Kommunist*, No. 9 (1956), pp 22–6. See also *Istoriya Sovetskoi Konstitutsii (v dokumentakh) 1917–1956* (Moscow: Gos. izd. yurid. lit.), pp 400–2.
12 Trotsky, *Moya zhizn*, p 226.
13 *Pravda*, 8 November 1941.
14 Gromov, *Stalin*, pp 335–42.
15 Z. Mlynar, 'Kholod veyet ot Moskvy', *Problemy Vostochnoi Yevropy*, 1988, p 15.
16 Trotsky, *Moya zhizn*, p 59–60.
17 *Istochnik*, No. 5 (1996), p 81.
18 V. Chalidze, *Pobeditel kommunizma* (New York: Chalidze Press, 1981).
19 R.V. Daniels, 'Was Stalin Really a Communist?', *The Soviet and Post-Soviet Review*, Vol. 20, Nos. 2–3 (1993), pp 169–75.

Chapter 14: The Murder of Bukharin

1   *Istorichesky arkhiv*, No. 4 (1998), p 39.
2   N.I. Bukharin, *Problemy teorii i praktiki sotsializma* (Moscow, 1989), pp 337, 421.
3   *Voprosy istorii partii*, No. 4 (1991), pp 59–60.
4   XVII cyezd VKP(b). *Stenografichesky otchet* (Moscow, 1934), pp 124–5.
5   *Bukharin: chelovek, politik, ucheny* (Moscow, 1990), p 158.
6   Nadezhda Mandelstam, *Hope Against Hope* (New York: Atheneum, 1970), p 13.
7   N. Mandelshtam, *Vospominaniya* (New York, 1970), pp 25–6.
8   Yevgeny Gromov, *Stalin. Vlast i iskysstvo* (Moscow, 1998), p 277.

9   Joseph Berger, *Shipwreck of a Generation* (London: Harvill Press, 1973), pp 106–7; *Krusheniye pokoleniya* (Italy, 1973), p 138.

10 *Pervy Vsesoyuzny syezd sovetskikh pisatelei. Stenografichesky otchet* (Moscow, 1934), p 479.

11 *Ibid.*, p 671.

12 *Ogonek*, No. 48 (1987), p 29.

13 'Pisma I. G. Erenburga I. V. Stalinyu i N. I. Bukharinu', *Vestnik Arkhiva Prezidenta Rossiiskoi Federatsii*, No. 2 (1997), pp 109–18. It is evident from Stalin's notes that Bukharin sent him letters that he (Bukharin) had received himself.

14 Yu. G. Felshtinsky, *Razgovory s Bukharinym* (Moscow, 1993).

15 *Ogonek*, No. 48 (1987), p 30.

16 *Ibid.*, No. 2 (1988), p 22.

17 Roy Medvedev, *Nikolai Bukharin. The Last Years* (New York and London: Norton, 1980), pp 129–30.

18 *Voprosy istorii*, No. 1 (1995), pp 3–22.

19 The stenographic record of the February–March plenum of the Central Committee was published in *Voprosy istorii* in 1992–93.

20 *Voprosy istorii*, No. 2 (1992), pp 5–6.

21 *Ibid.*, No. 4–5, pp 32–6.

22 *Ibid.*, No. 6, p 3.

23 *Ibid.*, No. 2 (1993), pp 3–32.

24 *Ibid.*, No. 2 (1992), pp 24–5.

25 *Ibid.*, No. 10 (1993), pp 12–13.

26 *Tyuremnye rukopisi N. I. Bukharina. Kniga pervaya* (Moscow: AIRO, 1996), p 6.

27 *Ibid.*, p 32.

28 *Tribuna*, 9 October 1998.

29 *Tyuremnye rukopisi N. I. Bukharina*, p 195.

30 *Tyuremnye rukopisi Kniga vtoraya* (Moscow: AIRO, 1996).

31 *Ibid.*, p 333.

32 L. Feuchtwanger, *Moskva. 1937. Otchet o poyezdke dlya moikh druzei* (Moscow, 1937); George Davis, *Mission to Moscow. 1941* (New York, 1941); Arthur Koestler, *Slepyashchaya tma* (Moscow, 1990).

33 Roy Medvedev, *Let History Judge* (New York and London, 1971); *O Staline I Stalinizme* (Moscow: Politizdat, 1990).

34 Yevgeny Gnedin, *Vykhod iz labirinta* (Moscow, 1994).

35 From Sidney Heitman's preface to *The Path to Socialism in Russia. Collected Works of Bukharin* (New York: Omnicron Books, 1967), p 6.

36 A. Solzhenitsyn, *Arkhipelag Gulag*, Vol. 1 (Paris, 1973), p 410.

37 Stephen Cohen, *Bukharin and the Bolshevik Revolution* (New York, 1973), p 380.

38 *Za rubezhom*, No. 26 (1988), p 18.

39 Robert Conquest, *The Great Terror* (London: Macmillan, 1968), p 425.

40 *Sudebny otchet po delu antisovetskovo 'pravotrotskistskovo bloka'. Polny text stenograficheskovo otcheta* (Moscow: Yurizdat), p 678–9.

41 *Istochnik*, No. 4 (1996), pp 78–91.

42 *Izvestiya*, 3 September 1992.

Chapter 15: Stalin's Mother

1 *Voprosy istorii*, No. 4 (1996), p 45.
2 Svetlana Alliluyeva, *Dvadtsat pisem k drugu* (Moscow, 1989), pp 145–6; *Twenty Letters to a Friend* (London: Hutchinson, 1967), p 165.
3 Volkogonov, *Triumf i tragediya*, p 37.
4 *Iosif Stalin v obyatiyakh semyi (sbornik dokumentov)* (Moscow, 1993), p 6.
5 *Nezavisimaya gazeta*, 13 August 1992.
6 Radzinsky, *Stalin*, p 28.
7 *Pravda*, 2 January 1991.
8 Roy Medvedev, *Semya Stalina* (N. Novgorod, 1993), p 4.
9 *Obshchestvennye nauki*, No. 4 (1989), p 147.
10 *Izvestiya TsK KPSS*, 1990, No. 11, pp 132–3. The patronymic of Stalin's mother is spelled differently in various documents: Georgnevna, Gavrilovna, Gabrielovna. According to the new calendar, 6 December corresponds to 19 December.
11 Alliluyeva, *Dvadtsat pisem k drugu*, pp 188–9 (English edition, pp 213–14). The capital of Georgia was called Tiflis until 1936.
12 *Nezavisimaya gazeta*, 13 August 1992.
13 Radzinsky, *Stalin*, p 413.
14 *Zarya Vostoka*, 8 and 9 June 1937. The Writers' Museum was established in the 1930s on the site of the now restored church.

Index